"The Most Complete
Political Machine
Ever Known"

· CIVIL WAR IN THE NORTH ·

"The Most Complete Political Machine Ever Known"

The North's Union Leagues in the American Civil War

Paul Taylor

The Kent State University Press ⬛ Kent, Ohio

© 2018 by The Kent State University Press, Kent, Ohio 44242
All rights reserved
ISBN 978-1-60635-353-0
Manufactured in the United States of America

Cataloging information for this title is available at the Library of Congress.

22 21 20 19 18   5 4 3 2 1

"There are wars of opinion not fought out with the musket."

~*William T. Sherman*

"In such wars those who win are loyal, the defeated ones the traitors."

~*Calderón*

"Treason doth never prosper. What's the reason?

Why if it prospers none dare call it treason."

~*John Harrington,*

sixteenth or early seventeenth century

Contents

Union Leagues

Jonathan W. White

When Abraham Lincoln was a mere twenty-nine years old in January 1838, he exulted in the fact that Americans inhabited a peaceful and prosperous land, and that they lived under "a system of political institutions, conducing more essentially to the ends of civil and religious liberty, than any of which the history of former times tells us." The Founding Fathers had fought for this land and established this government; Lincoln's generation had received them as a gift. But now it was their responsibility "to transmit these . . . to the latest generation that fate shall permit the world to know." Preserving America's political institutions, Lincoln said, was a "task of gratitude to our fathers, justice to ourselves, duty to posterity, and love for our species in general."[1]

Clearly, from a young age, Lincoln believed the Union was worth preserving. And these ideas continued to motivate him into his adult life. In his 1852 eulogy for Kentuckian Henry Clay, Lincoln maintained "that the world's best hope depended on the continued Union of these States." Why? Because the United States offered more liberty and equality than any other nation in the world. Ten years later, in 1862, Lincoln told Congress what he believed the Civil War was really about. In fighting for the Union and giving freedom to the slave, he said, "We shall nobly save, or meanly lose, the last best, hope of earth."[2]

Union soldiers echoed the sentiments of their commander in chief as they marched off to war. In what is now one of the most famous letters of the Civil War, Maj. Sullivan Ballou of the Second Rhode Island Infantry spoke of "how great a debt we owe to those who went before us through

the blood and sufferings of the Revolution." Through his own military service, Ballou hoped to set an example for his two young sons so that they
might grow up to "honorable manhood." Other soldiers felt alike. "Our
fathers made this country, we their children are to save it," wrote one Ohio
volunteer, while a Connecticut infantryman was proud to fight for "those
institutions which were achieved for us by our glorious revolution . . . in
order that they may be perpetuated to those who may come after."[3]

For as important as the Union was to many Americans of the Civil War
generation, the concept of "the Union" has not received its due in the historical literature. In some ways it makes sense that scholars would be more interested in questions of nationalism in the Confederacy. After all, the Southern
states were attempting to create and define a nation during the Civil War.
The Union, by contrast, was merely fighting to preserve a preexisting nation. And yet we cannot begin to understand what motivated Northerners to
enlist and fight in the Civil War—and what prompted Northern civilians to
support the soldiers in the field—unless we probe what "Union" and "nation"
meant to them.[4] After all, as Gary W. Gallagher reminds us in *The Union War*,
belief in Union, "more than any other factor by far," motivated northerners
to fight and die for their country. For them, the American Union was "a democratic beacon shining in a world dominated by aristocrats and monarchs"—
a unique and exceptional nation that provided economic opportunity, political liberty, and the possibility of upward social mobility.[5] If the Union fell, no
other nation would be left on earth to carry the torch of liberty.

In this wonderful new study of the Union Leagues during the Civil War
Era, Paul Taylor brings to light new evidence about the ordinary men—and,
in some cases, women—who supported the Union from behind the lines
through the establishment of Union Leagues in cities, towns, and villages
throughout the North (and during Reconstruction, in the South). When
many of us think of "the Union League," we perhaps envision the spectacu-
lar 1865 building on South Broad Street in Philadelphia, or the elegant postwar clubhouse in New York City. And yet, as Taylor reveals, these groups
emerged not as the elite social clubs they are today, but as patriotic (and
sometimes secret) community-based societies dedicated to preserving a
nation that was smoldering amid the chaos of civil war.

Taylor deftly provides the context for the emergence of these grassroots
patriotic organizations, reminding us that Unionists did not simply encounter an enemy on the battlefield—they also faced strong, and sometimes violent, political opposition in the rear. Lincoln's critics—the Copperheads, or

antiwar Democrats—have received a significant amount of attention from historians. Tellingly, much of this scholarship has appeared during periods in which America has been involved in wars, most notably during World War II, the Cold War, the Vietnam War, and the post–9/11 era.[6] Scholars working in this field have probed the nature of loyalty and dissent in wartime. But the private citizens who organized to counteract the Copperheads have received far less attention. And yet they deserve it. In response to both real and perceived Copperhead threats, Union League clubs formed in communities "from Maine to California," ready to do partisan battle (and sometimes actual violence) against their political enemies in the North. As Taylor explains, "They attacked their 'treasonous' Democrat and Copperhead foes relentlessly" in an effort "to shape public opinion and achieve their war aims."

Pro-Union organizations took vital action to support the Union war effort by raising regiments and supplies and publishing patriotic pamphlets and broadsides. Much of this work focused on shaping Northern understandings of patriotism and loyalty. As Taylor explains, members of the Union Leagues became "*the* powerful propaganda machine for the Lincoln administration and the Republican Party" during the Civil War. They played a fundamental role in keeping the North united behind the war effort—and the Republican agenda—even when prospects looked dark. Indeed, when things were going badly for the Union and war weariness was sweeping through the land, it was they who reminded Northern soldiers and civilians why the Union was worth preserving.

Acknowledgments

———————⟨⟩———————

The author of any nonfiction book often benefits from the support and lar-gesse of others who assist with the author's research requests, advice, and even reviewing early manuscript drafts. This work is certainly no different and accordingly, I would like to acknowledge those individuals who gra-ciously gave of their time and talents over this book's five-year gestation period.

Most of the major characters in this work were private civilians, or state or national politicians during the Civil War, rather than military personnel. Much of their pertinent commentary and thoughts pertaining to the Union Leagues are to be found within their private correspondence and diaries as opposed to official government documents. Therefore, much of the re-search for this book was conducted within the Library of Congress, which is one of the nation's premier archives for such collections. I want to thank Michelle Krowl of that institution's Manuscripts Division for pointing out numerous underutilized or overlooked collections that proved beneficial to my research. I am also indebted to Patrick Kerwin of the Manuscripts Division who graciously helped me with some long-distance research. Gary Johnson at the Library of Congress's Newspaper and Periodicals Reading Room was likewise helpful in recommending little-known period newspa-pers that proved to be of solid value.

Specific individuals at archives from around the country also provided immense aid. In particular, I would like to thank Theresa Altieri, archi-vist at the Heritage Center of the Union League of Philadelphia; Kimberly Reynolds, manuscripts curator at the Boston Public Library; and Tammy Kiter of the New-York Historical Society's Manuscript Department for their research assistance and then kindly providing me with copies of im-portant documents from their collections. I am grateful to Rodney Foytik at the United States Army Military History Institute in Carlisle, Pennsylvania, along with the staffs at the National Archives in Washington, D.C., the York

County (Pennsylvania) Historical Society, Philadelphia's Historical Society of Pennsylvania, and the University of Michigan's Bentley and Clements Libraries for making my visits to their research facilities both productive and pleasant. I also cannot forget Katharina Fuller of Boyne City, Michigan, who studiously translated and transcribed several nineteenth-century, old-script, German-language newspaper articles.

I would be extremely remiss if I did not recognize Dwight Woodward and Avery Hicks of the Williamsburg (Virginia) Regional Library. Over the three-year period when I lived in that old colonial town, they cheerfully acquired dozens upon dozens of uncommon books, Civil War–era pamphlets, obscure dissertations, and rare microfilm rolls for me through their interlibrary loan program. I felt that many of these acquisitions were long shots at best when I first placed my request, yet time and again they delivered. My research would have been far more arduous and time-consuming without their superb assistance.

I also want to thank Jonathan W. White for his generosity in contributing an insightful foreword to this book. Equally helpful were J. Matthew Gallman, Robert Sandow, and a third anonymous historian who all carefully read my manuscript's early drafts as part of the publisher's initial review process. As is always the case, the thoughtful critiques and suggestions provided by these scholars made for a much better book than the one I originally submitted.

Lastly and far from least, I wish to express my gratitude to Will Underwood and all of the staff at the Kent State University Press. Their expertise and attention to detail has helped make this labor of love a hardcover reality.

Introduction

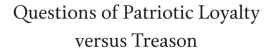

Questions of Patriotic Loyalty
versus Treason

In the early 1930s, psychology professor Dr. Donald P. Wilson began a three-year research study at Fort Leavenworth Penitentiary in northeast Kansas. The professor later recalled in his memoir what transpired when he told the story of President Abraham Lincoln to a European-born, convicted murderer. The prisoner's emotions ranged from sadness to anger as he concluded how Lincoln was, in his vernacular, a "right guy," a good man who saved his country while freeing the slaves held in bondage. The tough inmate was near tears as he decided that Lincoln and the Union were worthy of veneration, but angered that the noble president simply ended up "gettin' it in the back" upon the Civil War's conclusion. To the misty-eyed convict, the president's assassin, John Wilkes Booth, was simply "a ham," an "SOB" who got what he deserved in that Port Royal, Virginia, barn on April 26, 1865. For the rest of the day, the psychologist watched the convict and his fellow prisoners quietly sing the just-learned "Battle Hymn of the Republic" as they went about their tasks. This callous killer's patriotic emotions still resonated years later with the professor.[1]

Psychological studies such as Dr. Wilson's have shown that convicted felons are generally quite patriotic; however, "America" to them is not the government nor its citizens. America is an idea best represented by iconic symbols such as the Statue of Liberty, Mount Rushmore, the Iwo Jima Memorial, and, of course, Old Glory itself. Throughout our nation's history, patriotism has taken on different perspectives, based in large measure on what lens the citizen is looking through. What exactly is patriotism? What constitutes a loyal patriot? To whom or what is loyalty due—and under what conditions? These were all hotly contested questions for Northern citizens during the American Civil War, just as they are in our present day. The contrasting question, then as now, is: What exactly makes one a traitor and what should be considered treasonous activities? After all, if a convicted murderer can be an America-loving patriot, can a so-called traitor also be an upstanding, honorable man? The answers to those questions, how they were determined and by whom, together with the consequences of not being properly patriotic in the Civil War North are interconnected subjects that lie at the heart of this book.[2]

Defining loyal versus treasonous speech or acts are conundrums that have faced every government in times of political or military turmoil, whether the conflict was an internal rebellion or external war. It can be argued that civil wars elicit even stronger "black and white" definitions of loyalty and treason considering the intensity of brother fighting brother and family against family. The Civil War was certainly no different, especially in the tumultuous middle years. In fact, these questions manifested themselves more forcefully than perhaps any other time in American history. The American Civil War was the first significant occasion in the young nation's history where questions of loyalty and treason stretched from one end of the land to the other.[3]

Speaking out against potential hostility was certainly acceptable in the North during the months prior to the bombardment of Fort Sumter in April 1861, for few in the North sought war. Legislators and citizens across the Northern political spectrum were open to any solution that would prevent such a calamity, as long as the results did not mean disunion or dishonor. But with the attack upon that Charleston harbor fort, many Northern citizens changed their perception permanently: Secession speech had been replaced by treasonous violence directed against the republic. The Stars and Stripes had been desecrated, nation and honor were at stake, and it became imperative to many in the North that the Rebels must be taught a lesson. Three days after Fort Sumter surrendered, Lincoln called for 75,000 ninety-day state militia to march into the South and force the seceded states to recant. For the Republican Lincoln administration, preserving the Union was sacrosanct.[4]

Meanwhile, Democrats also proclaimed their virtue, which is patriotism's core element. Wrapping themselves in the flag, they laid claim to the moral high ground by their unwavering loyalty to the U.S. Constitution. For most Democrats, including the so-called "War Democrats," suppressing the rebellion and restoring the Union through military force was acceptable; however, the explosive slavery issue was not a legitimate rationale for war because of the simple fact that slavery was legal in much of the United States. Furthermore, slavery was a "hands-off" issue driven by the fact that almost all Northern whites were unrepentant racists by twenty-first century standards, viewing the African as the social, moral, and physiological inferior to the white man. Though most whites abhorred slavery and considered it morally wrong, those sentiments were trumped by its legality. Each state or territory had the right to decide for itself whether slavery would exist within its borders. Using military force to eliminate the South's "peculiar institution" was deemed a constitutional violation and an unlawful usurpation of power by the Federal government. This bloc of the Northern population viewed themselves as true patriots. Often referred to as the Civil War's political *conservatives,* their convictions held to a narrow, literal interpretation of the U.S. Constitution, the nation's laws, and the civil rights guaranteed to each *white* person within them. As the war ground on, they considered Lincoln's Emancipation Proclamation and the Enrollment Act mandating conscription to be unconstitutional. Vitriolic Democratic editors denounced the war, encouraged young men to avoid enlisting, and condemned the "black Republican" politicians who were risking white lives in order to free black slaves. After Lincoln's Proclamation and the Enrollment Act went into effect on January 1 and March 3, 1863, respectively, this anti-Lincoln and antiblack portion of the Northern populace was routinely referred to as "Secesh," "Butternuts," and worse by their Republican enemies. One of the harshest epithets used to describe an anti-Lincoln, antiwar Democrat was "Copperhead," first used in 1861 as a comparison to the poisonous snake slithering along the ground. When Peace Democrats attempted to turn the tables on that epithet by wearing the "Lady Liberty" copper penny as their symbol of pride, Iowa's Gov. Samuel Kirkwood referred to the newly styled breastpins as "the emblems of moral treason." Regardless of the term, every American of that era knew those words were derogatory and by utilizing those nicknames, Republicans engaged in a type of verbal shorthand that questioned the loyalty and integrity of Democratic partisans. Their reputation, deserved or not, became one of peace at any price, subversion, and even outright treason.[5]

Numerically speaking, many but certainly not all of the Northern antiwar, anti-Lincoln dissidents came from the poor, unskilled working class who had emigrated to the North from the Ohio Valley as well as poor European immigrants who had settled in Eastern city slums. This latter scenario was often true for the poverty-stricken Irish, who had fled the late 1840s potato famine in their homeland seeking a better life in the United States. Unlike other European immigrants, however, the Irish had been engaged at home in a protracted war against what they construed as a foreign English government; therefore, many did not feel loyalty toward the state that other immigrants felt, though certainly an antiwar ideology also played a role. Furthermore, conscription into the British Army provided an additional impetus for the Irish to leave their old country. For that reason, a possible military draft in the new world was likewise viewed doubtfully. Working-class German American Catholics were another ethnoreligious group often found in Democratic circles. Like their Irish immigrant brethren, German American Catholics disdained what they saw as the three "-*isms*" permeating the Republican Party: prohibitionism against alcohol, antislavery abolitionism, and Know-Nothingism, the early to mid-1850s nativist political movement that was resolutely anti-immigrant and anti-Catholic. Within political circles, many legislators held to a literal interpretation of the Constitution, which maintained each state had the right to determine for itself whether it would preserve slavery. Furthermore, these men viewed the Union as a mere association of the individual states, with any state free to leave the Union if it so desired. Though devoted to their country, they believed the national government did not have the legal right to force the seceded states back into the federal Union.[6]

Concurrently, Lincoln administration supporters viewed any public dissension from government policy as treasonous sympathy for the enemy. If treason was deemed the greatest crime under the law, it was because the government's highest duty was self-preservation. Americans have seen similar positioning even in modern times with the overseas affairs in Iraq and Afghanistan. Defining treason in theory versus current reality may often be politically ambiguous.[7]

Lincoln was careful not to describe the seceding states in any manner that might be construed as a de facto acknowledgment of their actions and legitimacy, opting instead to use the term "so-called Confederate States." If the Southern states had the right to secede and form a new government, then Lincoln did not have the right to raise an army, send it into those states, and force them back into the Union at the point of the bayonet. With such recognition, Confederate soldiers would have the international status of belligerents and all recognized rights under the international rules of warfare. Such theoretical talk ended on April 12, 1861, when Confederate batteries opened fire on Fort Sumter. Dissenting speech had been replaced by subversive action—the secessionists' attempt to kill Union soldiers and destroy federal property. Thus, from the war's outset, the Lincoln administration, its political allies, and the pro-Lincoln press portrayed the Confederacy and its purported Northern sympathizers as black-hearted insurgents guilty of treason.[8]

The reader should note that treason is the only crime defined in the United States Constitution. Article 3, Section 3 of that document states: "Treason against the United States, shall consist only in levying War against them, or in adhering to their Enemies, *giving them Aid and Comfort* [italics added]. No Person shall be convicted of Treason unless on the Testimony of two Witnesses to the same overt Act, or on Confession in open Court." The intentional use of the phrase "overt act" meant Union-leaning politicians and judges would not be able to cite mere speech or a suspected conspiracy as an act of treason, thereby eliminating the ability to use a treason allegation for partisan purposes.[9]

The legal challenge of alleging treason was first illustrated in the Civil War era by the October 16–18, 1859, raid by John Brown and eighteen followers against the Federal arsenal at Harpers Ferry, Virginia. In what many consider the rebellion's opening salvo, Brown attempted to obtain arms in order to inspire a slave uprising throughout the South. Several town residents were killed in the brief skirmish, but the locals held their own, forcing Brown and his men to take refuge in the arsenal's firehouse. United States troops, led by then-Lt. Col. Robert E. Lee and Lt. J. E. B. Stuart soon arrived and attacked the building, killing at least six of Brown's men while capturing him.[10]

The state of Virginia was stunned and outraged by Brown's actions and intentions, for an armed slave revolt was what white Southern society feared most. Brown and his men were certainly guilty of something, but exactly what? Was Brown's crime an act of war or the simple murder of local townsfolk? Seeking to give a political face to its indignation (and fear), Virginia charged Brown with treason against the state, as opposed to the felony charge of murder or military belligerence. This charge illustrated the emotional appeal of alleging treason against an accused, as opposed to his actions being viewed as mere dissent or even simple criminality. As George Fletcher pointed out, with such a charge Virginia "converted Brown's acts of violence into a calculated act of betrayal." By making such a claim, Virginia alleged Brown owed loyalty and fealty to that state, even though Brown was not a Virginia resident or a Virginian by birth. Furthermore, by charging Brown with treason, Virginia maintained it was a sovereign entity and enjoyed a relationship with its citizens that demanded loyalty, despite the aforementioned fact that Brown was not a Virginia citizen or resident. Brown was found guilty and hanged by Virginia on December 2, 1859, only three months after his trial ended. He walked up the gallows' steps unrepentant, a man who considered himself to be of a "different nation" and values than Virginia alleged, and quickly became the North's first martyr.[11]

In the John Brown case and throughout the Civil War, the angry cry of "Treason!" was often the pro-Union accuser's outraged sense of the South and its Northern sympathizers' betrayal. Moreover, making lofty accusations was one thing, gaining a conviction in a court of law was quite another. When Tennessee's fifty-seven-year-old "Parson" William G. Brownlow thundered that Democratic antiwar dissidents had but two rights, "the right to be hanged and the right to be damned," he gave voice to this dilemma. If they were not to be hanged because a legal conviction for treason was too problematic, they were certainly going to be openly damned within the court of public opinion. For many Northern Democrats on the receiving end of the treason accusation, they believed it was easier for their opponents to lump the Lincoln administration's political opposition in with traitors rather than trying to do the right thing the right way. From conservative Democrats' vantage, the ends could never justify the means. "The Constitution was not constructed upon a sliding scale," advised an Illinois senator to his colleagues. When a Union League formed in Doylestown, Pennsylvania, in the summer of 1863, the local Democratic paper complained only seven of the league's 130 members volunteered to help defend the state during the Rebel invasion that culminated at Gettysburg. "It is easier to abuse Copperheads than fight rebels," concluded the editor. As this work will show, what was often left out of Democrats' arguments was that their adherents had indeed often engaged in overt, subversive violence against pro-Union civilians or federal authority in an attempt to undermine the war effort. In many (if not most) instances where a civilian was arrested for subversive violence or conspiracy to carry out the same, the arresting authorities had solid cases.[12]

Despite the precedent of the John Brown case, the Lincoln administration's ability to secure treason convictions was going to be difficult at best, due in large measure to the legal writ of habeas corpus. *Habeas corpus* is a Latin phrase that means "you shall have the body" and by the start of the Civil War, the writ of habeas corpus had been a cornerstone of anglophone jurisprudence for over two and a half centuries. In essence, it required the arresting authorities to literally bring the accused before the court, where formal charges would have to be put forth or the accused set free. Lincoln's suspension of the writ was designed to allow the Union military to arrest suspected secessionists and hold them indefinitely, rather than see the accused tried in a civil court, where embarrassing acquittals were a distinct possibility. The modern debate over detaining suspected Islamic terrorists at Cuba's Guantanamo Bay military detention facility and whether or not these men should be tried in a civil or military court raises some, but not all, of the same concerns. In the president's opinion, suspending the writ was comparable to cutting off a limb in order to save a life, but you would never sacrifice a life in order to save a limb. Lincoln and his Cabinet knew that actually trying these men for treason would prove to be far more difficult than the arrest. This would be especially challenging in the still-loyal border states of Delaware, Maryland, Kentucky, or Missouri if the presiding judge held some personal sympathy with the Southern cause.[13]

Adding to Lincoln's legal dilemma was the fact that death was the only permissible penalty for treason when the Civil War started. Since no statutory sedition laws were in effect, those who spoke out against the war could receive only the death penalty if charged and convicted of treason. Everyone knew the federal government could not hang every antiwar Northerner or Confederate soldier.[14]

This is one reason why Lincoln and his allies viewed Copperhead pronouncements against the war and their sometimes violent antiwar protests as a significant threat to the home front. "Must I shoot a simple-minded soldier boy who deserts," asked Lincoln rhetorically, "while I must not touch a hair of the wily agitator who induces him to desert?" Within this growing "culture war," Republicans became convinced that antiwar or antidraft speeches and violent protest were treasonous activities because they offered "aid and comfort" to the enemy. For those Northern individuals who admitted assisting Southern family or friends, but claimed opposition to secession and, therefore, were not guilty of treason, the Lincoln administration occasionally had such persons banished under guard into the Confederacy, well beyond Union lines. Such deportations allowed administration authorities to ignore civil trials while smugly stating they were allowing the individuals to give a sincere expression of their feelings in a more appropriate theater. After all, "It is but just to our government and laws," claimed one Union military tribunal, "that the shield of its power should not be thrown over those who are inimical to it, and are giving active aid and sympathy to its enemies." Rejecting the very idea of a loyal opposition in the midst of a civil war, the tribunal concluded, "The claim to protection by the government implies the reciprocity of fealty." How to manage the "free speech" issue proved to be a vexing dilemma for the Lincoln administration, since managing the war efficiently mandated some regulation of public communications, which stood in stark contrast to the war's objectives.[15]

In addition, the very nature of revolution or the right of rebellion against what one considered a tyrannical government was dismissed by steadfast Union loyalists. Arguing that while man's right to revolution existed in the abstract, it ended when a society had established "a free popular government with all its appropriate institutions and a constitution duly regulating the administration of that government, and itself amendable by the people." If such a society existed, as staunch Unionists believed it did within the United States, then an armed uprising against a free constitutional government without justifying conditions was never a right, but merely a crime. If Lincoln the lawyer and his political allies were well aware of how challenging and imprudent going after treason convictions would be in a civil court, they were also well aware that the court of public opinion would be a far easier setting in which to solidify their definitions of what constituted patriotic loyalty versus treason.[16]

The entire debate over loyalty and treason reached the boiling point as summer 1862 progressed into fall. Repeated military defeats, economic worries, and staggering casualties all combined to prompt many Northern civilians to question the war's viability and cost. The public's frustration exploded into anger when Abraham Lincoln issued his preliminary Emancipation Proclamation in September. While many Northerners were willing to risk their lives to restore the Union, relatively few saw the benefit in jeopardizing white lives or livelihoods to free black slaves.

These disgruntled voices only grew louder. Prowar advocates labeled them as "peace at any price" traitors who blamed blacks for everything while always arguing that Lincoln's decisions were wrongheaded at best and unconstitutional at worst. Antiblack and antidraft street riots broke out in several Midwestern towns. Pro-Lincoln men were physically attacked and saw their farms vandalized by Copperheads. This growing civilian disenchantment led to significant Republican defeats in the November elections. As 1862 ended, Union confidence was at rock bottom.

Across the North, ardent pro-Union men realized their country needed a patriotic stimulus, as well as an organized means of countering their Copperhead adversaries' treasonous statements and physical violence against loyal, pro-Union men. For as William Stoddard, one of Lincoln's personal secretaries later wrote of those days, "There is no Confederate army in the field that is so dangerous as the political army now assailing the administration." A new sense of *nationalistic* patriotism needed to be introduced into the populace, one that would supplant the dominant regional or sectional loyalties that had worked against a national consciousness since the country's founding. Loyalty toward the national state had to replace the dominant moral sympathy for others as the proper mechanism for generating proper American allegiance. As Elizabeth Duquette noted, "Consistently opposed to sympathy's poor politics and local allegiances, loyalty encouraged a movement of both moral norms and political practices away from feeling by suggesting that rational reflection provided a more stable basis for national affiliation."[17]

Furthermore, those loyal, pro-Union men argued how it was essential that the *right type* of patriotic fervor and loyalty manifest itself. For loyalty to be considered proper, it had to be unconditional and directed not merely toward constitutional precepts, but toward the Lincoln administration and all of its war policies. Since the Confederacy had ready access to Northern newspapers, any anti-Lincoln, antiwar, or Southern-sympathizing editorials surely gave "aid and comfort" to the Rebel enemy and were therefore equated with treason.

These generally middle-aged, civilian men created what became known as Union Leagues: quasi-secretive "clubs" whose potential members had to possess "unqualified loyalty to the Government of the United States, and unwavering support of its efforts for the suppression of the Rebellion." Their mysterious member initiation rites featured prayers, oaths, songs, and patriotic symbols that were likened to a religious ceremony. Members vocalized the League's nationalistic viewpoint in speeches and served as campaign workers. They served as an armed "home guard" to protect their families, neighborhoods, and federal authority against Copperhead violence. They helped recruit white and colored military regiments, and when deemed necessary, employed social and commercial ostracism as a means of enforcing loyalty and stifling dissent that shocked polite society. On a murkier level, some members displayed no hesitation in smashing Democratic presses and serving as a form of civilian secret police for the Union military. The Union League crusade and its various offshoots spread like wildfire across the North. By the end of 1863, it seemed as if every hamlet from Maine to California had formed its own council.

In a singular sense, the Civil War–era Union League was what is now known as a "pressure group," defined as an organized assembly of individuals who share a common opinion, values, or point of view and who try to influence the policies of government or business to their end. While many groups may operate independently of the government, others can also work hand in glove with the government. This was the case with the Union Leagues, for though they initially raised a nonpartisan banner, by the war's last year they were in open collaboration with the Lincoln administration, its Republican allies, as well as the Union military.

Obviously, such groups have to strive for attention in order to be heard and achieve success. As modern studies of public opinion and propaganda have shown,[18] it is often far easier to rally the masses *against* a particular idea or person rather than *for* a specific cause. The Union Leagues and their loosely affiliated publishing societies explicitly illustrated this precept. For in their goal to shape public opinion and achieve their war aims, they attacked their "treasonous" Democrat and Copperhead foes relentlessly, as do many modern pressure groups.

Famed landscape architect Frederick Law Olmsted knew this well when he first conceived the idea for what became the Union League Club of New York by writing to a colleague, "It is easier to profess true hate than true love." The Union Leagues, their kindred publication societies, Republican political allies, and sympathetic newspaper editors worked this concept ceaselessly in convincing the Northern populace of their shared conviction that pro-Southern secret cabals were lurking throughout the North. It became the duty of every loyal and true patriot to counteract their treasonous activity by joining his local Union League council and voting the Republican ticket.[19]

My personal "aha!" moment arrived when I discovered this last point. I realized that the often angry, partisan media considered so prevalent in today's culture is not a new phenomenon, but rather has its roots in antebellum and Civil War–era journalism. As I delved further into the Union Leagues, I realized their story intersected with two of my keenest interests: Civil War history and contemporary politics. It became apparent to me how some of the most important political issues in our current news cycle are strikingly similar to the serious political debates faced by the Union Leagues during the Civil War. For instance, as I type these words in the summer of 2016, our nation is watching a relatively small but elite faction of a major political party attempting to replace that party's very popular and apparent presidential nominee with someone more to their liking. The parallels to 1864 will become obvious.

Placing Lincoln's controversial Emancipation Proclamation alongside the modern Iraq War's divisive switch from the publicly approved search for weapons of mass destruction to contentious nation-building allows us to compare each era's response to a president who added a second, highly provocative reason for continuing a bloody war—when that war was originally commenced based on only one widely agreed-upon reason. An examination of those two historic events also allows us to compare and then ask how a president's supporters should respond to antiwar protesters whose actions were viewed by administration loyalists as more sympathetic to the enemy than toward the nation's own men and women in uniform. Do these protesters not enjoy the same public, free speech rights as those who agree with the administration?

The Union League movement faced all of these questions during the Civil War and answered them by declaring that anything less than unconditional support for the government was treasonous. The Leagues acknowledged that freedom of speech was always a cherished ideal in the abstract; however, in wartime, when the nation's survival was at stake, the civic obligation for all good men was to close ranks and join together. As Edmund Burke, the eighteenth-century Irish statesman observed, "When bad men combine, the good must associate; else they will fall, one by one, an unpitied sacrifice in a contemptible struggle." For the men who created and then led the Union Leagues, this meant obedience and unconditional loyalty to the Lincoln administration and all of its war policies. In their fight for public opinion, they argued there was no differentiating between the administration and the government. They were one and the same.

Abraham Lincoln certainly understood the need for winning the public's heart and mind. In one of his famous 1858 debates with Illinois Sen. Stephen Douglas, Lincoln remarked, "In this and like communities, public sentiment is everything. With public sentiment, nothing can fail; without it nothing can succeed. Consequently he who moulds public sentiment, goes deeper than he who enacts statutes or pronounces decisions. He makes statutes and decisions possible or impossible to be executed."[20]

Through collaborations with other related loyalty groups and their quasi-affiliated publication arms, the Union League movement published and disseminated millions of pamphlets and broadsides over the war's last two and a half years. This deluge of political propaganda represented a quantity unlike anything previously imaginable, all intended to ensure public sentiment was indeed molded to their favor. These documents contained speeches, sermons, and editorial points of view that alternated between outright propaganda for the Union cause, heartfelt appeals for support toward the Lincoln administration, as well as vicious attacks against the Southern slavocracy and their alleged Northern Democrat-Copperhead sympathizers. The Union Leagues' actions also went a long way toward swaying the North's citizenry not only about the war's ongoing necessity but also about its righteous evolution from a goal of solely preserving the Union toward one that also included emancipation for black slaves.

The recently concluded Civil War sesquicentennial brought forth several well-received books that discussed the issues of loyalty, treason, and duty during the Civil War.[21] Yet for much of Civil War historiography in general, the North's Union Leagues were presented as a mere footnote—benign, patriotic civilian clubs whose efforts had little impact on the Civil War's Northern home front or outcome. Other works portrayed the Union Leagues as the artificial, top-down creation of cynical Republican Party leaders who sought to create a loyalty-driven machine that would battle "treasonous" Democrats and the feared Knights of the Golden Circle. In modern jargon, this is known as an "Astroturf" campaign.

This book will challenge these two myths by showing how the Union Leagues began as a true organic, grassroots movement. In addition, it will argue that the Union League movement's eventual nationalization made it the North's *primary* arbiter of how loyalty and treason were defined within the North's court of public opinion, all with Lincoln's full knowledge and approval. The Union Leagues' ability to influence voter opinion and turnout manifested itself in the Republicans' 1863 election gains and, perhaps more importantly, Lincoln's reelection in the 1864 presidential contest. They overwhelmed their Democratic opponents in the propaganda war by convincing the public that Democratic loyalty was conditional at best. The Union Leagues were hardly benign and inconsequential. Rather, they became a million-man civilian army who waged a home front war against treason with the pen—and occasionally the musket—while their brothers in blue fought a hot war down South with the sword. Their success in helping to maintain Northern morale throughout the dark days of 1863 and 1864 demonstrates that a national army at war must have its citizens' emotional and physical support in order to succeed. Without that bond—as evidenced by the Vietnam conflict's latter years—military success will not be achieved.

Why have the Union Leagues been so overlooked within Civil War scholarship? Over seventy thousand books have been written about some facet of the Civil War since the rebellion commenced 150-plus years ago; nevertheless, this volume represents the first-ever, book-length published work to examine the entire wartime Union League movement. I believe there are several reasons. First, the movement's secretive nature and relatively short-lived existence did not lend itself to recording great amounts of published history. Though the aristocratic Union League clubs in Philadelphia, New York, and Boston have maintained their social club existence to this day, along with their voluminous archives, almost all of the small-town chapters throughout the North faded away soon after the war ended, their reason for being having ended. The minutes and records for only a small handful still exist. The published pamphlets that described the proceedings for wartime Union League conventions do still exist and provide great insight. Nonetheless, there is no single records cache for the Union League movement in any centrally held location. Historians must ferret out the specific Union League–related correspondence ensconced in various individual letters and diaries to gain a further understanding.

Lastly, scholars first examined the Union League movement during the early twentieth-century and then almost exclusively for its role in Reconstruction. It was not treated favorably, which did not generate excitement for a deeper examination. Only with the dawn of the civil rights crusade did scholars take a second glance and then only to slightly alter the historical interpretation.[22] Considering the current interest in Civil War home front studies, this book will hopefully become a welcome addition to that aspect of the Civil War era's growing body of knowledge.

This book begins with a brief history of secretive fraternal organizations and their psychological appeal to the nineteenth-century male. It continues with a discussion of the various border state "Union Clubs" that existed prior to the Civil War. The final chapter offers a contextual overview of how the Northern-based Union League of America migrated southward during Reconstruction to focus on organizing freedmen based on the twin goals of racial equality and Republican Party political dominance. The book's overarching focus, however, is from the summer of 1862, when the Union League movement was first created, how it blossomed across the North in 1863, and then charged ahead toward the November 1864 presidential election, when it had become *the* powerful propaganda machine for the Lincoln administration and the Republican Party.

Chapter 1

"Quiet Men Are Dangerous"

Civilian Antecedents of the Union Leagues

Man is a social creature, with character traits that result from the herd instinct. Throughout all of recorded history, he has sought companionship
and refuge with others of like mind. In times of strife, men of similar convictions gathered for emotional protection and security, as well as for physical defense. In times of peace and tranquility, men joined together based
upon the social metaphor of brotherhood and fellowship to pursue similarly held religious convictions, to advance a fraternal cause that will im-
prove the quality of human life, or to gather to enjoy each other's company
in an entertaining environment. Many of these latter gatherings resulted in
the formation of "open" organizations, such as the modern-day Rotary or
Lions Clubs, where any may join to share in the group's mission. Other
such gatherings gave rise to "closed" associations, where men of comparable wealth or social stature associated only among themselves. In such private groups, admittance is gained only through invitation, for the herd
wants agreement, not independent thought or criticism.[1]

It is this latter want that gave rise to the gentleman's club in the United
States during the first half of the nineteenth century. These clubs based their
structure and design on similar grand clubs that had permeated London
since the late eighteenth century. At its highest level, "society" was defined
by white men who belonged to these clubs. Among the earliest and most
important was the Union Club of New York City, formed in 1836 as a refuge
for "gentlemen of social distinction." In particular, it brought together the
monied elite in a purely social setting, where men of power and wealth could
dine with their peers and share their various business affairs, tastes, and in-

tellectual thoughts in a uniquely male domain that existed somewhere between the gentleman's public and private life. When the Union Club moved into a new building in 1855, it marked the first time that a building was utilized solely for club purposes, which stood as a testament to the increasing social importance of class-based segregated spaces. By the late 1850s, three smaller though no less important social clubs had formed in the city. Two were formed for aficionados of yachting and the literary arts respectively; however, in both cases meeting the era's definition of what constituted a gentleman was paramount for admission. In the twenty-five years prior to the start of the Civil War, similar exclusive clubs were formed throughout the Eastern seaboard's major cities illustrating that the patrician Union League clubs that formed in early 1863 in Philadelphia, New York, and Boston were not an entirely new concept.[2]

A semipolitical group with the Union League name existed in New York City as early as 1860, though it was completely unrelated to the better-known Union League Club of New York formed in 1863 and which still exists. This earlier League was politically conservative in tone, meaning that its core principles held to a strict interpretation of the Constitution and a fealty to the nation's laws, which included the right of any citizen to move his property into any territory without distinction. That meant a conviction that slavery was legal and, therefore, should not be tampered with by any governmental body other than the respective states. The League's doctrine further stated they could not support any candidate whose beliefs were not in harmony with theirs. To that end, numerous papers across the country were reporting in the early months of 1860 how the League's National Executive Committee had issued a proclamation for a convention to meet in July, when it would determine if the League should offer its support to any specific presidential candidate. Though its stated principles stressed that the League's motives were "of the purest patriotism," their doctrines would have pleased any steadfast Southerner. This early New York Union League opposed Lincoln in the 1860 presidential election and soon found itself on the outside looking in, vanishing from the political landscape soon thereafter.[3]

Such closed associations also existed in the South in the years before the Civil War. Most notable were the Knights of the Golden Circle, a militant, secret, oath-bound society created by George W. L. Bickley at Cincinnati in 1854 as a means of furthering American expansion southward. This was the era of "Manifest Destiny," a term coined in 1845 by *Democratic Review* editor John O' Sullivan in the belief that American expansionism was providential and preordained. For the Knights, their targeted "golden circle" encompassed the area of Central America, the Caribbean, and especially Mexico. Any man could join, Southern or Northern, as long as he prescribed to the Southern interpretation of Constitutional principles, which included slavery's preservation. Through the late 1850s and into 1860, Bickley was a frequent public speaker on the Knights' behalf while their Southern expansion goals and activities often appeared in Southern newspapers. When they realized that civil war could become a real possibility, Bickley and the Knights abandoned the notion of foreign expansion and aligned the group with Southern secession and antiabolitionism. Bickley described the Knights as "a nucleus around which Southern men could rally." The KGC, as the group became known, soon grew into the northern Union Leagues' archenemy, as well as the North's villain for all manner of anti-Lincoln plots and treasonable actions. Union-leaning men feared for their physical safety to such an extent that Kentucky's centralized Union Club published its own revelations of the KGC monster.[4]

Such semisecretive voluntary organizations whose goals were primarily political, reform, religious, or simply fraternal had existed throughout history. Benjamin Franklin, for instance, established a club in Philadelphia in 1727 dedicated to the cause of moral improvement. Known as The Junto, Franklin explained in his autobiography that members were to discuss any question pertaining to morals, politics, or natural philosophy. By the mid-nineteenth century, such private groups were extremely popular in the United States. For example, the Sons of Temperance was created in 1842 with the goal of reforming alcoholics and established simple initiation rites. The Know-Nothings, a short-lived and secretive political party from the early to mid-1850s, had taken their moniker from one of their initiation rituals, even though their candidates were officially designated under the American Party. Created from the Whig Party's disintegration coupled with schisms in the Democratic Party over slavery, their firm nativist beliefs and clandestine rituals attracted thousands of men to their organization.[5]

Perhaps the most famous of such organizations was the Masons or "Freemasons." The Masons were initially a Catholic-oriented order whose existence could be traced back to the skilled stoneworkers of medieval times. Cloaked in rites and ritual, Masonic meetings were closed to the public with members swearing an oath of secrecy as to what transpired in their meetings. When Arthur Newell revealed to his brother in October 1864 that he had "rode the goat" during his local Loyal League initiation, he was referring to a purported Masonic phrase that described the secret nature of its own initiation rite. Outside of their lodges, Masons utilized secret handshakes and other undisclosed signs of recognition. These clandestine acts were all later adapted by the Union Leagues, especially in the Midwest, where secrecy was often deemed necessary due to violence against pro-Lincoln men. By the start of the Civil War, the Masons had existed in the United States for almost 130 years and were well known at the time as a fraternal and charitable society with spiritual overtones. Its members included such luminaries as Union generals George McClellan and Lew Wallace, Adm. David Farragut, and Democratic Ohio Rep. Clement Vallandigham. On the Southern side, Gen. Lewis Armistead was a notable Confederate Mason.[6]

Beyond such self-evident wartime security, why was such an emphasis on secret ritual with religious and mystical overtones so important to the mid-nineteenth-century young male initiate? Mark Carnes contended that such devices provided passage, i.e., support and emotional guidance as he made his way into full manhood. The secretive fraternal order offered refuge from an increasingly secular domain laden with worldly and monetary burdens via a belief system that granted order and fellowship. Secrecy not only added an element of mystique to the organization while excluding so-called "outsiders," but also furnished an important emotional element of possession to members. The prospect of advancing within a hierarchical organization by degrees or ranks, such as in the case of the Masons and the post–Civil War Grand Army of the Republic respectively, likewise appealed to many men and were quite common within the country's fraternal organizations during the second half of the nineteenth century, or what W. S. Harwood labeled the "Golden Age of fraternity." Within both groups, a member's advancement was accompanied by a distinctive ceremony, which included secret grips and passwords, as well as an allegorical performance that showcased the group's underlying reason for being. These ranks offered social distinction while their quasi-military overtones offered a measure of camaraderie that young, middle-class men found appealing.[7]

Yet in many instances, it appeared that these fraternal groups' entire emphasis was on ritual with any additional core activities undertaken almost by chance. These orders were almost entirely middle class and masculine in nature with their stylized rituals closely linked to issues of gender and paternalism. Though the later Union Leagues would also have female chapters, membership was always strictly divided along gender lines.[8]

Similar organizations and clubs consisting of loyal Union men were formed in Kentucky and Missouri as much as a year and a half prior to the war's commencement in April 1861. The agitation and potential for bloodshed was particularly acute in both border states, for they were founded by pro-slavery men and were both culturally and geographically tied to the South. Not only were these men adept at getting sympathetic politicos into office, but into vote-counting positions as well. Just for good measure, the old time-honored tradition of importing voters from neighboring states was utilized as well as outright physical intimidation. Defiant Unionists were to be simply driven away. As the storm clouds of war began to darken the horizon, those who considered themselves loyal Union men began to gather together for both influence and protection.[9]

Since each state's loyalty to the North or South was still up in the air, avid supporters of both sides began to gather to help sway public opinion. January 2, 1860, saw a "Union" meeting in Maysville, Kentucky, and then a huge public gathering on February 22 in Frankfort, where resolutions were passed declaring the people were for both the Union and the Constitution, and that both must be preserved. In addition to the public gatherings designed for any who wanted to attend, private antisecession Union clubs were being formed in early 1860 once many sensed that civil war was a possibility. The Democratic-leaning *Covington Journal* reported in early July that such an organization had recently formed and was making a special appeal to the young men of that city. "*They* have no interest in the bitter personal quarrels of selfish old politicians . . . they detest sectionalism. . . . The Union Party is now the only national party in the country," it asserted. In Louisville, the sixth ward formed a Union Club on July 19 while the city's seventh and eighth wards did likewise one week later. Following Lincoln's election in early November 1860, Union meetings were a regular event throughout the state. Though these clubs were antisecession and dedicated to the Union's preservation, they avoided any endorsement of what many called the "Black Republican" party.[10]

The Union clubs that formed in Kentucky and Missouri through 1860 and 1861 were secretive in nature and designed so that their members might become known to each other in case any type of violence broke out against them—characteristics later adopted by the Midwestern Union Leagues in 1862–64. Meetings were usually held at night behind guarded doors. Members laid out plans as to how they were to communicate with each other via secret passwords, phrases, and handshakes. Most club founders were older family men who knew they were not fit for the regular army but stood ready to serve within a local home guard unit. All agreed that none but well-known and trustworthy Union men would be admitted. Unlike New England or the Deep South, where sentiments generally went only one way, "here on the border it was quite different," wrote Missourian Robert Matthews. "You did not know who was friend or who was foe." Like the Midwestern Union Leagues that followed them, these men were often not politicians, the wealthy, or professionals who always had a finger raised in the political wind, but men who made up the skilled trades, shopkeepers, small manufacturers, bookkeepers, and the like. Within weeks, the number of such men in the Louisville, Kentucky, area numbered close to six thousand.[11]

Following the lead of Kentucky, Union clubs sprang up throughout the land in 1860 and 1861. Some of these were aligned with the Democratic Party and certainly did not align themselves with so-called "Black Republicans" who held an abolitionist agenda. Yet they decried any secession talk. "It is difficult to tell whether there is greater danger to the Union in this crisis in the South or in the North," lamented an Ohio paper in August 1860. The sheet saw disunionists in the South and ardent abolitionists in the North, the latter who were "fully organized with secret clubs." It urged Union clubs to form throughout that state to help ensure that Democrats would carry the upcoming presidential election, which was the only way to save the Union. Such clubs' firm loyalty was to the Union, such as the Central Union Club of Dayton (Ohio), which was formed in September 1860 and was dedicated to the "defence [sic] and propagation of the principles of the Constitutional Union Party, as proclaimed in its national and patriotic platform, 'the Constitution, the Union, and the enforcement of its Laws.'" That simply meant that slavery was legal and should not be eliminated by force of arms. By January 1862, over sixty Union clubs had formed in Ohio to combat the growing peace-at-any-cost movement and were organized to the extent that they were able to conduct a statewide meeting in Cincinnati. All but six of these clubs were in Ohio's lower half, where Southern sympathies remained the strongest. The conference also noted in its proceedings that their expansion efforts had also resulted in clubs being formed in Wisconsin, Indiana, and one in loyal western Virginia.[12]

Just to the west of Kentucky lay the slave state of Missouri. It had entered the union in 1821 as the nation's twenty-fourth state due to what was known as the Missouri Compromise. That congressional act was the agreement between antislavery and pro-slavery factions as to how that institution would be regulated in the western territories and any future states that might arise. In return for admitting Missouri as a slave state, the act specified that slavery would be outlawed in any area north of the parallel 36 degrees 30 minutes north except within the boundaries of the then proposed state of Missouri. The Missouri Compromise kept the peace for over thirty years until 1854, when it was essentially nullified by the Kansas–Nebraska Act. That act allowed white male settlers in those territories, as well as any future territories, to vote under the concept of "popular sovereignty" as to whether slavery would be allowed in Nebraska or Kansas. The result was that pro- and antislavery men began pouring into those two territories in the mid-1850s in order to influence the future vote. Many Northern antislavery advocates and other Free-Soilers were aghast at the new act, which led in part to the birth of the Republican Party in 1854.[13]

It had become apparent that by the time of Lincoln's 1861 inauguration, Missouri's current governor, Claiborne Jackson, as well as most of the state's leading politicians, were openly sympathetic to the Southern cause. As in Kentucky, political clubs had formed in Missouri that were dedicated to the Union, such as the St. Louis Union Guard Club. In its resolutions, members declared their fealty to the Union. As a conservative group, however, they lamented Lincoln's election. Though the club stated their discouragement due to what they defined as the triumph of sectionalism, Lincoln's forthcoming presidency was not adequate reason to dissolve the Union as it existed.[14]

It was possible that union or disunion in Missouri might come down to which side gained control of St. Louis's massive armory. The lightly guarded arsenal was the largest weapons cache west of the Mississippi River and contained over 60,000 stands of arms, 150,000 ball cartridges, 45 tons of gunpowder, and dozens of cannons. Its seizure by secessionist forces would surely secure Missouri to the South. Union men had to act for it was also known that the arsenal's commanding officer, Maj. William H. Bell, was a Southern sympathizer. As a North Carolina native and an 1820 West Point graduate, Bell had deferred to the Southern-leaning state government while refusing to allow armed Unionist men to camp on the arsenal grounds.[15]

To counter this threat, St. Louis's loyal men gathered in early 1861 to form what became known as the Union Legion, twelve companies of men who armed themselves essentially out of their own pockets. The vast majority of these men were German-born and organized into paramilitary home guards, which were generally older married men recruited to serve only in St. Louis. These German immigrants held a particularly odious opinion of secessionists, not to mention the slaveholding aristocracy and the Puritan Sabbath.

Included in these armed groups were two German clubs that had formed for the 1860 election, one of which ominously called itself the Schwarzer Jaegercorp or Black Rifles, whom it was rumored would not ask for nor give quarter in a battle.[16]

The other, better-known group called itself the Wide Awakes, and it was the most similar, semisecretive forerunner to what became known as the Union Leagues two years later. Their first impromptu appearance was in Hartford, Connecticut, on February 25, 1860, when a group of young men spontaneously donned capes and torches to escort Kentucky's Cassius Clay, who was the evening's guest speaker as part of the then ongoing state governor campaign. Their formation as a marching club was completed a week later; their moniker coming from a local newspaper article pertaining to the Clay meeting that was titled "Republicans Wide Awake!" The phrase "Wide Awake" in a political sense, however, stretched back to the mid-1850s, when it had been utilized by the nativist Know-Nothings to symbolize the vigilance necessary against the alleged degrading influences from immigrants and Catholics.[17]

The German Wide Awake community in St. Louis was large and solidly Republican. Many had previous military training and had fled their homeland as political refugees following the failed revolts of 1848. "Germans had learned the bitter lesson of *Kleinstaaterei* [small-statism] in Germany," explained one immigrant, "and had no desire to transform the splendid, dignified union of the United States into a mass of independent, petty state sovereignties." A local German newspaper, *Anzeiger des Westens,* echoed that sentiment by asserting local Germans were not border raiders, Negro thieves, abolitionists, nor had they had anything to do with the John Brown raid. Nevertheless, they were strong slavery opponents and could be counted on to be present wherever free labor was being defended through law and order against the slavocracy's pressures. Such unflinching Republican support from the German community was frustrating to many pro-Southerners, whose perspective of Federal-state relations was the exact opposite. "Knowing nothing of the relations of the States to the Federal Government, nothing of the circumstances of its formation, nothing about the Constitution, [the Germans] could not comprehend that South Carolina had any more right to secede from the Union than St. Louis had to secede from Missouri," complained one ex-Confederate years later. "Owing his own citizenship to the United States and not to any State, he could not comprehend that to a Virginian loyalty and patriotism meant devotion to Virginia, and not to

Grand Procession of Wide Awakes in New York on the evening of October 3, 1860. (*Harper's Weekly*)

the Union." Furthermore, the Southerner noted that these Germans were strongly antislavery. Having no friends or relations from the South, they were extremely unsympathetic to that region's peculiar institution. Meanwhile, Blair began to turn the Wide Awakes into Union clubs. The clubs were open to all "unconditional Union men" and as they began to spring up in the town's various wards, their express goal was to fully cooperate with the military in combating pro-Southern forces.[18]

Wide Awake chapters soon formed across the country, throughout New England and the North and into the far west. Like the future Union Leagues, the Wide Awakes developed a national set of standardized rules while prospective members were subject to an initiation ritual and given secret passwords. Adding to the mystique was their quasi-military appearance, as members marched in martial precision during their midnight processions, all clad in matching glazed black capes and caps while occasionally chanting their marching cadence. Each member carried a torch lamp at the end of a sturdy wooden pole, which could also function as a weapon should any trouble break out. Dedicated to the Republican Party and its ideals, its members were generally young men in their twenties and thirties. A local Wide Awake chapter often escorted their candidate to the various political rallies in areas where the elections were contentious, their military appearance and potential weaponry serving as a not-so-subtle reminder to opposition rowdies to mind their manners.[19]

This organic and mounting wave inevitably caught the attention of Republican leaders. New York's Sen. William Seward—then the leading Republican presidential candidate—cheerfully addressed a large crowd of Wide Awakes at Detroit in early September 1860, showering the young men with praise. On September 13, at least 4,600 Wide Awake men in full regalia paraded up Broadway in New York City near midnight, their marching as disciplined as any regiment of crack soldiers. "What shall be done with this grand army of black republicans," asked the Democratic *New York Herald* with a hint of worry. On the day of election, they often monitored polling sites, challenging those not known to be legitimate voters. By the November 1860 presidential election, there were over four hundred Wide Awake chapters with upwards of 500,000 uniformed members. Meanwhile, Democrats watched the growing movement with apprehension. The Wide Awakes' black capes, steely martial bearing, and occasional noiseless processions moving as one stood in stark contrast to the boisterous and party-like cavorting that typified previous political parades. "Quiet men are dangerous," warned the *Herald*.[20]

The Union military also saw a potential alliance with the civilian Wide Awakes, as it would with the future Union Leagues. George Bickley had earlier proclaimed how his KGC was necessary as a counteracting organization to the Wide Awakes since that latter group was formed "to enforce Black Republican misrule upon the South." Now in a case of quid pro quo and fearing KGC-inspired violence against Abraham Lincoln at his Washington inauguration, Gen. David Hunter asked the president-elect, "Would it not be well, to have a hundred thousand Wide Awakes, wend their way quietly to Washington, during the first three days of March: taking with them their capes and caps? By a *coup-de-main* we could arm them in Washington." Meanwhile, George P. Bissell of the Hartford Wide Awakes assured Lincoln, "If you say the word, I will be there with from twenty to one thousand men, or one hundred, (any reasonable number) *organized & armed*."[21]

The Wide Awakes' youth and vigor provided the Union Army with some of its most fervent volunteers in the days following the start of the war. Only three days after the attack on Fort Sumter, scores secretly trained in Washington and Philadelphia. In St. Louis, the Wide Awake group was composed almost entirely of antislavery Germans, who were armed by Republican Rep. Francis Preston Blair Jr. The Wide Awakes slowly faded from view in the months following Fort Sumter, but their impact and influence were not forgotten. The idea of an organized civilian body with standardized rituals, acting as the paramilitary arm of the political party in power, and with the United States military's full sanction, was replicated by the Union Leagues three years later.[22]

An organization calling itself a Union League also appeared in Maryland—another border state where slavery was legal—with the intent of supporting the Union cause. Gerard Morgan, an official of that Baltimore-based group, later wrote that it had been formed "with the single purpose of opposing the secret machinations of the enemies of our government, upon the same principles of the Union Clubs of Kentucky," which Morgan claimed that they were in close contact with.[23]

Union clubs also formed as far west as California in 1860 and 1861. Though California was admitted as a "free" state into the Union in 1850, pro-secession sympathies burned hot as the 1860s dawned. Following the mid-April news that war had commenced, Republicans in San Francisco formed Union clubs within the town's twelve wards and soon had nine hundred armed men at the ready. Two days later, the party's central committee urged that similar armed clubs be organized throughout the state. When a rumor reached these men in August 1861 that five thousand Union troops were to be sent from the state to Texas, they urgently beseeched Secretary of War Simon Cameron to reconsider. "The hatred and bitterness toward the Union and Union men, manifested so pointedly in the South and so strongly evinced on the field of battle, is no more intense there than here," they asserted, also noting that the Knights of the Golden Circle had over sixteen thousand members in the state. Less than two months after the war's commencement, loyal men on the Pacific coast were reporting that "California is safe for the Union. We are forming Union clubs in every city, town and hamlet." Within two years, these California clubs were transforming into Union Leagues and home guards—and like the Wide Awakes, with a wink and a nod from the Union military.[24]

Fraternity, a shared pro-Union political conviction and a desire to spread that message, along with securing members' physical safety via the club's numerical strength, were all reasons why the pre–Civil War Union clubs formed in the year and a half leading up to Fort Sumter. Though their numbers and need would wane as 1861 progressed, their manner of organization, secrecy, and original underlying purpose served as an antecedent to the Union Leagues, which would be born in the dark days of summer 1862.

Chapter 2

"There Can Be No Neutrals in This War; Only Patriots or Traitors"

The Demand for Public Loyalty

Newly inaugurated President Abraham Lincoln realized that the Union's preservation hinged on maintaining federal control in the four border slave states of Maryland, Delaware, Kentucky, and Missouri. Slavery was legal in all four and though none had formally seceded, Lincoln knew their loyalty to the Union was tenuous.

In Kentucky, for example, many of the state's wealthy and affluent favored secession as the obvious way to preserve their peculiar institution. Since slavery was legal, however, others believed that defending the Union was the best way to protect slavery—that is, loyalty to Union and Constitution *for the benefit of* slavery's preservation. Most workingmen and the majority of the state's population, however, remained loyal Unionists. "I doubt not that two-thirds of our people are unconditionally for the Union," noted Sen. Garrett Davis to this end in a June letter to Union Gen. George McClellan. "The timid and quiet are for it, and they shrink from convulsion and civil war, whilst all the bold, the reckless, and the bankrupt are for secession." Yet by the Fourth of July, over twenty thousand people were in Lexington for a massive display of Union support that included a dedication of a statue to the late Henry Clay[1] and a parade that featured four companies of Unionist home guards.[2]

These home guard companies were grassroots, volunteer units who, like the Union clubs, had formed to meet what they considered a serious threat from Secesh or other disloyal elements within their communities who were purportedly plotting various forms of treason or insurrection. They were comprised of those men who, for whatever reason, had chosen not to enlist in the Federal volunteer regiments. Perhaps they were a family's sole bread-winner or possibly too old or ill to endure harsh campaigning. One study of such men in Illinois indicated they were generally financially well off and re-gardless of age, often ran large farms or businesses and thus incurred signifi-cant ongoing obligations within their community. Nonetheless, they were prepared to organize and arm themselves in order to protect their livelihoods and towns, as had their citizen-soldier forefathers from the Revolutionary War era. They believed this desire to protect the very income-producing as-sets that kept them from enlisting in the first place was, on a smaller scale, no different than protecting their state or the Union. This home guard concept was a key security element within pro-Union regions and would reappear in 1862 with numerous Union League councils forming their own companies.[3]

It was through the home guard organizing efforts of these average men that plans to take Kentucky into the Confederacy ultimately failed. Once the state legislature was safely in Unionist hands in the fall of 1861, how-ever, the need for the Union clubs slowly faded. That diminished need for these early Union clubs was due in large measure to a declining overt and public sympathy within Kentucky for the Confederate cause. Unionist men in the Bluegrass State began rapidly enlisting in the army or state militias while state and local authorities cracked down firmly on pro-Southern newspapers. Some sheets that existed for decades vanished almost over-night, including the *Lexington Statesman,* which was shut down for violat-ing a new state policy prohibiting "treasonable" public statements coupled with harassment by the local and state military authorities. Civilian author-ities often turned a blind eye toward such activity, just as they would soon do within the North.[4]

For pro-Union men, confronting "treason" in a border state like Kentucky that held widespread Southern influence was one thing; however, for loyal men to hear such talk in the North's own backyard was quite another. Even before the smoke cleared over Fort Sumter, the North was filled with public exhortations demanding loyalty and decrying treason. State legislatures from one end of the North to the other passed resolutions and military measures to show support for the war. At the capital, loyal Washingtonians angrily recalled how numerous Deep South politicians had resigned their congres-sional seats and headed home following their respective states' secession decisions during the 1860–61 winter. Mississippi's Sen. Jefferson Davis and his wife, Varina, were gone with Davis set to become president of what Lincoln referred to as the "so-called Confederate States." Louisiana's Sen. John Slidell and Florida's Sen. David Yulee had likewise left to assume new roles within the Confederate government while Adj. Gen. Samuel Cooper and Quartermaster Gen. Joseph E. Johnston had similarly resigned to head home.[5]

Now reality settled in as to how woefully unprepared the Union was to fight any war. The months leading up to Sumter only amplified the sad state of military affairs. The United States' regular army numbered barely sixteen thousand men and of those, only four thousand were stationed east of the Mississippi River. The majority were posted at far-flung forts in the distant west and Pacific regions. Almost one-third of the regular army's officer corps tendered their resignations in order to head home and don the new Confederate gray uniform. In Washington, the army's commander in chief, Gen. Winfield Scott, was well aware that the Union's lightly defended capital city was perilously situated between Virginia and Maryland. Its location bestowed a distinctly Southern flavor to its social life and culture. Not surprisingly, slavery was also legal within the city. Scott viewed an assault on Washington with such angst that in the event of a Rebel attack, the relatively few Union pickets were ordered to stand their ground until actually "pushed by the bayonet."[6]

Meanwhile, secessionists had raided U.S. arsenals and seized federal forts throughout the South. Samuel Wylie Crawford, an army surgeon stationed at Fort Sumter in the months leading up to its attack, viewed this situation and resignations of one-time close friends as heartrending. "We cannot repress the sadness that comes over us when we see one by one of our old comrades dropping away, men with whom we have many a bivouac in the far distant frontier," he confessed to his diary. For Ohio's Sen. John Sherman, who viewed the resignations from a political, somewhat more dispassionate vantage, such actions were a complete discredit to the regular forces. "The desertion of so many officers (treachery I had better say) . . . has so stained the whole regular course of officers that it will take good conduct on their part to retrieve their old position." At the West Point Military Academy in New York, Southern officers and cadets were deluged with letters from home urging them to resign and cease serving the vile Yankee government. These letters reasoned that no true man of Southern blood would ever raise his hand against his home state. "You shall never darken our doorway again" was the not-so-subtle warning for those who opted to stay. Eventually, over three hundred Southern cadets at the nation's premier military academy chose to resign their commissions in order to offer their services to the Confederacy rather than to the national government that was providing their education.[7]

The war quickly worked its way into Northern churches as well, with beliefs that stretched from pacifistic neutrality to hostile enmity. The latter feeling quickly became dominant within Protestant denominations as preachers began putting forth a patriotic message urging fealty to the government. This blending of secular patriotism with Christian duty was not uncommon—North or South—in the Civil War–era church. Leading Northern orators and ministers condemned the disloyal from their pulpits, using a religious metaphor to compare secession to the serpent, who "stole into the garden of Eden and whispered treason to Heaven in the ear of Eve. And now the serpent would seduce us from allegiance to our country."[8]

Treason against the national flag was equated to treason against God while patriotism became a type of sanctified worship. War was a tool for the righteous in their eternal battle against evil and the long-awaited opportunity to bring about moral revolution in the nation's character. For these educated men of the Lord who viewed themselves as the nation's moral stewards, the war became a sacred cause—what Peter Hall described as "that final fulfillment of the covenant that Americans had made in undertaking the political revolution of the eighteenth century." These Protestant ministers occupied a form of "bully pulpit," for like political parties, the church's weekly sermons provided the means by which individuals could receive information about the war's nature and interpret its meaning. In short order, clergymen across the North were readily blending the religious with the political by reading political tracts from their pulpits. They warned their congregants that God would strike them with vengeance if the Union cause was not voted on or carried out properly. As Victor Howard summarized it, the Northern Protestant church acted as the Republican Party's conscience and regarded itself as a pillar of the party's far-reaching agenda. Simultaneously, such sermonizing comparing patriotism to religious devotion also served many ministers' desire to increase the clergy's power and prestige. The slavery compromise measures that tainted the nation's moral purity in recent decades had now been usurped in primacy by the belief that the nation was engaged in a life or death struggle against an alien culture. In the summer of 1861, much of the Northern Protestant church viewed dissent against the war as sin to be purged, a perspective that by the summer of 1863 would align the church hand in glove with the Union Leagues.[9]

As weak as the North's military readiness was, of equal concern was the state of affairs within the Federal government at Washington, or what is known today as "internal security." While modern society has a rich history of civil liberty case law and watchdog social groups to protect the citizenry's individual rights, as well as established law to protect the national government's legitimate security interests, no such apparatus existed in 1861. Nor was there any type of legal history pertaining to civil rights. No one seemed to know who to trust, whose motives were pure or malicious, or the legal precedents to address those concerns.[10]

It seemed to many loyal men that the entire government was rife with Southern sympathizers. That was not entirely surprising since the Democratic Party had been dominant over the preceding twenty years with much of that influence driven by Southern men. The patronage and spoils schemes generated by the party system had inevitably resulted in Southern-leaning men holding influential positions. Indiana congressman and veteran politician George Julian believed in the days leading up to the war's commencement that Washington was "largely a city of secessionists," amply filled with treason supporters. Within Washington, "It seemed to be generally expected, if indeed not wished for," noted future army surgeon John Brinton, "that the southern states would win, and succeed in their attempt to withdraw from the union, and thus overthrow the national government." Those supporters included Southerners who brazenly walked the streets, proudly wearing badges or ribbons on their clothing that represented their home states, thereby symbolizing their pro-secession sentiments. "Treason is the common talk among Southerners even when salaried by Uncle Sam, and disunion badges are very plentiful," observed William Thayer, a Washington-based assistant editor with the New York *Evening Post*. "We used to think the 'covenant with death' abolitionists, who reviled the Union worthy of being mobbed. Here the disunionists are the cocks of the walk."[11]

Given how these pro-Southerners seemed to be everywhere and frustrated at how sensitive conversations were often carelessly conducted in front of open doors and windows, Union Gen. Samuel Heintzelman remarked that every window curtain in Washington hid two spies. The Supreme Court as well had tilted toward the South with decisions that benefited the idea of federalism, i.e., a concept that allocated power between state governments and the

national government in Washington. Overall, Southerners held a dispropor-
tionate share of both federal and high court seats within the judicial branch.
In looking back on those dark months, Lincoln frustratingly complained how
"Every department of the government was paralyzed by treason."[12]

The onset of war only amplified those concerns. Union loyalists wasted
no time in stating their conviction that Southern spies and Northern traitors
were lurking everywhere and embedded throughout the government. "The
man who thinks he has become disloyal because of what the Administration has done," wrote former Secretary of War Joseph Holt, "will probably
discover, after a close examination, that he was disloyal before." Unaware
that the war had started that very morning at Fort Sumter, Horatio Taft, a
U.S. Patent Office examiner, presciently recorded in his diary on April 12
that "Treason is in our midst. One hardly knows whom to trust. But I speak
my own sentiments freely as I have all the time and denounce 'seceders' as
Traitors." At the State Department, Polish-born translator Adam Gurowski
concurred with Taft, observing that "The secessionists in Washington—
and they are a legion, of all hues and positions—are defiant, arrogant, sure
that Washington will be taken." Secretary of the Navy Gideon Welles, a
Jacksonian Democrat from Connecticut, echoed a similar observation in
his diary, recalling how the Washington atmosphere in those early days
"was thick with treason." Welles admitted that his Democrats seemed to
sympathize with the Rebels far more than any Republican, not due to any
secessionist beliefs, however, but merely in the routinely political hope that
the Republican administration would fail. Republicans "were scarcely less
partisan and unreasonable," wrote Welles, carping against what he claimed
was the indiscriminate removal from office of any Democrat.[13]

Defections from Congress, as well as the courts and military, all conspired to weaken the country while those who left sought position or command within the insurgent forces. Those Southern-leaning men who had
stayed in Washington due to lucrative business interests now saw the fearful writing on the wall, whereas others felt honor-bound to leave the North.
"I must depart immediately," noted Southern-born John B. Jones, editor of
the *Southern Monitor* from his New Jersey office only days before the war
began, "for I well know that the first gun fired at Fort Sumter will be the
signal for an outburst of ungovernable fury, and I should be seized and
thrown into prison." As soon as his southbound steamer pulled away from
the dock, Jones breathed a sigh of relief, noting in his diary that many other
passengers did likewise. "Certainly, there was more vivacity," he wrote,

"since we were relieved of the presence of Republicans." The fear of prison was also felt by Littleton Washington, an avid Southern sympathizer who admitted in his journal that he was one of Washington's most outspoken secessionists. On April 16, sensing that Virginia was on the verge of seceding, he hastily began planning his departure. "I looked for martial law to be proclaimed any moment," Washington wrote, fearing he would not be able to escape and might end up in jail for the war's duration. His prison fears were not unreasonable for, as Mark Neely pointed out, many of the Lincoln administration's initial arrests were Confederate states residents who had been trapped in the North.[14]

Not all, however, who felt sympathy toward the South left their influential Northern positions. Many politicians and government workers stayed on in Washington or state capitals, hoping they might wield that influence in a manner beneficial to Southern aims. To loyal Unionists, this was tantamount to treason. It was this disdain toward the secession sympathizer, generated by their subversive acts and the feeble display of proper patriotic loyalty that contributed to the Union Leagues' birth throughout the fall of 1862. The notion that a Northern-based propaganda and loyalty organization was necessary during the war's initial months never crossed anyone's mind because most expected the war to end relatively quickly. This was evidenced by Lincoln's first call for volunteers, which was only for a ninety-day duration. Moreover, the very notions of "public duty" and correct civic behavior were vast unknowns in April 1861.[15]

Despite some early concerns over home front treason, the Fort Sumter bombardment generated waves of patriotic chest thumping and loyalty pronouncements throughout the North. "Patriotism is boiling over. Nothing is dreamed of but battles," observed a Dubuque, Iowa, reporter. Thousands of would-be volunteers were turned away from recruiting stations because the requested regiments were already filled. "There can be no neutrals in this war, only patriots or traitors," trumpeted Stephen Douglas, the esteemed Democratic senator from Illinois in his last public speech before his untimely death just over one month later. Politicians, preachers, editors, and civic leaders from both parties throughout the North urged that all political differences be cast aside and that all should now unite under the common banner of the Union, an early example of nascent nationalism, where one's deference to the Federal government equated to their degree of loyalty. This patriotic call to arms blossomed under the phrase "no party now" indicating that one and all were united in the cause.[16]

In Vermont, the *Daily Green Mountain Freeman* reminded its readers with typical enthusiasm that "The time has come when old party lines should be obliterated. There are and can be but two parties now. Those who are not for the Government, the Constitution, and the laws, are against them. *Those who are not patriots are traitors.*" On April 28, Rev. Albert Barnes reminded his Philadelphia congregation how the war was not in the defense of any political party. Rather, "party lines in this great movement have been obliterated, and should be," he asserted. In the Midwest, the *Indianapolis Daily Journal* extolled, "We are no longer Republicans or Democrats. . . . In this hour of our country's trial, we know no party, but that which upholds the flag of our country." Meanwhile, those Northerners who were against the war under any circumstances kept silent for the time being. "The less you say about it the better," advised Robert McClelland, Michigan's former Democratic governor, to his daughter.[17]

As the party in power, the Republicans eagerly advanced this desire for monologue far more than Democrats, who were used to a two-party dialogue. Some Democrats viewed the Republican motives with a cynical eye. The Republicans "conduct themselves as though 'patriotism' in these days is exclusively designed for the benefit of their party," complained Indiana's *New Albany Ledger*. Yet, with the country now facing an internal rebellion, most Democrats throughout the North were prepared to set aside party differences, as long as it was understood that the war's sole purpose was to preserve the Union and not to abolish slavery or to subjugate the South. Even the fiery Democratic mayor of New York, Fernando Wood, initially proclaimed, "I am with you in this contest. We know no party now. We are for maintaining the integrity of the national Union intact." With no national or major state elections on the immediate horizon, such political magnanimity was not difficult to achieve.[18]

While pro-Union men of all political leanings were rallying 'round the flag in the early months of the war, there was no doubt at the time that there existed a substantial number of Southern sympathizers employed within the government machine. Moreover, the mere opportunity to claim there was such nefarious activity provided an extremely useful propaganda tool to the Radical wing of the Republican Party. They learned this lesson well and would hone their techniques to a razor sharpness in the years to come. Led by senators Zachariah Chandler (Michigan), Ben Wade (Ohio), Charles Sumner (Massachusetts), James H. Lane (Kansas), representatives Thaddeus Stevens (Pennsylvania), George Julian (Indiana), and Secretary of the Treasury Salmon P. Chase, the "Radical Republicans" were those Northern Federal politicians, state governors, and a small cadre of politically appointed generals who had been strong antislavery advocates prior to the war, such as promoting a repeal of the Fugitive Slave Act of 1850. Along with the Southern "fire-eaters," a few of the Radicals had actually welcomed the war, believing it the only way to eliminate slavery.[19]

Once war came, they reminded Lincoln with their letters and private talks that slavery lay at the heart of the rebellion; that emancipation would surely be a consequence of the war if not an explicit goal. To that end, these men favored a highly severe and remorseless prosecution of the war against both Confederate soldier and civilian. The Radicals took the Rebels at their word with the latter's claim that they had seceded from the Union. As a consequence, the Radicals maintained that Southerners had forfeited any and all rights afforded Americans under the Constitution. From the Radical vantage, military aggressiveness should include confiscation of Rebel property and the use of black men in the Union war effort.[20]

Since so many Southern Democrats had resigned their seats in Congress, the Republicans now held firm majorities in both houses, with the Radicals as the largest faction. The war they envisioned was to be waged not merely against the Rebel armies in the field, but against the Southern civilian infrastructure that kept those armies clothed and fed. This belief stood in stark contrast to many conservative Union men who believed the war should be fought solely to restore the Union and only by white gentlemen rigorously observing all established rules of civilized warfare. The Radicals hated slavery and loathed the cavalier slave owner even more. Yet for many Radicals, humanitarian concerns for the slaves took a back seat to the possibility of using the black man as a tool to generate Republican dominion and economic control over a defeated South. Personal racism against blacks was not uncommon, even among Radicals, such as Ben Wade's antebellum comment to his wife that Washington was a "mean God-forsaken Nigger-ridden place." Even more far-reaching were the abolitionists who viewed the African as a man worthy of the freedoms espoused in the Constitution. Many of these Radical men were also leading members and spokesmen for the evangelical churches. Their moral commitment to abolition and their belief that the fight was a holy war were one and the same, for no longer could the American public evade or compromise on the slavery question. Possessing more than a little vindictiveness, the Radicals sought confiscation of Rebel property, immediate emancipation, and favored utilizing blacks in the war effort. As long as the threat of disloyalty existed inside the Washington bureaucracy, it would be convenient to blame military challenges in the field on home front treason. Their Democratic opponents could be labeled as Southern sympathizers with the subsequent opportunity to place their own like-minded colleagues in positions of power and authority.[21]

When Stephen Douglas passed away unexpectedly in June 1861, the Democrats lost one of their most powerful anti-Republican voices. Even though Douglas was certainly a healthy Lincoln critic, he had earned a considerable measure of respect across party lines and thus the title of spokesman for the opposition. His death created a vacuum within the Democratic Party's ranks that allowed the Radicals to run rampant with their cries of treason against any opposed to their actions. When Republicans cried out "No More Party" in an effort to create a unified front against the Rebels, their opponents soon viewed it to mean "No More Democratic Party."[22]

The concern over Northern home front treason was so intense that Edward Bates, Lincoln's attorney general, suggested only two weeks into the conflict that all government employees, "from the head Secretary to the lowest messenger," should submit to new "loyalty oaths." Like many of his loyal colleagues, Bates sensed that something was amiss in the way the government's new enemies were acting with open impunity and outright disdain for the rule of law. Such actions were highlighted by a pro-secessionist mob in Baltimore, Maryland, that attacked Massachusetts militiamen on April 19 who were rushing to Washington's defense. Those Union soldiers passing through Baltimore not only had to fight off the mob, but were forced to contend with severed telegraph wires, burned bridges, and railroad tracks that were taken apart, all of which convinced Union loyalists that secession sympathizers were also potential saboteurs. Other state militiamen refused to defend the Union while the aforementioned army and naval officers resigned their commissions rather than wage war against their Southern brethren. For the seceded Southerners to preach disunion in their home states was one thing, but for Northern men to openly flout secessionist sympathies was quite another. Asking rhetorically why this was so, Bates pounced on his answer: "Because we hurt nobody; we frighten nobody; and do our utmost to offend nobody," as he listed off in his diary all of the traitors' various transgressions, coupled with the weak and vacillating responses from the national government. As far as Lincoln's attorney general was concerned, it was high time to start separating the loyal wheat from the disloyal chaff.[23]

Lincoln's Cabinet agreed with Bates and quickly began disseminating the decision. The new edict soon included all army officers, who were ordered on April 30 to take a new oath of allegiance to the United States. Inside the government, Register of the Treasury Lucius Chittenden noted in his journal that Secretary Salmon Chase was "very firm and determined" on this issue. Chittenden was instructed "to turn out every clerk in my department of whose fidelity to the Union I have any suspicion."[24]

Across the North, plenty of Northerners were quick to denounce any of their neighbors whom they suspected of disloyalty. Home guard units, local politicians, and even police officers were all ready to cast doubt on anyone who questioned the administration's war policy, especially if that person aligned himself with the Democratic Party. Indiana Rep. George Julian, the fiery, pro-abolition Radical Republican, succinctly summed up this view when he later admitted, "Loyalty to Republicanism was . . . accepted as the best evidence of loyalty to the country," a sentiment the Union Leagues would come to heartily endorse. Not being able to ascertain what emotions truly lived in a man's soul, such outward signs were viewed as a self-evident display of one's patriotic fervor, for as one New Yorker crowed, "The loyal people are good judges and know by instinct what giving aid and comfort to the rebels means." Democrats discovered that anything less than wholesale support for the war was viewed as treasonous by many neighbors. It seemed to some Democrats that much of the North was infected with an unseemly case of war fever. Another New Yorker complained that the only sane people left in the country were those who "do not esteem cutting the throats of one's countrymen as proof of patriotism or rely upon the bombardment of a city as the best way of cultivating union and fraternal love with its inhabitants."[25]

In the rebellion's early days, this fear of pro-Southern skullduggery was so palpable that journalist Noah Brooks later wrote that it was impossible for postwar generations to truly appreciate how loyal Washington men "were constantly haunted by suspicions of secret plotting all about them." This anxiety within the halls of government set the stage for Wisconsin Rep. John F. "Bowie knife" Potter to come to the fore, so nicknamed for his choice of weapon when challenged to a duel in 1860 by Virginia Rep. Richard Pryor.[26]

The fear of disloyalty was so great in the halls of Congress that on July 8, 1861, the House of Representatives appointed Representative Potter to chair the just-created, five-man Select Committee on the Loyalty of Clerks. Its mission was to determine the number and names of those government

Wisconsin's Congressman John F. Potter (Library of Congress Prints and Photographs Division)

clerks and bureaucrats whose loyalty to the United States was considered doubtful, as well as those who had refused to take the new loyalty oath. By mid-July, the committee had sent letters to all department heads outlining the committee's purpose and seeking those names. Yet the initial support level from many department heads was tepid at best. When Benjamin French, the commissioner of public buildings, received an inquiry from Lincoln about the loyalty of specific employees employed at the White House, he replied, "As a matter of course, all sorts of stories . . . are brought to me, but I put no faith in anything I hear unless it be substantiated by 'proof as strong as Holy Writ.'" Though he admitted to the president that he had no desire to dismiss anyone, the clamor calling for heads to roll was so great that French felt having a few leave might be expedient.[27]

Potter likened his committee more to that of a grand jury rather than a court of justice. Its purpose was one of inquiry, not final adjudication, and its members wasted little effort in their investigations. From those steamy July days on into the congressional fall recess, Potter's committee stayed active, scrutinizing approximately 550 names while interviewing close to 450 "witnesses." Many of those witnesses provided factual evidence of disloyalty while others, acting anonymously, were merely looking to settle old scores. The *Washington Star* alleged that much of closed-door testimony was "a bundle of malicious perjuries." Other accusers were said to be merely "office seeking"—what the *Star* referred to as "the black plague of American politics"—hoping they might land the dismissed employee's salaried and, therefore, coveted government position.[28]

When Congress reconvened on December 2, 1861, so did the committee. Potter promptly asked all department heads for the names of those clerks who were dismissed due to the committee's prior investigations. Secretary of the Treasury Salmon Chase and Secretary of the Interior Caleb B. Smith ignored the request, prompting Potter to take to the House floor on December 30 seeking a resolution demanding compliance. Potter displayed little letup as 1862 dawned. "Every day new cases are being brought to the attention of the committee involving serious charges of disloyalty against persons entrusted with office, or employed in responsible situations with the government," declared Potter. From his perspective, the government was riddled with disloyal men, who, through "faithless professions of loyalty and obsequious protestations of personal regard" ingratiated themselves with those in authority in order to learn anything that might aid the secessionists. At the War Department, for instance, it was discovered that the departmental mail pouch, freely hanging in the hallway, was routinely rifled through by secession sympathizers looking for information that might be of interest to Confederate authorities. Potter viewed the threat as so great that he rationalized committee actions that were hardly in line with the rule of law. He freely admitted that as a general rule, those accused of disloyalty were not interviewed by the committee, were not informed of the specific charges against them, nor were they allowed to offer their own testimony. Such information was passed on to the various department heads for them to act as they saw fit. Ultimately, if an innocent man was thus removed from office, the action was to be merely regretted, considering the government's very existence was in peril. In any case, Potter reasoned, the dismissed employee was not going to be tossed into jail, but only returned to the honorable role of private citizen.[29]

Of course, those suspected of disloyalty viewed their situation in a harsher light. Lt. Col. William Maynadier, for example, was accused of shipping weaponry to the South prior to Fort Sumter in order to aid the then-forthcoming rebellion. Though formally exonerated by *both* the House of Representatives' Military Affairs Committee and Secretary of War Simon Cameron, Maynadier believed his name was still sent to Potter's committee after his acquittals solely as an act of political revenge. Infuriated at this attack against his reputation, Maynadier prepared and published a lengthy explanation of his travails. Despite the possibility and even likelihood of such machinations as the Maynadier case, Potter's committee and the actions of the departmental heads produced relatively little uproar, especially among Republicans and most of the general public. From their perspective, anyone refusing to give an oath of allegiance to the national government was suspect at best. When the pro-Republican *New York Times* reported in September 1861 that Simon Cameron was allegedly dismissing any War Department employee investigated by Potter, the paper opined further that it was "to be deeply regretted that the other Departments have been less ready to purge their ranks of disloyal men."[30]

When Potter's committee issued its final report in January 1862, its "reign of terror," as one Democrat had framed it, essentially came to a close. For Democrats, sincerely offered advice was censured while constructive criticism had been treated as treason. Yet within that criticism, Democrats overlooked the fact that subversive actions had indeed been underway within the Federal capital. Whether in the church, town squares, or in the halls of Congress, strict fealty to the Constitution's principles *and* political loyalty to the Lincoln administration were beginning to become one and the same, a perspective that the Union Leagues would start to intensify within a year and a half.[31]

Chapter 3

"A Fire of Liberty Burning Upon the Altar"

The Union Leagues Arise amidst Despair
and Disillusionment

From the military perspective, the year 1862 began with a string of successes for Union forces in the Western theater that generated some sorely needed good news for the North. The first significant Union victory of the war occurred on January 19 at the battle of Mill Springs, near modern-day Nancy, Kentucky. Fort Henry, located on the Tennessee River in northwestern Tennessee, was taken on February 6 by a then fairly obscure brigadier general named Ulysses S. Grant in a joint operation with river gunboats. Grant then marched his command twelve miles overland to the Cumberland River and after five days of skirmishing, received Fort Donelson's surrender on February 16. Grant's successes had the effect of forcing the Confederates to withdraw from Kentucky, and left much of western and middle Tennessee under Union control.[1]

From March 6 to 8, Gen. Samuel Curtis defeated the Rebels on an Arkansas battlefield known as Pea Ridge, giving the Union control over northern Arkansas as well as Missouri. In the far West, a 2,500-man Confederate force under the command of Brig. Gen. Henry Hopkins Sibley had invaded New Mexico territory with plans of western conquest, but those dreams were halted by Union forces at the March 28 battle of Glorieta Pass. On April 6–7 in southwest Tennessee near the banks of the Missouri River, Ulysses Grant overcame a disastrous first day at the battle of Shiloh. In what was the war's largest engagement to that point, Grant succeeded in driving the Confederates from the field on the second day with the help of fifteen thousand fresh troops under the command of Don Carlos Buell, who had fortuitously arrived via steamship the night before. Ultimate control of the Mississippi River was helped by the capture of Island Number Ten on April 7, just south of the junction of the Mississippi and Ohio rivers. The sequence of Union victories also extended into southeastern Georgia. Following a 112-day siege by combined army and naval forces, mighty Fort Pulaski, located at the mouth of the Savannah River, was reduced to rubble during a two-day bombardment on April 10–11 by Union batteries using the latest rifled cannon technology. By late April, New Orleans had fallen when Adm. David Farragut's Union fleet fought its way past the Confederate Mississippi River fortifications, leaving the defense of the Confederacy's largest city untenable.[2]

Along the Atlantic coast, Gen. Ambrose Burnside seized New Bern and Beaufort, North Carolina. Northern morale surged in March after Gen. Thomas W. Sherman's Union forces followed Burnside's Carolina success by occupying the Florida coastal towns of Jacksonville and St. Augustine. Predictions of the Confederacy's imminent collapse and the war's end were everywhere. By early July, Illinois Maj. Gen. John McClernand had written to his home state's congressional delegation urging that two divisions of his command be sent east from Tennessee in order to support the Union armies in that theater. "I am persuaded that no more important battles will be fought in this quarter," he asserted. "The strength of the rebellion is broken in the south-west." Even Secretary of War Edwin Stanton became caught up in the elation. On April 3, only a few days prior to the carnage at Shiloh, Stanton ordered all recruiting officers to stop their tasks, close their offices, and sell off all surplus. While the ever-increasing costs of the war may have played a part, Stanton, like others, believed the Union armies were large enough to crush the rebellion.[3]

Such euphoria was short-lived, however. In less than four months, Union fortunes turned so precipitously that a civilian draft was considered to make up for the manpower shortfall, and in the tiny town of Pekin, Illinois, loyal men were so fearful for their safety from antiwar neighbors that they banded together to form the Union League of America's first council.

The military chessboard in the Eastern theater was markedly different from the west and had been from the start. On July 21, 1861, in what was the Civil War's first major battle, Union forces engaged the Confederates near the northern Virginia village of Manassas by a meandering stream known as Bull Run. The green and untested armies fought all day in what many political prognosticators predicted would be the first and only grand battle of the war.

The Northerners seemed to have the upper hand through midday, but Rebel reinforcements arrived by train from the Shenandoah Valley late in the afternoon, a first in military history, which ultimately turned the tide. Soon the Rebel forces had their Union opponents retreating in full flight back to Washington in what became known as "the great skedaddle." For several days after, grimy and dazed Union soldiers streamed back into Washington in groups or individually, to the utter dismay of the North's citizenry. Northerners now realized the Southern men could and would indeed fight. Matters had not improved any three months later when the Union was again whipped in a much smaller engagement at Ball's Bluff, just outside of Leesburg in northern Virginia. The feelings of national unity and "no party" that so animated the country in the few months between the war's commencement and the Bull Run battle were over. Though Northern morale remained solid overall, the Peace Democrats who opted to keep quiet at the beginning now saw these military debacles as their opportunity to assert that war was not the answer.[4]

Following the Bull Run disaster, Union Gen. George McClellan was brought east due to several small victories he achieved near western Virginia's Rich Mountain in early July. A West Point–trained engineer and then a civilian railroad executive prior to the war, McClellan was a first-rate administrator and organizer of men. His new mission was to whip what was now known as the Army of the Potomac into fighting shape. Washington politicians believed that in short order, the thirty-five-year-old McClellan would have the reinvigorated Union soldiers boldly marching against the secessionists. That desire was especially true for the Republican Party's Radical wing, who assumed victory would smile on those who displayed the most hard-hitting aggressiveness. They were quickly disappointed, however, for the Union's grand eastern army had seemingly gone quiet. No forward movement was attempted after the Army of the Potomac had limped back into the capital on July 21.[5]

By late October 1861 the Radicals, led by Michigan's Sen. Zachariah Chandler, Ohio's Rep. Ben Wade, and Illinois's Sen. Lyman Trumbull were demanding action from Lincoln and McClellan. From their perspective, a military defeat was no worse than continued delay, and moreover, could be easily repaired by more recruits. The ever-cautious McClellan demurred, however. From the general's vantage, he would rather have a few more enlistees before a victory than swarms of them after a defeat.[6]

For the remainder of the year, the Army of the Potomac did little more than drill within their camps outside of Washington. Further adding to the

Radicals' frustration was that General McClellan was now bedridden, having contracted a case of typhoid fever in December. No military movement seemed imminent to Congress or Lincoln as 1862 began, which only added to their growing frustration. An exasperated Lincoln told a gathering of generals on January 10 that if McClellan had no immediate plans to use the army, he would like to borrow it for a while. Yet McClellan was beginning to act. He devised a plan that entailed sailing his entire command from Washington down the Potomac River, into the Chesapeake Bay, and then landing at Fort Monroe at the easterly tip of the Virginia Peninsula. By doing so, he would bypass any Rebel armies positioned between Richmond and Washington.[7]

McClellan's grand plan commenced on March 15. Over 120,000 men, plus 15,000 animals, 44 artillery batteries, and tons of supplies sailed from Washington over a two-week period before all were ashore. It was the largest gathering of military might the North American continent had ever seen. The army's lead elements left Fort Monroe on April 4 with only the haziest idea of what lay in front of them due to poor maps. The next month witnessed McClellan's siege of Yorktown, which was followed by a vicious engagement in the rain at Williamsburg on May 5.[8]

By the end of May, McClellan's army had advanced seventy miles up the peninsula to the gates of Richmond, near a railroad depot known as Fair Oaks Station. Sensing that the Union Army was split with its pieces isolated, Confederate Gen. Joseph Johnston attacked on May 31, driving his enemy back several miles until Union reinforcements arrived to stabilize the situation. More fighting occurred the next day, but the results were inconclusive. Though perhaps innocuous at the time, Johnston was severely wounded during the battle, which resulted in Gen. Robert E. Lee being placed in command of the Confederate forces. June 26 through July 1, 1862, brought daily carnage with what became known in history as the Seven Days battles. An almost nonstop series of large battles and small engagements occurred over those seven days throughout Richmond's eastern fields and forests. All but one of the battles ended with Union forces holding the field, nevertheless Robert E. Lee's relentless aggressiveness and audacity had so overwhelmed McClellan that the "Young Napoleon" viewed them as a defeat. By August 26, McClellan's grand army had abandoned the Peninsula and was on its way back to Washington. Historians have estimated that the number of Union killed and wounded during the Peninsula Campaign exceeded 25,000.[9]

As depressing as that was, the Union's military fortunes in the east con-tinued to deteriorate. Lee's Army of Northern Virginia marched north from Richmond and collided with Union Gen. John Pope's Army of Virginia, along with elements of McClellan's command, on the old Bull Run battlefield in northern Virginia from August 28 to 30. Three days of brutal carnage ended with the Union Army being swept from the field. While the bluecoats were retreating back through Fairfax County to Washington, another sharp fight occurred in the pouring rain at Ox Hill during the late afternoon and early evening of September 1. The short but deadly engagement saw Philip Kear-ney and Isaac Stevens, two of the Union Army's finest field generals, both killed by Rebel bullets. As the sun rose on September 2, Billy Yank was again limping back into the Washington defenses' relative safety. In a span of just over one month, Robert E. Lee had reversed the theater of operations from the gates of Richmond to the outskirts of Washington.[10]

Meanwhile, the Confederacy's Western forces had recovered from the Shiloh defeat in early April and were again on the march. Gen. Braxton Bragg moved his thirty-thousand-man Army of Mississippi into eastern Tennessee in late June and July where it readied itself to liberate middle Tennessee and eastern Kentucky. By late August, Bragg's forces were in motion and scored the first victory of their Kentucky Campaign at the town of Richmond on Au-gust 28. Lexington and Frankfort, the state capital, soon fell as did the four-thousand-man Union garrison at Munfordville in mid-September.[11]

These repeated military disappointments added to the growing northern despair. Washingtonians trembled with the thought that the North's capital might be attacked any day. Not merely tactical losses but the unspeakable carnage that came with them dissuaded many one-time glory seekers. The number of men seeking discharges from the army for one reason or another skyrocketed. For many, if an honorable discharge could not be had, then a dishonorable one would suffice if it meant passage home. At the same time, many boys in blue had no intention of dealing with such formalities. A typi-cal case was that of William Greene. The seventeen-year-old had joined the 2nd U.S. Sharpshooters in December 1861 and saw action in August 1862 from Cedar Mountain to Rappahannock Station. During the regiment's first seri-ous combat during the Second Bull Run battle, Greene and his unit fled the field. Writing somewhat cryptically that he simply "got tired out," Greene nevertheless walked twenty-seven miles to Alexandria seeking the sanctuary of a Union hospital. Greene was eventually sent to a hospital in Portsmouth

Grove, Rhode Island, where he continuously sought a discharge without success. Greene eventually walked out of the hospital and never returned.[12]

Overall, desertion and straggling had become rife in the Union Army. Other volunteers resorted to the more dangerous method of seeking out and surrendering to the enemy, knowing that at that point in the war, they would be paroled and sent home. On September 2, only one day after the conclusion of the disastrous Second Bull Run campaign, Gen. John Pope warned General-in-Chief Henry Halleck that "Unless something can be done to restore tone to this army it will melt away before you know it."[13]

The sinking feeling throughout the North was generated not only by military reverses but also by simple economics. This was especially the case in the Midwestern states. Once the war commenced, one of the national government's first efforts to subdue the South was to stop the flow of goods into Southern states. This had a particularly negative impact on those farmers and residents in the southern counties of Ohio, Illinois, and Indiana who used the Ohio and Mississippi rivers to transport their products southward and who considered New Orleans as their primary port. Most of this region's original settlers—described as the "sturdy, struggling, western farmer with his hand on the plow and a formal education that went little beyond the third grade"— had immigrated to this area mostly from the Upper South or Pennsylvania. The 1860 census indicated that some 475,000 residents in Illinois, Indiana, and Ohio had been born in slave states, while four of every ten residents in the Old Northwest had a Southern birth or parentage. Many of these émigrés still had kin in the South, some of whom were serving in the Confederate Army. Rural and localized in culture, they acquired a disdain toward the puritanical New England "Yankees" who had come to dominate the economies in the northern parts of those three states. Furthermore, it was the Yankee who was seen as wanting to instill his abolitionist and cultural values upon the rest of the land. Despite a lack of education for many, they were nevertheless a deeply political people, keenly aware of and interested in the social, cultural, economic, and political issues of the day that affected their lives. This heavily Democratic lower Midwest was the "storm center of American politics" and became a cultural battleground between Northern progressivism and traditional Southern individualism.[14]

Once the rivers were closed, business in the river towns grew stagnant, resulting in serious financial pressures as many farmers could not afford the higher freight costs required to send their products to the East via railroad. Businessmen could not pay workers who, in turn, could not pay their family's bills. Midwestern factories saw their Southern markets vanish while bank notes based upon Southern bonds collapsed in value. An Indiana "treason bill" supported by Republicans was designed to cut off produce sales to Kentucky, which southern county farmers opposed claiming it would ruin them. Their appeals, and similar ones for debt relief if such laws were passed, repeatedly fell on deaf ears. In the meantime, crop prices tumbled. By summer, the result was frequent sheriff's sales auctioning off the property of those unable to pay debts. Adding insult to injury were the denouncements from those in the North not affected by such realities, who complained that the farmers' patriotism was subordinated to base financial desires.[15]

Lincoln's home state of Illinois posed a particular dilemma for the president. The Prairie State was no mere outlier on the young nation's Western frontier. In 1860, it was the fourth most populous state in the Union with considerable wealth and influence. Nonetheless, like Indiana and Ohio, it held significant pro-Southern culture and sentiment. In fact, Illinois was the only state born out of the Old Northwest territory that had not eradicated slavery outright during its initial 1818 constitutional convention, as those state residents who already owned slaves were allowed to keep them. This sentiment was especially true in its southernmost counties which, geographically, dipped further southward than did most of Kentucky or Virginia. Like the lower half of Indiana and Ohio, this was a Democratic Party stronghold that held strong views on the proper relationship between the federal government and the respective states. Unlike the more nationalistic vision held by the Republicans and their Whig predecessors, many Northern Democrats subscribed to a strict states' rights or even a state sovereignty view of government, which were two separate views themselves. The former, as had been espoused by the late Stephen Douglas, put forth that power was shared between the federal and state governments, each having defined powers and responsibilities. On the other hand, state sovereignty, as championed by Southern "fire-eaters" and ardent Northern Copperheads, held that true power rested with each state. The U.S. Constitution served as a contract for common agreement between the states, but did not bind the state to any national government. The national government in Washington, in the eyes of state sovereignty adherents, was little more than an acting agent for the various states. For the national government to raise an army on its own accord, use it to wage war against fellow states for reasons deemed unconstitutional, and close off men's river livelihoods to advance those war aims had signaled to Midwestern Democrats the beginning of despotic rule.

Their rallying cry became "The Constitution as it is and the Union as it was." They began to push back and sometimes in violent fashion.[16]

By early 1862, the deteriorating military situation, economic concerns, and a growing antiblack sentiment prompted Illinois's antiwar Democrats to call for a convention to draft a new state constitution. The convention's delegates consisted of forty-five Democrats, twenty Republicans, and ten Union Democrats, none of whom lived north of Springfield. The convention adopted proposals that would severely restrict the governor's military powers and cut the four-year term to two. Convention delegates also redrew congressional district lines to help ensure Democratic success, all of which might lead to Illinois seceding from the Union as well. Just for good measure, the new proposals also barred blacks from moving into the state. Those free black men who already lived in Illinois would be prohibited from voting.[17]

The new constitution was defeated as a whole at the June election, though the two proposals regarding black immigration and suffrage carried by wide margins, a strong indicator of the state's antiblack prejudice and growing Peace Democrat prominence. Despite the Democratic failure, Republicans saw with a keen eye how war resistance was growing in the Midwest. In a letter to Illinois Rep. Elihu Washburne, Emanuel Stover warily noted the Republicans' "grand victory . . . though we have made a narrow escape. We have learned a lesson not to compromise with the enemy." The silence or low mutterings that the Peace Democrats had kept through 1861 had now clearly vanished in the political winds.[18]

By summer 1862, it was obvious that the Union armies needed more men. Stanton's earlier April edict closing all recruiting offices was now seen as a major blunder. A growing demand for factory labor coupled with the need for farm hands offered more motivation for men to avoid the war. Yet, as more and more citizens appeared to have doubts about the conflict, the Lincoln administration's response was to double down on its efforts with a carrot-and-stick strategy. In a contrived plan designed to appear as a willing acquiescence to Northern governors' pleas for more men, Lincoln issued a call on July 2 for 300,000 three-year volunteers. The carrot was the plentiful cash bounties offered by the War Department, individual cities, and the Northern states to those who enlisted. Should the call fail to generate enough volunteers, however, Congress created its stick in the form of the 1862 Militia Act, passed on July 17. That law gave the Lincoln administration the right to call up an additional 300,000 men for nine months' duty from those states who failed to meet their enlistment quotas, which Lincoln exercised on August 4. For most Americans, their only interaction with the federal government prior to the Civil War was either voting in a national election or a trip to the post office. States held real domestic power while the federal government's impact was minimal. Thus, "love of country" was actually a manifestation of a more localized or regional sense of pride. With the advent of this new military draft, the national government's reach into the daily lives of its citizens entered a new era. For the first time in the country's history, a man now had a potential life-and-death interest in national politics. As part of the Militia Act, any man subject to the draft was forbidden to the leave the country; historian William Marvel argued that this proviso transformed a military-age, male American citizen into little more than the equivalent of a paroled prisoner. Those Northern men who had no desire to don a blue uniform—whether for family responsibilities, business commitments, or ideological antiwar reasons—soon began to seek out any possible exemption or even "skedaddle" to Canada.[19]

Other Democratic men decided to take matters into their own hands, genuinely fearful that Lincoln and the Republicans' attempts at despotic, tyrannical rule were increasing. Harkening back to the libertarian rhetoric of the American Revolution, these Democrats believed government was legitimate only when it openly placed the rights of citizens first and operated within the Constitution's clearly defined parameters. They believed it their right and duty to resist when the "mass of the people" judged that the government had exceeded its authority. In parts of Pennsylvania and Ohio, troops were sent in to suppress antidraft disturbances. In Wisconsin, six companies of troops were required to quell a November 10, 1862, antidraft riot in Ozaukee County, which resulted in extensive property damage and the arrest of 140 men.[20]

In Indiana, Gov. Oliver Morton had pleaded as early as August 1861 to the assistant secretary of war for soldiers after repeated warnings that anti-Lincoln men were set to burn railroad bridges running from Indiana's interior toward Kentucky in an attempt to hinder troop movements. Now in June 1862, Morton implored Edwin Stanton to send arms so that Morton could distribute them to loyal men in order to combat what appeared to be a growing, anti-Lincoln cabal that was working to subvert the government's recruiting and tax collection efforts. Iowa Rep. James Wilson expressed similar concerns to Stanton, using the recent example of how a wounded Union soldier serving as a recruiting officer was assaulted by four Copperheads in the small town of Rome, Iowa. They threatened to hang the man if he did not immediately leave town. "Men in this and surrounding counties are daily in the habit of denouncing the Government, the war, and all engaged in it," complained Wilson, "and are doing all they can to prevent enlistments." U.S. Marshal David L. Phillips wrote from southern Illinois that "The Democracy is intensely agitated in all this region, and almost desperate—ready for anything." Phillips knew that the Copperheads were ready to drive out all Union men, and that "matters may come to point where bayonets will be needed almost any day. Of this Genl. [William K.] Strong is fully convinced."[21]

In response, Lincoln issued a decree subjecting anyone to martial law who discouraged enlistments or resisted the draft. Using a broad brush, Lincoln also applied his directive to anyone who might be guilty of any "disloyal" practice or of giving "aid and comfort" to the enemy. Almost all arrested were Democrats as they were the ones who were most opposed to the new developments. To Republicans, however, any opposition to their war aims was viewed as unwarranted and treasonable opposition to the government itself.[22]

This level of violent antiwar protest in the Midwestern states had never before reared its head and was a cold shock to Republicans and "loyal" Unionists. It seemed as if an earlier prophecy was coming to pass. On January 26, 1861, almost three months before the war started, the rabid Democratic editor of the *Detroit Free Press*, Wilbur Storey, threatened that if the North raised troops to march against the South, a "fire in the rear" would be opened by Northern antiwar forces against those men. Storey's quote and sentiment were used often by pro-Union men as proof of treasonous leanings lurking within the North. Now that antiwar sentiment was indeed at work within the region. The cheers and excitement that heralded the war's beginning a little over a year earlier now seemed like a distant mirage.[23]

Those fears came to life with ever-increasing and ominous reports that anti-Lincoln and antiwar men were banding together into secret societies and that loyal men needed to do likewise. In Illinois, Gov. Richard Yates asked Stanton for the authority to raise four, one-year home guard regiments of men over the age of forty-five who would serve within his state as well as neighboring Kentucky and Missouri. Their intent was to defend their homes against Rebel-sympathizing guerrillas. The men Yates had in mind were all officers of Illinois's State Agricultural Society, "who are gentlemen of high character, and who propose to enlist themselves."[24]

After being released from a Rebel prison, newly minted Brig. Gen. Orlando Willcox touched on these concerns at an August 18 Washington rally by advising that "each town should have its committee to know of a surety what were the sentiments of all who reside within their limits." The *localized* threats were generally the same: These antiadministration men were arming themselves with plans to overthrow the government; they were doing all in their power to discourage enlistments or hinder any possible draft; they harassed soldiers' families so that the soldier might desert; and if necessary, they would use force to free Confederate prisoners held in Union prison camps. This new reality of antiwar, antidraft violence as had occurred in the Midwest was now seen by loyal men as proof of their concerns. Fears abounded that the Knights of the Golden Circle had infiltrated the region and that their membership numbered in the tens of thousands. Even politicians were not immune. The KGC was deemed so threatening that at the 1862 Illinois State Convention creating a possible new state constitution, rumors surfaced alleging that a majority of the convention's delegates were KGC members. "That this [KGC] society was secret was presumptive proof that it was treasonable and the enemy of every honest man," opined *Harper's Weekly*. The Republican cry of treason reached a fever pitch, prompting a heightened state of awareness in pro-Union men throughout the North.[25]

Recent scholarship has shown that the last KGC "castle" was formed in August 1861, in Texas. As a consequence, the Knights' influence throughout the South slowly began to wane as its members focused more on the Confederacy's survival. Yet in the dark days of summer 1862, its mystique was still spreading rapidly into the Union's Midwestern counties and towns.[26]

Due to this real threat, the grassroots Union clubs that existed in the border states in 1860–61 multiplied into the Midwest during the summer and fall of 1862. This growth was spurred in large measure by the conviction that the KGC menace was growing coupled with riotous Democratic resistance to the militia draft. With ever-growing concerns about the war's course and home front treason, Union men began gathering together for shared political interest, power in numbers, and mutual protection. For as one Indiana man complained, "It is unsafe for a Union man to express his sentiments on the streets." A statewide organizational system was soon developed where the individual clubs in a given town would work together with a newly formed, larger statewide chapter. Many of these clubs were considered subordinate to the larger state chapter and were furnished with ample instructions for club formation and protocols. For example, the Subordinate Union Club of Indiana North #14 was formed in Lafayette on June 18, 1862, while the charter for subordinate club #6 was issued on June 16, 1862. A penciled annotation on that latter document dated 1890 noted that the club was "organized to counteract the influence of the democratic Knights of the Golden Circle, an organization intended to assist the rebellion." These new Union Clubs were to be "organized upon a military basis," having centralized power within the state. Each club's mission was the same: to offer unqualified support for the Lincoln administration, to rally the good citizenry around the flag in the nation's hour of peril, and to provide protection to Indiana's loyal citizens from the treacherous actions of the so-called Rebel-sympathizing "secret societies," such as the KGC. Therefore, for safety's sake, the Union clubs' own secrecy was paramount. Cryptographic alphabets, cyphers, and secret signs were issued to club officers, along with how they were to be handled and codes disseminated. The club's initiation rituals were likewise standardized and kept secret. Each new initiate was to be instructed only in "the salutation, badge, and manual signs," but not told the passwords or "rallying cry."[27]

Out of this legitimate fear arose the first council of what soon became known as the Union League of America. It was organized on the third floor of the building at 331 Court Street in Pekin, Illinois, on June 25, 1862. This organization has often been credited as being the first true Union League, which is not entirely accurate. It was, however, the first such group to form under what later became known as the Union League of America national umbrella. This claim of being first is a slight bit of revisionism that was effectively promulgated by Illinois and the Pekin League in the years to follow. As touched upon in Chapter 1, patriotic and loyalist groups that gave themselves the Union League name had existed well before the Pekin gathering, such as the politically conservative organization operating in New York during 1859–61. Other examples included a Union League that formed in October 1861 in Clearfield, Pennsylvania, along with the Union League that was created in Baltimore during what a past member called "the days of darkness" in the spring of 1861. A German Union League existed in New York City in October 1861 for the purpose of advancing German interests in local politics. In addition, the *Chicago Tribune* had reported back on April 11, 1862—well before the Pekin gathering—that a Union League existed in both Nashville and Memphis. These were all isolated groups at the time that were not yet part of any larger framework. The Pekin Union League was comprised of twelve prominent men from Tazewell County, some of whom had experienced firsthand the ravages of being Union men in portions of Confederate-held east Tennessee. In order to find some measure of collective safety, they sought refuge within Tennessee's mountains during the 1861–62 winter "with the blood hounds of Jeff. Davis on their tracks." There they grouped together to proclaim loyalty to the Union, thereby creating the Tennessee leagues. For these Union League founders, violence against Unionist men was a real and ever-present danger that led them to form their new organization.[28]

Those Tazewell men included attorney John W. Glassgow, Dr. Daniel A. Cheever, postmaster Hart Montgomery, Maj. Richard. N. Cullom, Alexander Small, Rev. J. W. M. Vernon, George H. Harlow, Charles Turner, Jonathan Merriam, Henry Pratt, and Levi F. Garrett. Basing their new organization on the ideas and principles previously enacted at similar alliances in the Volunteer State, the new league, with its "fire of liberty burning upon the altar," provided a measure of support and protection for its members while giving them a voice in their support for the Union. For these men, their new League's fundamental purpose was "to sustain and encourage the administration in its efforts to put down treason and traitors; to preserve the Union in its whole territorial integrity; to maintain the laws, and to keep inviolate the principles of the constitution and the Declaration of Independence."[29]

The Pekin men appointed agents to spread the word throughout neighboring towns and counties and within only a few weeks, they learned that their work was paying dividends. Similar councils were organized in the Tazewell County towns of Groveland, Delavan, and Tremont. In neighboring Peoria County, new councils were created in the towns of Peoria and Kingston. To the southwest, Union League chapters had formed at Virginia and Beardstown in Cass County. Jacksonville, Springfield, Decatur, Clinton, and La Salle likewise soon formed councils, all created by average men who were committed to repelling the treason they sincerely believed to be in their midst. Not to be outdone, a Chicago council was created on August 19, 1862, by Joseph Medill, editor of the *Chicago Tribune* and a staunch, fiery Radical Republican. Once formed, each council was given the authority to spread the news and form other councils throughout the state.[30]

This type of organic recruitment was undertaken by council agents and members speaking face to face with their friends, relatives, fellow church members, business colleagues, and acquaintances about the League's mission and objectives. This preexisting social network was crucial to the early success of the Union League movement, for as political scientist Jo Freeman wrote, disgruntled masses by themselves do not create movements; there must be some type of interconnecting linkage between adherents. New movements are at a distinct advantage when they can utilize existing social structures rather than having to create them from the ground up.[31]

If a member felt a new contact was a suitable candidate with proper political beliefs, the member presented the applicant's name at the local council's next meeting for consideration. The council members would debate and then vote on the application. If approved, the new member was initiated into the council at a following meeting. Those denied membership were not told why, though in some instances, they were allowed to reapply in six months. The relative few, extant minutes from Union League council meetings are rife with the names submitted and then either approved or denied, usually at the next weekly gathering.[32]

A new member's initiation was a ritual laden with symbolism that was akin to a solemn religious ceremony. An altar draped with an American flag, the Holy Bible, copies of the Declaration of Independence and the U.S. Constitution, swords, gavels, sickle, anvils, or any other "emblems of indus-

Civil War–era flag-draped altar with Holy Bible—Espy Post 153, GAR Room, Carnegie, Pennsylvania. (Author's Collection)

try" were all utilized in a darkened initiation room lit only by candles. Most important was a censer of incense and alcohol, which was used to kindle the "fire of liberty" located in front of the altar. After the council's officers were seated in their designated locations, the assistant vice-president left the room to bring in the new initiates. Before escorting them in, however, he first explained to them the object of the Union League and then obtained their pledge of secrecy to anything that might transpire during council meetings. More questions followed pertaining to their belief in the principles set forth in the Declaration of Independence along with loyalties toward the United States of America and to the Union League. If the candidates were deemed "loyal and worthy," they were led down a walkway to the altar with the council members on either side of them. Songs and prayers followed, and then the president led the new initiates in their swearing-in ceremony.[33]

Whether a group of loyal Union men coming together called themselves a Union Club or Union League, the ensuing growth of semisecretive Unionist organizations in the lower Midwest alarmed Democratic newspapers, especially when their Republican-leaning counterparts had been beating the drum against the KGC for quite some time. "We know of no good motive or apology that a party in power, controlling both the State and National administrations, can have for organizing such associations," complained the *Indiana State Sentinel* in late July after hearing repeated reports of mysterious Republican clubs forming throughout the state. Democrats simply feared Republican intentions, those motives allegedly being "for the same object that a hard-pressed rogue cries 'Stop thief'—to divert attention away from its own party rascalities."[34]

In Illinois, the pro-Union *Daily State Journal* dismissed the Democrats' "cock and bull" stories that raised alarm over the Union Leagues. The *Journal* was especially contemptuous since those same Democratic papers had appeared so calm and unmoved by the proven existence of the KGC and its nefarious activities. For instance, the *Indiana State Sentinel*'s editor, Joseph J. Bingham—whose paper had complained about the new Union clubs—also happened to be the chairman of Indiana's state Democratic Party and a KGC member himself. The *Daily State Journal* asked that if the Union League did truly exist, its name implied a pro-Union society, then why were Democrats concerned unless they harbored Southern sympathies?[35]

By early September, the new coalition had christened itself the Union League of America. New chapters had spread so quickly through Illinois that a meeting of the various councils was scheduled to be held in Bloomington on September 25 that would draw representatives from twelve counties. At that gathering, the League men standardized organizational processes, council security, and rituals. The executive committee issued charters to new councils while making sure that every member renewed his loyalty pledge. A state constitution was also created along with new bylaws. Considering the League's belief that secrecy was paramount, new hand signs, passwords, and handshakes were introduced in lieu of what was previously utilized. To finish matters, the delegates prepared a new member initiation ritual featuring lit candles, oaths, prayer, and song that maintained a religious ritual's seriousness and majesty. That was not mere hyperbole, for a Wisconsin council president reverently recalled decades after the war how as part of the ceremony, the Holy Bible was laid upon the council's altar over which hundreds of initiates swore to protect the laws and federal government with their influence, property, and lives if need be.[36]

Many of the aforementioned Union clubs soon pledged their support to the new Union League and were given formal charters. By October, the new Illinois-based Union League estimated its membership at three thousand to five thousand and by year's end, it claimed almost fifty thousand loyal men enrolled in its ranks. Despite that impressive growth, it was still a far cry from the purported 350,000 men in the North who were said to be members of the Knights of the Golden Circle, two-thirds of whom were reported to be drilled and organized.[37]

Acting under the authority of *Chicago Tribune* editor Joseph Medill, who was earlier elected chairman of the Illinois League's State Executive Committee, Chicago attorney and Washington lobbyist John Wilson set out to organize similar councils anywhere feasible within the northern United States. With his marching orders in hand, Wilson established a Union League in Washington on October 27. The fifty-five-year-old, Irish-born Wilson had a ready audience. Wilson had previously served as the federal government's commissioner of the General Land Office from 1852 to 1856, a position now held by James Edmunds. The two men easily talked shop as Wilson convinced Edmunds to head the new Washington Union League. Over the next weeks, Wilson did likewise in Pennsylvania, New York State, Maryland, and Connecticut.[38]

Some historians have asserted that the Union Leagues were essentially an artificial, top-down construct created by cynical Republican editors and politicians as a way to whip up patriotic hysteria against Democrats via their sympathies with the phantom KGC and other "traitorous" secret societies. While some Republican politicians certainly began to realize by mid-1863 how these new patriotic societies might provide the perfect propaganda antidote to the KGC and Democratic aspirations, the early Union Leagues were all true plebeian organizations dedicated to local protection and national loyalty.[39]

The growing chorus of the peace-at-any-cost men coupled with military stalemate generated fear for the stability of both Union and state governments. The result was that some fifty thousand men were credited to Illinois alone in the League's first year of existence. Joining his local Union League council served as a means for the common Northern man (who was often too old for the military) to take some measure of action against the frustration generated by repeated military defeats and the anxiety that pro-Southern traitors were all around him. If "a fire in the rear" did indeed break out, they would administer a strong counterfire. For many of those men whose age, health, or family commitments prevented them from enlisting, joining a Union League was better than doing nothing, and helped to regenerate Northern confidence.[40]

The Union's military defeats in the summer of 1862 sapped Northern public and army morale. Had Union armies been marching triumphantly throughout the South, there is little doubt that Republican political fortunes would have been far brighter. The reality was that a year and a half of war had left the Union no closer to restoration than it was when the conflict started. Furthermore, the immense cost in blood and treasure was forcing the government to adopt policies that cut against the grain regarding individual rights, the role of the state, and long-held racial beliefs. For numerous Republican-leaning officers, Democratic priorities and beliefs were much to blame, the result being that Democratic policies were preventing the Rebel army from being "exterminated" and "Radical" officers from being promoted. "Too many officers from 2nd Lieuts. on up to Maj. Generals believe the Rebels to be half right and we three quarters wrong," complained one officer to Radical Rep. George Julian in early 1863. "I am thoroughly sick of hearing continual slang from the likes of Army officers about Abolition War, Niggerism and cannot believe that those who talk that way can be very desirous to *subjugate* the Rebels." Even the pro-Democratic *New York World* expressed worry that the recent letters received from the boys in blue "are not pitched in the right key. They show demoralization and want of heart" due to the recent military setbacks.[41]

In the meantime, Confederate Gen. Robert E. Lee had no inclination to give "those people" a respite.[42] While the North was licking its wounds and debating policy, Lee and his 55,000-man army splashed across the Potomac River on September 4 into Maryland in what was the first Confederate invasion of the North. Lee knew he could not attack Washington directly despite the bluecoats' demoralized condition because that city's defensive fortifications were almost impregnable. Nor could he sit still and rest since northern Virginia's farms and fields were devastated after a year and a half of war, giving him no way to feed his hungry army. Having regained the initiative, Lee and Jefferson Davis did not want to see their army withdraw back toward Richmond, therefore the two Rebel chieftains agreed that the former would march forward into Maryland, a border slave state, with the hope of recruiting more men for his command and putting ever more pressure on the North. As for food, Maryland's lush farms and fields would provide ample resources for Confederate stomachs. An added bonus was the confidence that just one more victory, especially on Yankee soil, might be the impetus for Britain and France to give formal diplomatic recognition to the Confederacy.

Lee's Maryland invasion certainly aroused the local population, though not in the way the Confederacy had hoped. While eastern Maryland in and around Baltimore held significant Southern sympathy, the middle and western part of the state was reliable Unionist country. Few locals answered the Rebel call as the gray-clad army marched along, singing "Maryland, my Maryland." Having received the news that the Rebels had invaded their state, Cumberland's loyal men organized themselves into a home guard to protect their town "against traitors at home and enemies abroad." Lee's veterans would have to look for more recruits elsewhere. East of the Blue Ridge Mountains, a newspaper correspondent with the Army of the Potomac noted that several Union League meetings had been held near Middlebrook, Maryland. He claimed there were twenty or so chapters in the area, all part of the "great secret society for the defense of the Government" of which he had earlier written.[43]

Not only did Lee's army fail to attract a significant number of Marylanders into its ranks, the victory sought by the Confederates was not forthcoming, either. On September 17 at Antietam Creek, near the tiny village of Sharpsburg, Union and Confederate armies collided in what became the single bloodiest day in American history. Over 23,000 men were killed, wounded, or missing in what was a drawn battle. Lee effected his escape back across the Potomac the night of September 18, giving Lincoln and the North what appeared to all as a major strategic victory.[44]

For months prior to Antietam, Lincoln had been considering a proclamation to free the slaves as a military measure. Having a battlefield victory in his pocket prior to the announcement was deemed crucial, however, for as Secretary of State William Seward remarked to Lincoln, such a declaration on the heels of one defeat after another would be seen as "our last shriek on the retreat." Given the repulse of the Rebels at Antietam, Lincoln saw his opening. On September 22, Lincoln released his order, known as the Preliminary Emancipation Proclamation. The edict proclaimed that any slaves held in areas still in rebellion against the United States on January 1, 1863, would be free. With a stroke of his pen, Lincoln had altered the Union's initial war aims. Abolition was now formally linked to restoring the Union as official war policy.[45]

By the addition of such a lofty, moral goal to Union war aims, Britain and France realized they could not be seen as aiding a belligerent power striving to keep men in bondage. Britain had outlawed slavery in 1833, therefore any formal recognition of the Confederacy would have been a diplomatic nightmare. With 20/20 hindsight, however, the likelihood of England's involvement on the Confederacy's behalf ended on March 10, 1862, the day after the USS *Monitor* and the CSS *Virginia* staged their legendary duel of ironclads off Hampton Roads, Virginia. The *Monitor*'s successful defense against the *Virginia*, coupled with the *Virginia*'s easy destruction of two wooden Union warships, would have certainly given Britain's Royal Navy significant pause. As Thomas Sebrell pointed out, while the "monitor"-class warship was not ocean-worthy, it was ideal for defending the American coast. If Britain sought to intercede militarily on the Confederacy's behalf, its troops would need to cross the Atlantic via its wooden-hulled navy. Any battle near the American coast between those British warships and the Union's ironclad monitors would have resulted in a charnel house for the former.[46]

Nothing generated more shock and consternation in the Northern loyal states throughout the second half of 1862 than Lincoln's Emancipation Proclamation. The outrage was especially pronounced in Indiana, Illinois, and Ohio's southern counties, where Southern culture and influence remained strong. For virtually all Democrats and some conservative to moderate Republicans, the proclamation was considered proof positive that the war really was all about abolition and not the noble reunification of the country that Lincoln had pledged from the beginning. Illinois's Republican Sen. Orville Browning and Judge Thomas Drummond were two of Lincoln's many friends who expressed surprise and disappointment. They considered the proclamation unfortunate and of dubious constitutionality. Most of all, though, it would unite the Rebels more forcefully than ever. By early December, lawyer and ex-Ohio senator, Thomas Ewing, had confided to Browning that the Emancipation Proclamation had ruined the Republican Party in Ohio.[47]

The Democratic reply was not so much unruffled as outraged. To the Democratic *Indiana State Sentinel,* the Union Leagues and their purported Radical allies could now be more accurately described as the "Emancipation Leagues." The editor of Canton, Ohio's *Stark County Democrat* railed that the Proclamation was just "another step in the nigger business, and another advance in the Robespierrian highway of tyranny and anarchy."[48]

For many private Americans all across the North, their antiblack racism exploded when they learned of the president's new edict. Even for many committed Union men, fighting for flag and country was one thing, but risking one's life on the battlefield to free what was universally viewed as a degraded race was quite another. Such reaction was exactly what pro-Union conservatives and moderates had feared. They realized that not only was emancipation unpopular, but also dangerous in that it might tear apart a fragile Northern agreement regarding the necessity of war. Emancipation and the rightful place of blacks in American society were a can of worms that most Americans wanted to ignore. Regardless of whether Northerners considered themselves antislavery, proslavery, or indifferent, virtually all mid-nineteenth-century whites held to a racist view of blacks with the lone exception of Radical abolitionists. Washington socialite Elizabeth Blair Lee, sister of Postmaster General Montgomery Blair, put forth a typical opinion: "I am an abolitionist for the sake of my own race—Contact with the African degenerates our white race—I find the association with them injurious to my child—keenly as I watch to prevent it."[49]

The Democratic attack against Lincoln's proclamation and Republican racial policies was blistering. Their venomous attacks stressed that Republicans' real aim was social equality between the two races. Playing on whites' almost universal racial prejudices, Democrats pointed out how black refugees were already migrating into the Northwest at a torrid pace. Camps of escaped slaves, known as "contrabands," mushroomed near the perimeters of army camps. Secretary of War Edwin Stanton unknowingly played into his opponents' hands by sending hundreds of fugitive blacks into Illinois to help gather crops during the upcoming harvest, since so many white farmers were away in the Union Army. Outraged whites rioted, forcing the authorities to return the blacks to camps south of the Ohio River. In early July, striking Irish dock workers in Toledo, Ohio, had rioted after being replaced by free blacks at the lower, original wage. A similar disturbance in Cincinnati soon followed—all examples to loyal Union men of the violent lengths anti-Lincoln men were willing to undertake. Even the prospect of military promotion could not overcome ingrained racial animosity. When Ohioan Andrew Evans learned from his son, Sam, in early 1863 that the latter was recently promoted to major in a newly formed "colored" regiment, he replied, "I would rather clean out Sh—t houses at ten cents per day, than take your position with its pay." Meanwhile, the Ohio Democrats' campaign slogan of "The Constitution as it is and the Union as it was" was amended by adding "and the Niggers where they are." At an Indiana campaign rally, young Democratic women clad in white dresses proudly stood on both sides of a banner urging their fathers to "save us from nigger husbands," while in Martinsville, a livid Democratic woman declared that she wished every Unionist woman in town could be forced to sleep with a black man. At the other end of the political aisle, antislavery leaders rejoiced and made Lincoln's proclamation the key reason for their Republican support.[50]

Despite Democrats' and Southerners' frantic warnings of sexual relations or intermarriage between black men and white women—what they later termed "miscegenation"—actual relationships of that nature were quite rare. Republicans even ridiculed their opponents for giving voice to these anxieties, for such fears implied that middle- and upper-class white women found cross-racial liaisons socially desirable. Quite the contrary, virtually all white women of the era refused to cross into this cultural no-man's-land because they knew it would have meant forfeiting their social standing due to the ongoing dictates of the era's public opinion. This was especially the case for white Southern women after the war, even when considering that the supply of eligible white men was devastated by the conflict. Only in communities with a long-standing liberal view of social intermingling between blacks and whites, such as New Orleans, did white women consider relationships with black men. Even among Radical abolitionists, who were the loudest proponents of racial intermarriage if the man and woman so desired, keeping marriage and sexual relations only between whites was considered the preferred option.[51]

Given the anger of Democratic attacks, Republicans were compelled to respond as the 1862 fall elections drew near. In Civil War–era America, the election calendar ran nearly all year long. Most local elections occurred in the late winter or early spring while state, congressional, or presidential voting took place in the late summer or fall. Thus, political partisan warfare never seemed to disappear.

The Republicans' dilemma was pronounced. They certainly could not point to the battlefield as a source of success, nor did they wish to discuss mundane topics like tariffs or governmental corruption. Therefore, the Republican propaganda machine began to ramp up with the nascent Midwestern Union Leagues playing a part. Support for the administration and rallying the public often took the form of League members handing out editorial pamphlets to the public. These propaganda pieces, often printed by the Midwestern Union Leagues themselves, were often essays or speeches from prominent politicians or preachers putting forth the Republican loyalist position. For example, four hundred such copies of a speech by former Indiana Gov. Joseph A. Wright were printed in late September 1862 and sent to Indianapolis with a directive to distribute them immediately. "There is nothing which we know of that contains so good an exposition of the *duty* of the American citizen at the *present* time as this document," stated the sender's instructions.[52]

One of the foremost propagandists in the Lincoln administration was Secretary of War Edwin Stanton. Though ostensibly a War Democrat, Stanton soon adopted a hard hand to both subordinates and enemies, garnering him the trust of the Republican Radicals. Propaganda quickly became a tool for the Radicals in their efforts to win the hearts and minds of the public toward their agenda. Stanton, along with the Congressional Joint Committee on the Conduct of the War, became leading mouthpieces for the effort.

Earlier in February 1862, the War Department had taken control of all telegraph lines, which gave it the ability to control its message and make the first impression in the public mind. News from the front—which a worried public most wanted and waited for—was effectively managed by the administration. It tolerated a free press because in large measure it went around those editors by monitoring the war information it fed to the newsrooms. Such propaganda techniques were not lost on the Union Leagues.[53]

Meanwhile, War Department memoranda to the newspapers were intentionally given the appearance of official bulletins, which administration personnel knew would help to control the narrative and secure such news squarely on any major newspaper's front page. These acts were not lost on the Democrats, who quickly began to attack Stanton and his propaganda machine.

Stanton's battles were especially pronounced with the Associated Press, the North's largest news-collecting agency. The AP was controlled by Democrats at the time and they were not going to let Stanton run roughshod over them. Stanton discovered this shortly after taking office when an innocuous speech he had made to railroad men was reported as if the new secretary had praised George McClellan, whom Stanton disliked.[54]

In another manner of propaganda, Republicans spewed forth all kinds of tales highlighting alleged battlefield barbarities by the Confederates. Fantastical tales abounded of Rebels torturing wounded Union men on the Bull Run battlefield and then boiling the bones of the Yankee dead so that they could be kept as souvenirs. The Radical-led Congressional Committee on the Conduct of the War gathered testimony that spoke of Union prisoners being intentionally starved and beaten at Rebel prisons. The intent of this propaganda was to increase the Northern population's level of hate toward their Southern enemy, the belief being that Confederates' more intense malice toward the North translated directly into their greater military success. These propaganda efforts were rarely made against specific individuals or Rebel leaders, but against the Confederate Army as a whole and, by further implication, Southern society. Later in the war, the Committee published a lurid account of such atrocities purportedly committed by the Rebels. "Let Lincoln send a copy of this book to every home," wrote one Northern diarist, convinced it would have a more positive impact on recruitment than any draft or bounties.[55]

If the Democratic low blow was a virulent strain of antiblack racism, then the Republican retort was to use a broad brush and intentionally paint any Democrat as a disloyal, pro-Southern Copperhead, even though most rank-and-file Democrats supported the war effort. As the election neared, this cry increased as pro-Unionists linked any type of wartime dissent as disloyalty to both flag and government. When the 14th Michigan Infantry left for the seat of war in February 1862, its new regimental banner featured the sewn inscription "We come not to war on opinions, but to suppress Treason." This innocuous statement was a subtle affirmation that the Lincoln administration's prowar policy was the one correct opinion. The Democrat's plea for free speech was only "a sanctified cloak for treason." In a decision that would have surely pleased the eastern Union Leagues' future leaders, the Methodist Episcopal Church urged its "Christian and Patriotic women" to form local groups to uncover those who were opposed to the war and then publicly shame them as traitors. "Hunt them out. Make the place, the society, the neighborhood too hot for them," it urged. Opposition to the war was equated to a lack of patriotism, which easily flowed into one being viewed as a traitor.[56]

A highlight of their efforts was to trump up a quote attributed to Maj. John J. Key, a staff officer for Gen. Henry Halleck and the brother of McClellan staff officer Thomas Key. When Major Key was asked after the Antietam battle why the retreating Rebels had not been vigorously pursued and destroyed, Key replied, "That is not the game. The object is that neither army shall get much advantage of the other; that both shall be kept in the field till they are exhausted, when we will make a compromise and save slavery." Lincoln was incensed when he heard this report, summoning the major to explain himself. When Key admitted his words, Lincoln promptly dismissed him from the army as an example to others. Republicans everywhere used Key's sentiment as a sample of the treasonous, antiwar sentiment lurking within the Democratic Party.[57]

The Union armies' sad military state in mid-1862 was matched only by the Democratic Party's dismal political fortunes and condition. Since the death of Stephen Douglas in mid-1861, no politician had emerged as the standard-bearer ready to take over Douglas's prior leading role. Moreover, the party's unity had been weakened by secession and considerable infighting. The faithful hoped that if the party conservatives could carry New York in the upcoming elections, they could bring considerable pressure upon Lincoln and force him to clean out the Radical Republicans' growing influence within his administration. Adding to their woes was the realization that the party lacked the full support of any major New York newspaper. By the fall of that year, however, several prominent Democrats, including Samuel L. M. Barlow, had joined forces with Manton Marble, then the night editor of the *New York World*, and in short order it became one of the leading Democratic voices in the country.[58]

At first glance, the fall 1862 election results struck a hard blow against the Republicans. Though they still maintained a congressional majority, their losses were significant since the Democrats gained thirty-two seats. Such defeats spoke to the degree to which the Northern populace had tired of the war and the processes by which it was being waged. In Lincoln's home state of Illinois, both the state legislature and its congressional delegation turned Democratic. Next door in Indiana, Democrats won nine of the eleven congressional seats up for vote while securing both houses of the state legislature, all of which left Republican Gov. Oliver P. Morton on a political island. In Ohio and Pennsylvania, the extremists took over both parties while the center eroded. Democrats gained the governor's chair in both New York and New Jersey. In New York City, the Democratic candidate for governor, Horatio Seymour, won over 70 percent of the city's vote as well as taking the statewide vote. Democrats also secured all six of the city's congressional seats.[59]

A closer examination, however, showed the results were not as damning as first considered. Democrats won only in areas where they were traditionally strong while their gains in Congress's House of Representatives were the smallest for any minority party in an off-year election in over a generation. Meanwhile, the Republicans picked up five seats in the Senate plus the knowledge that a difference of only a few thousand votes in Ohio and Pennsylvania would have kept those states in the Republican column. In any event, the Republicans offered plenty of excuses for the defeat: Solid Union men were in the armies and not at home, and state laws had prevented them from voting. Concurrently, the Democrats were guilty of fraud. These were excuses as old as the republic.[60]

Historian Mark Neely has argued that following the November 1862 election, Republicans considered Democratic opposition as seditious when it was nothing more than "politics as usual." As the party in power, Republicans deemed the very concept of political opposition in the midst of a bloody civil war as unpatriotic at best and treasonous at worst. At a minimum, it was certainly the case that Northern political infighting gave "aid and comfort" to the Confederacy. After all, the Confederates realized almost from the outset that they could not defeat the numerically superior North on the battlefield. Therefore, their overarching war strategy was to simply outlast the North by generating unremitting war weariness in the Northern population through endless military stalemate.

Yet it can be argued that in some instances, Northern opposition was indeed subversive. Straightforward public expressions of sympathy for the Southern cause were rampant. Many Copperheads openly encouraged men to avoid enlisting or to desert the army once in. Copperhead rallies often turned violent, and in 1862 and 1863, deadly antidraft, anti-Republican, and antiblack riots broke out in Northern cities. Physical assaults by Copperheads against enlisting officers and pro-Union men were well documented. At the same time, the newspapers were filled with reports describing the gatherings of pro-Southern, "dark lantern" secret societies that were drilling and arming in order to bring about the promised "fire in the rear." This was especially the case in those Northern states west of Pennsylvania. While hyper-partisan rhetoric was as old as politics itself, Americans who had experienced, witnessed, or simply read about these disturbances knew these new threats had an air of legitimacy. Little wonder then that tens of thousands of working- and middle-class, pro-Union men sought safety and comradery within the burgeoning Union Leagues.[61]

Of course, not all prowar Northerners were abolitionists, nor were all Democrats disloyal Copperheads, despite the Union League's later broad-brush efforts to paint the latter as such. This was especially frustrating to those Northern Democrats who considered themselves staunch Union supporters. Following their tremendous success in the November 1862 elec-

August Belmont (Library of Congress Prints and Photographs Division)

tions, August Belmont, a steadfast War Democrat and that party's national chairman, felt compelled to advise an English baron that Britain and France may have misinterpreted the Democrats' intentions given their victory. While Democrats did want to see the South retain its rights as guaranteed by the Constitution *and* remain within the Union, Belmont felt strongly that Democrats would "not accept of any compromise which has not the reconstruction of but one Government over all the thirty-four States for its basis." Belmont continued to offer advice and sagacity to the Lincoln administration through the summer of 1863, at which time communications dwindled. Belmont was still the Democratic Party chairman, and to have communication and official contacts with men he would soon be trying to oust from office would be seen as having questionable decorum.[62]

As bad as the political situation was, the military chessboard for the Union worsened further. After replacing the soldiers' beloved George McClellan with Ambrose Burnside as head of the Army of the Potomac in early November, Burnside's new command was thoroughly whipped by the Rebels at the battle of Fredericksburg on December 13 to the apparent delight of Northern Copperheads. "McClellan's friends chuckle and secretly rejoice over the result. The opponents of the administration are doing all in their power to break it down," groused Republican Ohio Rep. William P. Cutler in his diary after seeing the smiles. Concurrently, an Illinois man complained to Rep. Elihu Washburne how "Every defeat or check that our army meets with in Virginia strengthens the cause of the home secessionist." Those opponents did not have to be powerful politicians or military men, either. They could be average citizens, the type that Connecticut housewife Mattie Blanchard described as those who "get over to the store and have a glorious time over the news if it is in favor of the south." "They had ought to be shot," was Mattie's preferred solution. Such misfortunes only soured Northern spirits even more.[63]

The gloom that permeated the pro-Union North as 1862 ended was as deep as at any point in the war. In the past seven months the Union's Army of the Potomac had suffered one military reverse after another: the Peninsula Campaign had ended in ignominious flight from that Virginia finger of land. The three-day Second Bull Run engagement, only thirty miles west of Washington, from August 28–30 was another disaster. While the fight at Maryland's Antietam Creek on September 17 had ended in a strategic defeat for Confederate plans, it had nonetheless featured a Confederate army proudly marching unopposed across the Potomac and into Union territory. The December

13 battle at Fredericksburg, Virginia was the Army of the Potomac's crowning catastrophe from the past seven months. In the meantime, Lincoln's Emancipation Proclamation evoked bitter controversy throughout the North. It was easy to pinpoint all of this disappointment as the collective reason for the Republican's perceived rebuff in the fall 1862 congressional elections. Lincoln, his political allies, and the pro-Republican Northern public began 1863 the same way they began 1862: frustrated, depressed, and on the ropes. "If there is a worse place than Hell, I am in it," groaned Lincoln as 1862 was drawing to a close. The pro-Union public needed a significant injection of hope, morale, and patriotism.[64]

Chapter 4

"A Refuge Rather Than a Resort for Loyalty"

Philadelphia, New York, and Boston Lead the Way

The 1862 election results sent an irrefutable message to steadfast, prowar Lincoln loyalists. Such a stinging rebuke was not only obvious by the voting patterns, but also seemed apparent on every Republican's countenance. "The hearts of loyal men everywhere were depressed," recalled Philadelphian poet and playwright George Boker, such that "public spirit sank into an almost helpless lethargy, and doubt and distrust had crept into the minds of the most sanguine." The Union Army's quartermaster general, Montgomery C. Meigs, gauged the country's mood accurately when he wrote to Union Gen. Ambrose Burnside: "Exhaustion steals over the country. Confidence and hope are dying."[1]

Morale was sinking not merely through the populace but even within the halls of Congress and at the White House. Massachusetts's Sen. Charles Sumner wrote that "there are senators full of despair" and that even Lincoln confided to him that he feared the "fire in the rear" more than the military outlook.[2]

Throughout their gentlemen's clubs and dinner parties, Philadelphia's leading Republican men took note of the gloom and realized that something had to be done to rally the public. How to accomplish such a broad goal was the key for unlike our modern era, no manner of "public relations" or propaganda agency existed at the state or federal levels during the Civil War. Any limited concept of national loyalty was promoted solely by private organizations or individuals, each perhaps with their own agenda. These generally middle-aged to elderly Philadelphia men stood atop the city's intellectual, business, social, and cultural houses. As with men of similar age, wealth,

George Boker (Library of
Congress Prints and Pho-
tographs Division)

and stature in New York and Boston, they viewed themselves as the patrician fraternity within their respective cities, morally obligated to act under
noblesse oblige as a standard of conduct or action, for an active political life
was deemed a sign of social respectability. Moreover, these forward-looking
men sensed that for the country to continue its geographical and economic
growth, the primacy of the nation must supersede the individual states. The
Republican-leaning *Harper's Weekly* editorialized on this point when the war
began, noting that if the federal government was not paramount, then the
bond that bound the states was no greater than a mere treaty with England
or France, which any party might annul at their whim. From the political
and cultural perspective of these men, it was their honorable duty as the
city's elite to guide the working classes as a means of preserving secular stability. Jacksonian Democracy—opposed to the idea of an educated elite but
favoring greater involvement of the common man in civic and governmental
affairs, and which dominated civic life for over a generation—stood as the
primary hindrance to a more nationalistic outlook.[3]

Even worse than the depressed attitudes of Philadelphia's loyal men were
the constant smirks from the city's Copperheads, who were by no means a

minority within the City of Brotherly Love. Renowned English novelist Anthony Trollope wrote in his *North America* travelogue that when he visited Philadelphia in late 1861 en route from Boston to Washington, it was the first time he encountered secessionists who openly proclaimed themselves as such. Yet while many Democrats disapproved of Southern secession and wanted to see the Union remain whole, a significant number held long-standing business ties to that region and therefore empathized with the South's grievances. Much of this commercial interest was further strengthened by years of social interaction and marital relationships. A result was that Pennsylvania had long been considered a Democratic state with half of its leading city's population firmly anti-Lincoln. Nevertheless, politics had often been kept at arm's length as many of Philadelphia's elite fraternized openly at exclusive organizations such as the Wistar Party, named for Dr. Caspar Wistar, who had gathered since the turn of the century to enjoy their polite society. The coming storm clouds of war altered much of that congeniality. Many of Philadelphia's leading businessmen viewed the president as a threat to their profitable business dealings with the South.[4]

All of this was painfully apparent to those upper-class, pro-Union men who were members of the long-standing Philadelphia Club. Founded in 1834, that club was considered the oldest "Gentleman's Club" in the country and whose membership included some of Philadelphia's first and most prominent families. Membership in the Philadelphia Club was deemed a pinnacle of social success and status in antebellum Philadelphia. Escalating tensions between the club's Southern sympathizers and more pro-administration Union men became so intense after the war broke out, however, that each group soon socialized in separate rooms at their club, with little interaction or talk between the two. Philadelphia's Union men were convinced that their bitterness was justified. They recalled how just a few months earlier following the Second Bull Run disaster and Lee's subsequent September 1862 Maryland invasion, Southern-leaning men were cheerily predicting that Philadelphia would soon be taken by the Confederates. Once the Rebels were in the city, these Copperhead men would set up General Lee's headquarters in the James Dundas mansion at the northeast corner of Broad and Walnut streets. At the same time, the front doors of leading Republicans' homes were to be brandished with large X's so that those men could be easily scooped up by the arriving Confederates.[5]

Matters only worsened as year-end approached. Philadelphia diarist Sidney Fisher wrote that he was "disgusted" as to how Charles Ingersoll, one of the city's leading anti-Lincoln Democrats, exhibited "exultation and delight" at the Union Army's Fredericksburg defeat. George Boker was likewise stunned and angered at the ascension of Southern sympathizers in Philadelphia. "The alarming fact," wrote Boker, "was that this class of people was obtaining social supremacy. Their defiant and outspoken treason converted all convivial meetings into disagreeable wranglings, or drove into seclusion the more modest and peaceful patriots." Tensions within the Philadelphia Club erupted after one Union man observed, "This place reeks of Copperheads." A physical altercation and lawsuits ensued, prompting many proadministration men to leave the club in early December 1862.[6]

At the behest of Boker and Judge John Innes Clark Hare, just over a dozen men secretly met at the home of fifty-one-year-old attorney Benjamin Gerhard on November 15, 1862, to discuss what might be done to counter the growing threat. Hare was an obvious man for the new idea. At forty-six years old, Hare was one of Philadelphia's elites, a staunch Unionist, and vice-president of the Law Academy of Philadelphia. In that latter role, he was considered by many to be Pennsylvania's most eminent jurist. The group met again a week later on November 22, and it was then that they adopted the Union Club of Philadelphia as the group's initial name. Other cofounders included Morton McMichael, the publisher of *The North American* and a future Philadelphia mayor, and Charles Gibbons, an eminent attorney and ex-Pennsylvania state senator. In discussing membership requirements, the final wording stated "unqualified loyalty to the Government of the United States, and unwavering support for the suppression of the Rebellion." Since the beginning of the war, the words "loyal" and "loyalty" held significant meaning. They connoted healthy patriotism over rank partisanship; those who were not loyal faced the "scarlet letter" of traitor. For men like Boker, a demand for loyalty was obvious for as he later stated, "Once the sword was drawn, it struck me that politics had vanished entirely from the scene—that no more politics remained—that it was a mere question of patriotism or disloyalty." With such characterization, these men were defining and then institutionalizing how they, and future Union Leagues around the country, would delineate a patriot as opposed to a traitor.[7]

Four more weekly gatherings followed, each one generating more attendees than the one before and which were quickly becoming Philadelphia's center for Union sentiment. Yet the growing club realized that there must be more to their meetings than just pleasant weekend dining and discussion. Some manner of focus and reorganization was necessary. The seventh meeting on December 27, 1862, was that lynchpin. Held at the house of forty-four-year-old Dr. John Forsyth Meigs, one of Philadelphia's leading physicians, the members approved an organizational name change from the Union Club to the Union League, what member John Russell Young later called "one of the grandest and most potent influences in the war." The minutes from that meeting noted that they were organizing "for the purpose of counteracting the effects of traitors in the northern states to destroy the American Union." No wine was to be served at meetings, no games other than billiards could be enjoyed, and most importantly, no one was to be admitted who was reluctant to offer unqualified support to the Lincoln administration and all of its war measures. The new Union League's initial, typeset Articles of Association listed the names of 253 of Philadelphia's leading men. An analysis of those men revealed, perhaps somewhat surprisingly, that seventy-five were Republicans, 135 Democrats, and forty-three whose political affiliations were not confirmed. Such a breakdown showed there were plenty of elite Democrats in Philadelphia who considered themselves pro-Union patriots desiring to fully put down the rebellion. This initial nonpartisanship was not forgotten in later years for in 1888, member Edwin Benson recalled how "there is a fine old ring of patriotism about the title of *War Democrat* which will cling to those brave and gallant gentlemen, so long as memories of the war shall endure." These membership numbers demonstrated that at least initially, this important organization's political makeup was true to the "no party now" ideal.[8]

The League's first president was sixty-two-year-old attorney William Morris Meredith, who had served as secretary of the treasury under President Zachary Taylor and was the current attorney general for Pennsylvania under Republican Gov. Andrew Curtin. Meredith's new position added immediate stature to the group, not only because of his public reputation but because he served as a member of the ill-fated 1861 Peace Conference in Washington that tried but failed to keep the Southern states from seceding. By accepting his new position, one Philadelphia League historian later wrote that Meredith's presidency "betokened a rule of judicious tolerance that might draw conservatives and waverers into the association."[9]

George Henry Boker was the Philadelphia League's secretary from day one and he soon proved to be a tireless workhorse. At thirty-nine years old, Boker was the prototypical silk-stocking man of leisure whose political ideals were staunchly pro-Union. Considered charming, intelligent, and handsome by his peers, Boker was an aspiring poet whose work had garnered some critical acclaim during the antebellum years. Far more importantly, he was the son of a wealthy Philadelphia bank president whose prominent lineage was well established by the time of Boker's birth in 1823. When Boker graduated from Princeton at the age of nineteen, he took his position as one of Philadelphia's elite, earning the era's desired reputation as a polished gentleman with just the requisite amount of social reserve. These latter realities provided him ample time to throw himself into building up the nascent Union League. He described Philadelphia's new League as "a refuge rather than a resort for loyalty." It was to be a social institution, "where true men might breathe without having the atmosphere contaminated by treason." Boker would serve as the Union League of Philadelphia's secretary from 1863 to 1871 and then as president from 1879 until his resignation in 1884. Later League publications considered Boker "if not the soul, in a large degree the brain and hand of the club and league" during its dark, early days. No man in the United States would come to be more of a force in turning the Union Leagues into a viable political power during the Civil War than George Boker.[10]

Cofounder John Russell Young, the twenty-two-year-old managing editor of the *Press* in Philadelphia, echoed Boker's defensive sentiment by advising his publisher, John Forney, how "our policy is never to attack in these times. It is meant to fortify our own friends." Such perspectives would be short-lived.[11]

By mid-February, the *Press* was a strong editorial advocate for Philadelphia's growing Union League. Since Forney was a founding member, the *Press* soon became the de facto Philadelphia mouthpiece for the Union League. Boker showed no hesitation in asking Young to make various announcements in the Philadelphia *Press* on the League's behalf: "I need not ask twice, nor in two ways, for I know that your heart is in the cause."[12]

By late winter and early spring of 1863, speaking to the Union League of Philadelphia was essential for any politician or prominent civilian seeking to burnish his pro-Union, loyalist bona fides. To properly accommodate its members and guests, the League opened a new, elegant clubhouse located at 1118 Chestnut Street on February 23, 1863. Food, drink, and speeches abounded, which included remarks by Pennsylvania's Gov. Andrew Curtin and industrialist James Milliken. "Its name, and the flag that floats over it, its very existence," the League later proclaimed, "are a standing rebuke to the traitors."[13]

The Union League of Philadelphia's weekly meetings quickly featured an impressive list of Republican guest speakers. Former Baltimore mayor Thomas Swann appeared on March 2, urging that the federal union must be preserved. Frederick Douglass spoke on March 18, followed by Delaware's Gov. William Cannon the next week. In early April, Indiana's Gov. Oliver Morton appeared. The League's organic success was becoming apparent to many who initially cast doubt or even declined membership. Included in that group was Sidney Fisher, who initially feared that such a group looked too much like mob rule but now had a change of heart. In his March 11 diary entry, Fisher cheered the previous night's speeches, "all urging a vigorous prosecution of the war and an uncompromising determination to crush the rebellion and reduce the South to absolute submission, at any sacrifice." As was to become all Union Leagues' standard fare, rebellion sympathizers were denounced with great bitterness. Meanwhile, word of the Philadelphia's new Union League was rapidly spreading.[14]

The political leanings and relations of New York's business and cultural elite were similar to that of Philadelphia. New York was the preeminent financial center for the South, its banks financing the South's cotton trade and other cash crops. Three-fourths of the nation's imported goods entered the country via New York's ports. When the Civil War started, most of New York's leading merchants, bankers, and industrialists supported the war solely to restore their commercial interests to the prosperous, prewar status quo, not to challenge the South's "peculiar institution." Though perhaps antislavery in the privacy of their homes, many New York elites decried abolition in public, lest profitable business dealings be jeopardized. So great were the economic ties that one young man named Abram Dittenhoefer came to believe that New York was a virtual annex for the South, the latter being the best customer of the former. "Our merchants have for sale on their shelves their principles," Dittenhoefer dryly noted, "together with their merchandise."[15]

Culturally, New York exhibited significant Southern sympathy as well. The cotton trade was New York merchants' most important business and its continuity allowed Southern belles to lavishly spend their families' money at upscale New York retailers. Meanwhile, they also attended the city's fashionable finishing schools, with their matronly mothers accompanying them "in season" in order to show them off to the young, eligible Southern men who frequented the city. After thirty years of socializing and intermarriage, the Southern elite and their way of life was well entrenched within New York society's highest levels.[16]

As the rebellion dragged on and Union losses mounted, New York's prowar upper class began to see a causal link between emancipation and the war's end. While long-time abolitionists had always held this view, many Democrats and Republicans now realized that slavery lay at the root of the rebellion and its termination the only way toward peace and reunification. For Radical Republicans, the war represented a life-or-death struggle between two alien social systems: Northern free labor and the Southern slavocracy. Lincoln's Emancipation Proclamation went into effect on January 1, 1863, and it represented the opening salvo in a new recalculation of the war's purpose for New York's patriarchy.[17]

As mentioned previously and similar to Philadelphia in 1834, an exclusive gentleman's club was formed in New York in 1836. The club christened itself the Union Club of New York with its membership limited to four hundred of the city's "most distinguished citizens." According to one diarist, the Union Club patterned itself after the great clubs of London, though New York in 1836 was still a much smaller city. Unlike London, New York possessed no uniformed police force while fire stations were comprised entirely of volunteers. Just like Philadelphia, however, its members were not immune to opinionated discussions on the then-upcoming Civil War. Some of the club's members were Southern men who eventually resigned or were later dropped from membership due to nonpayment of dues after they headed south. Two prominent Southern members in that latter category included Judah Benjamin and John Slidell, who later became Confederate secretary of state and commissioner to France, respectively. When three Democratic club members paid Benjamin's dues after they fell into arrears, pro-Union members protested vehemently, claiming Benjamin was a rebel in arms against the United States and that he had no business being in a pro-Union association. Once other pro-Southern men were allowed to quietly resign from the Union Club rather than being ceremoniously expelled, a number of members more loyal to the federal government quit to protest the club's lenient handling of these Southern sympathizers. Some of those who resigned then went on to form the Union League Club of New York. Yet in spite of the mass resignation legend, the Union Club's records reveal that most of those new Union League members also remained Union Club members throughout their lives.[18]

The men who created the Union League Club of New York also possessed deep roots within the United States Sanitary Commission, the tireless civilian body of men and women who collected and distributed all manner of medical and relief supplies for the Union armies. Officially sanctioned by President Lincoln on June 9, 1861, the Sanitary Commission was directed

Sanitary Commission Group (*left to right*): William Holme Van Buren, George Templeton Strong (treasurer), Henry Whitney Bellows (president), Cornelius Rea Agnew, and Oliver Wolcott Gibbs (Library of Congress Prints and Photographs Division)

to focus its efforts toward "the inspection of recruits and enlisted men; the sanitary condition of the volunteers; to the means of preserving and restoring the health, and of securing the general comfort and efficiency of troops; to the proper provision of cooks, nurses, and hospitals; and to other subjects of like nature."[19]

Though the Sanitary Commission's membership and activities spanned all of the Northern and Midwestern states, its commissioners and executive committee were all leading men from New York high society. The initial twelve-man commission included Dr. Henry W. Bellows, a prominent, Harvard-educated, fifty-seven-year-old Unitarian clergyman, who served as the Commission's president and strategist. His congregation at All Soul's Church included numerous members of New York's business and intellectual elite. George Templeton Strong, a genteel forty-one-year-old New York attorney with significant ties to the city's business community, served as the Sanitary Commission's treasurer. Frederick Law Olmsted, a forty-nine-year-old former journalist and current landscape architect, served as executive secretary for the Commission. Another member of future Union League importance was thirty-nine-year-old Dr. Oliver Wolcott Gibbs, considered one of the leading chemists in the nation. These men knew each other well, considered themselves friends, and were of one mind when it came to purpose.[20]

As part of New York's cultural elite and monied class, these men shared a common *nationalistic* belief system that bound them together, which was expressed in a civic and social obligation to perpetuate American civilization's continued advancement. While the Sanitary Commission had the appearance of "a humanitarian or beneficent organization," its high-level purpose was to advance the commissioners' political ideal of instilling a sense of national life into the populace, as opposed to one that focused only on city or state and the attendant petty jealousies that accompanied such a limited perspective. Strong angrily revealed this view in his March 11, 1861, diary entry when, frustrated at the apparent inevitability of civil war, remarked "The bird of our country is a debilitated chicken, disguised in eagle feathers. We have never been a nation; we are only an aggregate of communities, ready to fall apart at the first serious shock and without a center of vigorous national life to keep us together." These men saw through the North's early enthusiasm for the war, which they realized was only a reflection of county or state pride, rather than a true conversion to nationalism. Advancing a more national life would be accomplished in part by working through organizations in a manner that would elevate the character of the poor and working classes. The elites viewed poor immigrants with a skeptical eye, believing their cultural values and commitment to the new nation to be questionable. Through the mission of providing much-needed aid to the Union Army, they sought to create a national, Christian-based organization guided by leading men who would build upon that goal by focusing on the North's patriotic emotions. Though led by male intellectuals, the Commission's initial grassroots success was generated by the scores of women and their patriotic labors to gather, package, and ship the various supplies to the field. Its leadership focus was on the trained professional.[21]

Like his fellow Sanitary Commission members, by late 1862 Olmsted believed a dangerous gloom cloaked the North and accordingly, its people needed a patriotic stimulus. For all their national concern, however, as New Yorkers these men were most alarmed over the political condition within

Frederick Law Olmsted (Library
of Congress Prints and Photographs Division)

their home state and its largest city; one that was increasingly divided by
class, ethnicity, politics, and political loyalty. Over the past fifteen years, huge
numbers of poor Irish immigrants had settled in New York. In fact, in 1860
just over one quarter of New York's 813,000 residents were Irish. Most of
these new immigrants identified with the Democrats' "common man" ideals.
That loyalty was repaid as New York Democrats fought for Irish freedoms
both here and abroad, combated Republican nativism by stoking class resentment, and developed a party line that touted Irish jobs while promoting
antiblack racism. As a result, many of these immigrants believed the Civil
War was not their fight; they feared and loathed blacks as competition for
manual labor jobs. Furthermore, many poor Irish disdained much of the elite
class who displayed ample nativist sentiment against them in the past. Both
social classes were well aware of the scornful typecasts each held of the other:
Rich, greedy, Protestant Republicans who wanted the poor man to fight his
war versus the corrupt, ignorant, Catholic immigrant who cared little about
his new homeland. It was a tinderbox waiting for the match.[22]

Meanwhile, fifty-two-year-old Horatio Seymour, a reliable anti-Lincoln
Democrat, was headed to the governor's chair for a second time. Sensing

Seymour's apparent lack of conviction in fighting to preserve the Union, English journalist William Howard Russell aptly described the new governor as "an ingenious gentleman who thinks the Union can be best maintained by not attempting to govern it at all." At the same time, another anti-war Democrat, Fernando Wood, was seated as New York City's mayor with Democrats also in control of local city government. Only five of the city's seventeen newspapers were clearly pro-Republican. Of the twelve remaining, nine were proslavery and of those, five espoused the Copperhead line. The anti-Republican, anti-Lincoln sentiment was so widespread that another British journalist visiting New York in early 1863 perceived the city as "incurably Copperhead, and at least nine-tenths Secesh." In February 1863, a Union Navy officer returning to duty after a visit to New York remarked that he was practically taunted by city residents because of his blue uniform. Every saloon or public place he visited, the officer observed rampant Southern support. Years later, noted New York attorney and Union League member George Bliss recalled that "if [Confederate President] Jeff Davis had been running against Abraham Lincoln in 1862 he would have won New York City by 60,000 votes," Though obviously exaggerations, these sentiments were reflective of the significant Peace Democrat–Copperhead sentiment within the city and perhaps not that far off the mark.[23]

Based on Horatio Seymour's election and the danger that heralded to Republicans, Oliver W. Gibbs wrote to Olmsted in early November 1862 suggesting that some manner of social club needed to be created that would promote loyalty to the Union, thereby becoming the first Sanitary Commission member to ring the alarm bell. Olmsted heartily agreed in his November 5 reply to Gibbs. More letters followed between the two men, as well as face-to-face discussions between Gibbs and George Strong at the former's home on December 1. These early discussions by Sanitary Commission members about the need for a new loyalist club gave birth to Henry Bellows's famous postwar remark that "the Union League Club [was] the child of the United States Sanitary Commission." In Olmsted's reply, he stressed the club's methods must be built around its nationalist aims. In this initial proposal, the idea of mere loyalty to the Constitution and Union were insufficient for membership. Olmsted deplored the idea of a European-style "hereditary aristocracy" or privileged class and wanted an organization based on a "natural" aristocracy of the mind that might provide a leading light for others. These ideas would combine economic, political, and cultural pursuits, but not necessarily ingrained within political parties. Of course, men of wealth, culture, and stature should lead the way, Olmsted reasoned; however, he also envisioned creative men in the literary field becoming part of the new organization. Not to be forgotten were wealthy and promising younger men who might be properly educated toward Republican principles and the Union cause. These elite New Yorkers' Republican politics were also steeped with old Whig Party principles, believing that the educated elite should guide the country forward. From their vantage, they represented a benevolent patriarchy, whose social duties included instruction to the masses on civic responsibility, honest labor, and social reform. As with their Philadelphia brethren, their public benevolence stood not only as a means of protecting their business interests, but also as a means of implementing secular order into an unruly world. These men sought, in part, a "cultural reclamation" of New York. These values stood in opposition to the common man virtues espoused by Jacksonian Democrats, whose vision of unfettered democracy looked too much like mob rule to Republicans. Unlike the original Midwestern Union Leagues created in the last half of 1862 as an organic, middle-class, bottom-up means of safety and promoting loyalty, the aristocratic Eastern Leagues envisioned an upper class–led organization that would promote a new manner of nationalistic identity.[24]

Olmsted and Gibbs soon learned of the Union League of Philadelphia's recent formation and its membership requirements. After a heated internal debate within the Philadelphia League as to whether it would be a pro-Union *and* a pro-Republican organization, cooler heads voted that unwavering loyalty to the Union was sufficient, thereby welcoming Democrats who fully supported a war to restore the Union, but may have disagreed with Lincoln and his Republicans on lesser issues. Olmsted and Gibbs were not impressed, believing the Philadelphia League's membership requirements as stated in its founding document were not strong enough. "Any rogue could drive a four horse coach through it," complained Olmsted. "Everybody who has been in Fort Lafayette could swear to it. Loyalty means lickspittle to save the Union with some men." His new vision was not that of a staid gentlemen's club uttering hollow words to loyalty and Union, but a forceful weapon to be used liberally against the Union's enemies. "Now is the time in question to crush the spirit of secession in our affairs, and I have done my best to make this an irresistible battery for that purpose," wrote Olmsted in early 1863.[25]

The call for the new loyal organization went out on January 15 in a confidential circular sent to select "men of social, financial, and political distinction." The letter advised the recipient how "the urgency of the present great national crisis, and the revolutionary schemes which unprincipled men are plotting to accomplish, make it the immediate duty of all loyal citizens to organize themselves as to give the most efficient support to the national cause." Two weeks later on January 30, the first informal gathering occurred at the home of Dr. Gibbs. Initially the new group referred to itself as The National Club, as it was believed by many of those present that such a name was more representative of the group's character. Some felt that Union League Club might be construed to link the new organization with the plebian Union Leagues in the Midwest or with the Union League of Philadelphia, since both Eastern cities considered themselves unique and distinct from the other. Nonetheless, at its next meeting on February 6, the name was officially changed to the Union League Club of New York. Sixty-four men signed their names as charter members. When the new club held its first official meeting in March, fifty-six-year-old Robert B. Minturn, one of the country's leading merchants and shippers, was elected to serve as the New York League's first president. Its object was "to cultivate a profound national devotion, rather than state or sectional feeling."[26]

To Gibbs's, Olmsted's, and Strong's dismay, however, the Union League Club of New York's membership requirements were closer to the Philadelphia League than what they had originally envisioned. As far as Olmsted was concerned, it contributed to his lessening involvement with the club, as well as a slow withdrawal from the Sanitary Commission. Strong was more understanding, conceding in his diary that "No one can be expected to pledge himself to uphold whatever any set of men at Washington or elsewhere may hereafter think proper to do, and on the other hand, no one can expect to be admitted to a club designed to sustain government who goes about denouncing the damned idiocy of Secretary this, and the corruption of Secretary that." Though Gibbs attempted to defend the membership parameters to Olmsted, he admitted, "I wanted it to sound like a trumpet, but find that it was necessary to begin with a whistle." Despite that initial disappointment, one of the New York League's most important early actions was establishing a committee to investigate the possibility of creating or working with affiliated organizations throughout the country.[27]

Even with Gibbs's misgivings, the first of many trumpets was sounded by Rev. Henry Bellows on February 1, 1863. In his sermon at New York's All Souls' Church on that Sunday evening, Bellows delivered a thundering oration on the loyalty due the national government in these troubled times. Bellows's sermon was titled "Unconditional Loyalty" and was inspired by a dinner he recently attended at Washington's Willard Hotel, which included Secretary of State William Seward as one of the guests. Throughout the evening, Seward repeatedly compared Lincoln to Christ and the president's travails to the Lord's work. Bellows built his sermon around the biblical verse, "And the government shall be upon his shoulder,"[28] lecturing his flock that now was no time for petty political ideology. Such partisan schemes, Bellows argued, were similar to the businessman who publicly and self-righteously proclaimed honesty and integrity as worthy principles, but then made quiet exceptions in dealing with his own creditors. Rather, support was owed unconditionally to the president and the government, for "The head of a nation *is* a sacred person, representing, for the time he holds his office, the most valuable and solemn rights and duties of a people. 'The Government' is 'upon his shoulder,'—and the Government is the mighty pillar that fastens in order and holds to safety the ten thousand varying interests, rights and obligations of a nation." Unspoken in Bellows's sermon was the religious and political belief that a citizen's unwavering loyalty to the Lincoln administration and its policies was sufficient; an emotional state that did not demand any type of physical action or personal sacrifice. The *New York Times* printed the sermon in full in its February 6 issue and soon thereafter, Bellows's oration was republished in pamphlet form. Olmsted considered it a "grand work," and by the end of 1863, over thirty thousand copies had been distributed to Union soldiers in the field. Though not a publication initially sponsored by the blossoming Union League, it nonetheless represented one of the first of over four million pro-Union pamphlets printed during the course of the war that put forth the League's position on what constituted proper loyalty and patriotism.[29]

Within a few weeks, the moderate Republican *New York Times* endorsed the new Union League. The *Times,* considered one of the most important papers in New York as well as the country, purported that loyal men lagged behind the disloyal in organizing, to the point that treachery and treason were virtually on public display. That treason, according to the *Times,* was manifested by the Copperheads' alarming growth via the Knights of the Golden Circles' secret operations. It was essential for the Union Leagues to act as a counterweight to the KGC. "The wayfaring man," wrote the *Times,* "though a fool, needs no longer have a glimmering doubt as to their essential disloyalty."[30]

By early spring, Secretary of State Seward was also on board with the idea of a patriotic society promoting loyalty. He wrote letters to the Union

Leagues, asking that his name be placed on the rolls. "If providence could disappoint the dearest hopes of mankind," he pledged, "let not my name be found among those who proved unfaithful." Those who proved themselves faithful were numerous. When the Union League Club of New York officially opened its new clubhouse at the corner of 17th Street and Broadway via an evening reception on May 12, 1863, its membership roll stood at 350 and would continue to grow.[31]

The urge to publicly profess loyalty and inspire public patriotism was quickly manifesting itself throughout the Eastern seaboard. Having learned of what transpired in Philadelphia, fourteen of Boston's leading Republican men were urged by John Murray Forbes to start their own loyalty club. Born in Bordeaux, France, in 1813, Forbes established himself as one of the country's leading railroad industrialists and land developers during the 1850s. Like many of the country's wealthiest businessmen, Forbes considered himself a Whig at mid-century. He later admitted to being indifferent to the black slave's plight in his younger years. Following the murder of abolitionist editor Elijah Lovejoy in 1837, however, Forbes became vehemently antislavery, to the point of meeting with John Brown at Forbes's Massachusetts home. By the turn of the new decade, Forbes was a steadfast Republican and Lincoln supporter.[32]

Forbes's concern was that he was witnessing in Boston what upper-class Philadelphians and New Yorkers saw earlier in their respective cities: a growing suspicion that the Lincoln administration was losing favor with a large portion of Boston's conservative business establishment, which often found refuge in the Somerset Club. Formed in 1852 by members of the defunct Tremont Club, the Somerset was deemed the pinnacle of antebellum Boston's club society. As the war dragged on into the second half of 1862, pro-Lincoln men were becoming ever more frustrated with their Somerset colleagues who found fault with every Lincoln word or action. Their concern also extended to what they were hearing on Boston's streets. "The state of feeling," wrote former state legislator Martin Brimmer, "was more conspicuously critical than patriotic. Some privately denounced the war in all its aspects; some attacked indiscriminately all the acts of the government, and [others] peppered their remarks with a liberal supply of sarcasm. . . . We agreed that a club of some sort was greatly needed to serve this purpose [of loyalty]." Therefore, these men sought a means to counter it through the power of their own loyal organization, yet one devoid of party politics.[33]

Adding fuel to their fire was the recollection of a late January 1863 visit to the city by Gen. George McClellan, which resulted in scores of conservative merchants and bankers closing their businesses in honor of "Little Mac's" arrival. Republicans however, were less enthusiastic. "The Hero of one hundred ungained Victories,—the conqueror in his own bulletins, is at present in Boston, and but a few people remain calm," wrote Charles Eliot Norton, the thirty-five-year-old editor of the *North American Review* and member of Boston's emerging loyalty club. Though still technically "awaiting orders" following his November 1862 dismissal as the Army of the Potomac's commanding general, McClellan was considered the leading Democratic candidate for president in the 1864 elections. One Boston socialite who witnessed the general's appearance felt there was more fanfare than she could ever remember. "Beacon St. laid down and begged to lick his shoes," she wrote, though adding that McClellan apparently disliked the extreme level of attention. Local Republicans concluded this trip was an early attempt to establish Democratic opposition against Lincoln, even though the presidential election was still over eighteen months away. In this vein, the Springfield

Charles Eliot Norton, c. 1903 (Library of Congress Prints and Photographs Division)

Republican quipped that no man ever traveled to Boston unless he wanted something, and at the same time, no one was ever invited unless the town sought something from him. In this particular case, what was apparently wanted was a new president. That the onetime Army of the Potomac leader was now the darling of the antiwar, i.e., "treasonous," Democrats irked pro-administration Republicans incessantly. "McClellan has succeeded in establishing the position of a party leader," wrote Ohio's Sen. John Sherman, "and now enjoys the bad honor of being cheered by a New York mob of thieves and scoundrels."[34]

The new Boston initiative was gaining traction and by late February, Charles Eliot Norton proudly wrote that Boston's new loyalty club was already at two hundred members. A circular seeking possible members emphasized the need for keeping "the public opinion of New England sound, and as nearly as possible unanimous." The club served as "a rallying point for gentlemen of intelligence, public spirit, and social prominence, who believed that the Union could be preserved, and that it could be preserved by the announced policy of President Lincoln." Simply put, wrote one of its founders, "We want a place where gentlemen may pass an evening without hearing Copperhead talk."[35]

Complimentary toward Philadelphia's show of loyalty, Norton dryly wrote how Boston could achieve the same if only the city had "a few more out-and-out secessionists." In fact, the new Boston club was set to adopt the Philadelphians' articles of association until conservative Republicans demanded additional guarantees that the new organization was not a Radical nest run by abolitionists. This prompted Norton to record that the new association would be known as the Union Club, as the word "League" was deemed too offensive to some. Other Boston conservatives refused to join for they regarded the new club as merely an "abolition concern" or a "Jacobin Association," regardless of its designation. This name concession was an attempt by the Boston club to be more politically inclusive, as opposed to the Philadelphia and New York leagues who intentionally sought a degree of exclusivity. Yet, in a display of pragmatism, Norton realized that all the loyal clubs, lectures, and pamphlets in the world would not make any difference unless they were accompanied by military victory.[36]

At the Boston club's formal inauguration on April 9, newly elected president Edward Everett laid forth the club's objective, which he described as "the active and earnest cooperation of all good citizens in the loyal support of the Union, the Constitution, and the Government of the country in the present great crisis of affairs." The esteemed, sixty-nine-year-old Everett had served the public long and honorably as a congressman, senator, Massachusetts governor, and ambassador to Great Britain. With a desire to show the elder statesman the proper respect, Everett's speech was described as "an eloquent and finished production, as are all his oratorical efforts." Nevertheless, his selection as the club's initial president was considered a surprise pick by some. In actuality, though, his selection was another backroom bid for "respectability" and to entice members from Boston's conservative community to join, considering Everett's sterling reputation for integrity and reasonableness. The wily Everett knew the occasional importance of style over substance. "The truth is that the conservatives here and elsewhere are about as far gone in one extreme as the radicals in the other," he grumbled into his journal. As a conservative, old-line Whig, Everett's election as president was meant to show that the new Union Club was not to be entirely dominated by Radical Republicans from top to bottom—a goal shared by the Philadelphia and New York Union Leagues.[37]

Chapter 5

"We Are Learning to Draw the Line Between Treason and Loyalty"

Union League Ostracism and Democratic Resentment

Republicans were delighted when they realized that the initial Democratic reaction to the Union Leagues was generally one of raised eyebrows, some outright contempt, along with surprise and apprehension. "The Copperheads . . . see the defeat of their treasonable plans," boasted Pennsylvania's *Raftsman's Journal,* while in neighboring Ohio, the *Western Reserve Chronicle* observed how some "wiseacre politicians of the Copperhead persuasion" were thrown "into a spasm of mental trepidation" by the Union Leagues' recent birth. In Philadelphia, the elite class's social protocols were governed by a decades-long set of arbitrary and irreversible rules often determined by those with Southern leanings. To now be excluded from a club populated by many of the city's leading citizens based on something as crass as politics was considered a daring offense. Despite the Philadelphia League's nonpartisan claims, Philadelphia's Democrats were still outraged and concerned. One Democratic-leaning paper published the names of the Union League's new members while threatening to sack their homes within a few weeks. The more prominent members carried ax handles to meetings as self-protection against physical threats. Others saw themselves hung in effigy on lampposts.[1]

Upon first learning of the Philadelphia League, the highly partisan and Democratic *New York World* dripped with sarcasm, referring to the City of Brotherly Love as "a rather droll place." Its latest "egg laying" was the creation of the new Union League, a place that would serve ample amounts of "patriotic chloride" for the "flatulent loyalists" gathered inside. The *World* and its editor, Manton Marble, asserted that the Union League of Philadelphia was essentially an invention of John Forney, the Philadelphia *Press* publisher, administration office holder, and "toady." Those Democrats who were seduced by the Leagues' allegedly nonpartisan siren song, wrote the *World*, "must not object if they are spanked and sent supperless to bed." For many, if not most, Democrats, the Union Leagues' patriotic front was just a cloak for a gang of highly partisan party operatives. Such gloves-off, hard-hitting journalism was as old as the republic, yet in the midst of a war for the nation's survival, many Republicans felt the *World* and its young editor had crossed a line.[2]

In the case of the *World*, crossing a line was a bit of an understatement. The *World* was born in 1860 as a religious-oriented and Republican-leaning daily that sold for one penny. However, its refusal to print police reports or theatrical news and related advertising led to early financial problems. Soon after merging with the *Courier and Enquirer*, the paper was purchased in April 1862 by twenty-seven-year-old Manton Marble, who used a significant amount of borrowed funds. With the note coming due in September, Marble went searching for investors. He ended up selling shares in the paper to none other than August Belmont, Samuel L. M. Barlow, and other conservative New York Democrats who agreed to the deal only if Marble would support their political point of view. Marble showed no hesitation, for while his purchase of the *World* was a pure business decision undertaken as a means of entering the publishing arena, his personal political beliefs were quite in tune with his new investors. Marble was a committed War Democrat when the war commenced, believing hostilities were necessary and justifiable solely in bringing the South back into the Union. Yet he became increasingly frustrated with what he considered the unconstitutional means being used to fight the war, both in the civil and military arenas. Lincoln's Emancipation Proclamation was the last straw; Marble believed the president's edict was the pinnacle of his unconstitutional acts. By late 1862, the paper, now renamed the *New York World*, became the spokesperson for the anti-Lincoln Copperhead perspective and the arch enemy of New York's Republican dailies.[3]

James A. Dix, the thirty-nine-year-old editor of the *Boston Journal* and one who mentored young Marble when the latter was the *Journal*'s aspiring theater critic, felt compelled to caution his young colleague "for the sake of old associations and friendships." Hoping that the *World* might adopt a more patriotic tone, Dix reminded Marble how "fair, honest, and legitimate criticism of the measures of the administration is justifiable, but the sweeping, factious, and intemperate partisan warfare which the *World* has waged is unpatriotic and disloyal." As far as George Strong was concerned, Dix's sentiments were too kind and cautious. Strong felt that any person associated with "the daily treason of that infamous paper," even as a mere theater or opera critic, should be shunned by polite society. In public, the Union Leagues would have applauded Dix's remarks quite fervently, yet privately, many members concurred with Strong by equating "legitimate criticism of the administration" with "intemperate partisan warfare." As Republicans put forth, "In time of peace we may oppose the policy of the Administration . . . but in war if we do so in a manner to weaken the Government we strike hands with the enemy." In the midst of a bloody civil war, "loyal opposition" was an oxymoron.[4]

Regardless of Dix's and the new Union League's intents, the *World* declared a "second uprising" was already underway due to growing disenchantment with the war. Any political organization in favor of the war and a purportedly secret one at that was certain to garner Democratic contempt. Ohio's *Portsmouth Times* editorialized how the Union League was simply the Know-Nothings resurrected, "with all its abhorrent surroundings, its oaths, and its midnight conclaves." The Democratic *Daily Ohio Statesman* opined that the organization's use of the word "Union" in its name was no different than if "an association of infidels should call itself Christian." Upon learning that a Union League chapter was set to form in its southwestern Pennsylvania town, the *Bedford Gazette* warned its readers to stay away and to "stand aloof from the rotten carcass of abolitionism." The Leagues were nothing more than the "same old skunk in a new hole." In short order, Boston's new Union Club was being sarcastically referred to by Southern-sympathizing men as the "Sambo Club" due to its proabolition sentiments, while the city's Irish Catholic newspaper, the *Pilot*, denounced the Leagues, referring to them as "associations of the basest politics" that were led by "unscrupulous cunning men." To practically all Democrats, the new Union Leagues' patriotic front was merely a Trojan horse for their abolitionist desires.[5]

Even conservative to moderate Republicans were becoming frustrated with the growing power of the "ultra" Republicans, many of whom had found a kindred spirit within the burgeoning Union Leagues' allegations of treason against Democratic criticism. They were "more violent, denunciatory, and intolerant than ever," complained Illinois's Orville Browning, a personal friend of Lincoln's who had recently been defeated in his U.S. Senate reelection bid. "They snap like rabid dogs at everything that stands in their way or crosses their path." Like the Democrats, Browning was angry how the "ultras" considered themselves the "exclusive patriots" and if any of their plans failed, it was not because they were poorly conceived but because they had been stymied by Rebel sympathizers.[6]

From a bare-knuckles political viewpoint, Democratic aversion toward the burgeoning Union Leagues was understandable. Their partisan antipathy, however, was quite different from those Northerners who seemed to truly admire Southern slavocracy culture. In Boston and New York, some leading Democrats had long viewed Southern slaveholders with respect, considering them splendidly aristocratic and possessing a degree of idleness any gentleman should envy. Typical of that perspective was Richard Lathers, the New York head of the Great Western Marine Insurance Company. Lathers spoke freely of his admiration for the Southern planter by referring to them as "gentlemen of culture" and possessing a gold-plated standard of public and private integrity that Northern society often lacked. In Boston, John Murray Forbes complained to a friend how the wealthy Bostonians who focused their days on wine, tobacco, cards, and billiards tended to identify with the secessionists. "They are apt to think of themselves as aristocratic and gentleman-like, and they look up to the idle slave owners with respect as being more permanently idle than themselves." A lengthy letter in the Republican and proabolition *New York Daily Tribune* observed this Northern cultural phenomenon in Baltimore following that town's April 1861 riot. Though Maryland was a slave state, the missive pointed out there were very few slaves actually living or working in that important port city. Since Baltimore's residents seemed to have little economic interest in slavery, the author concluded the town's Southern ardor was primarily racist and caste-driven, i.e., that it was somehow noble to be proslavery. No matter how low on the economic or social ladder a white man may have been, it was gratifying and psychologically important to know there was at least one race or ethnicity below him. It is, therefore, no surprise that the men who founded the eastern Union Leagues, some of whom were ardent abolitionists, viewed such Southern admiration with contempt.[7]

The men who established the elite eastern Union Leagues were not surprised in the least by the vitriol levied against them. Philadelphian George Boker later recalled how such men viewed the new Union Leagues with "hatred and alarm." In New York, attorney and Sanitary Commission member George Templeton Strong reveled in the Democrats' discomfiture, recording in his diary how "It is delightful to perceive that 'respectable' Copperheads [also described by Strong as 'dirt-eaters'] begin to be aware of this club, and to squirm as if it irritated them somehow."[8]

These aristocratic, eastern Union Leagues were a new concept for the Civil War years represented the first time social clubs were established on a purely political basis, and not solely on caste, wealth, or other qualities deemed essential for a gentleman of the era. Unlike the Midwestern Leagues or Union Clubs created in mid- to late 1862, which were open to any loyal man regardless of wealth or standing, the elite Union Leagues' prospective members would have to meet upper-class characterizations of what consti- tuted a gentleman of the finest sort. This meant, of course, that the political values and loyalty of prospective members would have to pass the strictest subjective tests of the League's founders. These Eastern patrician leagues publicly stressed party affiliation was irrelevant, as long as the prospective member possessed an unwavering loyalty to the administration and *all* of its war efforts. In New York, the well-known Copperhead banker William Duncan publicly frowned on the League's creation. Yet he was urged by his Democratic friends to join the club in order to get an inside scoop. Sensing his application would be declined and not wishing to suffer such public embarrassment, Duncan announced to his friends, somewhat sanctimo- niously, how he felt duty-bound to decline. Meanwhile, George Strong, who chaired the New York League's new Committee on Admissions, noted in his diary with sardonic humor how Duncan was consistently mentioned within the League's clubhouse "as a convenient familiar specimen of the class we would not admit on any terms."[9]

Who to accept into the club and who to exclude did present concern for some members. The agreed-upon solution was to let the purported disloyal element self-select themselves away from the club. Judge John I. C. Hare proposed that the developing Union League of Philadelphia should have a very clear set of publicly stated, pro-Union principles and values. If a man declined to join because of those beliefs, the League and the public would see his "true colors." Such a policy of "inviting self-exclusion insured the sturdiest unanimity of the Unionists."[10]

Merely refusing membership to men whom the Union Leagues deemed insufficiently patriotic was hardly the extent of conveying their values and seriousness of purpose. When the upper-class Union Leagues in Philadel- phia and New York were formed in late 1862 and into early 1863, its bour- geoisie members were also determined to send a stern public message to

WINNING AND WEARING.

DOUBTFUL CITIZEN—*Sir, do you sell Copperhead Badges?* I want one.

PATRIOTIC STOREKEEPER—*This is the only badge you Copperheads deserve.* (Doubtful citizen wears it for some days.)

"Winning and Wearing"—Doubtful Citizen: "Sir, do you sell Copperhead badges? I want one." Patriotic Storekeeper: "This is the only badge you Copperheads deserve." (Doubtful citizen wears it for some days.) (*Frank Leslie's Illustrated*, May 23, 1863)

those whom they, and they alone, deemed disloyal if not outright traitorous. Their method of conveying such sentiments was through the well-worn tactic of social ostracism, known colloquially in modern society as "the cold shoulder" or "the silent treatment." This became one of the weapons utilized by the Leagues in this new home front civil war. George Boker wrote in the Philadelphia League's first annual report how outspoken treason became so odious that "loyal men forsook many of their old associations rather than encounter its impudent presence." In fact, Boker was considering such action as early as August 1861. In a cordial meeting at the time with Boker and future Union League cofounder Charles Gibbons, Philadelphian Sidney Fisher wrote in his diary how the two men were discussing means by which "social opinion" might be brought to bear on those who were speaking out against the government and the war. In a discussion with the two men, Fisher rejected their idea, believing then it looked too much like mob rule, though he had since changed his mind.[11]

Yet only a little more than a month after the Philadelphia Union League was formed, Mark A. DeWolfe Howe, the rector at Philadelphia's St. Luke's

Episcopal Church, was eagerly sanctioning such actions. In a letter to Boker, he stated his conviction that "not only should armed rebellion be crushed by the hand of power, but sympathy with it should in social and commercial life meet the frown of the patriotic and the true. Disloyalty must be made unprofitable." A few years after the war ended, Boker recalled how "such a policy of exclusion was vehemently denounced, both in private and in public, by the most able of the sympathizers with the South." Judge John Hare concurred with their ostracism policy, suggesting League members "withdraw from all social relations with disloyal men, and set up a society of our own," while New York newsman Sinclair Tousey urged "Loyal men should shun all such as moral lepers," just as if by associating with them would lead good Union men toward pestilence and death.[12]

This level of Northern ostracism was not limited to the Union Leagues or to the public's social and commercial interactions. For example, teachers and administrators who failed to show proper loyalty were publicly harassed in the newspapers or even dismissed from their positions. In time, every candidate seeking public office, those already in office, even average citizens who failed to garner Union League approval were automatically deemed disloyal. Many were "invited" to move south, or at a minimum, were branded with the "scarlet letter" of Copperheadism.[13]

Churches were another loyalty battleground. A Pennsylvania Democrat recalled that his Unionist friends from before the war considered him a traitor after the rebellion began and thought he should be hanged. His alleged crimes, he claimed, were only in defending slavery and condemning the war. In the name of the greater patriotic good, such unconditional loyalty expectations also stretched from the pew into the pulpit. While the federal government kept a keen eye on potential disloyal sentiment coming from ministers and reverends, it was the preachers themselves who were often most likely to ostracize their fellow Northern evangelists. In the South, of course, Union generals whose troops occupied Southern towns easily arrested those pro-Confederate ministers who preached disunion with hardly a glance from their civilian superiors in Washington. Though these "disloyal" ministers were a distinct minority in the North, it was nevertheless simply impossible for many staunchly pro-Union ministers to conceive how any of their brethren could still stand in the pulpit and call the reasons for, or the justice of, the war into question. For these pastors, an essential role in their ministry was to sustain their flock's morale in the face of repeated military reversals. Even the mere suspicion of disloyalty could have dire consequences, such as an Illinois minister who recalled after the war how his Democratic leanings and refusal to join the Union League left him ostracized and financially destitute. As mentioned earlier, many Protestant ministers placed patriotic loyalty toward the government on the same plane as Christian duty. At its base level, some ministers equated such dubious fidelity as a fundamental lack of Christian spirit worthy of the gallows. "I expect to meet some of these [ministers] in heaven," wrote one pro-Union preacher, "but before that, I expect to see them hanged upon earth; and I shall rejoice in that hanging."[14]

Those Northern men of social standing, economic means, and spiritual influence who were sympathetic to the South could certainly exercise their free speech First Amendment rights; however, Union League members strove to make sure there would indeed be a social price to pay. If the Union Leagues deemed one's words or actions disloyal, League members would sever commercial relations and terminate any friendship bonds, not only by ostracizing the offender but also via economic embargo. As Indiana Rep. George Julian put forth, "We are learning to draw the line between treason and loyalty."[15]

Indeed, Article II of the Union League of Philadelphia's Articles of Association instructed members to use "every proper means in public and private" to "discountenance and rebuke by all moral and social influences all disloyalty to the Federal government." This was construed by members that they should cease business dealings with Democratic secession sympathizers. On October 3, 1863, a Union League council in greater Boston debated this very idea, noting they should make their social, political, and *business* influence felt within the community on behalf of loyalty to the national government. "If motives of patriotism and loyalty to the best government that ever existed among men are not strong enough to restrain factions and damaging opposition," the Council asserted, "then the influence of patronage refused by the loyal should bear its potent weight. The sensitivities of the pocket nerve will quickly dictate a more seemingly patriotic course at least by such Copperheads." In Washington, D.C., the *Evening Union* protested that League men were seen hanging up the business cards of its members, while proscribing those businesses whose owners were not League members. "Ostracism is added to Bastilles, and dissidence from the policies of 'the powers that be' is denounced as treason," railed the paper.[16]

Such marketplace ostracism also worked in reverse as employers were willing to dismiss employees deemed disloyal. A Michigan Southern Railroad employee was dismissed by the company superintendent for being "blatant in his Copperheadism." When Seth Thomas Jr. of family clock-making fame discovered his valued foreman and other workers wearing Copperhead lapel pins at his Plymouth Hollow, Connecticut, workshop, they were summarily let go. After the foreman demanded to know why he was being fired, Thomas replied, "I'll tell you, sir. I may possibly employ traitors to my government in my shop, but if I do, it will be because I do not know who they are, but when I see a man *openly* announcing his treason, *and wearing the sign,* he cannot work for me any longer." While Thomas reacted to what he deemed unacceptable treason, other business owners took a more proactive approach, such as a Pennsylvania factory owner, who demanded in an 1863 memo to his primarily German employees that they "give more credence and confidence" to his political opinions. In what was clearly a warning regarding their future employment, the owner advised that the only acceptable opinion was to fully support the Lincoln administration, adding the old adage, "he who is not for us is against us."[17]

Some Democrats fought back, of course. New York Democrat Daniel S. Dickinson decried the use of ostracism against any "who fail to fall down and worship at the sound of the secession psaltery and sackbut." Severn T. Wallis, a Maryland state legislator who languished for fourteen months in a federal prison on disloyalty suspicions yet with no formal charges ever levied against him, railed against Republicans' attempts to set themselves up as the loyalty judge and jury. "You have accordingly borrowed from the vocabulary of despotism, the name of 'disloyalty,' to designate that undefined and undefinable offence—not known to free institutions," wrote Wallis to Ohio's Sen. John Sherman. Yet "With like propriety and consistency you have adopted the catch-word of 'loyalty,' to indicate the equally undefinable public virtues and excellences which you would have it believed that yourselves and your partisans embody and monopolize."[18]

After reporting how a Union League council in Cincinnati recommended local businesses, churches, and boardinghouses shun any man who bought or read an opposition newspaper, the Democratic *Detroit Free Press* asked rhetorically what type of society would exist if Democrats responded in kind. The paper could only surmise that the Union Leagues "must have some terrible design to fulfill, or they would not propose such revolutionary and barbarous measures." The Detroit paper's fear soon spread into Sollarsville, Pennsylvania, where a staunch Democrat named Joseph Wise wrote to his cousin, informing her party strife "was extending into the Churches and the social circle—Democrats and Abolitionists pass each other by almost as the ancient Israelites did the Leper." As for ostracism, the man explained how "The Democrats [are] refusing to pay the Preacher because he is an Abolitionist—Bully for them say I!!"[19]

In spite of Democratic pushback, Boker and his Union League colleagues soon viewed their tactics as a success, for the Copperheads "were shut up within their own small coteries; they were forbidden to vent their treasonous utterances within the hearing of patriotic men. In vain they complained of social ostracism and threatened us with reprisal." This Union League–generated war of silence and ostracization, or the fear of such, was soon noticed at all levels of society and eventually spread across the country. Bostonian Edward Whipple observed how the impact of his city's new Union Club "was to make patriotism fashionable . . . by informing the rich and fashionable people that they would lose caste if they became Copperheads." In Connecticut, many citizens refused to acknowledge former governor and Secretary of the Navy Isaac Toucey when they passed him on the street since his antiwar position was well known. Farther south in New York, William Cullen Bryant, the sixty-eight-year-old abolitionist editor for the *New York Evening Post,* sensed public opinion toward the war was correcting itself and that the people were becoming more agreeable toward emancipation. "I look for the time," wrote Bryant, "and it is not far off I believe, when to be called an anti-abolitionist will be resented as an opprobrium." Meanwhile, the wife of a Democratic New York judge complained to her diary, "It is extraordinary to hear the violence that the Republicans indulge in against the Democrats. They hate them worse than the secessionists. . . ."[20]

Politicians also started to notice how this upstart movement was impacting Washington's political winds. Massachusetts's Sen. Charles Sumner mentioned to John Jay—Union League member and the abolitionist grandson of the country's first chief justice—how "The Democrats are becoming patriotic, & all are now hopeful," while Sen. John Sherman likewise detected a subtle shift away from rampant public displays of Southern sympathy. In a letter to his brother, Gen. William T. Sherman, the senator noted, "The tone of popular opinion is more patriotic. There are fewer noisy Butternuts, and most of these think their bad talk is only fair opposition to the administration." Thus, we see how the popular present-day phrase, "dissent is the highest form of patriotism," carried very little weight with the Union Leagues and the Lincoln administration, as is often the case with any party in power.[21]

Boker, Hare, and their Union League colleagues knew then what modern scientific psychological studies have since confirmed: the act of social ostracism can have devastating impacts on the psyche of the unfortunate recipient. As the psychologist and philosopher William James noted in 1890, "We have an innate propensity to get ourselves noticed, and noticed favorably, by our kind. No more fiendish punishment could be devised, were such a thing physically possible, than that one should be turned loose in society and remain absolutely unnoticed by all the members thereof." Modern psychological studies have shown ostracism deprives people of a sense of belonging to others, which is a universal human impulse and in its absence, can lead to physical and mental illnesses. Moreover, these studies have shown subjects will alter their perceptions and behavior in order that others not regard them with suspicion or belittle them; in essence, that they will not be excluded or rejected by other members of society. As one historian observed, "The fact that . . . status could be accorded or with-drawn at will by influential social circles without having to be justified in terms of any formal, explicit criterion made [club membership] a curiously subtle and effective mechanism of social control." The Union League's ac-tions against those whom they considered disloyal or traitorous signaled the opening salvo in a civil war among the North's civilian population, with their weapons of choice being ostracism and media propaganda. The bat-tlefield quickly became the North's court of public opinion.[22]

George Strong put such practices into play only days after the New York League's formation. In his February 9 diary entry, Strong sardonically noted how he visited the Century Club two nights earlier "for the sole purpose of showing a cold shoulder to two or three of its habitués who seceshionize [*sic*], or, what amounts to the same thing." As pleased with himself as he was with his results, Strong recorded his success "in manifesting to them my desire that we may be better strangers." The scorn directed at William B. Reed also fit into the new Union League tactic. Reed was a distinguished Philadelphia lawyer who was so vehemently outspoken against the war that a portion of one of his speeches was later used by the Republicans in an anti-Democrat campaign document. Upon seeing a close friend on the street who was a member of the newly created Philadelphia Union League, Reed approached his colleague in the usual manner with an outstretched hand and verbal pleasantries. Reed's soon-to-be-ex-friend refused to shake his hand and solemnly declared, "I do not know you, sir" and then walked away. They never spoke again. Reed's relationship with his many influential friends who were now League members quickly faded, prompting the man to move to New York. He was received by the loyal men no differently in that town. The modern act of "unfriending" those on social media with differing political views may be recognized by twenty-first-century readers as serving a similar function.[23]

Though most acts like this occurred in a face-to-face manner, some played out across the miles. After enjoying a close friendship spanning more than twenty-five years, ardent Republican James F. Chamberlain informed his Democratic friend Ansel McCall in June 1862 of his decision to decline McCall's invitation to visit his upstate New York home. "Our views of public affairs are not sufficiently coincident," explained Chamberlain, and their inevitable arguments would damage the friendship. One year later, Chamberlain wrote to McCall informing him he was breaking off all communication so that their relationship might remain intact. Other than a brief letter in 1886, Chamberlain never again reached out to his one-time friend.[24]

Nor was such an exclusionary tactic limited to civilians. Those volunteer soldiers who deserted from the Union Army faced public shame and social ostracism if and when they returned to their hometowns, for the Civil War was one where communities generally received consistent information on the whereabouts and actions of their enlisted men. Whether from reports telegraphed from soldier correspondents or firsthand accounts from men visiting home on leave, the typical private knew his conduct was probably going to be known by the folks back home. This was especially the case if those men had come from communities that were resolutely prowar in their outlook. In many cases, those deserters who relocated and reinvented themselves elsewhere often settled in areas where support for the war had been weak. Modern "identity theory," which places extreme importance on one's self-image and the opinions and expectation of others within the hometown, helps to rationalize such behavior.[25]

Chapter 6

"This Is the Time for Pamphleteers and Essayists"

The Pen Begins to Fight Alongside the Sword against Copperhead Dissent and Violence

Despite their impressive 1862 election victories, leading New York Democrats became convinced they needed some manner of organization to counter what they saw as the growing Republican propaganda movement. Adding to their concern was a disturbing trend in how Republican elites were reevaluating the war following Lincoln's Emancipation Proclamation. These Democrats had always been committed to the war and remained so, but *solely* as a means to restore the Union and not to effect radical social change. After Democratic Party chairman August Belmont sent a letter to New York railroad lawyer Samuel Tilden on January 27, 1863, suggesting it was "high time for conservatives to go to work and make a powerful demonstration in our city," twenty-two prominent New York Democrats met at Delmonico's restaurant on February 6 to discuss that concern. (Social ostracism also extended into upscale New York eateries, with the Democrats gathering at Delmonico's while Republicans preferred Maison Dorée.) The Democrats' solution was to create the Society for the Diffusion of Political Knowledge (SDPK.), whose motto was "Read—Discuss—Diffuse." The SDPK's overall goal was to capitalize on the sagging morale within Northern public opinion. Its tactic was to utilize printed pamphlets to make the public aware of constitutional principles and rights at both the federal and state levels. Then by extension, how the Lincoln administration and its congressional allies had usurped those rights. As one Democrat had earlier stressed, "This is the time for pamphleteers and essayists, and if we expect to save constitutional liberty, no time should be lost in furnishing food for reflection." Belmont was absent, though other prominent Democrats were present that chilly February night. The attendees included Tilden, New York attorney and financier Samuel L. M. Barlow, *New York World* editor Manton Marble, and the newly elected governor of New York, Horatio Seymour, among others; they were all leading Democrats who were used to wielding influence and power, and were disturbed by their new status as the administration's allegedly disloyal opposition.[1]

The Society's new president was seventy-one-year-old Samuel F. B. Morse, a well-known painter and a man who fervently believed with all his heart—like many other Americans of the era—that human bondage was ordained by God, approved of in the Bible, and a blessing for the African slave. Morse's real claim to fame, however, was having invented the electromagnetic telegraph and Morse Code, then in use throughout the land by both governments and armies. He was gratified that the SDPK would be properly funded, assuring his cousin that the Society "was backed up by millionaires, so far as funds go, who have assured us that funds shall not be wanting." As for tone, Morse

Samuel F. B. Morse c. Civil War years (Library of Congress Prints and Photographs Division)

wanted to ensure the Society's papers strove to avoid "any display of that violent rancorous spirit which characterizes our opponents." Their pamphlets were intended to appeal to the reader's intellect rather than raw emotion. With both the nascent SDPK and the Union Leagues convinced of their own righteousness, they would soon battle each other in a home front war to be waged for the hearts and minds of the Northern public. This political warfare for the national soul was to be fought not with the sword, but with the pen.[2]

The Delmonico's meeting originated as a gathering of Democrats with vague ideas as to what they wanted to accomplish; however, it was immediately vilified in New York's Republican-leaning press. Though the Democrats had agreed to strict silence regarding the gathering, the *New York Evening Post* still learned of the event and managed to sneak a reporter into the meeting. At evening's end, subscriptions for the new initiative were solicited among the attendees, with several men coming forward to pledge $500 each. In early 1863, that was an immense sum of money equivalent to almost *two years'* wages for a man performing hard and unskilled manual labor. With satisfied smugness, the *Post* rhetorically asked the next day if those same men "had contributed with equal liberality to the encouragement of volunteering, and the other patriotic objects which claim popular sympathy." Such desire for secrecy coupled with a formal plan to publish anti-Lincoln propaganda only stirred the Republican pot even more. Yet a few Republicans quietly viewed the whole affair as a blessing in disguise, including Boston's John Murray Forbes, who admitted, "I am very glad to find that the doings of [the] Delmonico Copperhead conclave have stirred New York up to the importance of spreading light in dark places."[3]

Samuel Tilden and his colleagues were outraged by the *Post*'s story and wasted no time in saying so the next day in a letter published in Marble's *New York World*. Believing an article like the *Post*'s would usually be worthy of only silent contempt, Tilden rejected the paper's claim that the meeting had an air of "revolutionary intrigue" about it, or that its purpose was to countenance a change in Lincolnian policy by radical means. The *World* weighed in on the matter as well, asking rhetorically, "What law or principle of right, is violated by the meeting of gentlemen who choose to hold certain perfectly legitimate political opinions and to take steps for the dissemination of those opinions?" It condemned the *Post* for referring to these men as "a secret conclave of treasonable conspirators bent on upsetting the government and demoralizing the army." David M. Turnure, a prosperous sugar broker and New York Democrat, was not only aghast at the *Post*'s political insinuations, but at the breech of social etiquette as well. In a lengthy missive comparing the SPDK and the Union Leagues, Turnure asked how the *Post*'s editor could so grossly assail men who were one-time close friends. Then, "in violation of all the rules governing society and gentlemanly intercourse," the reporter "smuggles himself into that room as a spy and informer, and the odious affiliation of traitor and conspirator is applied to all present save one." The answer to Turnure's rhetorical question was that as far as the Republican press and the new Union Leagues were concerned, the gloves had come off.[4]

Though they made gains in the 1862 fall elections, Democrats were still the minority party, both in congressional seats and in the growing volume within the partisan newspaper wars. As was often the case over the next two years, Democrats who trumpeted their loyalty often found themselves on the defensive, in part because of repeated acts of Copperhead-generated violence against loyal men and the Union war effort. For the *New York World* and its novice editor, Manton Marble, the response was to label Republican attacks as purely political and that the Democrats' real transgression was winning several states in the fall 1862 elections by opposing emancipation and indiscriminate arrests. In any case, the Democrats repeatedly pointed out, slavery was constitutionally legal. Changing the Constitution was undertaken at the ballot box, not at the cannon's mouth. Perhaps seeking to downplay the whole Delmonico's affair, Tilden admitted to a colleague within weeks that the Society's plans were not fully developed. Moreover, Tilden felt it "had not become a movement of much importance or definiteness of aim when it was brought into sudden notoriety by the attacks of the extreme Republican press."[5]

Morse knew the Society faced a daunting challenge, believing they had to "dispel this popular delusion" that slavery was the war's root cause. From Morse's vantage, the real villain was abolitionism or antislavery. Since Morse felt the abolition disease was "long-standing and deep-seated," the cure could not be expected to be anything other than slow.[6]

The SDPK's announcement regarding its formation and purpose caught many pro-Union New York men off guard, awakening them to the realization that some type of media counteroffensive was needed. They knew it was imperative that "loyal men" win the propaganda war for the hearts and minds of the Northern public. Many citizens were still open to the reason and arguments of what was meant by true loyalty and civic duty.

Driven to action, Columbia College president Charles Butler called a meeting of like-minded men to his 14th Street home on February 14, 1863, only eight days after the SDPK first met. The sixty-one-year-old Butler was a highly respected attorney and philanthropist, and also happened to be the brother of Union Gen. Benjamin Butler. At his overflowing house that evening, New York's Loyal Publication Society was born; its mission to distribute "journals and documents of unquestionable and unconditional loyalty throughout the United States," and especially aimed toward the Union armies fighting so hard to suppress the rebellion. If the soldiers were properly instructed, they would surely vote the Republican ticket.[7]

Butler was elected permanent president that evening with thirty-six-year-old John Austin Stevens Jr. as permanent secretary. The son of a prominent New York banker and a Harvard graduate, Stevens's selection was a sound choice for his current occupation was as secretary of the New York Chamber of Commerce. Both men also happened to be members of the then-embryonic Union League Club of New York.[8]

George Strong attended the February 14 gathering, too, and observed how the new organization would stand "in opposition to the surreptitious workings of the gang of Belmonts and Barlows and Tildens," a clear allusion to the SDPK. Strong, however, was no admirer of John Austin Stevens, which gave the former some doubts about the new Society, believing "there were too many old talking hacks of doubtful antecedents" attending and that it could develop into competition for the developing Union League. Sensing just such a conflict, the new group declined to undertake any initiatives other than printing and distributing "loyal" propaganda documents. Moreover, keeping an official arm's-length distance from the New York Union League would help to preserve a nonpartisan appearance.[9]

As was the case with the Union League Club of New York, the Loyal Publication Society's new members represented a deep and mostly wealthy cross-section of New York's business leaders and intelligentsia. Included in that group was Oliver W. Gibbs, who was an initial member of the publication committee and a Union League Club of New York cofounder. The new Society functioned through three distinct committees totaling twenty-eight men and an initial budget of just under $10,000. The front-line, seven-man publication committee targeted newspapers and pamphlets to be distributed, as well as selecting new articles or manuscripts for publication that would best serve the Society's mission. A twelve-man finance committee gathered and monitored the Society's operating funds, with one committee member to serve as the Society's treasurer. Lastly, a nine-man executive committee oversaw distribution for all of the material prepared by the publication committee. Within weeks, its presses were rolling in the new media battle. Pamphlets consisting of new works by the era's leading thinkers were the chosen medium, with topics that ranged from rebutting various Democratic objections against Lincolnian war policy to explaining the rationales for the war itself. The primary audience was the various army corps, though the Society also prepared pamphlets targeting specific issues and constituencies. A case in point was its first pamphlet, *The Future of the Northwest in Connection with the Scheme of Reconstruction without New England: An Address to the People of Indiana* by War Democrat Robert Dale Owen, dated March 4, 1863. The first of forty-three pamphlets the Loyal Publication Society prepared and distributed in its first fiscal year, Owen's work targeted the Hoosier State's residents with an argument against the Democrats' peace-at-any-price faction. Its thesis was that if the South and Northwest were able to merge, it would give that section a controlling majority in Congress, much to the Union's detriment.[10]

By late winter 1863, another publication group was underway in New England, though its size and focus was almost the opposite of the New York publication society. As far back as April 1860, Boston's John Murray Forbes felt there should be a Republican-oriented publishing committee working at "spreading light in dark places." In July 1862, Forbes revisited the matter and concluded that excellent newspaper articles or editorials trumpeting loyalty needed to be reprinted and distributed throughout the North. He personally read enough of these to realize the tremendous propaganda value they might transmit to the common man or woman. By reprinting them in single sheet, "broadside" format, they could be shipped to important newspapers throughout the North for easy copying into their daily or weekly editions. In Forbes's opinion, the broadside's relative low cost made it a more viable weapon than pamphlets because he believed newspapers would reach the largest number of readers.[11]

On March 9, 1863, Forbes sent out an invitation to select Boston gentlemen inviting them to partake in a new society "for the publication and distribution of sound doctrine and information upon public affairs." The new organization was christened the New England Loyal Publication Society and by late March, its small executive committee was set and in motion. The sole editor was Charles E. Norton, who fully "consented to take over the laboring oar" from Forbes, after the latter was asked by the Lincoln administration to visit England in a diplomatic attempt to stop the British from outfitting Confederate cruisers. By spring, and as discussed previously, Norton was also heavily engaged in Boston's new Union Club. As was the case in New York, there was no official tie between Boston's Union Club and the New England Loyal Publication Society, even though members of the League or Club were often Publication Society members. Both publication societies often worked together to advance their mutual mission of promoting loyalty to the Union. In many instances, Union League reading rooms stocked the latest broadsides from the Society while older copies were bundled up by the League for shipment to more isolated towns and villages. Norton later recalled how the Society "printed at irregular intervals . . . a Broadside containing selected or original newspaper articles. . . . These Broadsides [were] printed in good type, on good paper, and on only one side of the sheet, so as to be convenient to copy from. Our circulation was between one and two thousand copies," and were distributed primarily as newspaper inserts and not through a direct mailing to individual citizens. Considering the relative small cost of printing a single sheet compared to printing and creating a pamphlet, the Society generally printed as many copies as possible. Extra sheets were then used for distribution throughout the military, for use in hospitals, and even as campaign literature.[12]

So while New York's Loyal Publication Society focused on new essays published within pamphlets, the New England Loyal Publication Society generally utilized reprints of previously published newspaper articles or editorials. Individuals and various organizations received the broadsides; however, the prime targets were the editors of small-town newspapers. Norton's rationale was that many of these editors were often strapped for time and money; they also often struggled with ideas as to what to put on the front page. Because the New England Society did not ask for recognition, editors were often all too happy to use the broadsides Morton sent free of charge. The net effect of Norton's strategy was that the New England Loyal Publication Society became the unseen coeditor for hundreds of newspapers throughout the North while those small-town, partisan editors became the era's version of the modern press secretary, doling out the administration's public position on any given issue. This was an important point during political campaigns for the men who ran the Publication Societies, and the Union Leagues realized every local or state election constituted a small step toward nationalizing the war effort. Frederick Olmsted fully realized this last point. While he agreed that the diverse publication societies were better than nothing, he would have preferred to see a single, centralized publication society that would eliminate much of the inevitable duplication of efforts.[13]

Like the Radicals, Norton viewed the Civil War as a to-the-death struggle between two wholly incompatible civilizations. In his first original editorial for the Society, Norton described the conflict as "two adverse conditions of society;" on the one side the "champions of government and law" with his enemy described as "the supporters of privilege." Forbes concurred, urging Norton that their initial focus should be in the Western and border slave states, especially by explaining to the average border state man how he had more in common with Easterners than with the slave aristocracy. As for Northerners, a consistent propaganda theme was needed in order to maintain good morale. If the Union armies suffered military reversals, it was the people's obligation to find strength in adversity.[14]

While the New York and New England publication societies were being organized, the Union League of Philadelphia's Publication Committee was also formed "in order to disseminate correct information tending to promote unfaltering loyalty among the people." This three-man committee had its birth at the League's February 17, 1863, Board of Directors meeting. At that session, distinguished attorney Benjamin Gerhard motioned that a three-man committee be formed with the power to print and distribute loyal reading material to the public. If more men were needed, they would be added from the League's membership rolls. Any and all required funds were to be raised entirely by voluntary subscriptions among the members at $250 each. Through their Monday evening meetings, a sum of $35,000 was soon raised to support the mission. Their sense of urgency was clear: "The machinations of Traitors must be met—their schemes must be exposed and counteracted, the people furnished with facts."[15]

So great was the initial success that the committee's initial investment was quickly depleted. Furthermore, the workload became so extensive that three men were insufficient. Consequently, the Board of Publication was created on March 2 with Gerhard as president. Unlike the New York and New England publication societies and their respective town's new Union Clubs, the Board of Publication was a direct affiliate of the Union League of Philadelphia. It quickly became the largest and wealthiest of the three primary publication societies. The new Board consisted of twenty-seven men working through three subcommittees—finance, publication, and distribution—each consisting of nine men. The Board obtained a small apartment solely to house, fold, and mail the various materials. Meanwhile, committeemen sought out literary talent both internally and from the community. When Judge Hare asked diarist Sidney Fisher to write some articles "of a popular character" for the Union League, Fisher seemed especially captivated by the new venture's deep pockets. "It has a publication fund of $100,000 and is constantly printing thousands of copies of pamphlets to spread thro' the country," he noted, while the "reactions of sentiment against the insidious and treasonable schemes of the 'Copperheads' . . . are strong and universal." Fisher's positive impression was warranted, for through the first two years of its existence, a dozen clerks were employed continuously to process the Board's pamphlets. On March 12, it was agreed that each pamphlet would have an initial print run of ten thousand copies unless some other specific number was required. In the ten-month period from the Board's formation until the end of 1863, over one million pamphlets were distributed. Most were printed in English; however, some were also printed in German to attract those foreign-born men whose antidespotism ideology was in line with many Republicans.[16]

Though these three similar publication societies maintained no formal ties or bonds with each other, they nonetheless maintained a friendly working relationship and collegial relations, which was not surprising, since they all shared a common enemy. All three groups instituted a system by which each society would share its publications with the other two. Occasionally one publication society would even reprint a pamphlet or broadside that originated with another. At the same time, the societies subscribed for extra copies of "loyal" newspapers, which would be sent to voters or sympathetic editors still sitting on the political fence. An important additional reason for cross-cooperation was that the political content of the pamphlets and broadsides issued by the societies, as well as the SDPK, generally seemed to represent the consensus of the parties; little factional party warfare crept in. Taken as a whole, the publication and distribution efforts of these three societies resulted in a flood of political literature reaching the average man and woman unlike anything before in the nation's short history.[17]

Not only did the quantity of pro-Union literature surpass anything previously seen, its physical appearance was also novel. With an eye toward visual marketing, Philadelphia's Board of Publication utilized vibrant pink, green, or blue paper for their pamphlet covers. Big, bold block lettering was used on both pamphlets and posters to attract the reader. All of this material served one overarching Union League goal: To encourage the Northern reader toward a higher sense of nationalism rather than regionalism; that loyalty was owed to the national government in a time of war.[18]

The use of the privately printed pamphlet as a means of conveying thoughts and ideas had a long and ubiquitous history in the United States dating back to the seventeenth and eighteenth centuries. For example, the American Tract Society traced its roots to 1814 as a Boston publisher of religious pamphlets. Political partisans also gravitated toward their use, including lawyers and judges, who utilized them to speak out on the various constitutional or other legal issues of their era. In an age where speeches and newspapers were the dominant tools of choice for political parties, the pamphlet served as the vehicle for delivering the best speeches or editorials to the public at large, since they were often too long to be reproduced in a newspaper. They were seen by authors and readers alike as a call to arms that reminded the reader why he was a Whig, Republican, or Democrat in the first place. These pamphlets were inexpensive and often given away free to local individuals or organizations. With a small page count of anywhere from just a few pages to no more than several dozen, they were considered easily portable and easily shared. In numerous ways, these early pamphlets were the precursors to manifestos that appeared as advertisements in twentieth-century newspapers.[19]

The Union Leagues and their allied publication societies sought to build on this tradition. As in previous generations, the pamphlets' messages utilized a military theme to warn of imminent disaster to the nation's most important interests if the authors' positions were not enacted in their entirety—glorious battles against enemies leading to ultimate victory. The Union Leagues' idea for publishing and distributing vast quantities of pamphlets to the American citizenry was based in large measure on the high literacy rate for antebellum Americans. This was especially true in the military, where over 90 percent of white Union soldiers were deemed literate. It was routine for Americans to share newspapers and to read aloud to friends, family, or comrades with interpretive discussions to follow. To satisfy reader demand, some four thousand newspapers and journals were in existence in the United States in 1860 and they were read voraciously by both civilian and soldier. While most publications were small and created for local consumption, a large percentage of those overall numbers were published in the major Eastern cities. Printing vast quantities of a political pamphlets with distribution targeted across the land to both the home front and the men on the battlefield became the era's version of mass communication. Since the three publication societies from New York, Boston, and Philadelphia were all created within one month of another, the Civil War's last two years can be argued to be the golden age of political pamphleteering.[20]

The Publication Societies immediately set about broadcasting their message and works across the country. Indiana's Gov. Oliver Morton advised the local Union Club that a portion of the funds they raised should be used to rent a room for storing the various Union League pamphlets that were now flooding the country. If this was accomplished, Morton advised the Club that the large quantity of pamphlets sent to Indiana could be consolidated there as well as any future publications from the Publication Societies.[21]

The forty-year-old Morton was a combative Indiana native who was born for politics. He was an astute Republican and stalwart Lincoln ally. Prickly in temperament, Morton was callous and lacked any sense of humor. He considered politics akin to warfare, with his opponents deemed merely enemies to be crushed. Yet during the war, he showed himself to be a true "soldier's friend" and Union League ally. As part of his care and concern for the needs of his Indiana regiments, Morton made sure appropriate Union League reading material reached the army in abundance.[22]

Unlike their Democratic opponents, Morton and other Republican men knew the Union Leagues retained an unspoken partner in disseminating their pamphlets and literature, and that friend was the U.S. Postal Service. Missourian Montgomery Blair was the man serving in Lincoln's Cabinet as U.S. postmaster general. Forty-nine years old when 1863 dawned, Blair was an antislavery political conservative. Nonetheless Lincoln viewed him as a reliable ally, and in his duties, Blair's efforts satisfied the president. During his tenure, he instituted several policies that greatly enhanced mail distribution, including free delivery in cities and sorting and distributing mail while in transit on postal railroad cars. For the military, he instituted the program where each regiment had its own postmaster, while allowing servicemen to send mail home unstamped with the postage due paid by the recipient.[23]

Though the nearby smaller Eastern Leagues were an obvious distribution point, in the middle and far west such matters posed more of a challenge. It was not uncommon for mail to occasionally disappear. Furthermore, ever since the summer of 1862 when the War Department took over post office supervision, pamphlets sent out via the mail could be confiscated and newspapers suppressed if the local civilian or military authorities deemed them to be treasonous. Despite cries of "free speech," many Democratic antiwar editorials and letters from home argued the war's illegality to the point of practically promoting desertion and discouraging enlistments—facts not lost on the Union Leagues and part of their reason for being. Two Illinois men, for instance, were charged with advising young men to maim themselves or to take harmful drugs in order to escape the draft. A young Michigan man was dismayed to read the various letters urging soldiers to desert or resign and to "do no more for the 'nigger.'" The provost marshal for Indiana's 11th District reported that his territory was dominated by Copperheads and antiwar, secret society members, all of whom "opposed the war in every way they could, and threw every obstacle in the way of the execution of the laws, discouraging enlistments and counseling resistance to the draft." Meanwhile, the "Union Leaguers," those "gallant knights of Darkness," earned bitter enmity in Democratic papers for painting their entire party as cowardly traitors. This new heated conflict within the Northern press was certainly greeted by Confederates. From the Union League perspective, the Rebels obviously gained "aid and comfort" by such vitriolic antiadministration arguments that therefore equated the dissenting speech to treason, despite Democratic protests to the contrary.[24]

To Quartermaster Gen. Montgomery Meigs, suppressing these newspapers was simply a matter of good military security, which translated into protecting the public interest. Moreover, what was good for the goose was good for the gander as Republicans alleged that Democratic dailies received a far wider circulation in the army than Republican papers when Democrat George McClellan and his like-minded lieutenants were in command of the Army of the Potomac. In the current environment, failure to suppress earned officers the enmity of the loyal press back home. After Gen. Stephen A. Hurlburt and Gen. Jeremiah C. Sullivan banned the vehemently anti-Lincoln *Chicago Times* from their districts, Gen. Ulysses Grant overturned their decision, earning Grant the vilification of *Chicago Tribune* editor Joseph Medill, a staunch Lincolnite. "Last night the editor sent down 3000 copies of his treasonable issues to do their work of poison in Grant's department, to breed more mutiny and demoralization," complained Medill to Illinois Rep. Elihu Washburne. From Medill's vantage, such action revealed Grant's true sentiment. "He stands confessed as a copperhead and openly encourages the dissemination of secession and treason in his army." Despite Grant's veto, suppressive action against "treasonous" literature had already occurred in places as diverse as Baltimore, Maryland, New York, and Plymouth, Indiana. Since small-town postmasters were appointed federal employees, most were loyal Union men who had migrated to the Midwestern states in the years prior to the war. They would do all they could to ensure that "loyal" reading material like Union League pamphlets reached their proper destinations.[25]

Moreover, citizens with staunch Republican congressmen often wrote to their representatives urging the replacement of those local postmasters who were not considered sufficiently loyal. One man in McConnell's Grove, Illinois, wrote in early July 1862 of wanting a "secession Democrat" postmaster removed immediately from office. "The position he occupies gives him opportunities to do our country injury," he complained. "He has done his utmost to defeat the election of any and all Republicans."[26]

While the Democratic press spewed a combination of sarcasm and venom toward the new Union Leagues, nothing raised their ire in the spring of 1863 more than the new and hated national "draft" law. For the first time in the country's history, the federal government passed legislation to raise a national army without any approval or input from state governments. With repeated Union military disasters such as Second Bull Run and Fredericksburg in August and December 1862 respectively, the number of new volunteers needed to fill out the Union armies was simply failing to come anywhere close to meeting the need. Even worse, the two-year term of enlistment for many of the original 1861 regiments was set to expire in May 1863, while the nine-month men from the previous summer would be heading home soon as well. To deal with the crisis, Congress passed the Enrollment Act of 1863, which was to go into effect on March 3.

The Act stated that any able-bodied, single male citizen of the United States between the ages of twenty and forty-five, or any foreign-born man in that age bracket who intended to become a citizen was subject to the new national draft. Married men between the ages of twenty and thirty-five were also within the new law's parameters, though there were some exemptions such as for widowed fathers. The most egregious provision from the Democrats' view was how the Act allowed any man to exempt himself from the draft simply by paying a $300 fee to the federal government through what was known as the "commutation clause." Or, he might gain an exemption by hiring a substitute to go in his place, the fee being negotiated between the two. In either case, the funds required were exorbitant by working-man standards. It became apparent those most likely to avoid conscription were well-to-do. As a consequence, resentment ran deep in working-class towns and neighborhoods. These were often the enclaves of Democratic support.

Following the creation of the Office of the Provost Marshal General in March 1863—a War Department office designed to oversee the new Enrollment Act and address anti-Union espionage—its Washington headquarters sent orders to each state's provost marshal instructing him to print official notices only in loyal Republican newspapers, "upon first assuring yourself that the sheets selected are not opposing the government." Printing government notices was considered a desirable form of steady revenue for Civil

War–era newspapers and awarding such contracts to loyal papers by the party in power had a lengthy history within the country. Accordingly, this form of journalistic ostracism was fully in keeping with social and business exclusionary tactics proposed earlier by the Union Leagues. The rising influence of Philadelphia's Union League was further felt in the summer when an officer from Pennsylvania's Provost Marshal's office sought the League's advice in ascertaining "sound Union newspapers" within the Keystone State.[27]

After being forced to swallow Lincoln's Emancipation Proclamation, which went into effect on January 1, the Peace Democrat–Copperhead faction went apoplectic with the new Enrollment Act and its evasion provisions. One Democratic soldier spoke for many like-minded Northerners when he wrote home stating that Congress seemed determined to "not leave an able bodied man at home in the north. Their policy seems to be to take all the white men and kill them off for the sake of freeing a few niggers. I don't feel much like fighting to free niggers at the expense of my life." The same day the Enrollment Act went into effect, another bill passed that gave Lincoln the ability to suspend habeas corpus anywhere he desired. Many Democrats and even some Republicans were outraged, claiming all of this was simply unconstitutional. Taken together, these new laws represented a one-two punch to Lincoln's political opponents that confirmed their worst fears as to where the country was heading. These new laws drove many Northerners who were in favor of a war to preserve the Union—but were reluctant to see poor white men used as cannon fodder in order to free black slaves—into the antiwar camp.[28]

Most of the boys in blue who were already fighting in the trenches cheered the new conscription act within their letters to their loved ones back home. George Whitman of the 51st New York Infantry wondered just how many of his acquaintances were "fortunate enough to draw prizes in Uncle Sam's lottery" and then smugly admitted, "I know quite a number that I should be pleased to hear, would have to shoulder a musket, and take their chances With the rest of us." Soldiers in the field generally felt little empathy toward those hale and hearty men who always seemed to offer any excuse as to why they were not in the army. In fact, some Union soldiers wrote of a stronger, *manly* respect for their gray-clad adversary than for those able-bodied men back home who "skedaddled" away if their name was called during the draft lottery or, worst of all, actively spoke out against enlistments and the war. "I think the rebels at home far meaner than the rebels of the South," concluded an Illinois bluecoat following the enrollment act's passage. "The latter has courage enough to meet me in open conflict while the former poor miserable sneaking hound, seeks to creep up in the dark and strike his dagger at my heart." Though he was shivering in a tent with snow seeping in through every crevice in Virginia, a Maine soldier explained to a female friend that he would rather endure his current state than exchange it for the comforts of home, if the latter was "purchased by the loss of all manly principal and loss of Patriotism such as these Copperheads enjoy now."[29]

Pennsylvanian Anson Shuey likewise held less disdain for Rebels than for home front dissidents, whom he described as "the meanest traitors the country is disgraced with." In a letter to his wife, Shuey explained, "I have more respect for an armed traitor than for Sneaking cowardly copperheads too mean to fight for his country and too cowardly to fight against it." Henry C. Bear of the 116th Illinois Infantry possessed similar antipathy. "You may tell evry man of Doubtful Loyalty for me, up ther in the north, that he is meaner than any son of a bitch in hell. I would rather shoot one of them a great deal than one living here," Bear assured a relative. Rejecting the idea of any moral equivalency between a Rebel private and a Northern Copperhead, Bear concluded, "There may be some excuse for the one but not the other." Another young soldier simply wished he could have all the Copperheads in his trench so he could then push them up and out to the other side of the breastworks, which is where they belonged, being every bit as rebellious as those wearing butternut and gray.[30]

For Wilbur Fisk of the 2nd Vermont Infantry, such men were "fighting against their country and against their God—fighting in the service of Satan and Jeff Davis and they are fools if they think they will win in the end." With a deluge of letters and newspapers reaching the front, the typical Union soldier was well aware of the Copperhead threat back home and in their replies, made sure their kin were well aware of their soldierly contempt. These pro-Union letters were often shared by relatives with sympathetic local newspapers, which published them as an example of a Union soldier's proper patriotism and duty. Many letters simply viewed draft resisters as cowards lacking in the manliness required to accept their civil duties. "I still feel very confident of success if the people at home will support us," stated one Ohio soldier in late August. "Keep cowards from attacking us in the rear while we are trying to wind up this infernal Rebellion." Thaddeus Capron of the 55th Illinois voiced a comparable sentiment, informing his father how glad he was to learn that his hometown aid society was being maintained and that a Union League had been organized. "I tell you it cheers us up to know that friends at home are working for us and the cause."[31]

As the 1863 summer rolled past, the constant Copperhead vitriol toward the draft, emancipation, and the war these young Northern men were fighting caused some to rethink their Democratic sympathies. After all, it was starting to dawn on many Union soldiers that a black man in a blue uniform could stop a Rebel ball just as good as a white one while others had witnessed slavery's horrors firsthand during their marches throughout the South. "I think the copperheads of the North have overdone themselves and in trying to bite the loyal citizens they have missed their mark and bit themselves and are now writhing in agony from the effects of their own poison," mused Andrew Davis of the 15th Indiana Infantry to wife. "And I think the Conscript bill will cause some of them to writhe worse than ever before many months. They may talk Politick and treason at home as much as they please but they cannot inculcate their damnable doctrines into the soldiers who are in the field."[32]

The man considered to be the most notorious Copperhead by proadministration supporters was forty-three-year-old former Ohio Rep. Clement Vallandigham. After Vallandigham was arrested by Union Gen. Ambrose Burnside on May 5, 1863, for giving a treasonous speech in Mount Vernon, Ohio, the *New York World* fired broadside after broadside against the legal pretext for the arrest. Vallandigham's arrest, however, suddenly gave the peace movement an element of respectability by showing that the despotic prophecies Democrats had warned against might actually be coming true. Leading Democrat and SDPK member Samuel Tilden gave voice to this in a letter to Brooklyn's Mayor Martin Kalbfleisch. "Of what avail are elections if we are not at liberty to discuss the measures which we may rightfully seek to have adopted or rejected by means of the election?" Tilden asked rhetorically. As Tilden and his fellow Democrats saw it, the country's entire system of government rested on the individual's right to discuss and print their thoughts on the great issues of the day. Take away that right "and there is nothing left to distinguish our political institutions from those of Turkey, or from those of France, except that in the latter, despotism has grown experienced, politic, and artistic."[33]

Anti-Copperhead soldiers also loathed Vallandigham, especially those from the Midwestern states. A commissary officer reported that when Vallandigham passed through their camp near Murfreesboro, Tennessee, a guard detail from the 93rd Ohio Infantry had to be dispatched to keep the other soldiers from attacking him. That history has often painted Vallandigham with the scarlet *T* for traitor speaks to the long-lasting success of Republican propaganda.[34]

Rep. Clement Vallandigham of Ohio, leader of the Copperhead movement against the Civil War (Library of Congress Prints and Photographs Division)

With all of their editorials proclaiming the war's unconstitutionality, its lack of merit, or the poor likelihood of its success, Northern Peace Democrats overlooked or underestimated the Union soldiers' desire to see the war through to its conclusion. "We begin to look upon this war as a necessity—a war for a great principle," wrote John Bennitt, the surgeon for the 19th Michigan Infantry. "It is not a question of *negro* slavery simply, but a question that applies to every individual." For Bennitt and others like him, the essential question was whether the United States was going to bequeath to its children a country where the strong had the right to enslave the weak, regardless of color. "This is the issue," Bennitt stressed. "Let the Copperheads understand this distinctly, & there would be a change of front with many of them." Simply put, many Union soldiers' letters as well as the Union League—Publication Society pamphlets and broadsides worked in concert to portray Peace Democrats as little more than cowards avoiding the fight while criticizing those doing the dirty work. Moreover, the Copperheads angrily denounced the war while seeming to offer only tepid pronouncements of support for the boys in blue. Meanwhile, the Union Leagues' public declarations put forth rabid support for the soldiers, a sentiment that would pay dividends in the year to come.[35]

Chapter 7

"The 'Loyal Leagues' Are Really Effecting Public Opinion"

The Broad-Based Loyal Leagues and "No Party Now"

Almost all of the young men who enlisted in the Union armies at the war's commencement considered patriotism to be a primary motive. Knowing that their friends and relatives back home were watching their movements and were also supportive of their travails gave the soldiers an important emotional boost. Home front loyalty toward cause and soldier was what Jörg Nagler referred to as "the psychological touchstone on which to base national cohesiveness." Soldiers demanded political conformity from the folks at home because only a cohesive loyalty between Northern soldier and civilian would lead to victory. The sometimes violent antidraft and antienlistment activities undertaken by the Copperheads against the Union war effort underscored this conviction. Soldiers made little effort to differentiate between antiwar political speech and violent subversion directed against federal authority and loyal citizens. Ardent Union League men understood and echoed this belief. In referring to the Leagues as "the reserve corps of our armies in the field," a New York state executive emphasized it was "as important to have a pure and healthy moral sentiment here—to have a tone of pure loyalty at home—as it is to sustain our armies in the field."[1]

Still, while the Northern men who were huddled in the Union's front lines certainly appreciated their home communities' harsh rhetoric decrying treason, many came to realize that mere words were a far cry from those same men actually picking up a musket to join them in the trenches. "If anyone is very keen to shoot or hang Rebels, let them come down and he can have a chance to try it on. I presume there is less danger in losing one's life up there than here," mused Lt. Samuel Evans of the 59th United States Colored Troops (USCT) in November 1863. "If we are compelled to fight the South into the Union, it is soldiers we want," declared an Iowa officer. Not overly impressed with the Union League's mission, he bluntly complained, "These meetings are very good places for loud-talking patriots to go and to talk about suppressing the rebellion"; however, "one of these meetings is the last place to go for recruits." Of a similar mind was the 149th New York Infantry's George Collins, who advised his mother in February 1863 while encamped in the Virginia mud that "those flowery speeches (I believe they call them patriotic speeches) sound a little different when read down here." Even men of the cloth perceived a difference. While expressing his approval upon learning that a Union League council had been formed in Boston, the 2nd Massachusetts Infantry's chaplain wrote in March 1863 how he belonged to an even better one out in the field. "It numbers seven or eight hundred members, and it bears the title of the 'Massachusetts Second,'" he dryly noted. "There is room for a few more members in it now. It had more, but they are buried at Winchester, at Cedar Mountain, at Antietam, and at many a wayside grave." These men and their brothers in arms appreciated the pro-Union sentiment, but what they really wanted was more Northern men to join them at the front. In the case of the elite Union Leagues in New York, Philadelphia, and Boston, however, almost all of their members were well past military age, having reached their forties and beyond. With a Civil War soldier's average age being around twenty-five, the plebian Midwestern Union Leagues more likely contained the men sought by the Union soldiers.[2]

Though some may have been unaware of yet another Union military defeat at the May 1–6 battle of Chancellorsville, by early to mid-May Democrats sensed the political winds were changing. The mountain of letters from soldiers railing against "skedaddlers" and those Copperheads who spoke or acted against the draft were routinely published in Northern papers and were read by both parties. The ongoing growth of the Union League movement also showed Democrats that Republicans were quite prepared to fight back in the war for public opinion. Iowa jurist Charles Mason admitted that many of his fellow Democrats were greatly depressed. "There is a disposition on the part of many to let the next election go by default," he wrote. Even party leader August Belmont sensed a shift. Writing to a British general on May 7, 1863, Belmont knew the Northern populace were now determined to fight the war tooth and nail until the national government was reestablished. He admitted "a decided change has taken place" and even his party's most strident peace-at-all-cost men, whose number and influence had increased in the fall due to Republican mismanagement, were now "entirely put in the background" for the time being.[3]

In spite of the success the Union Leagues and Publication Societies experienced in getting their new organizations off the ground, much of the North's mood was still quite somber in the spring of 1863. Other than the tactical draw (though strategic victory) at the battle of Antietam on September 17, 1862, the Union's Army of the Potomac experienced repeated disasters during the second half of the year, starting with the Seven Days battles in July 1862, the August 28–30 battle of Second Bull Run, and at the battle of Fredericksburg on December 13, 1862. On the home front, the controversies surrounding the Emancipation Proclamation and the new draft law only added additional discord.

Proadministration politicians, speakers, and newspaper editors strove to rejuvenate the sagging morale by resurrecting the "no party now" sentiment that so animated the country in the spring and summer of 1861. With the disappointing military results so widespread in mid- to late 1862, however, Northern unity fell by the wayside. Leading the new charge was Francis Lieber, a sixty-one-year-old German American professor at Columbia College who was also a Union League Club of New York member, cofounder of the Loyal Publication Society, and chairman of the Society's seven-man Publication Committee. Considered by all as a Radical Republican, Lieber authored the famous General Orders No. 100 for the army, published on April 24, 1863, which for the first time ever set down on paper the lawful rules of warfare. Lieber was distraught over the North's sagging morale at the end of 1862 and shortly thereafter asked a friend if "an able, lofty, penetrative pamphlet" might help to counter the Democratic threat. Having not forgotten the morale issue, he became aghast at what he witnessed one month later on a train trip home to New York. In a letter to Sen. Charles Sumner on February 10, Lieber complained, "The cars, on my return from Washington, were full of discharged soldiers, and such loud, nasty, infernal treason I have never believed my ears should be destined to hear. I changed cars, but it was everywhere the same." As an intellectual émigré, Lieber stayed in touch with many European liberals, explaining the Union cause and urging their support for it. With an eye toward home front support from the German and French communities, the Loyal Publication Society eagerly reprinted any positive replies from the European intelligentsia.[4]

Francis Lieber (Library of
Congress Prints and Photographs Division)

Lieber's most important moment came on April 11 at New York's Union
Square, where the eloquent professor delivered a speech titled "No Party
Now; But All for Our Country." In his discourse, Lieber reiterated the ideal
that the country's current travails should be beyond partisanship. The issue
was not one of politics, but of patriotism, "and we hold everyone to be a
traitor to his country, that works or speaks in favor of our criminal enemies,
directly or indirectly." For Lieber and all League men, loyalty was the preeminent civic virtue in a free country. Loyalty was "patriotism cast in the grace-
ful mould of candid devotion to the harmless government of an unshackled
nation." Not surprisingly, Lieber's speech was rushed into print by the Loyal
Publication Society and went through multiple printings. In the process, it
became one of the most famous political pamphlets from the Civil War. Yet
despite Lieber's (and the Union Leagues') public plea for nonpartisanship
and "no party," Lieber's speech read like a Radical Republican treatise with
its support for abolition (slavery as "the poisonous root of the war"), the
draft, and Southern subjugation—all topics most Democrats abhorred.[5]

Other proadministration men expounded on the "no party now" theme.
Just two days prior to Lieber's speech, Edward Everett spoke at the formal

inauguration on April 9 of Boston's new Union Club. Everett declared, "We propose no party action; we aim at no party ends; and we invite the fellowship of all good and true men." In a June 25 letter to the Philadelphia Union League and published by its publication board as antiparty propaganda, eighty-three-year-old Horace Binney, an esteemed Philadelphia attorney and 1830s anti-Jacksonian congressman, lamented the rise of party dominance in government compared to George Washington's era. "If there be any practical distinction between the government and the administration, party has made it, and not Washington," Binney argued. "It is a distinction disloyal to the Union" and "reduces loyalty to the degraded rank of personal favors to personal actors in the government." Though still controlling both the White House and Congress, the 1862 congressional elections delivered quite a blow to the Republicans. This attempt to get the Democrats to call off their attacks was a propaganda effort designed to retake the moral high ground with cries of Union one and forever. As one Indiana newspaper had framed it, Democrats were now expected to join the "no party 'Union party' party." Another complained that "all agreeing" simply meant "all abolitionists." An upstate New York paper asked if all Democrats were Copperheads and Copperheads were traitors, then why was it safe to have Democrats in the army? Conversely, since the "Leaguers" were patriots and patriots were the only true Union men, then better to fill up the ranks with only League men. "Men who blow their own trumpets about their own greatness should be compelled to prove their acts," asserted the paper. Now, as in the past, many Democrats were galled at Republicans' nonpartisan pretensions coupled with their attempts to define patriotism and loyalty. Of special annoyance to Democrats was how the Radicals and Union Leagues persisted in labeling prominent, loyal Democrats as traitorous Copperheads.[6]

As 1863 rolled on, the growing success that the Union Leagues enjoyed in publicly defining loyalty angered Union-devoted Democrats and even caused some Republican moderates to raise their eyebrows. In a case of the squeaky wheel getting the grease, the Leagues, their publication societies, and their allies were beginning to set the definitions of what constituted proper loyalty and patriotism. Edward Bates succinctly identified the frustration. As Lincoln's attorney general and a political outsider in Lincoln's Cabinet, he later complained how "The radicals are making great efforts to create the belief that they are *the* Union men, and all others are against the Union. And they succeed in driving on some *cowardly patriots,* who reluctantly go along with them, for fear of being denounced by them." Lincoln's secretary, John Hay, was even more frustrated, informing Bates, "The whole spirit of [the Radical] faction is contempt of and opposition to law."[7]

The Radical and wealthy bourgeoisie who created the Union League Club of New York envisioned it from the beginning as an organization that would target strictly the pro-Union cream of New York society for membership. As Frederick Olmsted had originally proposed, it was to consist of men who formed the "natural aristocracy," i.e., those men whose education, business acumen, and cultural accomplishments had brought them to the top of their respective fields. Considering its upper-class nature and, therefore, the relatively finite number of potential applicants, some members saw the benefit in creating a "brother" loyalty group whose ranks would be far more broad-based. According to early New York Union League member John Austin Stevens Jr., such a group would "bring a direct influence to bear on the working classes" and would be open to all who professed fealty to the Union and its war efforts.[8]

What some saw as the new Union League's hard-line position of *unconditional* support for the Lincoln administration, coupled with the desire to create a pro-Union loyalty organization anyone could join, led to the creation in New York of two new loyalty-based Leagues. They were organized at essentially the same time as the Union League Club of New York and the Loyal Publication Society were coming into existence. While both groups shared a considerable overlap in their stated loyalty objectives and were never really competitors, their target audiences were different.

The first of the two working-class New York groups was named the Loyal League of Union Citizens and it was formed by Mayor George Opdyke and Democrat Prosper Wetmore in early March 1863. The two seemed an odd pairing at first glance, yet both illustrated the new organization's overarching public loyalty goal. Opdyke had become wealthy years earlier as a clothing manufacturer. Now at fifty-seven years old, he was a combative, antislavery politician who was a proud cog within the Republican Party's Radical wing. The sixty-five-year-old Wetmore also possessed some background in the public sphere, including a term in the New York state legislature. A wealthy dry goods merchant and author, Wetmore was a conservative Democrat who had denounced abolitionists as early as 1835. Though he had a military background, having joined the New York State militia in 1819 and eventually becoming paymaster general, Wetmore possessed little passion for the current war, but nonetheless desired to show support to the government. Despite Wetmore's credentials, George Strong loathed the man and considered him a phony, referring to Wetmore in his diary as "the embodiment of corrupt, mercenary, self-seeking sham-patriotism" and whose loyalty possessed a "doubtful antecedent."[9]

The Loyal League's new constitution proudly declared its "unconditional support of the government" and was open to any man regardless of wealth or social status. It separated itself, however, from the Union Leagues by the qualifier "in all its *Constitutional* efforts to suppress the rebellion." This conservative constraint appealed especially to War Democrats, who, while wanting to see the rebellion suppressed, felt Radical Republican policies regarding civil liberties had gone too far. Considering the rebuke they had suffered at the polls back in November, Republicans saw this new blend of loyalist organization as a way of seeking common ground and, therefore, beneficial in bringing War Democrats into the Republican camp. Sensing New York still held far too much dejection and pro-Southern sympathy, its February 28 draft proposal urged all loyal citizens to gather for the purpose of "reaffirming their determination to sustain this government in its efforts to quell the rebellion." In a friendly letter to George Boker, Wetmore explained that his league was noticeably different in scope than Boker's Union League of Philadelphia. The Philadelphia League, from Wetmore's vantage, existed to cultivate and circulate loyalty as a social science. The Loyal League's mission was "to produce effect upon the popular mind of the country thro' the agency of public meetings."[10]

The Loyal League held its first rally in a grand and packed meeting at New York's Cooper Institute on March 6. Presiding over the gathering was *New York Evening Post* editor and abolitionist William Cullen Bryant, and which also featured several Union generals in attendance. Bryant, renowned attorneys David Dudley Field and James T. Brady, Judge Charles P. Daly, and Democratic Party leader John Van Buren all delivered patriotic speeches at what was New York's largest public gathering in support of the war since the conflict had begun almost two years earlier.[11]

The New York newspapers covered the event extensively. The *Times* headline proclaimed "Monster Mass Meeting" with a reported four thousand people in attendance. Even though the event was scheduled to start at eight o'clock, the doors had to be closed by seven o'clock. The Democratic reaction was swift and predictable, condemning the meeting as merely a way to reverse the previous elections. In the *Times* rebuttal, it pointed out the growing

John Austin Stevens Jr. (Collection of the Newport Historical Society)

Union and Loyal League movements were designed "simply to array the loyal men of the country in support of the national unity and integrity, without regard to past party distinctions."[12]

While Wetmore and Opdyke were forming their conservative-leaning Loyal League, John Austin Stevens Jr. had not forgotten his earlier desire to see a more broad-based loyalty group. Following a disagreement with Union League Club of New York members—which George Strong described as the Club's refusal to view Stevens as the "first violin"—Stevens resigned from the club and set about forming the Loyal National League. It was a patriotic organization geared toward middle- and working-class proadministration Republicans. The League's pledge committed members to an unconditional loyalty toward the government along with "an unwavering support of its efforts to suppress the Rebellion." Years later, Stevens explained how the new group was designed to showcase the average New York citizen's loyalty and to "put an end to temporizing schemes." This put the Loyal National League more in line with the Radicals. Its stated object was to join together all loyal men from all trades and professions without regard to wealth or position. No mention was made of constitutional restrictions, which clearly set the Loyal National League apart from Wetmore's Loyal League of Union Citizens.[13]

In a response to the Loyal League's initial March 6 meeting at Cooper Institute and its second gathering at New York's Academy of Music on March 14, the Loyal National League held its first grand rally on March 20 at the Cooper Institute. Like the March 6 gathering, speakers and speeches were plenty. Charles Butler, the president of New York's Loyal Publication Society, presided over the meeting. Union Gen. John Cochrane and Gen. Andrew J. Hamilton gave rousing speeches, as did New York Republican Rep. Roscoe Conkling. In the days prior to the meeting, the new League placed announcements along with a loyalty pledge requiring a potential member's signature at various offices and newspaper counters throughout the city. As a consequence, attendance was somewhat lighter than the March 6 affair as only those who had signed the pledge were admitted. The requirement for a written pledge further separated the Loyal National League from the Loyal League of Union Citizens, the former quickly pointing out that since the latter required no such bond or commitment, it was therefore not a true "League" in any sense of the word.[14]

The executive committees of both organizations contained many of New York City's leading business, political, and intellectual elite. In what was a keen sense of political acumen, these men realized two such groups were necessary, especially with the Loyal League of Union Citizens, whose aim was to bring more conservative men and War Democrats into a full-throated backing for the administration's war efforts. When word of the new resolutions reached Lincoln friend and moderate Orville H. Browning, the Illinois Republican could find no reason for criticism. "I can see nothing objectionable in them . . . nothing that can be offensive to a loyal man of any party."[15]

At the Loyal National League's initial gathering on March 20, General Cochrane addressed an audience question concerning what differences existed between the two Loyal Leagues. He replied that while there may be some minor discrepancies between the two Loyal Leagues, there was no critical difference. "These misunderstandings, when we are all united in one common purpose, are but additional incentives to energetic action," explained Cochrane. The pro-Republican New York press concurred. The New York *Evening Post* felt the chief differentiator between the two was the Loyal National League's "air of sterner determination to support the war to its last results," nonetheless it endorsed both groups. The *Times* simply saw strength in numbers. "If all these various Union Associations work in unison and with a single spirit of patriotic duty, it will not be easy to estimate the extent of the benefit they will confer on the national cause."[16]

To Democrats, however, the two new Loyal Leagues were merely opposite sides of the same coin. "The spirit of rivalry between these Loyal Leagues is to be evinced in striving to outdo each other in professions of loyalty and efforts to support the government," chortled the *Brooklyn Daily Eagle*. "Both declare they never, never will desert Mr. Lincoln, as long as he is President and has an office or a contract to give out," its sarcasm masking Democratic anger at the growing Republican refusal to acknowledge the concept of a "loyal opposition." The *Detroit Free Press* railed against how the word "traitor" was becoming "sadly perverted" and what it saw as the growing Republican canard of loyalty versus disloyalty. From its vantage, the paper opined how "Every household, every community, is a loyal league," and if any citizen was dissatisfied, it was only because of the immense waste in national blood and treasure. Since it was obvious to the *Free Press* that all Northerners wanted to see the war prosecuted to a successful close, the Loyal Leagues really had no reason for being other than as a purely political entity. The SDPK chimed in as well, calmly pointing out how neither Loyal League had ever put forth "one word of indignant remonstrance against the unconstitutional measures of the Administration."[17]

Both Loyal Leagues continued their New York gatherings well into the spring. The Loyal National League held another rally on April 11 to commemorate the Fort Sumter battle, with the Loyal League following that rally with a huge gathering on April 20. George Strong attended the Loyal League meeting on April 20 and felt the event was more "imposing" than the Loyal National League's event from a week earlier. "They say the former is a machine run by [moderate Secretary of State William] Seward, and that [Radical Secretary of the Treasury Salmon P.] Chase pulls the wires of the latter," noted Strong in his diary. There was an element of truth in that as numerous Chase supporters sat on the Loyal National League's general council or executive committee, including founder John Austin Stevens Jr., who was a close Chase ally and friend. Chase was invited to speak at the April 20 rally, but when he replied that he could not attend, Stevens had Chase's written reply promoting loyalty while rebuking treason printed and distributed widely among politicos and the military. Even though George Strong had incorrectly given little credence to the puppet-string rumors, they nonetheless served as a valuable cautionary tale: "These stories show how watchful we must be in our Union League Club to keep above suspicion of mere political partisanship."[18]

Loyal National League

MEETING!

An adjourned meeting of the Loyal National League of Ravenna will be held at the TOWN HALL, on **Friday Evening, March 27th,** to commence at 7 o'clock. The meeting will be addressed by ALPHONSO HART, Esq., and Rev. JAMES E. WILSON. Good, patriotic songs may be expected. The public generally are invited to attend. By order of the Executive Committee.

Loyal National League newspaper advertisement, March 25, 1863 (*Portage County, Ohio, Democrat*)

Like the Union Leagues, chapters for both broad-based Loyal Leagues spread throughout the city and eventually throughout the North. As Henry Bellows later acknowledged, the like-minded Union and Loyal Leagues "were all the fruits of a common feeling of necessity for organizing public sentiment against the threatened loss of nationality." In the case of the Loyal National League, it ultimately reached thirty chapters just within the state of New York. Several prominent men who organized the New York Loyal Leagues assisted in organizing Leagues in other states. They were part of a speaking tour illustrating Bellows's postwar assertion that all League men were "animated by the same heart." Pamphlets reporting on the proceedings of each large meeting were printed in quantity by both organizations and distributed throughout the land. Along with the pamphlets and broadsides produced by the Publication Societies, a veritable high tide of "loyal," pro-Union propaganda began to be disseminated throughout the North that soon drowned out any similar Democratic effort. Pamphlets spawned more pamphlets as well-reasoned arguments prompted a flurry of responses that transcended faction. A *New York World* reporter who happened to drop in on a League meeting saw that the piles of postpaid circulars stacked neatly on tables, all ready for the mail, were larger than ever. So great was the torrent that upstate New York Democrat O. W. Smith wrote to Samuel Morse—president of the Democrats' Society for the Diffusion of Political Knowledge—to complain about the "immense supplies of reading matter in the shape of speeches and Loyal League documents [that] are flooding the country." He urged Morse that the Democrats must immediately counter because the effectiveness of the various League and Publication Society distribution efforts was becoming self-evident: "You can hardly go into a public office or store, but you will see such documents on tables, counters, and even posted up in the shape of handbills. The 'Loyal Leagues' are really effecting public opinion seriously with their meetings, documents, etc."[19]

Despite the two Loyal Leagues' apparent contradictory membership requirements, the similarities outweighed the differences. In fact, both shared some of the same men on their respective executive committees, from conservative and War Democrats to a sprinkling of Radical Republicans. The *New York Tribune* echoed the "no party now" rallying cry and endorsed the new Leagues' crossover senior leadership by stating, "This is as it should be. Party is forgotten when the existence of the nation is at stake." New York's *Independent* concluded that "both bodies are essentially one, and represent, together, the great mass of loyal people of New York." Most notable of the cross-serving men was Radical Republican George Opdyke, who was a co-founder and vice-president of the Loyal League of Union Citizens yet also served as a vice-president with the Loyal National League. The wealthy entrepreneur and retailer Alexander T. Stewart, Loyal Publication Society member Francis Lieber, financier and banker Morris Ketchum, dry goods merchant Seth B. Hunt, banker and New York Union League member George Cabot Ward, and New York politician William Orton all served as officers or executive committee members for both of the new Loyal Leagues.[20]

At the same time as the New York elites were developing their offshoot Loyal Leagues, the Union League of Philadelphia was also creating a proletarian group that any loyal man in Philadelphia could join with a dues structure favorable to the middle and working classes. Christened the National Union Club, the association was housed across the street from the Union League of Philadelphia and was considered a "brother" association. The League described its new offshoot as being "without distinction of party, in support of the war; and a proper response to the uprising of the loyal men in New York and elsewhere." "This is no ordinary party club," stated a request to Ohio's John Sherman asking the senator to speak at the group's upcoming inauguration. Rather, it considered itself "an organization which in material, in plan of action, in spirit, and in probable numbers, promises to exert a vast influence upon the events before us."[21]

The National Union Club's initial rally resulted in one of the largest public gatherings Philadelphia ever witnessed despite the damp cold and heavy snow covering the streets and sidewalks. Held at the Musical Fund Hall on March 11, 1863, the crowded event featured many leading orators from both parties, including Pennsylvania's Gov. Andrew Curtin, Wisconsin's Sen. J. R. Doolittle, and Tennessee's Gov. Andrew Johnson. Noted Philadelphia attorney Benjamin H. Brewster spoke as to how just such an organization had long been needed and that a public gathering as that night's was indispensable for awakening the public to the treasonable dangers all around them. When it was apparent that the crowd outside the hall exceeded those inside, an outdoors meeting with speeches was hastily assembled for the gathering throng. Philadelphia's *Press* newspaper covered the event lavishly, which was not surprising as its editors were also Union League members. Its headlines proclaimed "Union for the Sake of Union," "No Party but the Party of the Country," and "Treason Rebuked," which were all standard pro-Union buzz phrases.[22]

The creation of the common man, Loyal Leagues and the National Union Club were an acknowledgment by the social elites of what political scientists Glenn C. Altschuler and Stuart M. Blumin referred to as the growing "rude republic." The term described a youthful and growing nation where many of its working-class citizens ascribed to the egalitarian political virtues of the common man while disdaining deference to the elites, in particular, Olmsted's "natural aristocracy." These "separate but equal" Union and Loyal Leagues, as created by patrician elites, provided the means for them to engage in noblesse oblige among their peers without having to wade into the unseemliness of street-level politics.[23]

A brief ray of hope penetrated the Northern gloom in early July when word reached the home front of two stellar Union military victories. During July 1–3, Union Gen. George Meade and his Army of the Potomac had battled Robert E. Lee's Confederate Army of Northern Virginia on the rolling hills and farms outside of Gettysburg, Pennsylvania, following Lee's second Northern invasion. When the figurative smoke cleared on a rainy Fourth of July, Lee's battered army was again retreating southward to the safety of Virginia. Both sides suffered a combined 53,000 casualties in what was the

largest battle ever fought in the Western hemisphere. As the North was receiving this good news, the word also arrived of the Confederate surrender
at Vicksburg, Mississippi, following a forty-seven-day siege of that Mississippi River bastion. With Vicksburg's surrender, the Union Navy now controlled the river, thereby cutting the Confederacy in two. For the first time
in a long time, the Union military scored major victories and as a result, the
Union Leagues' past exhortations that the war must be continued started
to resonate with much of the North. In New York, the Loyal Leagues fired
a one-hundred-gun salute. Horace Greeley's *New York Daily Tribune,* perhaps the North's most influential newspaper and one that had previously
espoused reservations about the war, now reversed itself. With such important victories under the North's belt, peace meetings as advocated by the
Democrats "would be hailed as an exhibition of weakness, a proclamation
of discord on the part of the loyal States, and would reestablish the insurgent leaders in the fast-waning confidence of their long-suffering dupes."[24]

The stunning victories at Gettysburg and Vicksburg provided a brief up-
lift from long months of often violent home front discord over the war's
course and the means by which it was now being fought. Organized antidraft mobbing had taken place in Pennsylvania in October 1862 and then
in Wisconsin one month later in November. A vicious, antiblack riot in
Detroit on March 6, 1863, had left several dead and many more homeless.
Much of the black neighborhood in that Great Lakes city was burned to the
ground by the rioters.[25]

Physical violence against draft enrollment officers was particularly acute
once those men begin to fan out across the country in June 1863 to register
men for the new draft. The provost marshal for Connecticut's first district
reported that two buildings belonging to his officers had been torched. He
had been threatened to his face that the draft would be resisted by force
if necessary, "not only by men of no character and position in this community, but by men prominent politically, socially, and officially in various
parts of the district." In Schuylkill County, Pennsylvania, the provost marshal reported that on June 4, two of his officers had been shot at. On June
17, over four hundred men from the 15th Ohio Infantry were dispatched to
Holmes County, Ohio, following an attack against a draft enrollment official by four men who were arrested, but later forcibly freed by local antiwar
residents. That same month, an officer was ambushed and shot dead in Sullivan County, Indiana. His assassins were never brought to justice. Those
incidents are just a few examples of many that resulted in thirty-eight Bu-

reau men being murdered while carrying out their enrollment duties over the final two years of the war. An additional sixty were wounded. More "fortunate" officers routinely had rotten eggs thrown at them or in more severe cases, saw their barns burned with all livestock inside. Such Copperhead-initiated violence against federal authority in Northern towns served to remind Union League men why they had formed in the first place and that their opponents' "fire in the rear" threats were more than just words.[26]

None of that violence, however, approached the scale of what transpired in New York City in mid-July. The city's long-simmering brew of political, ethnic, and class strife reached the boiling point on Saturday, July 11. The cauldron exploded on July 13.

On Saturday, July 11, the first-ever draft lottery was held in New York at the provost marshal's office on the corner of 3rd Avenue and 46th Street. Grumblings against the new draft law were heard throughout the day as 1,236 names were pulled out of the lottery wheel, though the crowd's behavior was generally restrained. The resentment was generated toward the new law's apparent class-based provisions that allowed any man to avoid service by either hiring a substitute or paying a $300 commutation fee to the national government. Such a fee was well beyond consideration for most workingmen and in many cases, that sum was equivalent to a year's wages. Resentment quickly festered toward the wealthy, typified by New York's Union League members, as those being most able to afford and take advantage of the commutation provision. An air of unease permeated the city on Sunday, July 12.[27]

This bitterness and anger was primarily manifested in New York's dirt-poor Irish enclaves. As discussed in Chapter 4, fully one-quarter of New York's 1860 population were Irish immigrants. In fact, over 12 percent of *all* Irish immigrants to the United States were living in New York City, most of whom were packed together in filthy tenement housing primarily in lower Manhattan. Upon seeing the squalor, a young well-educated Frenchman wrote how he was repulsed by the "pitifully wretched . . . wooden hovels, these long, muddy avenues and this swarm of paupers." It was common for three or four families to be crowded together in a small, two-room flat. Clean sanitation was nonexistent while disease and pestilence were rampant. With the enactment of the March 1863 draft law, many of the Irish working poor now believed they were going to become the Union Army's much-needed cannon fodder; a loathsome prospect, for many recalled the British Army's mandatory conscription provisions that contributed to their flight in the first place. When recently elected Democratic Gov. Horatio

Seymour publicly warned in New York on July 4 that "The bloody and treasonable and revolutionary doctrine of public necessity can be proclaimed
by a mob as well as by a government," many interpreted Seymour as saying
that the time had come to take to the streets.[28]

The relatively calm atmosphere on July 11 vanished when the draft process
restarted on Monday, July 13. Unlike the draft on July 11, which was held in
only one location, Monday's draft was scheduled to be held at numerous offices all over town. In what amounted to coordinated efforts that had to have
been preplanned, protesters went to anywhere workingmen were located—
factories, wharves, foundries, etc.—and implored them to join in the demonstration, forcing the work sites to shut down. Others returned to the site of
Saturday's draft and severed all the telegraph wires in an attempt to disrupt
police communication. When the crowd was large enough, the ringleaders
and their followers destroyed the lottery equipment and then began to burn
the office. The uprising was underway.

In short order, the rioters began taking out their anger against any symbol of Republicanism or the well-to-do. Those targets included the fine Fifth
Avenue Hotel because "that's where the Union Leaguers meet!" yelled some
in the crowd. Dozens of men were beaten for no reason other than that they

Charge of the police at the *Tribune* office (Library of Congress Prints and Photographs Division)

were attired in fine clothing. The rioters also turned their destructive intent toward Republican newspapers. Finding stern resistance at the *Times,* however, the roving mobs then tried to destroy the offices of the Republican *New York Tribune* and the home of Republican Mayor George Opdyke.[29]

The mob's most vicious rage was soon transferred from Republican symbols toward blacks of any age. These were the people whom the rioters viewed as the unwelcome reason for the draft in the first place, as well as working-class labor competition. From the Irish vantage point, they had come to this country simply to work hard but peaceably and raise their families. As one Irish newspaperman had editorialized, Irishmen from Detroit to New York had "rushed into a fight at which no interest of theirs was at stake." A visiting Englishman wrote what was known to all by noting how the Irish "habitually dread the freedom of the negro, lest he should become a competitor in the labor market." Labor was not the sole issue, however. Social caste played an immensely important role in Irish racist emotions. "The Irish hate the Negroes, not merely because they compete with them in labor, but because they are near to them in social rank," Philadelphian Sidney G. Fisher had stated within his diary. Finishing his thought, Fisher concluded, "Therefore, the Irish favor slavery in the South, and for the same reason the laboring class of whites support it—it gratifies their pride by the existence of a class below them."[30]

For four days from July 13 to 16, mobs consisting primarily (though not exclusively) of New York's Irish underclass waged war against the city police, shutting down New York City in the process. According to George Strong, who was an eyewitness, the New York mob was a "perfectly homogeneous" rabble composed of "the lowest Irish day laborers. . . . Every brute in the drove was pure Celtic—hod-carrier or loafer." Strong loathed the Irish and was amazed at the fury of their women, whether "stalwart young vixens" or "withered old hags; all were cursing the 'bloody draft' and urging their men to mischief." Such destruction even included burning the city's Colored Orphan Asylum to the ground. The two hundred black children who lived at the four-story brick structure on Fifth Avenue barely escaped with their lives. Those blacks who fell into the rioters' hands were mercilessly pummeled, always with a reference that they were the reason for the war and the hated draft act. Many not merely beaten were killed outright, including one man who was attacked by a crowd of four hundred with clubs and paving stones. After he was dead, the crowd hung him from a lamppost and set his corpse on fire.[31]

For John Lauderdale, a surgeon at New York's Bellevue Hospital, the sights and results of the rioting were heart wrenching. The hospital's alarm bell sounded for days, signaling the arrival of more victims with burns, fractured skulls, or gunshot wounds. A solid Unionist, Lauderdale had little sympathy for the majority of his patients. "Tis a pity that more of these demons were not shot down, more especially the leaders of the infuriated mob, those copperhead leaders," he wrote to his sister. Lauderdale readily noticed one constant from one victim to the next, regardless of age or gender: "They all say they were not participants, but merely lookers on." This included a bruised and battered gunshot victim whose pockets contained several bills of Confederate script.[32]

The various rampaging throngs numbered in the hundreds and were comprised primarily of young, working-class males. Dozens of disciplined police officers waged hand-to-hand combat in the streets with the rioters. So great was the peril that troops from Gen. George Meade's war-weary Army of the Potomac, still encamped near Gettysburg, Pennsylvania, were sent to New York with all haste. The rioting was finally quelled after these battle-hardened veterans arrived on July 16 with orders to shoot to kill if the rioting continued. In many instances, that order was obeyed well. The New York riots were by far the deadliest the nation had ever seen with a death toll estimated at 105 to 120 lives. Property damage was estimated at over $1.5 million, all of which only added to the draft-related civil tension spreading throughout the North. Most of those killed were white rioters shot dead by Union soldiers.[33]

The Union League Club of New York's perspective on the riot was one of pity and benevolence toward the city's black victims. In the weeks to follow, a Committee of Merchants for the Relief of Colored People was established by New York businessmen to raise funds and collect clothing for those blacks who had been left destitute by the riots. By late September, almost $42,000 had been raised, with over half of that already distributed. Though not an official Union League Club of New York undertaking, at least twelve of the General Committee's nineteen members were League men.[34]

As for the working-class white rioters, the Union League's position was one of disdain and contempt. Some Union League members had urged the authorities to impose martial law when the rioting started though the military ultimately rejected such action. Police Commissioner Thomas Acton and Superintendent John A. Kennedy ended up leading the early street fights against the demonstrators. Kennedy, in fact, was severely beaten by the rabble early on. Both men were Union League members, which meant there was little League sympathy for the Irishmen who had taken to the streets. "For myself, personally, I would like to see war made on the Irish scum as in 1688," admitted George Strong in his diary. Further, he sensed a movement afoot to resurrect the early to mid-1850s nativist leanings of the Know-Nothings. Strong rationalized that such actions were understandable given the recent atrocities perpetrated by the Irish "canaille." The lack of national loyalty and violent rebellion displayed by the rioters toward lawful authority demonstrated one of the overall Union League movement's initial reasons for being and in its opinion, revealed the depth of their enemy's sympathy toward the South. While upper-class Democrats may have held to the most publicly racist beliefs, the anti-Irish nativism displayed by New York's patrician businessmen, as typified by George Strong and his Union League colleagues, was the most overt.[35]

Frederick Olmsted was not overly concerned with the riots damaging the Union League's positions. In a letter to his friend and *London Daily News* correspondent, Edwin Godkin, Olmsted wrote, "I don't think the riots will harm our enterprise. How I wish it was started & we could pitch in." Noting that he considered the leading Copperhead–Peace Democrats to be coconspirators to the riot, Olmsted sternly advised, "I think you should take the ground that the most dangerous foes of the republic are in New York City, that the government has now the right and the duty to put them down; that from this moment to the end of the war, government should deal with New York and other insurrectionary towns and districts, as it does with Baltimore & Nashville and New Orleans. Let [Samuel L. M.] Barlow & [James G.] Bennett & [Rep. James] Brooks and [August] Belmont & [George Gardner] Barnard & the [Fernando and Benjamin] Woods & [John U.] Andrews and [John] Clancey be hung if that be possible. Stir the govt. up to it. I didn't mean to omit Seymour." These men, along with "the mob" they allegedly inspired, were referred to by the Republican *New York Times* as "the left wing of Lee's army."[36]

The New York riots certainly captured the League's attention along with the realization that they needed to aggressively defend their property. Some members had armed themselves with muskets and posted themselves at their clubhouse windows during the riots. As a result, the Union League house suffered "not so much as a cracked windowpane" during the tumult, despite the rioters' efforts to attack Republican symbols. A visiting *New York Times* journalist to the New York League's headquarters in August duly noted the home's opulence and furnishings. Yet in stark contrast, he also described the "vast wooden shutters or shields of unpainted pine, bullet-proofed themselves and pierced for musketry." These heavy buffers were designed to cover the ground-floor windows, just in case any of the disaffected attempted another riot against Republican institutions. The journalist was also shown an impressive weapons cache, controlled by the club's "Chief of Ordnance," which could be utilized by members from the headquarters' iron balcony against any threatening intruders. Such an article in a major newspaper was clearly designed to serve notice to the New York League's enemies that it intended to defend itself.[37]

This antidraft, antiblack rioting did not stop with New York either. Serious, though less destructive, street riots also occurred in Boston; Portsmouth, New Hampshire; Rutland, Vermont; and Troy, New York, in the days following. When word of the riots reached the Union soldiers fighting down South, many were outraged, just as the middle-aged and elderly civilian Union League men were. As with the ongoing Copperhead-initiated resistance to the war effort that so many soldiers had earlier read about in family letters or newspapers, this deadly rioting proved yet again to the soldiers and pro-Union civilians that a treasonous cabal was on the march within the North, with the intent of sabotaging a just war to save the Union. Union League men realized they had to be more earnest than ever with their dual goals of promoting national loyalty while defending their homes and families. As for the boys in blue, most were pleased with the army's direct involvement in quelling the riots. "The example in New York City will have a *soothing* effect on Butternuts," wrote Col. Elijah Cavins of the 14th Indiana Infantry. "No better medicine could be given than a few doses of grape and cannister, mixed up with a reasonable quantity of cold lead and steel—the latter in the shape of a bayonet." There were even words of warning for Copperheads and their sympathizers: "We are coming home soon," proclaimed Samuel Fiske, "and we shall not fire *blank cartridges* at riotous 'friends' who resist the laws, and fill our streets and houses with blood."[38]

Chapter 8

"Neutrality Is Allied to Treason; Indifference Becomes a Crime; and Whoever Is Not with Us Is Against Us"

A Union League of America Council in Every Town

Whether they called themselves a Union League or a Loyal League, organized societies dedicated to promoting fealty to the Lincoln administration's policies and combating subversive acts mushroomed throughout Northern counties and small towns in the first half of 1863. This growth was concurrent with but uniquely separate from the prominent and fiercely independent Union League Clubs, which had generated so much press in Philadelphia, New York, and Boston. The driving engine behind this organic growth was the newly christened Union League of America (ULA), first formed in Illinois in the summer of 1862 and then spread like a spider web from there. The Illinois men found much of their early work slow going, considering the gloom that blanketed the North toward the end of 1862. League Secretary George Harlow recalled of no lower point than the dawn of 1863. "Treason and traitors were rampant all over our state," he later wrote. The opposition controlled the Illinois state legislature, with their decisions and pronouncements "bringing the blush of shame to the cheek of all honest men." Lincoln's personal friend, Orville Browning, saw the same picture as Harlow. "Not a few of the democratic leaders are traitors at heart—are in sympathy with rebellion, and had rather the government was overthrown that that it should be saved by a Republican administration," he observed.[1]

On the home front, Illinois Unionists complained to Illinois's Gov. Richard Yates that Rebel sympathizers and antiwar dissidents were showing their "hatred and fiendish malice" by poisoning horses and destroying young orchards belonging to loyal men. Mr. A. Babcock appealed to Union Gen. Jacob Ammen in Springfield for help in stopping the "secessionist traitors" who had destroyed his fences, his four hundred fine young fruit trees, and were intent on driving him and other loyal men out of the area. "What are we to do?" asked Babcock. "Must we tamely submit to those vile miscreants and allow them to destroy our property, to insult us daily as we meet them on the public roads?" More often than antidraft riots, localized Copperhead subversion against the war took the form of terrorizing neighborhood Unionists, who then sought protection and support within their local Union League. A frustrated Mrs. Rankin McPheeters of Sullivan, Illinois, echoed all of these grievances, informing her husband that "The seceshionest [*sic*] here are a great deal worse than those in the south. I have a natural hatred towards them."[2]

These Copperhead-generated outrages prompted Union League men to respond in kind in an ever-growing cycle of violent retaliation, with each side claiming its acts justified in lieu of the other's violence. That each side proclaimed itself the keeper of both the Constitution's ideals as well as law and order created a paradox. Whether Copperhead or Union League man, each individual claimed himself heir to a "democratic heritage" that transcended normal governmental practices, and in the process, sought to deny his opponent full participation within the American republic in the name of the people—what Paul Gilje referred to as "the unraveling logic of a democracy unleashed."[3]

To plan their next steps, the Illinois Union League's Grand Council called for a second meeting at Springfield to be held on January 14, 1863. Delegates from only seven counties were present, which added to the despair. Seeking guidance, Harlow and Daniel Wilkins met with Governor Yates to inform him about the League's current meeting, its goals and objectives, and to ask him for any advice and assistance he might provide. As a firm Republican, Yates was fully supportive of the Union League's intentions. He advised them to persevere, to keep expanding into every Illinois town, and that he would readily provide whatever support he was able to. Being the shrewd politician, Yates voiced his confidence that such an organization could be of immense value to the current government. With a renewed sense of purpose, the Union League's executive committee met six days later in Peoria to plan a new strategy. By early February, the Springfield chapter boasted over four hundred loyal members.

Meanwhile, in Chicago, Joseph Medill's *Tribune* was urging all loyal men to organize a Union Club or League in every Illinois town. Governor Yates was advised how Leagues were forming throughout the state and that Madison County, close to St. Louis, would be thoroughly organized within ten days. "We are about ready and able to take care of home troubles in any event," declared an Illinois Unionist regarding the League's determination to prevent Copperhead subversive acts.[4]

The progress that Yates urged was indeed well under way and continued throughout late 1862 and into early 1863. Despite the Illinois League founders' temporary pessimism, new councils were being formed throughout the upper Midwest states of Iowa, Michigan, Wisconsin, Indiana, and Ohio, as well as into some Eastern states, including the District of Columbia. It was there that the nascent Union League of America hit its first stumbling block by encountering what would be known today as a "turf war."

Formed in late October 1862, the new Washington council assumed it should be the ULA's official home and dominant chapter since Washington was also the seat of the national government. Specifically, Washington was the one place in the country where every state had some form of representation, not only within the congressional delegations, but also at the various government departments and by frequent visits from prominent state-level politicians and private citizens. The Washington council quickly acted in that leading capacity. Word then reached the Illinois founders that the Washington council was authorizing branch chapters in the East, with it as the central organization. As far as the Washington men were concerned, they were aware of no national organization or any plans to create one. To add insult to injury, the Washington council was now calling for a national convention on its own authority to discuss transference of ULA headquarters from Springfield to the nation's capital.[5]

In an attempt to circle the wagons, the Illinois Grand Council called for a convention of delegates from all Midwestern Union Leagues, which was to be held in Chicago on March 25. Considering all the past recruitment and council creation they generated in the Midwest, no upstart Eastern League was going to steal their thunder. Numbers would tell their story, such as Wisconsin delegates, who bragged that some twenty thousand Badger State men were now Union League members. Over 404 Illinois councils were represented at Chicago along with delegates from Ohio, Indiana, Michigan, Wisconsin, Iowa, and Minnesota. The convention formed a committee to determine what next steps should be taken to unify the disparate Leagues.

In order to resolve the jurisdiction questions, a two-day national ULA convention was scheduled for May 20–21 in Cleveland, Ohio, at which point a Grand National Council would be created.[6]

To the Illinois men's credit, they admitted that some manner of national coordination was imperative. The Washington council, meanwhile, had made plans to call for its own national convention in its hometown on July 4, but relented upon learning of the Cleveland proposal. In order to give every state a voice in the matter, each state council was allowed to send two at-large delegates to the forthcoming Cleveland convention, plus one additional delegate for each federal congressional seat. At the opening gavel, 171 delegates were seated representing fifteen Union states along with delegates from Tennessee, Maryland, and the District of Columbia. Only Maine was absent. The atmosphere was reported as upbeat and civil. The proceedings included numerous resolutions proclaiming unconditional loyalty to the Union, as well as rousing patriotic speeches from Postmaster General and Lincoln ally Montgomery Blair, Radical Ohio Rep. John A. Bingham, leading Philadelphian and orator David Paul Brown, abolitionist Union Gen. James Lane, among others. Ex-Ohio Rep. John Hutchins received thunderous applause when he remarked how the assembly had gathered "as Union Leaguers, and our Democratic neighbors hate a Union League as the devil hates holy water, and for the same reason."[7]

The convention's business debates regarding League consolidation were serious yet amicable, though the results in retrospect seemed almost preordained, in spite of Illinois's protest that its Grand Council should serve as the parent organization. The delegates voted that since Washington was the seat of national government, it was only logical for the city to also be the headquarters of a now-nationalized Union League of America. Christened the National Grand Council, the Washington leadership immediately started unifying any and all loyalist organizations from around the country.[8]

An important discussion point on that very topic was how to handle the new Midwestern loyalty groups who referred to themselves as Strong Bands since they also sent representatives to the convention. The Strong Band was the brainchild of *Chicago Tribune* editor Joseph Medill and attorney John Wilson, who were both Radical members of the initial Illinois Union League. Created in late 1862 to early 1863 when the Illinois movement was feared to be ebbing, this spin-off organization was headquartered in Chicago, making it strategically situated to take advantage of the "Old Northwest's" large, Radical German population. They used newspapers to advertise their mes-

January 6, 1863.   jan15-89w4

S. B.

" Union for the Sake of the Union."

THIS PATRIOTIC FRATERNITY, being now
prepared to establish its branches in Cass
County, invites to membership all loyal citizens of
whatever party or sect. Its aims are the following:

1. To preserve, through all coming time, the
unity of the United States from disintegration and
decay.

2. To secure to posterity our birthright of freedom of conscience, speech and action.

3. To afford to people of other lands an asylum,
a refuge from tyranny, oppression and political
wrong.

4. To perpetuate the memory of the founders of
this great Republic and of their worthy and immortal successors.

5. To teach, by covenants, emblems, and solemn ceremonies, the harmony, strength and beauty
of National unity.

For full information, Constitutions, By-Laws,
&c., apply for the present to John Trimble, Jr.,
D. D., Box 6295, Chicago Illinois.

Strong Band news-
paper advertise-
ment, January 5,
1863 (*Cass County,
Michigan, Republi-
can*)

sage, utilizing just the initials "S. B."—an abbreviation that antiabolition
Democrats derisively interpreted as "Sambo Brothers." Others found the
abbreviated nomenclature confusing and wondered if the group was legitimate or just a "catchpenny" movement. The group's name was borrowed
from the German word *Bunds,* which, in Napoleon's final years, "accomplished so much in uniting the discouraged peoples of Prussia, Holland, etc.,
in defense of their country." The Strong Bands' target audiences were liberal
Germans who loathed slavery, possessed a martial spirit, and desired a more
vigorous prosecution of the war than Lincoln had exhibited so far. From
Medill and Wilson's vantage, the Strong Bands possessed a vision even more
radical than the Union League. In a circular sent to prospective members
in late 1862, the group described itself as a fraternity, while its method was
"essentially military. Its nomenclature, paraphernalia, covenants, laws and
ceremonies are warlike in their structure."[9]

Though Medill and Wilson desired an alliance between the Strong Bands
and the Union League, no such tie was ever formalized. At the May 20 Cleveland convention, Wilson proposed a resolution, suggesting any loyal organization brought under the Union League umbrella should not be required

to disband their lodges, as long the group's goals were in harmony with the Union League's. When the time came for a decision, Wilson's resolution was voted down. The convention simply "did not deem it expedient to connect a military organization with the U. L. of A." This decision also displayed the pro-Lincoln Union Leagues' willingness to curb those Republicans it deemed too critical of the administration.[10]

Though miffed with the verdict, Wilson and Medill's Strong Bands continued their existence. For Democrats who learned of the Strong Bands, or "S. B.'s," they were considered just another abolition conspiratorial society. In Michigan, Democrats accused the governor of being the group's secret head. When the Democratic *Daily Ohio Statesman* learned that a Strong Band had purportedly formed in Ohio's Republican-leaning Warren County, the paper admitted it knew of no better home for such an organization. "Abolition cut throat associations are at home in that fanatic-ridden county," it opined. Despite its notable presence in the Union's Midwestern states, the Strong Bands never achieved numbers comparable to the Union Leagues, nonetheless, their influence and existence was routinely acknowledged in the "Old Northwest."[11]

Republican newspaper coverage of the Cleveland convention was favorable, though not unanimous. Few saw any issues with a "secret" organization promoting a pro-Union perspective while battling the nefarious anti-Lincoln societies such as the KGC. "The Cleveland proceedings will encourage loyal people at home and the soldier in the field," observed the *Cincinnati Gazette's* reporter. Ohio's Republican-leaning *Portage County Democrat* described the "immense gathering" as "a complete success" that the paper wholly approved of. The Republican *Daily Cleveland Herald* was a notable exception, opining that while it supported the League's principal aims, it abhorred secret organizations, believing they rendered too much power to "demagogues." At this early stage of the Union League movement, some viewed all manner of "secret societies" with suspicion, especially in light of the KGC's subversive activities.[12]

A Union League advocate, however, had a ready explanation for such doubters. Writing in Illinois's *Centralia Sentinel*, which had christened itself "The Voice of the Loyal League," the author acknowledged that whether a secret society discussion centered on the Union Leagues, the Masons, or the Sons of Temperance, the sticking point was the organization's secretive nature. "I am a loyal man. Can the League make me more so?" was a common question. Hopefully not, was the author's firm answer. Men should be loyal based on their principle and conscience and not from external influences. The League's great positive influence was in its organization, as with the church. "You say you are a Christian. Does the church make you more so?" was an analogous rhetorical question. The Union League's vital power lay in its loyalty precepts, not its secrecy. That latter issue was merely a defense against traitors and its enemies who would wish to destroy it, just as the Christian church had to meet in secret during its early days. After all, the League pointed out, men would not carry revolvers if there were no thieves. In any event, the League well knew that those who opposed it did so for far more than conscientious reasons, for men of conscience are rarely to be feared. The Union League viewed itself as a force for good that was devoid of politics, unless treason was considered politics. Members believed that any man who viewed the Union League as a partisan political organization was either a simpleton or a rogue. How could any loyal man oppose the Union League, especially if he happened to be a member of another secretive fraternal group, such as the Masons or the Odd Fellows? There was only one possible answer: That man hated the pro-Union cause, which the Union League advocated for, and was therefore not a loyal man.[13]

Back in Washington, the Republican Party's moderate faction solidified its presence within the Union League leadership with the Cleveland convention's election of James M. Edmunds as the new president of the Union League of America's Grand National Council. The White House also gained eyes and ears into the new League's hierarchy since William O. Stoddard, one of Lincoln's personal secretaries, was elected as grand secretary. Stoddard described Edmunds as a "tall, stooping, sagacious-faced, humorous-looking, tobacco-chewing, carelessly dressed, elderly man." In spite of Stoddard's unflattering depiction, a far more salient fact was that Lincoln trusted Edmunds and considered him a close personal friend. Edmunds also had an ally in Treasury Secretary Salmon P. Chase, the most radical member of Lincoln's Cabinet, who noted in his diary that Edmunds was welcome in his office "at any time."[14]

The fifty-two-year-old Edmunds was a veteran politician who had been appointed by Lincoln to serve as the commissioner of the General Land Office, a branch of the Department of the Interior that oversaw the surveying and disposition of public domain lands. It was an important and plum assignment, one that the president himself had hoped to land in an earlier

James M. Edmunds
(Zebina Moses, *The Sons of Michigan and the Michigan State Association of Washington D.C.* [Washington, D.C., 1912], frontispiece)

HONORABLE JAMES M. EDMUNDS,
COMMISSIONER OF THE GENERAL LAND OFFICE.
Elected December, 1862, as First President
of the
Sons of Michigan Society of Washington, D.C.

time. Edmunds's office epitomized Washington's inner workings, for it was a position laden with patronage and back-scratching opportunities. As one historian described it, Edmunds "applied the grease that kept the cogs of government humming."[15]

Though born in New York, where he first worked as a teacher, Edmunds moved to Michigan in 1831 to enter the world of commerce at Ypsilanti. In 1853, he moved to Detroit to join the booming lumber business. Concurrent with his business pursuits, Edmunds entered state politics in 1839, winning several terms as a Whig in the state legislature. He served as the Republican State Central Committee's chairman from 1855 to 1861 while seated as the controller of Detroit from 1859 to 1861. While in Michigan, Edmunds allied himself with Zachariah Chandler, a one-time Detroit mayor, Republican

Party cofounder, and then a Michigan senator who became a leading figure on the Congressional Committee on the Conduct of the War. By early 1861, Edmunds' and Chandler's friendship spanned several decades. When Chandler asked President-elect Lincoln to appoint Edmunds to the commissioner of the General Land Office position, Lincoln readily agreed. Now with Edmunds and Stoddard seated in their respective ULA positions, Lincoln would know of all Grand Council debates and decisions, either from Stoddard or Edmunds. Any actions the ULA took or declined to take from here on out certainly had Lincoln's tacit approval. Furthermore, the fact that the ULA's Grand National Council president could walk into the offices of three of Washington's most powerful Republican politicians at virtually any time certainly garnered significant influence for the now nationalized Union Leagues.[16]

Despite its new leading role in Union League of America affairs, Washington was little more than the seat of American government. The town was hardly an economic or cultural center on par with the larger Eastern cities that were forming their own independent Union Leagues in the spring and early summer of 1863. Furthermore, the city's social environment was noticeably different than in Philadelphia, New York, or Boston and had been throughout the antebellum era. Its 1860 population stood at 61,122, roughly one-third that of Boston, one-ninth of Philadelphia's, and one-thirteenth of New York's. Moreover, one-third of Washington's population maintained Southern political leanings, as well as "a distinctly Southern air of indolence and sloth," according to reporter Henry Villard. Ohio's Sen. John Sherman later described Civil War Washington as "an overgrown village," its 61,000 residents "badly housed, hotels and boarding houses badly kept, and all depending more or less upon low salaries, and employment by the government." Sewers and paved gutters did not exist. A British visitor remarked that the entire city seemed populated primarily by politicians and Negroes; "a howling wilderness of deserted streets running out into the country, and ending nowhere." By 1863, Washington was practically one large hospital, its perimeters filled with massive, hastily constructed buildings designed to warehouse and care for thousands of sick and injured Union soldiers.[17]

Yet despite its obvious differences from the larger Eastern cities, its politicians had developed a bond with each other that transgressed party lines. In the 1850s, for example, the men who became known as the Radical Republicans worked hard to remain socially acceptable within the Democratic majority. They often appeared at the city's important social functions, even though they were disdained by some Democrats for their perceived political fanaticism. Refusing to allow politics to intercede against manners, they were willing to set aside their beliefs in social gatherings. When they sought solace amongst themselves, Saturday nights at Dr. Gamaliel Bailey's house became the center of their social life.[18]

While Washington, D.C., was a place known for heated legislative battles, the city consisted of a close-knit political community that put forth a vibrant social and cultural existence. It was within this latter realm that the nation's politicians engaged and confronted the era's vexing questions. Once outside of Congress, various senators and congressmen often shared the same boardinghouses or hotels, irrespective of party. Meanwhile, these legislators and their families attended the same churches and philanthropic organizations. Whether elegant or small, official state functions and numerous dinner parties allowed politicians who battled by day to intermingle on a more friendly and intimate basis by night. This constant interaction of sectional rivals allowed for a more collegial atmosphere to develop within Washington society. Yet despite such sociability, the secession crisis during the 1860–61 winter strained some relationships. For example, Varina Davis, the wife of Democratic Sen. Jefferson Davis, announced in Washington following Lincoln's election in early December 1860 that she would no longer associate with Republicans.[19]

Washington's Southern culture only worsened matters after Fort Sumter. Moreover, as a onetime Democratic haven, that party's antiwar faction began to speak loudly following the Union's 1862 military reversals. "There seems to exist a great number of peace men, men who are willing to make peace on any terms 'only stop the war,'" observed Horatio Taft in early February 1863. Taft believed the Knights of the Golden Circle to be a real threat, ready to overthrow the government if they considered it necessary to bring about their peace. He was not far off the mark, for a KGC chapter (known as a "castle") had existed in Washington since before the war, all the while its members were drilling purportedly "within earshot" of the White House. As a consequence of his concern, the fifty-six-year-old Taft planned to join the new Union League. "It is intended to have the unconditional Union Men in this City and all over the Country ready (at a moment's warning, 'armed to the teeth') for any emergency." At the other end of the country, thirty-three-year-old Dustin Cheever of Clinton, Wisconsin, was writing in his diary how he had also joined a secret Union League for two principal reasons: "to support our government and . . . to put down traitors." Across the country, average men like Taft and Cheever were convinced that anti-Lincoln or pro-

Southern secret societies to be a real threat at the time and reacted accordingly. As historian Mark E. Neely Jr. concluded in his Pulitzer Prize–winning study of Northern civilians arrested for treason or disloyalty during the Civil War, no detainments of alleged Southern sympathizers were undertaken by Union authorities with anything less than grim determination and seriousness of purpose. Crass, partisan politics was rarely, if ever, a factor.[20]

Though Civil War historiography has often lumped the various Union Leagues and Loyal Leagues into one homogeneous grouping, I want to reiterate that the Eastern, aristocratic Union Leagues formed in New York and Philadelphia by each respective city's elite men, along with the Union Club in Boston, were never formally tied to the more broad-based and national Union League of America. The Philadelphia, New York, and Boston organizations all chose to retain their autonomy, though there was ample respect and cooperation across all groups.

As a result of inquiries from other cities as to what they had established, the Union League of Philadelphia illustrated that coordination by creating a two-page form letter explaining their purpose in great detail. This was to help facilitate the ULA's rapid, national expansion and served as a good example of necessary collaboration. All that needed to be filled in was the addressee's name, date, and salutation prior to mailing to any point throughout the North. A copy of the Philadelphia League's articles of association and bylaws were also included to help give the prospective new council an idea on how to organize. This method of organic growth was geared toward the rural community whose citizens routinely met in taverns, church pews, or schoolhouses for any type of public gathering. Once a location was decided, the League recommended weekly or at least monthly meetings to listen to local orators or transact "such business as may be necessary for upholding proper sentiments in the neighborhood." Showing a public, united front against the common enemy was deemed critical. The communique again stressed the League's nonpartisanship, but that it was paramount for members keep a keen watch for home front disloyalty. "Our armies can cope with the armed rebels," it asserted, "but it is for us, and it is our imperative duty, to keep watch and ward over our domestic foes." In so doing, the Union Leagues were slowly nationalizing their fight by transforming an average citizen into the federal government's local overseer.[21]

Throughout the first half of 1863, Union Leagues formed in eighteen states and were still organizing all across the North, from New England to the Pacific coast with no letup in sight. "I rejoice to hear of their success and great increase, which I read of in almost every paper," wrote a Union soldier in Tennessee in early spring. The *Washington Chronicle* sagely prophesized in April that "Before six months have transpired these Leagues will have gathered such multitudes, and will have such an over mastering influence on behalf of the perfect and entire Union of these States, that not a dog of all the miserable traitors in the land shall dare to wag his tongue."[22]

Examples abound of small towns and hamlets all across the North whose men came together to form Union League councils. Tiny New Hampshire led the way with the formation of its state council on January 2, 1863, its charter issued by the new Union League of America. When the new council held its first mass rally on February 25 at Concord, two thousand new Union League men paraded through the streets in a show of strength, shouting their support for Republican candidates along the route. At the League's council meeting, delegates decried the recent Democratic State Convention's platform, accusing the party that there was "not one word of condemnation of the rebellion in its speeches or resolutions." At that convention, Dr. Nat Batchelder, a member of the Rockingham County Democratic Committee proudly proclaimed, "I am a Rebel. . . . because I am in favor of a free government for white people and not for niggers. . . . Go home and vote the Democratic ticket." To these New Hampshire Union League men, such proclamations were worrisome at a minimum, if not outright traitorous. "We believe that the ringleaders and instigators of the proceedings are hand in glove with the 'Knights of the Golden Circle,'" they proclaimed, "and are determined to break down the present government." Just like Washington's Horatio Taft, Wisconsin's Dustin Cheever, and the countless average men who joined ULA councils throughout the North, these middle-class New Hampshire men took it for granted that the Knights' potential "fire in the rear" was a palpable threat and responded in kind.[23]

In an example of the initial controversy over the Washington council's self-appointed authority, James Edmunds wrote to Connecticut's Mark Howard on February 10 affirming that the Freestone State's Grand Council was approved by Washington. Its new charter was enclosed with the correspondence, and once the charter's blank spaces were properly filled in with the appropriate names, that information was to be mailed back to Washington. Connecticut's state elections were on the horizon and it was imperative to both Edmunds and Howard that all loyal men commit to the task at hand. "Endeavor to spread the League as rapidly as possible, and keep the G[rand]

N[ational] C[ouncil] posted in regard to your movements," Edmunds instructed. Six copies of the Union League's initiation ritual and notes on how to organize were also included.[24]

In Leavenworth, Kansas, loyal men became increasingly alarmed throughout the winter of 1862–63 at the pro-Southern talk all around them. A KGC chapter was said to exist in town and that it met routinely at the offices of the antiadministration *Evening Enquirer*. Having heard of the Leagues but not knowing who to contact, twelve loyal men gathered together in Leavenworth on February 9 to form the "Union League no. 1 of Kansas," making it the first such council west of the Mississippi River. The small town of Brownsville, Nebraska, responded by forming a Union Club and holding their first meeting on February 28. Both received their charters soon thereafter.[25]

Rhode Island soon joined the movement as well, its first council forming in Providence on February 28 with forty-four-year-old Albert Sanford as president. In one month the Providence League enrolled over 325 members throughout seven wards. Small New England towns in Massachusetts quickly followed Boston's lead by creating their own Union Leagues under the auspices of Union League of America's new national council. By the end of April, nearby Waltham had formed a Union League, "without distinction of party," that avowed its love for, and devotion to the Union. Their initial report thundered for unconditional loyalty from its citizens, claiming that "Neutrality is allied to treason; indifference becomes a crime; and whoever is not with us is against us." Such calls garnered the full support of Massachusetts's Gov. John A. Andrew.[26]

In early March, the men of Chester in southeastern Pennsylvania gathered to form a League, dedicated to the Union's preservation, as did the men of York, Pennsylvania, on April 20. In northeastern Pennsylvania, the editor of the *Pittston Gazette* urged his readers to "get up Union Leagues." In so doing, they would "join men of different parties who are throwing down old political creeds for the purpose of putting down the rebellion." By June, 180 councils had formed in the Keystone State. Even the relatively small state of Delaware was taking steps. On March 19, the Wilmington League was formed to generate the proper form of patriotism and fraternal feelings. Word of the Leagues quickly spread like wildfire to the Western states and territories as well. Union Leagues formed in Manhattan, Kansas, with the open invitation that all unconditional Union men may join to combat those "whose pro-slavery instincts lead them to justify assaults upon the Government but whose circumstances or want of manhood forbid the overt act."

In Nemaha County, Nebraska, men "came in procession, with banners and martial music, making a caravan about a mile in length" to form a League on May 2. Despite the nonpartisanship claim, Republican operatives were delighted with Iowa's Union League progress. In mid-March, Davenport's *Der Demokrat* rallied its German-language readers to the Union League, proclaiming the new society as "a political and legal undertaking that every free man should support." Less than a month later after winning state elections, one Republican organizer wrote to Iowa's Gov. Samuel Kirkwood exclaiming, "Our *Union* organization is perfect and we have good reason to be proud of the result of our first effort." Fearing the Copperhead threat, Iowa Union League members gathered later that summer in southeastern Henry County with plans to take matters to the next step of forming a military home guard and preparing a list of disloyal local Copperheads. And far to the north in Burnett, Wisconsin, fifty-three men from that small town gathered on March 7 to form a Union League. By late June, that far-off state boasted at least sixty-two councils.[27]

Newspapers and the telegraph quickly brought word of the new Union Leagues into the far West, prompting loyal Union men to organize just as the Eastern men were doing. A gold boom town in the Nevada territory christened Virginia City did likewise in the summer of 1863 and by the year's end,

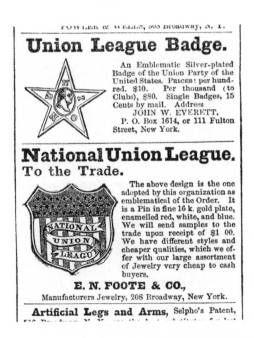

Union League of America badges, June 1863 (*Harper's Weekly*)

that town and its neighbor Gold Hill boasted a combined membership totaling 3,700. The new state of Oregon followed along with Gov. Addison Gibbs
helping to form its first council in December at Portland. Union League
lodges were soon created throughout the state. On October 14, the register
of the land office at Vermillion, in the Dakota Territory, reported to Lincoln,
"Thank God, by the exertions of the Union Leagues, we have been able to
Carry Both Houses of our Legislature."[28]

Even in far-flung California, Union Leagues were being created following
a March 15 incident when Union sailors and customs officials uncovered an
unfolding pro-Confederate plot to capture gold-carrying U.S. steamers in
Sacramento harbor. Following the affair, Gen. George Wright, in command
of the Union Army's Department of the Pacific, reported to Washington on
April 20 how "Great Union Leagues are everywhere forming, composed of
men sworn to uphold the Government and maintain the Union." In fact, the
California Grand Council for the Union League of America had officially organized only one week earlier. In his dispatch, Wright acknowledged that he
thoroughly approved and aided in the creation of the Union Leagues. Less
than two months later, Gen. L. H. Allen noted that he felt the majority of
California's organized militia would be comprised of Union League men.
Both men viewed this quasi-marriage of the federal government's military
arm with these civilian organizations as a "real strength" and would go a long
way to quieting Rebel sympathizers in California. Those Southern supporters
were feared to number in the tens of thousands. When California's twenty-
three-man Grand Council held its first annual meeting in San Francisco on
August 4, 1863, it reported that in just four months, over one hundred councils had formed within the state comprising some twenty thousand members. In addition, applications to form subordinate councils had already been
made in Oregon and the Washington and Nevada territories. For the remainder of the war, the very real possibility of the national or a state government
aligning itself with an "approved" paramilitary civilian organization to act in
concert with the federal army was viewed with alarm by Democrats.[29]

Union men in Baltimore formed a new "Union Club" similar to that of
Boston's in the spring of 1863 and distinct from the city's earlier 1862 league.
Like its Northern neighbor, the descriptive term "League" was deemed too
militant and political, hence the less threatening word "Club." Like the larger
Eastern cities with recently formed Union Leagues, Baltimore's overall Union
sentiment was often hidden while Southern sympathies seemed overt. Moreover, unlike Pennsylvania, New York, and Massachusetts, Maryland was a

"neutral" border state where slavery was still legal. In fact, Baltimore had its own KGC castle in operation by early 1859 to help protect that status, a scenario that was acknowledged and ridiculed simultaneously by Baltimore's pro-Southern *Daily Exchange*. Baltimore's sympathies were manifested by the KGC-led, pro-Confederate mob that attacked Massachusetts soldiers on April 19, 1861, who were merely passing through the city on their way to defend Washington. "There is no city in the Union in which domestic disturbances have been more frequent or carried to more fatal extremes, from 1812 to the present day," warned Union Gen. John Dix in September 1862 following his reassignment from Baltimore to Virginia. "Although the great body of the people are eminently distinguished for their moral virtues," Dix wrote, "Baltimore has always contained a mass of inflammable material."[30]

William Wilkins Glenn was one of the Baltimore men accused of being most eager to strike the match. As the thirty-eight-year-old proprietor of the *Daily Exchange*, a strong anti-Lincoln sheet, Glenn's incendiary columns were deemed so treasonous that he was imprisoned in a Fort McHenry jail cell from September 14 to December 2, 1861. Following his release, Glenn traveled to New York in the fall of 1862 to meet with leading Democrat Samuel L. M. Barlow and his associates, seeking some measure of support and backing from the New York Democrats. Though Barlow was an attorney by profession and a wealthy one at that, he was also the chief financial backer for the intensely Democratic *New York World*.[31]

Barlow and the others listened politely, but eventually refused Glenn's request, as they failed to comprehend just how earnest Southerners were. Glenn was flabbergasted that these men believed the South would readily return to the Union if only offered the right guarantees. In any event, New York contended with its own problems and could not come to Maryland's aid, a border state Barlow viewed with suspicion. "What we say here about liberty, is patriotism," declared Barlow. "When you say it there it is treason." An amazing statement from a leading Democrat that spoke volumes as to just how successful ongoing Republican–Union League efforts were to paint the entire Democracy with the broad brush of treason. "I came to the conclusion he was the most overrated man I ever met," Glenn later wrote, convinced that although Barlow may have been a good attorney and businessman, he was incapable of understanding the true depth of the nation's crisis. Glenn's frustration with Barlow spoke to *the* fundamental weakness within the Democratic Party's peace wing: The inability to come up with a concrete, reunification solution acceptable to *both* regions.[32]

Nothing changed with the start of 1863. Glenn recalled that while there were few social events over the 1862–63 winter, Baltimore's "society" sympathized almost entirely with the South. "The Union Shriekers who knew they would not be allowed to share in the amusements of the southerners gave information that the parties . . . were in fact treasonable gatherings," grumbled Glenn. Such complaints were confirmed by Frenchman Jérôme Napoleon Bonaparte in a January 1863 letter to his son. "In Baltimore, the disloyal are the most efficient, and although numerically fewer, they have managed to get & keep possession of the clubs, the society, and all the fashionable churches," complained Bonaparte. Even as the war was drawing to a close, pro-Southern Baltimoreans remained as intractable as ever. "Be very careful about admitting that you are a Unionist in Baltimore," warned a tolerant, Southern-sympathizing woman to a European visitor, since "people won't like it. . . . It will close all doors to you."[33]

A fifty-seven-year-old nephew of the famous French emperor, Jérôme Napoleon Bonaparte, held a strong affection for his adopted city and country. In early March, he decided to form a club "for Union people only," having concluded that the town in general and its oldest social organization in particular, the prestigious Maryland Club, were becoming far too pro-Southern in its membership and positions. By mid-May, over two hundred men joined what was christened the Union Club of Baltimore. Like its larger Eastern predecessors, loyalty to the government and devotion to the Union cause were paramount. Unlike the Union Leagues, however, its constitution forbade acting upon any political matter—a clear allusion to the fact that this was to be a patriotic organization only and not one that focused on constitutional or political matters.[34]

That was an important qualifier, for Baltimore and its unconcealed Southern leanings had attracted the Union military's attention, in particular Maj. Gen. Robert Schenck, who commanded the army's Middle Department VIII Corps from his Baltimore headquarters. Around the same time in early March that Bonaparte was contemplating his new Baltimore Union Club, Schenck learned of a Philadelphia bookseller whose store was stocked with portraits of Confederate generals, pro-Southern sheet music, and other Rebel literature. The Union Leagues certainly possessed no corner on propaganda as the Confederates also utilized it whenever possible, such as a children's mathematics textbook, which asked the question, "If one Confederate soldier can whip seven Yankees, how many soldiers can whip 49 Yankees?" Schenck ordered the material seized with further instructions requiring the bookseller to sign a parole stating he would not sell such "treasonous" material again. If the shopkeeper was recalcitrant in any manner, he was to be arrested and sent by the first available train to Fort McHenry in Baltimore's harbor, where he would be given ample time to silently reevaluate his actions. Schenck then sent a copy of his orders as a courtesy to Judge John I. C. Hare, who was also a cofounder of Philadelphia's Union League. Maintaining a unified nation was Schenck's primary concern, not civil liberties or the Constitution's first amendment free speech rights.[35]

With the Union's very survival at stake, many Northerners viewed such newspaper or bookstore suppression and the attendant "free speech" concerns as a lesser worry than having the country literally torn apart. Pennsylvania jurist Daniel Agnew addressed this issue in a Union League of Philadelphia pamphlet titled *Our National Constitution: Its Adaptation to a State of War or Insurrection*. "Must the government be ever thus exposed to the machinations of secret sympathy and treason?" Agnew asked rhetorically. His firm answer was no, that the government must possess "a power to muzzle the press when it runs mad; and to arrest and confine men, when they exhibit their traitorous proclivities. It is a question of life and death to the nation." George Strong was not so sure, but he was certain about the South's secession. "I dare say [the suppression] is 'unconstitutional,'" wrote Strong, "but I know of nothing so unconstitutional as armed rebellion against the Constitution." For Union League men like Agnew, Hare, and Strong, the bookseller and Copperhead presses had clearly crossed the line as to what constituted allowable behavior and speech. If such suppression helped put down the rebellion, then "I acquiesce in their suppression and exclusion as the lesser of two 'unconstitutional' alternatives," Strong rationalized. Loyalty and cohesiveness were paramount; with the nation's very survival at stake, the ends indeed justified the means.[36]

Following that matter, Bonaparte learned that the Maryland Club had been shut down by Schenck on June 27 due to its alleged Confederate sympathies in a suppressive action consistent with the prior bookstore affair. In the case of Baltimore's new Union Club, however, Schenck granted it permission to open, "satisfactory evidence having been furnished" that the Club was trustworthy and would not knowingly admit anyone whose loyalties were in doubt.[37]

Only in Michigan in the summer of 1863 did the Union Leagues suffer an expansion setback and that was merely temporary. Union Gen. Orlando Willcox, in command of the District of Indiana and Michigan, issued an independent order on June 30 banning all manner of secret societies within his territory. Believing that "none but the enemies of their country ever need disguises," Willcox's order was an attempt to play it down the middle, though he primarily aimed at the anti-Lincoln groups such as the KGC who were fomenting antidraft dissent in the upper Midwest. Willcox spoke at a war rally that night, yet he was clearly frustrated by the entire issue. "Nothing seems so sickening as to have to urge men to defend their own country," he wrote the next day. The Union Leagues would have surely concurred.[38]

By the time of its fall 1863 meeting, Michigan's Union League state council was urging its subordinate councils to continue their loyal work as far as possible, following the national Grand Council's determination that the Leagues were not the type of secret society Willcox had in mind. When a secret Union League council was said to have formed in Monroe during August, Democrats pointed out that Willcox's edict was apparently to be disregarded.[39]

It turned out that in the fall of 1863, southeast Michigan had reason to fear Rebel–Copperhead plots against it. The state's provost marshal general, Lt. Col. Bennett Hill, had constantly received reports from his intelligence officers and spies of plots against Great Lakes towns or the Johnson's Island prisoner of war camp on Lake Erie near Sandusky, Ohio, most of which he considered fantastical. In early November, however, Hill changed his tune due to the consistent intelligence gleaned by his men. "That some project of magnitude is in contemplation I feel very certain," Hill telegraphed to Washington on November 9, with the further note that he felt there were some two thousand Rebel agents and "sympathizers" in Canada. Two days later, Britain's minister to the United States put forth an identical warning as to how pro-Southern sympathizers lurking in Canada were plotting to seize Lake Erie steamers and then overwhelm the guards on the Johnson's Island prisoner of war camp. From there the freed Confederate prisoners could proceed to attack Buffalo and other Great Lakes cities. Secretary of War Edwin Stanton immediately telegraphed all Great Lakes governors and lakefront city mayors with the new intelligence and to be fully aware. With their plot exposed, the pro-Southern agents were forced to abandon their plans.[40]

The enhanced Union League presence in Michigan coupled with the reality of the aborted November raid led to a massive Union League rally in Detroit on December 17 that attracted over one thousand people. Radical Michigan Gov. Austin Blair reminded the throng that "Satan was the first rebel and Pharaoh was the first Copperhead," inferring that the fight to keep Old Glory "immortal" would be a long one. More League councils were formed, including one in the small Michigan village of Lexington on December 21. The membership roll for the small village of Brighton in Livingston County appeared to contain the name of every businessman and substantial farmer. By the end of 1863, Michigan's membership stood at 35,793. Nonetheless, there was still some concern that League vigilance was weak in the state due to Willcox's earlier, though now abandoned decree, coupled with a perceived lack of disloyal sentiment. In spite of the planned Great Lakes raid in November, most Michiganders believed the bulk of Copperhead disaffection was located in the southernmost counties of Indiana and Illinois, far away from the Michigan hinterland.[41]

Despite the earlier difficulties, with two Radical Republican senators and a Radical Republican governor in office, Michigan still stood solidly in the Republican fold, though its largest city, Detroit, did harbor significant Democratic sentiment. Its leading Democratic organ, the *Detroit Free Press*, sarcastically referred to the Union League as "a secret council of fumigators." In a speech four months later to the Union League council located in the small Michigan town of Romeo, twenty-five-year-old John Potter urged his brother members to dismiss such acrimony and to view their Union League as a type of school. "These loyal organizations are fast becoming one of the greatest powers in America," stressed Potter, and by taking advantage of the Union League's instruction, his fellow members would learn how to do their duty on the side of liberty. Repeating that theme, the Michigan Union League's state council urged that "All young men should be brought within the influence of the organization, before their opinions become fixed in the wrong direction.[42]

Unlike most of Michigan, some of those Hoosier or Prairie State towns were indeed significantly Copperhead in their outlook. In southwestern Indiana's Sullivan County, a heartland of Copperhead sympathy, James Thomas admitted to his father that "all of our relatives here are decided Copperheads and the idea of a Northwest Confederacy is freely talked of." From Thomas's Democratic perspective, the Union League was "an abolition organization" that was "armed by the administration and are faithfully carrying out the behests of their masters" by arresting Democrats.[43]

Though the leaders of Michigan's Union Leagues may have expressed concern over the commitment level in their state, General Willcox's concerns over secret society activity need not have applied to the Midwestern Union Leagues in general by the fall of 1863. The Union Clubs in the slave border states of Missouri and Kentucky formed in 1860–61 employed a strong element of secrecy in their membership and activities for their own physical safety. While the anti-Lincoln "secret societies" also maintained a strong secretive stance—believing that Democrats were in danger from League thuggery—the Eastern Union Leagues created in early 1863 were not as overt with their degree of secrecy, nor did they need to be. Despite their mysterious initiation rituals, which appealed to the male initiate's martial enthusiasm and desire for camaraderie, much of the proceedings were openly published in the various local papers to the chagrin of some members. Future U.S. president Rutherford B. Hayes, himself a Union League member, later explained to a Quaker friend, who scolded him for being associated with such a secret group that the League operated more like a family than an open organization. Some matters were simply personal or private, and should stay within the family's "four walls" rather than be made available for public consumption. "We do not tell who is rejected, or why he is rejected, or what cause it is that rejects him. That is a confidential matter," explained Hayes. Continuing his clarification, Hayes noted, "It is not a secret society; and yet if there are any gentlemen present who propose to put an account of our proceedings of tonight into the newspapers, I hope they will stop when they come to what I am saying. Leave that out—regard that as confidential." The Michigan Union League's State Grand Council reiterated this belief, advising that while it was not necessary to conceal a council's presence within any community, the League's actions and member names should stay private. Union Gen. Green B. Raum later recalled a similar lack of secrecy. After joining an Illinois Union League council while at home recuperating from battlefield injury, Green remembered that while the council's proceedings were private, the members gathered freely in public prior to the meeting. In fact, Raum stressed, "the plan adopted was to let it be known throughout the county who the members were. . . . The natural result of this policy was to bring together in this organization the friends of the Union."[44]

Some soldiers even went so far as to form Union League lodges in the field, having been empowered to do so when home on leave. "Tonight we initiated six new members," wrote Lt. Elisha H. Rhodes of the 2nd Rhode Island Infantry of one late-war field ceremony, recording how his hut was appropriately decorated with flags, sashes, and crossed swords suspended from the walls. "It made us feel a little solemn as the sound of the guns on our right was borne to our ears." No matter how inspiring the rituals back home may have been, they were not "half so impressive as when performed almost within range of hostile guns," recalled another Rhode Islander. Chaplains also took the initiative, such as Rev. Francis Springs, who organized a council with thirteen initial members at Union-held Fort Smith, Arkansas, in late 1863, under the authority of the Springfield, Illinois, League council. Springs understood the gravity of his act, writing how "such an association in this locality at any time previous to the occupation of the place by the Federal army, would have sent its originator & all of its abettors to the gallows." The movement had also spread to Northern parole camps for Union soldiers who were awaiting their formal exchange. At Missouri's Benton Barracks, Allen Geer of the 20th Illinois Infantry was one of approximately twenty soldiers initiated into a Union League in late July 1863. By the end of year, the Union League movement had entrenched itself across the North.[45]

Chapter 9

"We Are Not a Partisan, Yet We *Are* a Political Organization"

Women Enter the Fray as Midwest Dissent Boils Over

As the Union League of America movement spread throughout the country, the elite Philadelphia Union League's members decided to actively engage their organization "as an auxiliary force to the army and navy in the work of national unification." Seeking to show that its talk of loyalty and patriotism was not mere bluster, the Philadelphia League created public service organizations that were initially staffed by its members. These included a Soldiers' Claim and Pension Agency that offered legal and pension claims services to returning soldiers while another committee was formed to oversee the recruitment of colored troops. The League also offered its assistance to the Sanitary Commission and the Christian Commission. Nor was the church forgotten. Those clergymen who put forth loyal principles from their pulpits were harmoniously granted any privileges the Union League was able to offer. Another new committee wrote to Lincoln on May 5 urging that in conjunction with the creation of the new National Invalid Corps, preferential government employment opportunities should be awarded to those competent and deserving men who were honorably discharged from the military due to wounds, illness, or disabilities.[1]

In spite of these efforts, the Philadelphia League felt something more had to be done—meaningful acts with direct impact on the war effort, especially in light of repeated Democratic catcalls branding the Union League as all fluff and feathers. The League's answer was to raise and enlist a brigade (three regiments) of soldiers on its own, based on the call from Gov. Andrew Curtin for ninety-day men to help repel the Confederate's impending invasion of

Pennsylvania. On June 26, 1863, the Union League of Philadelphia took the initial steps toward their goal by advertising its intent in the local papers. Recruiting posters were created and placed by League men all over Philadelphia. To pay for all of this, League members raised $80,000 from within their wealthy membership. By July 6, one full regiment was already in place and ready to depart for the Pennsylvania state capital at Harrisburg. A second regiment was called for, then a third, and for good measure, five cavalry companies were also recruited and equipped. By year's end, the Union League Brigade was outfitted and in the field for the national government.[2]

In the spirit of the Union League of Philadelphia's progressive nature, its members also considered it crucial for the club to recruit and outfit a black regiment. After all, it was no secret that George Washington utilized free black men as soldiers in his revolutionary army, many even earning the general's praise. Some owners even manumitted their slaves so they might serve in Washington's ranks. Decades later, Gen. Andrew Jackson called for and received the aid of freedmen at the 1815 battle of New Orleans. Much had changed since then. While the large Eastern Union Leagues and their Radical Republican allies may have viewed recruiting black men into colored regiments as necessary and noble, others viewed it as reprehensible, for such work implied black soldiers possessed a level of equality with white soldiers few would admit to.

Black men had been allowed to serve in the Union Army since the summer of 1862, albeit reluctantly, and then only as teamsters, cooks, or as laborers building fortifications. By spring 1863, however, black men were granted the right to serve as volunteer soldiers in their own "colored" regiments since the white volunteer supply was not meeting the demand. Though not fully authorized by the federal government, the first all-black regiment was the 1st Kansas Colored Infantry, formed in fall 1862. The famed 54th Massachusetts Infantry followed later in the spring of 1863. After the Philadelphia men learned that over eleven hundred black Pennsylvanians had already been recruited for regiments in other states, the Union League formed their sixty-man Supervisory Committee for the Recruitment of Colored Troops.[3]

The Philadelphia League went about this task with the same fervor it attached to its original loyalty mission six months prior. They helped establish Camp William Penn as a training ground, eight miles north of Philadelphia and well out of sight of most citizens. The camp became the first and largest Union Army facility to train African American recruits during the Civil War. Concurrently, subscriptions for the venture were solicited by League members. The Supervisory Committee soon raised over $33,000 for the regiments' training and outfitting; by the end of September three regiments, designated the 3rd, 6th, and 8th United States Colored Troops, were ready for duty.[4]

Despite protests from many civic leaders, the League organized a parade for October 3 that would take the 6th USCT and a battalion from the 8th down Philadelphia's streets. The march was designed to showcase the colored regiments' martial ability and, therefore, refute long-held racist beliefs. This type of public display had long been the League's real aim. The city initially wanted nothing to do with the spectacle of black men carrying loaded muskets. As a compromise, officers were eventually allowed to carry a loaded sidearm; however, the 6th marched with empty muskets while the 8th carried no weaponry at all. There was to be no police escort, nevertheless, no clashes ensued along the parade route that was packed with both exultant and hostile spectators. "Moral bravery, quiet confidence in a just cause, loyalty and freedom, had triumphed completely in the face of a noisy opposition," a League historian later wrote.[5]

The reformist mindset that led Philadelphia's Union League members to expand their efforts on behalf of the war effort and black men in the spring of 1863 also took hold in the hearts of many Northern women. Like practically all political activities of the era, however, the Union Leagues were created by men as a male-only domain. Other than teaching or working as a seamstress, few vocational pursuits were deemed appropriate for antebellum women due to the era's social culture. Once the Civil War came, working-class women moved into more traditionally male spaces, such as retail or working in munitions factories, due to the market's increased labor demands or for needed income since their husbands were away at the front.[6]

With the Union League movement's growth apparent by spring 1863, and in a time when women wished to contribute to the war effort, female versions of the Union Leagues started to appear. What became known as Ladies' Union Leagues were progressive women's attempt to mirror the patriotic impulses inherent in the still forming, male-controlled Union Leagues. They were "a kind of side League, so to speak, with a distinct ritual and having only the alarm and distress signals in common with the U.L.A.," explained the Kansas Grand Council to two of its male members who had inquired about the new female-oriented Leagues.[7]

In many instances, these Ladies' Union Leagues were formed by middle- and upper-middle-class women who wanted to take a proactive, pro-Union role in the war beyond the traditional tasks of folding bandages or darning socks. Singing patriotic songs and prayer were an integral part of their meetings. The surviving papers of a Wisconsin Ladies' Union League show that writing letters to government agencies in order to secure relief for needy soldiers and their families, as well as gathering and donating food to hospitals for Wisconsin soldiers, provided two additional avenues of public work. Some two hundred Wisconsin families who faced destitution because their fathers and husbands were away at the front were kept clothed and fed by these Madison women. Des Moines, Iowa, was no different for their newly formed Ladies' League immediately alleviated the suffering of nineteen families who were in dire want from lack of food and heating fuels. The ladies of Marine Mills, Minnesota, opted to raise funds for the Sanitary Commission or, on occasion, used the money to buy cotton with which they made clothes for their soldiers.[8]

The experience of Mrs. Elvira Scott, a refined Missouri woman with Southern sympathies, demonstrated both the Southern disdain toward the Leagues and the pervasive lack of class consciousness within the female Leagues. On May 2, 1863, Scott went to St. Louis's Mercantile Library Hall to witness the formation of a Ladies' Union League that featured the full gamut of patriotic songs and speeches. She described a scene consisting of only a few men but close to fifteen hundred women, who "applauded boisterously, clapping their hands & stamping like men at a political meeting. They did not strike me as the elite of the city nor as particularly refined or elegant." An accurate sentiment, for one newspaper report described the crowd as "embracing all classes and conditions," which mirrored the male-focused Midwestern Union Leagues where social status was not an issue as with the aristocratic Leagues in Philadelphia, New York, and Boston. The speeches, according to Scott, were all in the same vein. They "heaped abuse upon the Southern people, the owners of Negroes particularly, until they culminated in the remark that they were fast mustering in, drilling, & arming Negro regiments to keep the South in subjection . . . without losing the lives of valuable white men who were not suited to the climate." Scott admitted in her diary how she could soon stand no more and quickly exited the building into the street, "with every vein throbbing with excitement & indignation."[9]

As word of the Ladies' Leagues spread, newspapers across the country reported favorably on the formation of such groups as in Martinsburg, Ohio; Madison, Wisconsin; in Springfield and Salisbury, Illinois, while urging other towns to do likewise. "The ladies of Cumberland would do well to take this matter into consideration," advised western Maryland's *Civilian & Telegraph.* "In a Loyal League, they could do much to sustain the government, and encourage the soldiers in the field." Loyal women observed what their fathers, husbands, sons, and brothers were creating within their male Union Leagues and responded in kind.[10]

As with the male Union Leagues, emulating loyalty pronouncements toward the government while decrying treason was fundamental to the Ladies' Leagues. They continued the home front war in areas where men did not, such as occasionally doling out blows to Democratic women or rooting out disloyalty in the retail marketplace. This latter effort was illustrated by the women of Bridgeport, Connecticut, who had formed a Loyal League in April 1863. Like their male Union League counterparts, they pledged "an unwavering support of the government in its efforts to suppress the rebellion" without qualifiers. Some predictable local controversy was generated by their resolution vowing to give their business only to those local merchants known to be truly loyal and patriotic while encouraging others to do likewise. One guest speaker stated how he had heard intimated in town that the Bridgeport women intended "to establish an officious and offensive system of espionage" within stores and families in order to ascertain patriotic sentiments. However, he dismissed such concerns, believing the League women would be culpable to trade with someone known to be a traitor to their country. Such a resolution and determination was in keeping with Union League tactics discussed earlier.[11]

While the Ladies' Union Leagues were for the most part forming within Midwestern towns and counties, another female-led organization was being created in the East at a national level. Headed by Elizabeth Cady Stanton and Susan B. Anthony, the Women's National Loyal League overtly advertised itself via its name as a way for the nation's women to show support and loyalty to the Union government, making it the first national women's political organization in the United States. After being repeatedly frustrated by accusations that Northern women collectively showed little interest in the war compared to Southern women, Stanton and Anthony replied by claiming Southern women knew all too well what their sons were fighting for, while Northern women generally did not. It was their new League's intention to show Northern women the true blessings of patriotic liberty.[12]

Stanton and Anthony were also ardent abolitionists and early women's rights advocates. Despite the patriotic tone of their new organization's name, championing these two issues was their new League's fundamental mission.

Elizabeth Cady Stanton (*seated*), and Susan B. Anthony (*standing*) between 1880 and 1902. (Library of Congress Prints and Photographs Division)

Their women's rights activism, abolishing slavery, and giving full equal rights to blacks manifested itself within the Women's National Loyal League's letters and circulars. Their antislavery message was a more strident one than Lincoln's Emancipation Proclamation seemed to offer for, as one activist complained, the president's decree was "more than I feared, but much less than I hoped."[13]

When women from all over the country met in New York on May 14, 1863, for the new Women's National Loyal League's first formal convention, the surface atmosphere was one of cooperation and purpose. Many delegates were excited at the opportunity for women to lend their patriotic support to the war effort. Letters from women in every Northern state, except Rhode Island, were shown pledging support. Before long, however, the convention's real purpose, as far as its founders were concerned, came to the fore. All seven resolutions put forth by the Business Committee pertained in some manner to the slavery issue while the fifth also pertained to women's rights; a resolution proclaiming loyalty toward the Union cause was noticeably absent. One speaker after another expounded on what she believed the

League's real purpose should be. When Susan B. Anthony exclaimed, "the hour is fully come, when woman shall no longer be the passive recipient of whatever morals and religion the trade and politics may decree," she received thunderous applause.[14]

The Women's National Loyal League's overt convention focus on abolition and women's rights stirred up noticeable internal controversy. Mrs. J. W. Hoyt of Wisconsin remarked how it seemed like she was present at an antislavery convention and not one that was supposed to be dedicated to devising the best ways in which women could assist the government in its current struggle against treason. In a lengthier speech later that day, Hoyt stressed that while she stood against any type of retrograde movement on women's rights, she was also apprehensive about dragging anything into the resolutions that was considered "obnoxious" to a good portion of the country. "The women of the loyal North were invited here to meet in convention the loyal ladies of New York," she argued, "not to hold a Temperance meeting, not to hold an anti-slavery meeting, not to hold a Woman's Rights convention, but to meet here to consult as to the best practical way for the advancement of the loyal cause."[15]

The notion of agitating against slavery—coupled with a desire for women to take a more active role in the political world—was simply not viewed favorably by all women of the era, or certainly all men for that matter. When David McKinney of the 77th Illinois learned from his sister of a new Ladies' Union League forming in Peoria, he warned her against such groups: "I don't approve & won't endorse the idea that women should form associations or leagues for the purpose of discussing the great issues of the day and make themselves notorious by their 'noisy babblings,'" he cautioned, "but I *do think* that by their *silent, united,* and *harmonious* efforts within sending material aid to the soldiers in the field . . . they are not going beyond their proper sphere. . . ." The colonel of the 77th, David Grier, penned a letter to his Peoria fiancé that was every bit as critical of the new Ladies' League as McKinney's. Such matters were better left to men, Grier argued, and furthermore, if women attended properly to their home duties, there would be little time left for public societies. Grier was pleased to read that his fiancé had decided not to join. "All such associations in my opinion are *Humbugs,*" he concluded. Anthony and Stanton acknowledged these obstacles, admitting that while women had always been heartily agreeable to charitable work that alleviated suffering, it was a challenge to arouse women to labor for a controversial idea or principle.[16]

The convention's vote tallies showed all seven resolutions passed unanimously except for the controversial fifth, which still passed with a large majority. Some speakers suggested that the matter of equal rights for women be deleted from the resolution, not due to any disagreement with the concept, but because it created controversy and distracted from the matters at hand.[17]

These abolition and women's rights conflicts within the Women's National Loyal League illustrated why the Ladies' Union Leagues met with little resistance when their focus was solely on patriotism and soldiers' aid. "This

A FIT FOR THE "LADIES' LEAGUE."

Mr. Lincoln, (to Mrs. Mannikins, of the "Business Committee"). "Well, ma'am, as the articles you wear don't seem to be large enough for you, I have the honor to present you, by the advice of Mrs. Lincoln, with a pair of mine. They may seem rather large; but, at the rate at which you are progressing, you'll fill them very well by and by!"

A Fit for the "Ladies' League" (*Vanity Fair,* May 30, 1863)

is no women's rights institution, or anything of the kind, gotten up by those aspiring to occupy the place of the sterner sex," explained a Ladies' Union League organizer in Iowa after learning about the Women's National Loyal League. "There is a sphere in which woman can act," therefore "It is our design to throw our whole, *our united influence, in favor of the Union*." For that reason, while some of the more zealous (and Eastern) abolitionist women within the new Woman's Loyal National League sought to have a more vocal antislavery position, most, especially those in the Western states, sought a more nonpartisan Union-oriented message. Most felt more comfortable with a statement offering unqualified loyalty to the administration and its military efforts rather than one that advanced a particular political agenda.[18]

With regard to furthering that message, New York's Loyal Publication Society also weighed in, showing its "brotherly" support for the new women's movement by publishing *A Few Words in Behalf of the Loyal Women of the United States by One of Their Own* in the summer of 1863. Written by sixty-two-year-old Caroline M. Kirkland, a noted American writer, the piece refuted Northern women's purported lack of patriotic zeal when compared to Southern women. "The feelings of Northern women are rather deep than violent," explained Kirkland. "Their sense of duty is a quiet and constant rather than a headlong or impetuous impulse." Nonetheless, the essay's subtle undercurrent suggested a more overt loyalty from Northern women would be a good thing.[19]

As was the case with the men who created the broad-based Union League of America, which was a separate association from the independent Union Leagues in Philadelphia and New York, the Midwestern Ladies' Union Leagues were not initially linked with Anthony and Stanton's Women's National Loyal League, though once the former learned of the latter, a desire to join forces often resulted. By the summer of 1863, Anthony and Stanton were urging women across the North to initiate auxiliary leagues in their respective towns and to stay in constant correspondence with the central New York organization as a means of supporting the war effort, which invariably meant an end to slavery. Whether a female-led patriotic group referred to itself as a Ladies' Union League or a Women's Loyal League, both should be viewed as part of the greater Union League patriotic movement that was gaining steam in the first half of 1863.[20]

While new Union Leagues, Loyal Leagues, and Ladies' Union Leagues were blossoming across the country, the original Midwestern Leagues and Clubs begun in the fall and early winter of 1862 continued to flourish throughout 1863. The bitter fall 1862 election results and the ongoing fear of KGC activity served as a clarion call for Republicans. The Midwestern Leagues, however, did more than just promote patriotism and battle their enemies with pen and paper. When the Illinois League's Grand Secretary, George Harlow, received an appeal just prior to the July 3 fall of Vicksburg claiming Union troops near the front were in dire need of various sanitary supplies, Harlow sent out appeals to every Illinois council. The effect, Harlow later wrote, was "magical." The "League Boys," as he called them, responded to the call and within six to eight weeks, over $25,000 was raised along with scores of supplies.[21]

At home, social and commercial ostracism against the alleged disloyal continued. Maj. Gen. Robert H. Milroy joined the Washington, D.C., League during a period of personal inactivity and while there, initiated new resolutions proclaiming, "it is the duty of every loyal man to by any means possible, pecuniary & social, to assist in driving these disloyal persons from our midst." To add additional weight, "every member of this league is prohibited from patronizing, associating with, or in any way encouraging any man or woman of known disloyalty in his or her trade, profession, or occupation."[22]

Nor were tactics limited to personal or business interactions. On the Midwestern home front, Union League members continued to view their organization not merely as a patriotic society, but also as an armed home guard or militia unit to be used for defense as necessary. Those twin goals occasionally merged as older home guard members used the unit as a recruiting tool to encourage the patriotic spirit within younger men. Still, while promoting loyalty and patriotism was the Union Leagues' cornerstone purpose, the need for loyal men to protect their homes against what they saw as a violent Copperhead threat was still a growing concern as already evidenced by anti-draft rioting, malicious property vandalism, and physical threat against pro-Lincoln men. In late August, Iowa's Gov. Samuel Kirkwood admitted that in order to assist provost marshals with their draft duties, he provided arms to Iowa's Union League men so they could keep down mobs and maintain order. Turning the smaller Union Leagues into a paramilitary arm of the Republican Party is exactly what a Pennsylvania Democrat had feared when he wrote: "I believe that something is secretly on foot to thin out the ranks of the Democratic Party. . . . that leagues of men calling themselves Union Leagues will be formed out of the Abolition party, and before we look around home guards will be formed under the authority of the general government, and composed of these men exclusively." Unlike their aristocratic Union League colleagues from the East's big cities, League members throughout the Midwest were working men situated far from rich wood-paneled parlors, brandy snifters, and leather chairs. The threats they faced were not necessarily the same as those in the Philadelphia or New York.[23]

This fear in the lower Midwest of armed revolt against Republican state authority by Copperhead–KGC members that had manifested itself in the second half of 1862 was still palpable as 1863 dawned and only increased as winter led into spring. On January 2, Indiana's Gov. Oliver P. Morton privately expressed his anxiety to his friend and confidant Calvin Fletcher that a conspiracy was afoot to take Indiana out of the Union by force. Fletcher was a sixty-five-year-old banker and civic leader who had lived most of his life near Indianapolis. Though it was years since Fletcher held elective office, he was nevertheless a devoted Republican who kept abreast of local politics. He noted in his diary how he heard all the stories about "extensive secret societies" being formed to topple the Union. As far as Fletcher was concerned, it was imperative for loyal Union men to arm themselves and meet the threat. He advised Morton to call in three trustworthy, loyal men from every county to hear the governor's concerns and then press the state legislature's Republicans to act accordingly. When those meetings were completed, the men were to go home and form their own secret societies in every remote town and county, resulting in coordinated action. When Morton confessed he could not pay the telegraph expenses, Fletcher furnished the governor with the required $100. It was the beginning of Indiana's Union League movement.[24]

Similar concerns existed near the southern border of Iowa. Back in August 1862, then-Radical congressional candidate Josiah B. Grinnell had pleaded with Iowa's Gov. Samuel Kirkwood to supply him with arms. "Secret societies are being organized to defy the draft and collection of taxes," warned Grinnell. "The traitors are armed. Our soldiers are defenseless." As spring arrived, those reports and fears increased. Governor Kirkwood pressed Secretary of War Edwin Stanton to send five thousand stand of arms and ammunition for distribution to Iowa's loyal men. "It is a fact," warned Kirkwood, "that unscrupulous men are organizing and arming for the purpose of resisting a draft under the conscription law." Without such weaponry, Iowa would be unable to suppress such acts.[25]

Oliver Morton followed suit, urging Stanton on June 29 to send him 25,000 arms and at least twelve pieces of artillery to Indiana in order to counter internal as well as external threats. In Morton's case, the external threat was quite real. Confederate cavalry Capt. Thomas Hines and his troopers crossed the Ohio River into southern Indiana from Kentucky on June 18 to see what KGC–Copperhead support Gen. John Hunt Morgan might expect in advance of his famous raid.[26]

Reports of anti-Lincoln and antiwar activity in Illinois were likewise constant. Dr. William White of Jefferson County was overheard advising his fellow Copperheads "to organize and drill publicly, not in the night as the damned abolitionists are doing." A Copperhead-leaning woman from Fulton County advised her husband in February that antiwar sentiment in their town was so great that "the Democrats won't let another man go to war from here." On April 23, Union League men in Marion County wrote to Gen. Ambrose Burnside with specific names informing the general how those Copperhead men "exulted in every defeat of our brave soldiers" and that they were holding their meetings in broad daylight with armed pickets turning away peaceable citizens on the nearby roads. Macon County Loyal League men wrote to Gen. Jacob Ammen in mid-May informing him of precisely when and where the local KGC chapter met and that every man there was armed with a shotgun or a revolver. "I had rather take my chances for safety with the army in the field than here," another pro-Union man fearfully wrote in late May. All of which led to comparable requests from Illinois for arms. On June 26, the Mt. Erie, Illinois, Union League branch requested guns from Governor Yates, flatly stating that they were organizing a home guard company for self-defense against what Christopher Phillips termed "wolfish war—one that was less to be won or lost than endured or survived."[27]

This profound fear felt by League men and other average, pro-Union civilians for their personal safety and that of their families was in line with the July 16 intelligence report from Lt. Col. James Oakes, Illinois's acting assistant provost marshal, who informed Washington that "seditious and turbulent elements" were to be found in practically all of his state's districts. His available troops were minimal as practically every available soldier was now at the front. "In case of any formidable and extensive resistance to the draft in Illinois we are utterly powerless, so far as the military is concerned." The news of the July 13–16 New York draft riot and what it portended should have been a wake-up call, yet Yates was frustrated with the difficulty he faced in securing those weapons from the federal government. An August 5 letter from Yates to Stanton begged for arms because "the Copperheads are armed and Union men are almost entirely unarmed," yet the plea went unanswered. Yates appealed to the secretary again on August 17, convinced that Illinois was defenseless against armed dissent. "Large bodies of men meet in arms in various parts of the State, in some cases 400 or 500 armed men, and applaud speakers who advise them to arm and resist the oppressions of the Government," he advised Stanton.[28]

A planned October 10 letter from Yates to Stanton again asked for more arms, plus organized regiments to protect the state from the Copperhead threat. If no troops could be had, then arms for Illinois's Union League members would suffice. Having not yet sent the letter, Yates added a postscript on October 14 acknowledging that ten thousand muskets had finally arrived, but insisted "that 10,000 stand of arms are insufficient to accomplish the purposes actually required to stay the tide of evil which treason openly proclaimed is spreading through the State."[29]

This manner of private, confidential, panic-filled correspondence from Republican state governors to the secretary of war—along with similar reports from military men in the field to their headquarters superiors—could hardly be considered concocted or public propaganda, but spoke directly to an immediate, on-the-ground concern of imminent danger. As with the Union Leagues, these men's fear of subversive conspiracy at home was every bit a sincere and powerful motivating force as was the Confederacy's overt rebellion. The 1863 fall elections would provide the next battleground, hopefully with only newspapers, pamphlets, and ballots as weapons.[30]

Those upcoming elections were primarily for state officials, nevertheless, everyone knew that like those of a year before, the results would impart some national sentiment. They marked the first nationwide opportunity for the burgeoning Union League movement to illustrate how its rapidly expanding membership could impact elections and, by extension, the war's course.

This was particularly noted in the Pennsylvania governor's race between Republican incumbent Andrew Curtin and Democratic challenger George W. Woodward, who was currently an associate judge on Pennsylvania's state supreme court. This contest marked the first occasion where the Union League of Philadelphia's nonpartisanship claim was abandoned in favor of open support for a Republican candidate. The Union League worked mightily on Curtin's behalf, raising over $150,000 for his campaign's war chest. Curtin ended up retaining the governor's chair, but only by a mere fifteen thousand votes. The League's direct and indirect work on Curtin's behalf was readily acknowledged by the governor and noted by all. As might be expected, the League went to great effort to explain its decision, claiming its right to abandon nonpartisan principles only if an elective office was in danger "of being conferred on 'traitors.'" In this instance, Woodward was given that epitaph due to his earlier publicly stated wish that the North–South demarcation line would "run north of Pennsylvania," coupled with having later voted against the Enrollment Act's constitutionality. From that moment onward, the Union Leagues invariably acted as an important adjunct of the Republican Party, though not always in full agreement with the Lincoln administration.[31]

The upcoming fall elections also helped to transform the Union Leagues into Republican propaganda organizations whose target was Northern voters. Carton after carton of the ULA's newly printed political pamphlets were arriving daily in Washington, allowing James Edmunds to advise his "brothers" that he could fill their literature needs almost immediately. With every shipment, Edmunds also included the League's new coded key "by which the secret work will be unlocked to you within a few days. Keep it close," he stressed. Meanwhile, state councils urged their subordinate chapters to maintain similar diligence and secrecy. "Never give the P.[ass] W.[ords] except in a low whisper," urged Wisconsin's Grand Council because "Copperheads are on the walk, and with all the cunning of the serpent . . . are making every effort to obtain a knowledge of our work."[32]

At the same time, the elections brought a predictable flood of Union League and Publication Society literature flowing into the Union Army camps, much of it acting as Republican propaganda. In many instances, the army officers themselves acted as the distributing agents. For those soldiers who held Democratic views, however, it was at times strangely difficult to acquire newspapers or pamphlets outlining their party's positions. Some army commanders ordered that no treasonable literature be allowed into the camps, and for many officers that meant anything pro-Democratic or anti-Lincoln. It was irrelevant whether the documents were originally published in the North or in Union-held Southern territory. The most famous directive of this type was Gen. Ambrose Burnside's Order no. 38. Issued on April 13, 1863, from his Cincinnati headquarters, Burnside's not-so-subtle decree proclaimed that anyone within his Department of the Ohio territory, "who commit acts for the benefit of the enemies of our country will be tried as spies or traitors." Furthermore, "The habit of declaring sympathy for the enemy will not be allowed in this department . . . It must be understood that treason, expressed or implied, will not be tolerated in this department." Two days later on April 15, District of Indiana commander Gen. Milo Hascall issued his General Orders No. 9 in support of Burnside's edict by criminalizing any words from the press or politicians that Hascall deemed treasonous.[33]

The impact of these orders on anti-Lincoln, Democratic newspapers was profound, with some even accusing the Union Leagues of being the diabolical puppet master behind the suppression. Additionally, this one-sided contest had an indelible impact on the Union soldier with Democratic sympathies and obviously angered Democrats to no end. "I am almost disposed to favor secret organization seeing how our antagonists have used it," groused Democratic jurist Charles Mason into his diary.[34]

This overt switch to Republican Party endorsement was entrenched on September 30, when George Boker wrote to Lincoln on behalf of the Union League of Philadelphia, informing the president he was now an honorary member of their organization. Lincoln's reply dated October 24 was cordial, advising the League how he had diligently endeavored to do his full duty as president and that the League's approval reassured him that he had not entirely failed. "I could not ask, and no one could merit, a better reward," his letter stated. Lincoln's reply was actually penned by his secretary, John Hay, with the president then signing his name below the letter, an act not uncommon considering Lincoln's busy schedule. This letter must have been distasteful for Hay, however, given his growing suspicion over the Union Leagues and what he saw as their steady drift toward the Radical agenda.[35]

The 1863 fall election results offered a strong rebound to Republican fortunes due in large measure to the improved military outlook, highlighted by the July victories at Gettysburg and Vicksburg. New Hampshire went first in the spring of 1863 and elected a Republican governor. Connecticut followed with similar results, thanks in good measure to Union League and Loyal League efforts to rally voters against the Democratic peace faction. Later described as "well organized, strong, and resolute," Connecticut's Union League men were also given arms by the governor to counter any antidraft or election violence that might be generated by disaffected Copperheads. Less regular voting measures included the several thousand, almost handpicked Republican soldiers who were given furloughs in order to go home and vote their party's ticket. Union soldiers who were known Democrats received no such benefits. When the votes were tallied, Connecticut's Unionists were gratified to see that the boys in blue who had voted did so overwhelmingly for Republican candidates, to the consternation of Democrats, who had completely misread the soldiers' shifting sentiments.[36]

In the fall, Ohio, Indiana, and Pennsylvania all returned Republican governors to office. In the case of Ohio, active Union League canvassing against Clement Vallandigham helped to deny his bid for the governor's chair. The

Philadelphia Union League's publication arm also became involved by distributing an anti-Vallandigham pamphlet containing Judge Humphrey Leavitt's legal explanation denying the Ohioan's request for habeas corpus. "Valiant Val" was crushed by over 100,000 votes, a strong rebuke to the nation's best-known Copperhead.[37]

Even in New York, where only minor state offices were up for a vote, anti-Lincoln Gov. Horatio Seymour's Democratic Party was defeated by about thirty thousand votes, prompting diarist George Strong to smugly note that "disloyalty is bad policy." The Union Leagues were even felt at the local level. When a Democratic candidate for county judge was defeated in the recent elections, he knew where to place the blame. "It is those people who get together in Peoples' Hall who defeated me," complained the man in referencing the local Union League. "They git together—three or four hundred of them—they sing a good deal; they pray a little; they swear them all not to vote the regular Democratic ticket- and they raise hell generally."[38]

In Washington, Treasury Secretary Salmon P. Chase sagely interpreted the results' significance: "The people are in earnest; and will push on the war and will maintain the integrity of the Republic against home traitors." All this in spite of the vulnerability Republicans had faced over a laundry list of Democratic grievances, which included the entire debate regarding the proper role of blacks in American society, the Enrollment Act, and Lincoln's suspension of the habeas corpus laws. Yet to the Republicans' benefit, many Northern citizens were beginning to view Democratic racism and their party's legalistic defense of slavery as highly suspect at a time when black men in blue uniforms were bearing as much of the war load as whites were willing to allow. Democrats, meanwhile, were well aware they had not achieved what they had hoped for and what the election results preordained. "There is no hope for a termination of the war until we have been much more severely punished for our sins," wrote Charles Mason.[39]

On December 9, 1863, the Union League of America opened its first "annual" convention at Union Hall in Washington, D.C. The delegates were all in good spirits; the fall elections had gone well for the Republican Party while the military chessboard held renewed promise. Though Union forces in the West had suffered a severe drubbing at the battle of Chickamauga, Georgia, in mid-September, they had rebounded by routing Confederate troops in Chattanooga, Tennessee, at the battles of Lookout Mountain and Missionary Ridge on November 24–25. Then on November 29, another Union command thoroughly repulsed a Confederate attack on Fort Sanders just outside of Knoxville, thereby maintaining federal control of east Tennessee. These successes only added to the gaiety. In fact, Washington's mood and physical appearance as a whole was consistently changing. Iowan Charles Mason noticed how there were a great many new faces in town while familiar ones seemed far fewer than when he had last been in the capital six and a half months prior. New houses were being built everywhere, patrons filled the theaters, while the general economic tone was one of solid prosperity. "Hilarity and self-satisfaction are everywhere manifested," he observed.[40]

Yet a far more serious countenance was on the Radical Republican faces who were assembling for the League convention. They became ever more convinced as 1863 progressed that Abraham Lincoln's backbone was weakening. He could not win reelection because he was too cautious and too nuanced to bring the war to a successful close. For several months, the Radicals had been considering one of their own for the upcoming 1864 presidential election. Salmon P. Chase was again considered that man. "In the most quiet way, your friends . . . should take action in reference to the political welfare of the country," hinted Brooklyn businessman Henry Bowen to Chase. Though Chase had performed magnificently as Treasury secretary in securing the means for the government to pay for the war effort, he believed from the outset that he was a better choice for the White House than its current occupant.[41]

These behind-the-scenes machinations were apparent to the politicos inside the party. During the fall, New York party boss Thurlow Weed had warned Secretary of State William Seward to be wary of the Leagues "into which Odd Fellows[42] and Know Nothings rush," as they were seeking to control delegate appointments on Chase's behalf. The politically moderate Seward readily believed Weed due to what John Hay described as Seward's "inveterate anti-masonic" prejudices.[43]

Even without Weed's warning, Seward had developed doubts as well. According to Hay, Seward admitted he had initially encouraged the Union League movement in the belief they could bring over those "honest" War Democrats and had therefore donated his influence and money as much as possible. However, like the Republican *Daily Cleveland Herald*, which had expressed displeasure with the movement's secretive nature during the Cleveland convention, Seward felt he had discovered a nefarious "wheel within this enterprise—a secret Know-Nothing Masonic order with signs and pass words." The secretary had no use for such Radical-led cabals, agreeing with Weed that the Radicals were doing all they could to secure delegate appointments for Chase in the upcoming presidential election.[44]

As part of the intrigue, members of New York's Radical-led Loyal National League, such as noted attorney David Dudley Field and John Austin Stevens, had attempted to gain control of the party with their Chase-for-president campaign at the epicenter. Field, in fact, had worked as a Chase man in the 1860 election before throwing his hat into the Lincoln camp after the election. At the Loyal National League's mass rally at Union Square on April 11, 1863, Field urged the throng that a firmer "moral courage" and commitment was needed than the government was currently displaying. The Loyal National League counted among its members a number of men who also held membership within the Union League movement. Now as the Union League of America's conference was getting underway, it seemed as if many Radicals had simply strolled across the street from the Chase-for-president conference to the Union League's convention.[45]

Despite such collusion, the convention as a whole was prepared to celebrate for 1863 was considered a year of stunning success. Few organized patriotic and loyalty groups of any stripe existed when the year dawned. Now, eleven months later, almost two hundred delegates were present at a convention representing nineteen Union states, the District of Columbia, and three Western territories. A lone, pro-Union delegate from Virginia was also seated. "There is scarcely a hamlet in the loyal states that cannot point to such an institution," the Union League of Philadelphia proudly stated in its year-end report. These men knew that the efforts from scores of their brothers, such as endlessly distributing literature, knocking on doors, and getting Republican voters to voting precincts, had played a key role in the recent Republican electoral successes. "It is not impossible that some of the political victories recently won, would have been realized without the intervention or aid of the Union League of America," proclaimed the Grand National Council's Executive Committee, "but it is certain that victory would not have been the rule and defeat the exception, but for the earnest and unconquerable loyalty of our organization."[46]

The Executive Committee reported 5,118 councils were now under the ULA umbrella with a membership brotherhood surpassing 800,000. Those numbers excluded the 968 men who were members of the autonomous Union League of Philadelphia, the 530 members of the Union League Club of New York, and the Union Club in Boston. If the numbers were to include all of the Loyal Leagues and Strong Bands from across the land, the number of men who were members of pro-Union loyalty groups could have numbered over one million, or just over 11 percent of the North's voting-age male population. Considering that roughly one-half of those males identified as Democrats, it is reasonable to conclude that approximately one in four adult Republican males were members of an organized, pro-Union loyalty group.[47]

Despite the comradery, there had been challenges. The national council in Washington had experienced difficulty in controlling what transpired in any given county or town council given the divergent local interests and an ever-changing membership. There were challenges at the state level as well. For example, New York's State Council acknowledged that its deputies, who were in charge of developing new councils and ensuring harmonious relationships between chapters throughout the state, had often declined to undertake the required travel as their territories were so large.[48]

In order to enhance nationwide consistency, a circular written by ULA President James Edmunds on behalf of the Grand National Council was sent out on January 1, 1864, surveying the previous year's work while laying out the duties and responsibilities for the upcoming year. Edmunds included a warning: No shirkers or those lacking in determination were wanted for it was imperative that pro-Union ballot-box wins be coupled with Union military victory in the field. "The success of the latter will be made practical and perpetual by the triumphs of the former," wrote Edmunds.[49]

Edmunds also included a reminder as to the Union League's cornerstone belief: "We do not work for men or factions, but for principles. We are not a partisan, yet we *are* a political organization. We will support only representative men. These we do not seek to designate, but we will require that they shall be radical and correct in theory, and earnest and vigilant in practice. We will judge men by their acts, and accept declarations only when they correspond therewith. We hold that those not in sympathy with our purposes should not be employed to execute our plans."[50]

Perhaps there was no better example of Edmunds's exhortations for members to judge men by their acts than that of the York, Pennsylvania, Union League's efforts to oust disloyalty in its midst. In mid-December, the council wrote to Edmunds urging that Capt. Charles Garrettson, an assistant quartermaster in Washington, be summarily dismissed. The York men knew Garrettson personally and considered him to be "a violent Copperhead" with no loyalty to the government. They alleged he had used his position for personal gain while stationed at Hilton Head, South Carolina, and that he had staffed his office with other antiadministration men. When Edmunds presented their case to the secretary of war, he included a letter from Rep. Thaddeus Stevens in which the Pennsylvanian wrote how he had always known Garrettson to be disloyal. The evidence was so detailed that on March 7, 1864, Lincoln dismissed Garrettson from the service. Garrettson may or may not have committed any actual crime, but his refusal to show proper support for the administration was sufficient reason for the Union League to successfully seek the captain's discharge. In essence, they acted as a secret vigilance community within their town.[51]

The Grand National Council's letter stressed 1864 would bring success only with a more "extended and perfect organization." To accomplish the goal, every congressional district or county was to have an active ULA agent in the field who would closely monitor the labors, numbers, and general health of each council in his territory. Those councils were to send the agent a monthly report, and any who failed to do so was to receive a personal visit from the agent. The reports were to include average attendance numbers for council meetings along with the names and addresses of council officers and those individuals who were to receive Union League literature. The agent was then to forward those local reports to the state councils and also note any election precincts that did not have a ULA council. It was the agent's responsibility to see to it that a council was created where needed. Any travel expenses incurred by the agent were to be paid from the local councils' collected dues.[52]

Once councils were up and functioning, it was the agent's responsibility to make sure they were well aware of their duties and responsibilities. In addition, he was to provide the council with guest speakers and Union League literature when requested. Every member was asked to subscribe to a "first class and radical" daily, semiweekly, or weekly newspaper. For those whose finances would not allow such an expenditure, an appropriate subscription would be provided for them. The council itself was to acquire ten or more weekly papers for general distribution as its budget would allow. Those papers were to be given to members who pledged to "place them in the hands of doubtful or hesitating men." And of course, all members were urged to bring any returned soldiers to the meetings as well as any young men whose political opinions might still be molded. With such an organizational outline in place, the Union League of America was ready for political battle in the 1864 presidential campaign.[53]

Edmunds's satisfaction with the Union League's 1863 results certainly spilled over to the various publication societies' activities. Over the course of 1863, the Union League of Philadelphia's Board of Publication prepared and distributed over one million pamphlets representing sixty-five titles. Eight of those sixty-five were German-language reprints of earlier English titles and were designed to speak directly to the 500,000 military-age, German American Northern citizens. As liberal, antislavery Germans were a key faction within the Republican tent, preparing pro-Union propaganda in their native tongue showed a shrewd political awareness. It was hardly hyperbole when the Union League of Philadelphia remarked in its year-end report, "There is scarcely a post-town, from Maine to California that has not received a package of our publications."[54]

New York's Loyal Publication Society reported at their first annual meeting in February 1864 that the organization had published forty-three pamphlets and distributed over 500,000 copies in every accessible state. New York obviously received the lion's share, while some states received relatively far smaller quantities, such as Massachusetts and Pennsylvania. Since they were the other two publication societies' home states, the LPS believed they were adequately covered with loyal reading material. At the gathering, Francis Lieber was elected as the Society's new president, offering in his remarks that he had reviewed the organization's output from the previous year as dispassionately as he would the work of any scholar. From Lieber's perspective, two-thirds to three-fourths of the society's publications held true, long-lasting merit, "while none breathed a spirit that was not truly loyal and patriotic."[55]

The New England Loyal Publication Society was equally pleased with its first-year results. In early 1864, the Society reported that they were sending their broadsides to 867 newspapers in thirty-one Union and Confederate states, the District of Columbia, and three Western territories. Each broadside was printed in an edition of approximately fifteen hundred copies at a bottom-line cost, including distribution, of about two and one-half cents apiece. It projected that if only two hundred of those newspapers regularly copied from the Society's broadsides, and if each paper had roughly one thousand subscribers with each subscribed copy being read by three people, then the Society's political viewpoints were routinely reaching up to 600,000 people.[56]

But how could they be sure? Were the broadsides actually being used or simply thrown away by editors, or pushed off the pages by the actual news? More importantly, were editors likely to resent outside efforts to edit their newspapers? To help answer that question, the Society often sent a written survey to its broadside recipients, not unlike today's polling techniques.

The survey responses were certainly gratifying to the New England Loyal Publication Society. "With hardly any exception [the replies] are written in a friendly spirit and are very gratifying and satisfactory to us," reported the Society's secretary. "Not infrequently papers have been sent to us with four or five articles, taking up several columns of the paper . . . Many editors report that they copy from the broadsides regularly every week."[57]

By way of comparison, the Democrats' Society for the Diffusion of Political Knowledge issued no more than fifteen pamphlets in 1863. Despite their gains and a strong sense of pride in what they had accomplished, the Union Leagues knew their greatest challenge as well as country's lay in 1864. The future of the United States was up for grabs in the 1864 presidential election.[58]

Chapter 10

"We Are Organizing Our Leagues and Getting Ready for the Great Fight of 1864"

An Open Arm of the Republican Party

When the quadrennial presidential campaign commenced along with 1864, the Democratic Party still viewed Lincoln and his policies with the same contempt as it had for the past two and a half years. Their convictions only intensified as the months sped past: They believed Lincoln's poorly considered war policies had led to a sea of crimson blood splattered across American doorsteps. The president was described as uncouth, a coarse buffoon, and "a third-rate lawyer . . . who once kept a whiskey still up a hollow, split 3,000 rails, and now splits the American Union." Democrats genuinely judged him tyrannical, his policies unconstitutional, his party corrupt, and a man who knew no limits if it meant keeping his party in power. They feared his constitutional interpretations presaged the end of a citizen's civil rights all in the name of political expediency.[1]

On the other side of the political aisle stood the Republicans, the majority of whom were supportive of President Lincoln and his policies, as was much of the army. The Republican Party understood that slavery lay at the heart of the rebellion and that its death was imperative for both the war's end and regional reunification. The party's satisfaction was not unanimous, however. The disaffected were prominent abolitionists and those politicians who were aligned with the powerful Radical Republican faction; staunch Republicans who preached unconditional loyalty to the federal government, but who wanted to see a bolder and harsher prosecution of the war than what they felt the president had done to date. Their differences with Lincoln, however, were more with tactics or style, rather than overarching goals. This general alignment was noted by Noah Brooks, the well-known reporter and friend of the president. "Upon all great questions, such as emancipation, confiscation, suspension of the writ of habeas corpus Act, and other kindred measures," wrote Brooks, "the Administration party, *per se,* is a solid column; but beneath all of this there is an undercurrent of dissatisfaction."[2]

The Radicals' influence within the Union Leagues had already been felt and would certainly continue. "These Union Leagues will control when we come to nominate a candidate as sure as there is a God in heaven," Charles Beasley warned Lincoln on January 8. The Radicals, however, were a numerical minority not only within the party but within the League movement as a whole, a fact they were never able to comprehend. Despite their overall agreement with Lincoln on slavery's centrality to the war and its need to end, their ire was further stoked by Lincoln's offer to the Rebels of an amnesty blueprint that the president outlined in his most recent message to Congress. Lincoln coupled his offer with a reconstruction plan that the Radicals deemed far too generous. After the president expressed a desire for leniency toward any Southern state that was willing to come back into the Union, the Radicals sought far sterner congressional restrictions on any state or Confederate who had engaged in treason against the Union. The Radicals preferred a more vindictive approach toward the South that was to be highlighted by enfranchisement and social equality for freedmen. While the Radical abolitionists sought this end due to a heartfelt belief in racial equality, more cynical Radicals sought it as a means of generating Republican political dominion over the defeated South. This reconstruction vision never waned and would come to life during the postwar version of the Union Leagues.[3]

Their final grievance was that Lincoln simply had not done enough to help the slaves, in spite of the fact that the president's actions during the war, such as the Emancipation Proclamation, had moved antislavery policy farther than where it had been prior. The Republican *Cleveland Morning Leader* aptly described this "domestic insurrection" after abolitionist Wendell Phillips publicly accused Lincoln of being willing to end the war without eliminating slavery. For these Radical men, their preferred choice for president was still Treasury Secretary Salmon P. Chase, who had done nothing to discourage the Chase-for-president rumblings since they began the previous fall. "[Chase] believed that he was indifferent to advancement and anxious only for the public good," Lincoln's secretaries, John G. Nicolay and John Hay later opined, "yet in the midst of his enormous labors he found time to write letters to every part of the country, all protesting his indifference to the Presidency but indicating his willingness to accept it." The Radicals bought into the Chase bandwagon wholesale, prompting their overall 1863 dissatisfaction with Lincoln's policies to boil over into 1864.[4]

Lincoln decided to seek reelection only in late 1863; nevertheless, if they could have their way, the Radicals wanted to see Lincoln replaced as the party's standard-bearer in the upcoming presidential election. Most Radicals acknowledged Lincoln's good intentions; however, his policies and actions were simply too conservative. Into this camp fell the influential Horace Greeley and his *New York Tribune,* the most widely circulated newspaper in the country. William Cullen Bryant, prominent editor of the *New York Evening Post* and a Union League Club of New York member, also desired a change. In fact, almost all of the Republican New York newspapers preferred a candidate other than Lincoln, with the exception of forty-four-year-old Republican National Committee Chairman Henry Raymond and his *New York Times.* Elizabeth Cady Stanton, a staunch abolitionist and cofounder of the Women's National Loyal League, also wished to see Lincoln replaced.[5]

Lincoln was well aware of Chase's undeclared candidacy and, therefore, wanted to act quickly on his own behalf. After letting it be known within Republican camps that he was indeed seeking reelection, Lincoln hinted that he would appreciate state endorsements. New Hampshire's state convention quickly endorsed Lincoln on January 7, much to the surprise of the Philadelphia Union League, which, according to John Hay, "saw their thunder stolen from their own arsenals" and were now scurrying about in order to get their nomination in place before such action became passé. The Philadelphia League responded on January 11 with their own endorsement of Lincoln. To organize their efforts, the Philadelphians created their Committee of Seventy-six, whose mission was to uncover and utilize all possible means of aiding Lincoln's reelection goal. The New York Republican Committee followed on January 23 along with the unofficial news that the Republican National Committee was set to endorse Lincoln.[6]

In all of this political wrangling, James Edmunds continued to stand by the president as a faithful ally and Lincoln knew it. Republicans saw in Edmunds a steady man who had Lincoln's trust and as a consequence, the old political pro was able to reassure skittish Republicans as to the president's true convictions. Edmunds had always disdained intraparty strife. "I can see nothing to be gained by a warfare among men of the same party," he had written five years earlier to his friend Sen. Zachariah Chandler. His position as the ULA's Grand National Council president only enhanced his influence and, by extension, the entire Union League of America. "From personal consultation with the President I know him to be entirely reliable on all the great issues of the day," Edmunds assured Mark Howard, a worried Connecticut Republican. "There will be no shadow of turning or wavering." As for the Radicals' plotting against Lincoln, Edmunds was resolute. "Mr. [David Dudley] Field's project stands no chance of success with the League," he again assured Howard on February 10.[7]

Despite Lincoln's apparent momentum, Washington's *Constitutional Union* printed a letter by Radical Kansas Sen. Samuel Pomeroy on February 20 that shocked everyone. What became known as the "Pomeroy Circular" was an open letter written on behalf of a coterie of Radical Republican legislators, urging the public to reject Lincoln's renomination and to support Chase for president. Chase hastily wrote to Lincoln the same day, admitting he had overheard how some Radicals were advocating his candidacy, but denying any knowledge of the letter prior to its publication. He swore fealty to Lincoln even though he was well aware of the letter's origins and the behind-the-scenes attempts for his nomination. Despite the embarrassment, Chase did not offer to resign.[8]

Seeking to keep his friends close and his enemies closer, Lincoln shrewdly declined to dismiss Chase after the circular became public, thereby painting the secretary into a corner. By keeping Chase in the Cabinet, the Treasury boss faced the public embarrassment of being seen as openly competing with the man he had sworn to serve. Had Lincoln fired Chase, the Ohioan would have been free to commence his presidential campaign unrestrained. Furthermore, if Lincoln accepted a hypothetical offer of resignation from Chase, Chase would have faced further public disapproval by appearing to have abandoned his president in time of need. The whole affair clearly backfired against Chase and was punctuated by Ohio Republicans in Chase's home state legislature endorsing Lincoln's renomination. Chase and the Radicals shelved his candidacy if only for the time being. Much could happen in the ten months between February and the November election.[9]

These party machinations deeply disturbed Lincoln's allies. Attorney General Edward Bates called the letter signers the "most shameless liars under the sun" and that the Radicals' "brazen impudence" was a betrayal to the Union Leagues. James Edmunds and his Union League of America would have concurred, as well as the Union League of Philadelphia. The ULA's growing influence manifested itself in the fall 1863 elections and it intended to maintain the momentum. As the year got underway, a loyal Lincoln man in Alton assured Illinois's Sen. Lyman Trumbull that "We are organizing our Leagues and getting ready for the great fight of 1864." Back East, Edmunds began receiving letters from prominent Republican senators requesting admission for their true Union friends into the ULA.[10]

The Union League of Philadelphia responded to the Chase conspiracy in March by reprinting James Russell Lowe's *The President's Policy,* which was first published two months earlier in the *North American Review.* The essay was a highly favorable review of Lincoln's December message to Congress and served the Union League movement as a de facto endorsement of Lincoln. The president even felt compelled to reply to the *Review,* expressing his hope that the article might be of value to the country, nevertheless fearing "I am not quite worthy of all which is therein kindly said of me personally." The Philadelphians followed in April with *The Will of the People,* in which its author, Henry Lea, personally advised Lincoln of his hope that the piece would "repel the attacks of radicals & Copperheads." The ULA's Washington leadership quickly issued *The Opinions of Abraham Lincoln, Upon Slavery and its Issues,* a sixteen-page pamphlet that collected all of Lincoln's antislavery remarks, just in case any wavering voter doubted the president's certitude on the issue. While a faction of ideologues within the Republican Party and the Union Leagues may have preferred a more Radical candidate, most of both organizations' membership stood solidly behind Lincoln.[11]

Despite the surreptitious Chase-for-president disturbance, if there was one issue that the pragmatic Lincoln and the Republicans' Radical ideologues could agree on, it was utilizing the black man in the Union war effort. With the Union League of Philadelphia having already raised three colored regiments in the summer and fall of 1863 and with two more in the training pipeline, the Union League Club of New York men felt they had to respond in kind. These New York men knew that as 1863 progressed, loyalty to the Union cause had become increasingly identified with support for black rights, especially in light of the July draft riots. On the surface, the wealthy Philadelphia and New York Union Leagues spoke of each other with high praise, yet a healthy competitive spirit clearly existed between the clubs and their respective cities. While there is no doubt that their loyalist pledges and antislavery politics were sincere, their memberships consisted of New York and Philadelphia's wealthiest and most successful businessmen, entrepreneurs, merchants, and financiers who had reached their station in life, in part, by embracing rigorous competition. This spirit manifested itself more fully in the forty years following the war's close with the reminiscences and histories of their respective Leagues, each one claiming how they preceded the other.[12]

Seeking a way to encourage enlistments, the Union League Club of New York had appointed a seven-man Committee on Volunteering on November 12, 1863, to address the matter. After initially focusing on ways to fill an existing white regiment, the committee abandoned the idea in favor of recruiting and outfitting a new colored regiment, a decision rife with controversy. When committee member Le Grand Cannon—who as a Union officer in Virginia had seen the plight of runaway slaves—made the suggestion to recruit a colored regiment, the other committeemen shivered. League president Jonathan Sturges was also worried, privately urging each committee member to reconsider. Allowing black men to serve as armed soldiers in the Union Army was still a politically volatile issue, for seeing such men marching in blue uniforms gallantly shouldering loaded muskets alongside white soldiers implied an image of equality that many Northern whites could not fathom. While some abolitionists and Radicals argued that allowing blacks to serve as soldiers was the righteous and progressive course, other moderates were more pragmatic or even cynical. They recognized that every black man who enlisted was one less white man who had to serve in order to meet a state's enlistment quota under the Enrollment Act. After all, noted Cannon, "Here we were having able-bodied negroes, who owed a service to this State, taken out of our State and filling the quotas in other States more advanced in their views."[13]

On November 22, the committee sent a letter to New York's Gov. Horatio Seymour seeking his authority and willingness for the venture. As an anti-Lincoln Democrat, Seymour had no interest in seeing black men in arms, therefore, he demurred, claiming he had no authority to authorize federal regiments; such power rested only with Secretary of War Edwin Stanton. The League men knew Seymour's game, however. While Seymour was technically correct, they were also well aware the secretary was not going to authorize any new regiments from any state, white or black, unless he first had that governor's tacit agreement. This federal–state understanding is why the League men wrote to Seymour in the first place and they believed he knew it.[14]

The League wasted no time in making their application to Stanton, which included a copy of Seymour's reply. To the League men, Stanton seemed incredulous upon reading their request, believing he would make a fool of himself by approving such a controversial appeal without a governor's approval. Furthermore, if Seymour was so politically obstinate as to insist on only white men for his regiments, then Stanton was perfectly fine with letting other states poach New York's supply of able-bodied black men.

By this point, however, the rich and powerful Union League Club of New York was not going to take no for an answer. When the committeemen gently reminded Stanton that their organization was comprised of over five hundred of the most wealthy and influential group of men in the country, that its financial support of and raising money for the government was unparalleled, and how the secretary's continued refusal might alienate that very support at a time it could be least afforded, Stanton saw the light and relented.[15]

The War Department informed the New York League on December 3 that its request was granted. The new regiment was to be officially known as the 20th Regiment United States Colored Troops (USCT) and would be mustered in for three years. No federal cash bounties would be paid to the black recruits, even though similar bounties were still being offered to whites. Of further insult was that a black soldier's monthly wage was to be $3 less than a white man's. Seymour never replied to the League's follow-up letter informing him of Stanton's favorable decision, nor did his office respond to the League's request for the governor to aid the recruitment in any way feasible.[16]

Despite any lingering doubts, it took only fifteen days for the new Union League regiment to be filled to its one-thousand-man capacity, a fact the War Department found difficult to initially accept and sent an inspector to confirm. When the League asked Stanton on December 31 for permission to recruit a second colored regiment, that request was likewise granted, with the new unit to be known as the 26th Regiment U.S. Colored Troops.[17]

The 20th USCT's training ground was on Riker's Island in New York's East River, a dismal rock later described by 2d Lt. John Habberton as "about the meanest place on earth." The training was slow going since no muskets arrived with the recruits. Meanwhile, the winter was brutally cold while the regiment's tents and heating were poor, prompting the New York Union League to provide a floor and small stove for each tent out of its own pocket. All were more than ready to leave when the training concluded at the end of February.[18]

Prior to the regiment's departure for the seat of war, the Union League Club of New York hosted a reception at its clubhouse for the regiment's officers. Habberton was pleasantly surprised by the experience, describing the League men "as mostly grey hairs" who possessed considerable money and brains, laid out a wonderful table, and were fond of good humor. "Each member of the club seemed to exert himself personally to do everything in his power to make things pleasant for us," remarked the young officer, "and they succeeded admirably."[19]

The 20th USCT's departure was scheduled for March 5, 1864. As far as the New York Union League was concerned, it was imperative for the regiment to receive a proper send-off in a manner similar to what the Union League of Philadelphia had staged the previous October. A grand parade and flag presentation ceremony were planned to showcase that not only had last July's rioting been quashed, but that the nation's laws were vindicated, the black man rightfully elevated, and the rioters' murderous actions against him avenged. This public display called for 350 hand-picked men from the regiment to arrive at the docks from Riker's Island, where they would then meet a band at the corner of 26th Street and 4th Avenue. From there both groups would march through the very heart of where much of last summer's draft riots had occurred, and then on to the Union League clubhouse. There the regiment would receive its colors. Each soldier in the regiment carried a loaded musket with an additional forty rounds, just in case any trouble broke out.[20]

The plans came off with little difficulty. Many white onlookers admitted to being duly impressed with the new regiment's martial discipline and manly appearance. Speeches abounded from Union League men and the regiment's colonel. Near the ceremony's conclusion, the wives, mothers, and daughters of the New York Union League members solemnly presented a hand-sewn, silken flag to the regiment's officers and enlisted men, describing the banner as "at once the emblem of freedom and faith, and the symbol of woman's best wishes and prayers for our common country." A light meal consisting of sandwiches and coffee was then provided for the troops prior to their departure. Good humor abounded, with soldier comments such as "This don't look like [last] July" and "How are you, rioters?" overhead by reporters. Once the festivities were concluded, 350 Union League members—one for each soldier present—led the regiment in a triumphant procession down Broadway to the foot of Canal Street, where the regiment boarded the steamer *Ericsson* for its journey to New Orleans.[21]

The entire ceremony's symbolism was unmistakable: The public act of New York's leading Republican white women solemnly presenting a flag to black men and then having the new regiment parade down Broadway with a band playing served as notice of the Union League's progressive power and sway. Any ethnic or racial stains perpetrated by the previous summer's draft riots were now washed away by this new black regiment and its Union League benefactors proudly marching together in what was still a Democratic stronghold. The ceremony served as a shot across the bow of the nation's darkest racial prejudices and illustrated the Union League's new nationalistic vision via this black urban poor and white upper-class joint venture. Over twenty years later at a Union League Club of New York banquet commemorating the event, the now-elderly League men who witnessed that day in March 1864 recalled it as their club's finest moment.[22]

The Democratic New York press responded predictably to the new black regiment and its much-ballyhooed farewell celebration. The *Herald* portrayed "the daughters of Fifth Avenue" affectionately presenting a flag to the black soldiers as "a pretty fair start for miscegenation." "Why," the paper surmised, "the phrase 'love and honor' needs only the little word 'obey' to become equivalent to a marriage ceremony." Racist reaction to the vision of black men in blue uniforms was hardly limited to Democrats, though their venom often seemed the most intense. The *Herald,* for example, routinely referred to abolitionists as "Niggerheads" within its pages as a crude attempt to counter the "Copperheads" epithet. Though many whites sought to elevate the black man from bondage and give him the right to earn and eat his own bread, virtually all Northern whites of the era still considered blacks an inferior race, regardless of their political loyalties. For example, one of the North's most passionate antislavery newspapermen was Horace Greeley, the owner-editor of the Republican *New York Tribune.* When Greeley proudly described the new 20th USCT as being "composed of stalwart, sturdy men, well adapted for the service they will see in the swamps of Louisiana and the prairies of Texas," he revealed a widely held racist belief that a black man's physiology was better suited than a white man's for working in a hot, subtropical environment. Along that same line, a politically conservative officer in the 14th Indiana Infantry writing from Virginia advised his wife how slavery was "a relic of barbarism" whose days were numbered. "Of course," he then wrote matter of factly, "I don't believe in negro equality, but on the contrary, I think they are an inferior race and ought not to be allowed to intermarry with white people."[23]

Union League members were not exempt from such ingrained ethnic and racial prejudices either, in spite of their Radical bona fides. George Strong was certainly in this group, yet he viewed the concern over recruiting African Americans into the army based solely on their skin color as no more relevant a question than whether the army would use black horses captured from the

Rebels. "Our consent to let the niggers enlist and fight is a heavier blow to the rebels than the annihilation of General Lee's army would be," he surmised. Treasury Secretary Salmon P. Chase concurred as well, which was in keeping with his Radical Republican ideology. In an earlier, published letter to the Loyal National League, Chase was adamant that "American blacks must be called into this conflict—not as cattle, not now, even, as contrabands, but as men. . . . Let, then, the example of Andrew Jackson who did not hesitate to oppose colored regiments to British invasion, be now fearlessly followed." This was an issue in which the Radicals and the Union Leagues outpaced much of their fellow Northern citizens. While many Civil War–era whites admitted to the numerical logic of recruiting blacks into the army, their in-grained cultural racism often counteracted such rationality.[24]

As winter blossomed into spring, all eyes started turning toward the upcoming campaigns, both political and military. Any Washington politician worth his salt knew the former would be heavily influenced by the success or failure of the latter. To help militarily, the Union Army accepted "100-day men"— raw recruits whose hundred-day enlistment was only to perform rearguard duties so the veterans currently handling those tasks could be freed up for hotter work at the front.

The Radicals were not content to sit on the sidelines since the earlier Chase-for-president disturbance had apparently blown over. A new alliance was formed between Radical Republicans and War Democrats under the Radical Democratic Party banner. Its sole mission was twofold: block Lincoln's reelection *and* prevent the Peace Democrats from gaining power. While such an alliance held obvious appeal for the Radicals, antiwar or Peace Democrats viewed their War Democrat brethren with a sense of betrayal. "The War Democrats and the Republicans all piss through the same quill," complained one bitter Democratic soldier. The new party held a convention in Cleveland on May 31 that was attended by only about 350 men who were determined to find a Lincoln alternative. Maj. Gen. John Fremont, a darling of the Radicals, was their nominee with retired Gen. John Cochrane as vice-president. Secretary of the Navy Gideon Welles was not impressed and described the gathering as "a meeting of strange odds and ends of parties, and factions" attended by "a heterogeneous mixture of weak and wicked men," while journalist Noah Brooks described the affair simply as "the Fremont harlotry." Back in October 1861, Fremont had issued his own emancipation decree in Missouri to the delight of that state's Radicals. Lincoln, however, was not pleased with Fremont's unapproved venture and rebuked the general by publicly rescinding Fremont's edict. Thus, New York and Missouri Radicals formed the two centers of opposition to Lincoln's reelection. In Missouri's case, Radical German Americans formed the core of Fremont's support.[25]

The Democratic press cheered the Cleveland convention, realizing how thousands of votes that would have gone to the president could now be siphoned off by Fremont, thereby increasing Democrats' chances. The Republicans and Lincoln, of course, ignored the whole affair. Nor did the Cleveland event have any impact on the upcoming Republican convention in Baltimore. During the previous winter, the Republicans had shrewdly designated their national committee as the Union National Executive Committee organization with their National Union Convention set for June 7 in Baltimore. By styling themselves as the Union Party, they implied that their Democratic opponents were the "disunion" party.

What did matter to Union League of America members was their own upcoming convention. Seeking to tie themselves to the National Union (i.e., Republican) gathering, the Grand National Council for the Union League of America set its meeting for one day earlier in the same city in order to maximize its influence. Its first order of business was to form a resolutions committee consisting of one delegate from each state, territory, and the District of Columbia. The committee's responsibility was to create the ULA's resolutions and declarations of principles for presentation at the upcoming Union Party convention. Those resolutions were then expected to be included in the party platform.[26]

The Baltimore Union League convention had an air of trepidation about it from the beginning. Some delegates were frustrated with Lincoln, while others were solidly in his corner. The former group wasted no time in delivering its criticism. William Stoddard, who was seated on the stage, recalled the early anti-Lincoln rhetoric was so "appalling" that he feared a quick vote might severely damage the president. The entire atmosphere changed, however, when Kansas's Sen. James Lane rose to speak. Denouncing all petty criticism toward the president, Lane thundered that rejecting Lincoln's renomination was tantamount to nominating Jefferson Davis, proclaiming disunion, and agreeing to the Confederacy's secession demands. With soaring oratory, the Kansan almost single-handedly changed the momentum toward the president. When a vote endorsing Lincoln was put forth, only nine delegates dissented.[27]

Stoddard was justifiably proud of how the Union League of America endorsed his immediate boss for a second term as president; however, in his recollections Stoddard overstated the convention's ultimate influence. He later wrote that "at least two-thirds of the delegates to the Grand Council were also delegates to the [National Union] Convention. They constituted a clear majority of the latter body as to mere numbers, and vastly more than a majority as to personal character, weight, leadership, and control. The National Convention, therefore, actually met first in the hall of the Union League." A later analysis of those numbers, however, reveals a different picture. The Union League convention featured 135 delegates, of which only thirty-five also appeared on the National Union Convention's printed list of 468 delegates who held proper credentials. Even if every Grand National Council delegate was also a delegate at the national convention, they would have represented less than one-third of the 468 total. Such numbers hardly reflect the Union League gathering as the real, though surreptitious opening to the Republican convention slated to start the next day.[28]

In retrospect, though, the private Union League of America convention still performed a valuable function. It was the place where its members who were dissatisfied with parts or all of Lincolnian policy could blow off steam in private, for there was little real doubt that the president would not be formally recommended for a second term. Grand Secretary W. R. Irwin for the Union League's Grand National Council had sensed this result earlier when he urged Illinois member John Bagby to make sure the Illinois delegation was in full attendance and would vote as a unit for Lincoln. "I think there is no doubt about it being nearly a unanimous thing both in the League and the Convention," Irwin predicted. "[The] New York and Massachusetts [Radicals] are our only thorns." What was most important was coming together in private so a unified front could be publicly presented the next day.[29]

As for the national convention, few planks in the party platform were of greater importance to Lincoln than antislavery. While the president was morally in this corner, he knew such a plank would appeal to Radicals and the Union Leagues. Even considering their overt lack of patience with him, Lincoln genuinely admired the Radicals as a group, realizing they were true patriots in the war. "I know these Radical men have in them the stuff which must save the State and on which we must mainly rely," he had earlier said to his secretary, further admitting that if push truly came to shove, he would have to side with the Radicals over conservatives. The president was shrewd enough to realize his victories were also the Radicals' victories,

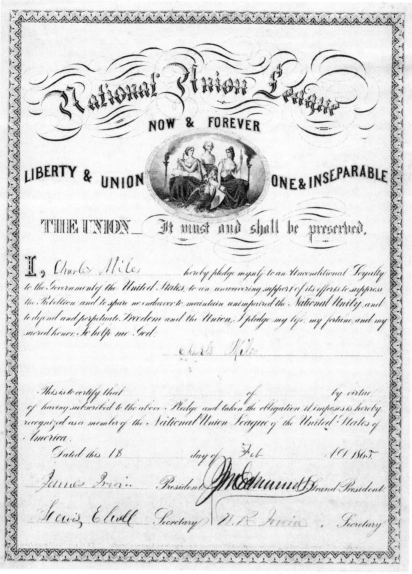

National Union League Pledge—"I, Charles Miles, hereby pledge myself to an Unconditional Loyalty to the Government of the United States, to an unwavering support of its efforts to suppress the Rebellion and to spare no endeavor to maintain unimpaired the National Unity, and to defend and perpetuate Freedom and the Union. I pledge my life, my fortune, and my sacred honor. So help me God. / Charles Miles / This is to certify that _____ of ____ by virtue of having subscribed to the above Pledge and taken the obligation it imposes is hereby recognized as a member of the National Union League of the United States of America / Dated this 18 day of Feb A.D. 1865 [Originally 1863] / James Irwin President. J. M. Edmunds Grand President. / Lewis Elwell Secretary. W. R. Irwin Grand Secretary (Courtesy of Archives and Special Collections, Western Illinois University Libraries)

the president insisted that any proper delegates be seated at the convention, including any Radicals who may be against him as to avoid any appearance of fraud.[30]

The Union Party convention was a boisterous affair, yet despite the rancor and the dissatisfaction with Lincoln by a contingent of Radicals, the president was unanimously renominated on the first ballot. Only the Missouri delegation had initially stood in his way. "The whole proceedings were a matter of course," noted Gideon Welles in his diary. In fact, few insiders ever doubted that Lincoln would be renominated. The words "Republican" or "Republican convention" were scrupulously avoided throughout the gathering, not only to present the party as reasonably moderate but to appease War Democrats who wanted to separate themselves from their Peace Democrat faction. As a further compromise, ex-senator and War Democrat Andrew Johnson of Tennessee was chosen to be Lincoln's new vice-president, though against the Union League of America's wishes.[31]

Despite Lincoln's convention victory, Attorney General Edward Bates was mortified with the proceedings—not that Lincoln was renominated, but how it seemed the goal of Missouri's Republicans was to defeat their party's leader. Secretary of the Navy Welles concurred with his fellow Cabinet member, complaining to his diary that the convention had actually hurt itself in that regard. To his own chagrin, Bates admitted that Missouri's Germans constituted the heart and soul of the Radical Republican movement in his home state.[32]

On the day after the convention, the Union League of America's Grand National Council notified Lincoln that it had formally endorsed the convention's results, its platform, and dedication to the party's loyal men. "We regard it as the imperative duty of all the members of the Union League to do all that lies in their power to secure their election," it pledged. It was time to get down to the real groundwork of defeating the Democrats. Lincoln was naturally gracious with his reply, thanking the League for their renewed confidence in him, though questioning whether or not he was the best man for the country. In a show of levity, Lincoln could not resist including one of the homespun anecdotes he was famous for. For this particular instance, Lincoln wrote how he was reminded of the story about an elderly Dutch farmer, who quipped to a companion, "It was not best to swap horses when crossing streams."[33]

On June 15, one week after the Baltimore convention, the ULA held a grand rally in Washington on the south side of the Patent Office lawn to formally ratify Lincoln's nomination. On the surface, this gathering was like most others in that it was designed to be full of entertaining pomp and circumstance, including ample martial music, artillery salvos, and fireworks. Underneath the surface lay a more important goal, which was to convey to the organizer's political enemies just how resolute the hosting party was along with showcasing their ability to bring out large crowds. For the ULA, it was time to start its serious campaign work.[34]

The Union League of Philadelphia's nonpartisan message came to an abrupt end with its endorsement of Lincoln for president in early 1864. Their uniquely political outlook on what constituted proper patriotism was now thrust into the spotlight. Only Lincoln's reelection, as well as the election of Republican candidates for lesser office, would win the war and save the country, which meant a vigorous expansion of Union League of America councils and their membership rolls. Organic growth was essential, for the League's leadership grasped that there was no functional difference between a Union League oath and a Republican vote. To the League members, however, what they viewed as patriotic work reigned above any political preference. Accordingly, they maintained their support for Republican candidates was not particularly partisan.[35]

Meanwhile, the Union League of America's similar claims of nonpartisanship vanished with the 1864 presidential campaign's commencement and its formal endorsement of Lincoln. All of the various Union Leagues and their offshoots, led by the elite Eastern clubs, were now firmly in the Lincoln and Republican camp. For many Republicans and their Union League allies, the idea of an opposition party in the midst of an internal civil war was intolerable. In a speech before the ULA's Washington, D.C., council, Rep. John Broomall of Pennsylvania spoke of this by asserting the rebellion was no longer merely one by slaveholders, but of an entire political party. From Broomall's vantage, those Democrats who loved their country more than their party had already left the latter to support the war with full vigor and enthusiasm. The Union Leagues were now poised to become a Republican forerunner to the modern political action committee.[36]

The ULA knew this was going to be a vicious campaign and promptly waded into the political muck. In fact, the Union League's declaration of war against their definition of treason had already started months earlier. Following Ohio Democrat Alexander Long's congressional speech predicting the war's failure and favoring recognition of the Confederacy on April 8, the Speaker of the House, Schuyler Colfax, brought forth a resolution to have

Long expelled from Congress for such treasonable utterances. Five days of acrimonious debate and speeches followed. The move ultimately failed, but Colfax did secure a formal congressional censure against Long. After learning of the affair, the Union League rushed a small pamphlet into print describing their resolution approving of Colfax's efforts and of their subsequent congratulatory meeting with the Speaker.[37]

Once the Republican's convention concluded in early June, the next important event in the campaign season was the Democrat's national convention, which was now scheduled to take place in Chicago on August 29. The convention had originally been planned for July 4, but had been postponed after some, but certainly not all, leading Democrats had urged delay so that the party might iron out its own differences and perhaps take advantage of a deteriorating military landscape. Rumors abounded as to what would transpire in Chicago, including one which held that the Democrats' real scheme of "peace at any price" would be masked by a "Trojan horse," pro-war platform that would be discarded once they were elected.[38]

In a propaganda ploy suitable for a modern spy novel, the ULA created an espionage campaign pitting neighbor against neighbor all across the North. Its "brother members" were sent secret circulars urging them to "aid in the work of foiling the traitors" by surreptitiously learning if any Chicago convention delegates or alternates lived in the member's neighborhood. If a delegate was uncovered, "two or more discreet and indefatigable" Union League members were to "work up the case against the parties." Working "secretly, quietly, and expeditiously," the members were to seek out information pertaining to the delegate's political views before and after the war began, his views on slavery, if he had previously held any public office, if he ridiculed the Union military, or had ever expressed a desire to see the Confederacy succeed. Once collected, all of this intelligence regarding the convention delegates was to be published in a "telling pamphlet" clearly designed to marginalize, if not destroy, the delegates' public reputations. If the circular's recipient could not or would not participate, or if no delegates lived in his neighborhood, he was instructed to destroy the instructional evidence. As is often the case with modern presidential politics, this Union League circular illustrated that in 1864, destroying your opponent's credibility by any means necessary was deemed every bit as important as making the case for your own policies and programs.[39]

This type of no-holds-barred tactic by Union League members against their enemies was hardly new, however. As previously discussed, all manner of social, commercial, and employment ostracism toward perceived Democrats had occurred earlier. Ministers and teachers who were not deemed properly loyal sometimes lost their positions. Informal cooperation between the civilian Leagues and the Union military had even become routine. This "criminalization of political differences"—as has been alleged in our modern era—took the form of League members notifying local military authorities of suspected disloyal men in their midst, such as the aforementioned case of Capt. Charles Garretson in York, Pennsylvania. Loyal men as well as the Union military felt no hesitation in utilizing the Union League as a form of secret police for the federal government. Kansas City's ULA council president notified Gen. Clinton Fisk, the Department of North Missouri's commander, that John W. Reid, a former Missouri Democratic congressman, had fled to Kansas City after being ordered out of Independence. After learning that Reid had been expelled from Congress and even served in the Confederacy, eight League men "advised" Reid to move on when they found him in Kansas City. The League men believed this entire chain of events would be of "great interest" to Fisk. Gen. William S. Rosecrans, in command of the Union's Department of Missouri, was even more direct, urging Fisk to "tell loyal league societies that they can best serve the interests of the State by keeping you promptly and fully advised of all rumors of rebel or bushwhacker movements." This civilian–military cooperation also worked in the opposite direction. When General Fisk reached out to the St. Joseph, Missouri, Union League for information pertaining to the loyalty of a suspected secessionist named John Pendleton, the League replied, "It would be difficult to prove any special act of treason. Yet Union men all esteem him a rebel."[40]

In the meantime, the Union Leagues' "no middle ground" position on loyalty to the government continued unabated. The "unconditional loyalty" preached by Henry Bellows in early 1863 continued well into 1864 with a sermon by Rev. Jacob Cooper entitled "The Loyalty Demanded by the Present Crisis." Cooper was a Southern Unionist from Kentucky, which was where his sermon first appeared. Reprinted by the Union League of Philadelphia in May 1864 and then sent forth throughout the North, Cooper asserted that given the tremendous opposition and challenges faced by the federal government in staving off the rebellion, "none deserved so much lenity from loyal men for mistakes in judgement, or measures of questionable legality."

Therefore, any criticism of the administration's war measures or actions was tantamount to being in favor of the Confederacy.[41]

The sentiments expressed in pamphlets like Cooper's and the aforementioned ULA secret circular campaign were not merely part of a "politics as usual" operation. Republicans and Union Leaguers sincerely believed their Peace Democrat–Copperhead enemies were part and parcel of a treasonous plot to tear the nation apart. This conviction again manifested itself in 1864 with the arrival of a new, anti-Lincoln cabal known as the Order of the Sons of Liberty.

Born in early 1864, the Sons of Liberty evolved from an earlier, short-lived shadow group known as the Order of American Knights, which was created in the fall of 1863. Both were successors to the KGC, whose flame was dimming as 1864 dawned. All of these secretive, Democratic-led groups shared one point in common: their belief that the Lincoln administration had committed numerous unconstitutional acts and was seeking despotic rule. Clement Vallandigham was a founding member who publicly proclaimed the group was benign. He claimed the new organization existed solely to protect its members from Union League harassment, the administration's usurpation of Democrats' lawful rights, and to elect Democrats to office. Democrats in general and the Sons of Liberty in particular likewise felt the need for a secretive, mutual protection association against arbitrary arrests and conscription. For Republicans, however, the Sons were just the latest secret cabal created to foment violent unrest against lawful authority.[42]

Vallandigham's concerns over Democrats' safety were not without merit. Violence against Democrats and their printing presses stood at the top of the list of concerns. "Almost every week lately we hear of the destruction of a Democratic paper, attempts at the same, or outrages upon democrats," complained the Michigan *Grand Haven News* in March. The paper felt it knew who the culprits were, too, alleging such deeds were the handiwork of "the despicable midnight abolition 'loyal leaguers.'" If the League men did not do the work directly, they would then incite soldiers to complete the task. The Lancaster, Pennsylvania, *Eagle,* Mahoming *Sentinel,* and the Wauseon *Press* were all said to have fallen to League torches.[43]

Democrats were also concerned about the quantity of Union League propaganda that was now blanketing the nation. In Pennsylvania, the *Bedford Gazette* urged the state's Democratic leadership in mid-July to stop its "masterly inactivity" and step up its messaging efforts. Democrats were confused, considering that the party's national Society for Diffusion of Political Knowledge had announced on the title page of its first three publications that "When a party in power violates the Constitution and disregards state-rights, plain men read pamphlets." The *Gazette* urged the state committee to join in the fray, stressing that if the organization waited until August, it would be too late since the Republicans had already been engaged for months in sending out its own speeches and pamphlets. For example, just one month earlier the editors of the *Republican* in Norristown, Pennsylvania, advised a benefactor that they were going to provide county Union Leagues with large quantities of their newspaper at below-cost prices in order to "circulate truth and educate the masses." The *Gazette* further warned that the Loyal Leagues were springing into action throughout the state and it was imperative "the baleful influence exerted by these devilish agencies should be counteracted." To Republican and League men everywhere, though, the influence they sought to generate was simply part of a righteous war against those seeking to destroy the Union.[44]

Keeping pro-Union citizens engaged in the home front treason battle was crucial since the actual fighting war had ground to a stalemate. Beginning in early May with the battle of the Wilderness, the armies of Gen. Ulysses S. Grant and Gen. Robert E. Lee had fought in a seemingly never-ending death struggle that took them from just west of Fredericksburg into the trenches south of Petersburg by mid-July. Unlike earlier in the war when the armies would fight a grand battle and then pause for months to regroup, the fighting over the past few months had continued almost nonstop. Over sixty thousand Union men were killed or wounded in the process, resulting in allegations that Grant was no general, but a mere butcher. The Eastern theater fighting was not limited to Confederate Virginia either. For the third time since the war began, a Rebel army crossed over the Potomac River and into Maryland on July 5. In this most recent instance, it was Gen. Jubal Early and his fifteen-thousand-man command who invaded the Old Line State with orders to disrupt railroads and threaten Washington if possible. In Baltimore, Union League men remembered their oaths to defend their home and swung into action as best they could by forming home-guard companies. That apparently suited local Copperheads just fine, who, according to the German *Der Lacha Caunty Patriot,* had shouted, "Let the Union League go chase the Rebels out of Maryland!" The government meanwhile, was said to be in dire need of horses and was confiscating as many from disloyal citizens as possible.[45]

Union Asst. Adj.-Gen. Samuel Lawrence was impressed with the League's efforts and reported so to Gen. Lew Wallace, who would be fully engaged with the Confederates only fifty miles to the west on July 9 at the battle of Monocacy. "Matters are progressing favorably here," remarked Lawrence. "The Union Leagues are forming companies, and as fast as the companies are reported, I send the captain a copy of the circular herewith enclosed, so as to prepare them for a call. They seem pleased with it. I think they will raise twelve or fifteen full companies." From July 10 to 15, Baltimore's Union League men formed an ad hoc militia stationed as a reserve force on Baltimore's west side.[46]

Early's men scored a hard-fought victory at Monocacy Junction, about forty-five miles west of Baltimore, but as Washington was their real goal, they lost precious time in the process. They bypassed Baltimore and turned south on July 10 for a drive on Washington, prompting Grant's Chief of Staff Henry Halleck to request that Gen. Abner Doubleday stay within the capital to organize all of the city's Union and Loyal League men for defensive work. In addition, convalescents, Invalid Corps men, marines, and Navy Yard mechanics were all rounded up to join the one-hundred-day green troops who were manning the capital's perimeter defenses. This ragtag force could not have comprised more than six thousand men; nevertheless, every loyal man was readily accepted in case of any attack from Early's battle-hardened veterans.[47]

The Rebel attack against Washington turned out to be more of a skirmish line probe. It took place in front of Fort Stevens on the city's north side over the July 11–12 time frame. The affair featured the now-legendary instance of Lincoln standing on the parapet to gaze at the attacking Confederates through field glasses, only to be ordered by a young Oliver Wendell Holmes Jr. to "get down, you fool!" as bullets whizzed by. It marked the only time a sitting U.S. president has come under direct enemy fire. On the Confederate side, Early soon realized that just-arrived reinforcements from the Army of the Potomac had now made the Yankee capital too heavily defended, therefore he abandoned the offensive and returned to Virginia almost unmolested on the 13th. With the threat over, the Union League men were asked to turn in their government-issued muskets and were then dismissed with the thanks of the local military authorities. As part of the larger picture, the Union possessed an overwhelming numerical superiority versus the Confederates in men and materiel, nonetheless loyal Union men were forced to comprehend that a relatively small Confederate force had almost seized Washington, D.C. Was all of the bloodshed and angst really worth it?[48]

Those middle months of 1864 were the North's summer of discontent. War concerns had prompted gold to spike in value, which caused the North's recently issued paper money—known as "greenbacks"—to tumble accordingly. With Gen. William T. Sherman's Western armies stalled outside of Atlanta and Ulysses S. Grant's Army of the Potomac wallowing in fetid trenches east and south of Petersburg, Virginia, the North's morale was at a low point not seen since the winter of 1862–63. Concerns over Copperhead-led, antidraft violence against loyal men—which Union League men had combated for two years—had now reached the highest levels of the Union military. On August 11, Maj. Gen. Henry Halleck sent a confidential communique to Lt. Gen. Ulysses S. Grant suggesting that Grant should be prepared to withdraw troops from the Petersburg trenches and send them into the Northwest to quell potential antidraft violence. It was imperative, stressed Halleck, that the draft be enforced or else the army's manpower would suffer. Halleck admitted he had never been a big believer in "secret society" plots, but army intelligence was now so consistent that the matter could no longer be ignored. "Are not the appearances such that we ought to take in sail and prepare the ship for a storm?" Halleck wondered. That storm would arrive in less than a month.[49]

In an angry letter to Illinois Rep. Elihu Washburne, Chicago *Tribune* editor Joseph Medill echoed his country's frustration: "Has it occurred to you that since July 4, '63—ten months since our mighty military paraphernalia costing over three millions a day to maintain, has not advanced a mile upon the enemy. With 800,000 soldiers on the pay rolls and 650 war vessels in commission, we stand exactly where we did ten months ago." Lincoln himself seemed to see the handwriting on the wall. Considering the dismal state of affairs, the president sensed he was going to be beaten in the upcoming election and "unless some great change takes place *badly beaten*," he reportedly said to Gen. Schuyler Hamilton in early August.[50]

Chapter 11

"Once More Rally Around the *Flag*, and Your Work Will Be Complete"

A Bitter and Partisan Election

As July dragged into August, nothing seemed to be going right for the Lincoln administration and the Union cause. Civilian morale was plummeting, along with the Treasury Department's funds to pay for the war. Meanwhile, the ghastly body counts continued to rise. The Union armies' outlook seemed as bleak as ever, which meant Lincoln's election prospects in November were just as grim. The Radicals, with Union League men among them, were simply not going to sit on their hands and watch their party's election prospects swirl down the drain, for nothing was as potentially calamitous to them as a Democratic victory that would sweep the peace-at-any-price men into power. Lincoln certainly concurred, writing in his then-private August 23 memorandum that if he lost the election, it would be his duty to cooperate with the Democratic nominee in such a manner "as to save the Union between the election and the inauguration; as he will have secured his election on such ground that he cannot possibly save it afterwards." The Radicals were still convinced a different candidate was sorely needed and again, their eyes shifted toward Salmon Chase. The Treasury secretary had resigned his office on July 1, which left Chase and his friends free to plot against Lincoln and hopefully steal the nomination. Meanwhile, jubilant Democrats gleefully watched from the sidelines and predicted victory based on Republican dissension.[1]

Following a flurry of correspondence, approximately twenty-five Radical Republicans from New York and Massachusetts met at the home of former New York mayor George Opdyke on August 18 to plot strategy and plan for a new convention at Chase's hometown of Cincinnati in late September. This followed a similar meeting, which was held at attorney David Dudley Field's home on August 14. Opdyke's guest list read like a "who's who" of prominent Union League and Union Club Radicals from New York and Boston, and included the likes of Opdyke, John Austin Stevens Jr., Parke Godwin, Francis Lieber, and John Forbes. Those Union League men who replied stating they could not attend but were in sympathy with the meeting's intent included John Jay, Massachusetts's Gov. John Andrew, and Gen. Benjamin Butler, who sent Col. J. W. Shaffer to the meeting as his eyes and ears. Chase was also invited, but he coyly responded that he could not attend and that New York Union League and Loyal National League member William Curtis Noyes would serve as his representative. Their goal was to save the Union by convincing Lincoln to step aside and then replace him with a candidate more amenable to the Radical viewpoint. "There are but two things that could save us—a telling victory, or rather the taking of Richmond, and Mr. Lincoln's withdrawal," Lieber grumbled.[2]

In addition to their Loyal League or Union League involvement, Francis Lieber and John Austin Stevens were influential members of New York's Loyal Publication Society and had been since day one. Stevens, in fact, sat on the Society's Publications Committee and was also the Society's secretary, while Lieber was the organization's president. Given these men's antipathy toward Lincoln's reelection, it was not surprising that with the lone exception of *Lincoln or McClellan?* not one of the thirty-three pamphlets' titles issued by the Society in 1864 could be construed as overtly pro-Lincoln, but simply pro-Union and/or anti-Democrat. In the Society's second annual report issued in February 1865, Stevens defended this point: "While [the Society] has often disappointed the eager partisan," wrote Stevens, "it has never offended the just patriot, and has won golden commendation even from those whom it would not lend itself to serve." Stevens's rationale was in keeping with League doctrine stating that loyalty was owed to the Union and not any particular individual. There is little doubt that the Radicals who sought a replacement for Lincoln acted with anything other than the purest of patriotic motives. Nevertheless, this 1864 Radical-led mutiny against Lincoln stood out as the one time during the Civil War when Union League men appeared to be in open revolt against the president.[3]

The White House staff was well aware of the Radical intrigues. After arriving home in Illinois for a respite, John Hay wrote to his fellow secretary, John Nicolay, complaining how he was completely fed up with the "diseased restlessness" infecting certain "growling Republicans." Hay had even been asked to speak before the local Union League council, but declined, knowing "the snakes [Democrats] would rattle about it." As far as Hay was concerned, "If the dumb cattle are not worthy of another term of Lincoln, then let the will of God be done & the murrain of McClellan fall on them."[4]

The Union League of Philadelphia's Board of Publication offered an entirely different perspective. Having endorsed Lincoln's candidacy as early as January 1864 and then creating a seventy-six-man committee to oversee that goal, six of the thirty-four pamphlets issued by the League's Board of Publications during 1864 explicitly featured Lincoln's name in the title and stood as a ready endorsement of the president's policies and reelection. The subject of several, in fact, dealt solely with the exigencies of reelecting the president.[5]

In the meantime, in addition to its unconditional support of Lincoln, the Union League of Philadelphia vigorously continued its efforts at recruiting new white and "colored" regiments for the Union war effort. Two more colored regiments, the 22nd USCT and the 25th USCT, were recruited in early 1864 and soon followed the League's original three into the field. On the white side of the ledger, the "Fourth Union League Regiment," officially designated the 183rd Pennsylvania Infantry, was mustered in for three years in early 1864. A ninety-day and a one-year regiment, designated the 196th and 198th Pennsylvania Infantry respectively, followed in the summer of 1864. More regiments soon followed. Late in 1864, three more "Union League Regiments" were formed, christened the 213th, 214th, and 215th Pennsylvania Infantry regiments. When the final numbers were tallied, the Union League of Philadelphia had raised over ten thousand men for the Union war effort and spent over $108,000 in the endeavor.[6]

Democrats were not going to passively watch the Republican fireworks. As expected, they formally nominated War Democrat George McClellan for president with Ohio's George Pendleton, a notable Peace Democrat, as vice-president at their August 29–31 Chicago convention. For those Northern voters who may not have been familiar with the Ohioan's record, a new Union League of Philadelphia pamphlet set forth a blistering critique of Pendleton's Copperhead bona fides. Predictably, the party platform was one that pleased even the most strident antiwar Copperhead. It condemned the war as a total failure with Lincoln as the architect. Peace without any preconditions was also called for yet, specifically, how peace *and* reunification were to be obtained was left unsaid. Such a platform was even more remarkable, considering that the Peace Democrat–Copperhead faction was a numerical minority view within the Democratic Party as a whole. Yet the words and speeches that flowed from the Democratic convention, along with the actions of groups like the earlier KGC and now the Sons of Liberty allowed Radical Republican and Union League men to successfully reinforce their mantra that treason was part and parcel of the Democratic Party. "If Mr. Jeff. Davis had been platform-maker for the Chicago Convention," wrote Horace Greeley, "he could not have treated himself more tenderly nor his enterprise more gently than they have been in the actual Platform." This Union League–generated patriotic stain would haunt Democrats for the next generation.[7]

George McClellan took seven days following his nomination to release a statement that essentially repudiated his party's antiwar peace plank. It was impossible, he wrote, for him to look his gallant, blue-clad soldiers in the face and tell them that their labors and sacrifices had been in vain, that the Union was now being abandoned. In a private letter on October 20, McClellan reaffirmed his beliefs: "I intend to destroy any and all pretense for any possible association of my name to the Peace Party.[8]

Nevertheless, as the Democrats' official standard bearer, George McClellan was publically portrayed by the Union League to be practically a traitor to the Union cause. The Union League of Philadelphia's new official newspaper, the *Union League Gazette*, decried McClellan's and the Democrats' stance on the issues. Describing him as a general once authorized to head an army dedicated to the preservation of the country's laws, today he stood "at the head of a political party . . . whose aim and purpose are subversive of the liberties and institutions of the nation." In that same report, it referred to the Democratic Party as no better than a "guerrilla operation."[9]

In truth, the more grizzled Republican political operatives were probably delighted with what they had read coming out of Chicago for the Democrats' words would only reinforce Republican stereotypes, a belief that some moderate Democrats sadly shared. That latter group included prominent Democratic strategist Dean Richmond, who, according to John Hay, had admitted that half of his party appeared to be traitors. A *New York Times* correspondent at Chicago reported how over the entire convention, he never heard one word uttered in favor of the war while a reader would "look in vain for one sentence of speech, or letter, or resolution that condemns the rebels of the South." A *Cincinnati Gazette* reporter informed his readers that the saddest thing he heard from convention speakers was the "evident delight" with the Union's military setbacks. Yet with Lincoln being harangued by Democrats and a small but influential contingent of the Radical Republicans plotting against him virtually in the open, those waning August days were the darkest of his presidency. "This morning, as for some days past," he wrote on the 23rd, "it seems exceedingly probable that this Administration will not be reelected."[10]

Then, like dark storm clouds suddenly parting to let in the sun's bright warming rays, the Northern malaise lifted on September 3, 1864, two days after the close of the Democrats' convention. Early that morning, Gen. William T. Sherman telegraphed Washington to report that the Rebels had evacuated Atlanta during the night, following his armies' forty-two-day siege of the city. "Atlanta is ours, and fairly won," reported Sherman. The Deep South's most important railroad hub and manufacturing center was now under Union control. Only a week earlier, Northerners learned that the Union Navy captured Mobile, Alabama, which had struggled as the sole Gulf port east of the Mississippi still under Rebel control. Then by late September and further north in Virginia's Shenandoah Valley, Union Gen. Philip Sheridan's Army of the Shenandoah began wreaking havoc on every Confederate grist mill, barn, and farm it could lay its hands on. Such activity was possible because of Sheridan's recent battlefield victories. The triumphs included a stunning defeat of Gen. Jubal Early's command on September 19 at the battle of Third Winchester and then a follow-up victory against the Rebels on September 22 at Fisher's Hill. This string of victories helped Northern morale to soar. For the first time in years, Union victory and the end of the war seemed promising. Within a few short weeks, one positive battlefield result after another had enabled Lincoln's reelection chances to flip from doubtful to likely. Chase and his conspirators saw their hopes slipping away in a new rush of war euphoria that benefited Lincoln immensely. He advised his allies to abandon their scheme and to support the president for the duration. For the remainder of the campaign, the Radicals and all Union League men were focused on their real enemy, the Democrats.[11]

Meanwhile, new District of Illinois commander Gen. Halbert E. Paine realized he had walked into a hornet's nest of Copperhead discontent. Between Rebel guerrillas and "domestic traitors," Paine reported to the Northern Department's adjutant general that he was quite inclined to believe all of the intelligence his men had brought him of looming insurrection. Then in August, Union Army spies and intelligence officers hit the motherlode by uncovering two clear-cut conspiracies. The first occurred in mid-month when officers learned of and seized sixty-four cartons of navy revolvers and ammunition in Indianapolis and New York that were targeted for a planned

Copperhead uprising in the Old Northwest. Indiana's Gov. Oliver Morton trumpeted the seizure as proof positive of the treasonous Democratic plots he had railed against for months. Then, while working hand in glove with Confederate agents in Canada—a treasonous act in and of itself—the Sons of Liberty had laid concurrent plans to free Confederate prisoners at Chicago's Camp Douglas prisoner-of-war camp during the Democrats' Chicago convention. Area Copperheads were feared to have guns and ammunition hidden on their farms in order to supply the escaped prisoners. The plans called for the escapees to cut a swath of armed destruction throughout Illinois in a designed effort to take several states out of the Union. Yet nothing transpired. When the plot's leaders heard repeated (and planted) rumors that Union troops were pouring into Chicago and that the Camp Douglas garrison had been increased to around five thousand men, the plot was called off. Harrison H. Dodd, the grand commander of the Sons was arrested on treason charges. Before his trial began, Dodd escaped from prison but was convicted in absentia and sentenced to death. Five more men were also arrested and were to be tried before a military commission. The charges against one man were dropped after he agreed to testify for the prosecution; of the remaining four, all were found guilty and three were sentenced to death. All charges were later commuted, however.[12]

The political benefits to Republicans with such an exposé were quite evident. After the convictions and sentences, the Philadelphia League responded by issuing a pamphlet titled *The Great Northern Conspiracy of the "O.S.L.,"* only weeks before the election, as a reminder to undecided voters what a vote for the Democracy represented. While Republicans may have utilized these events for maximum political benefit just prior to the election does not negate the fact that the Union military had acquired reams of evidence proving the conspiracy.[13]

With the campaign heading into its final weeks and finally feeling some wind in its sails, the Union League intensified its campaign efforts. In Connecticut, Yale professor, John Porter, urged all League men to continue forming new councils and distribute campaign literature with grim determination. His printed circular included a list of campaign pamphlets currently available from the state council with pricing, just in case any council's stock was running low. League field agents were positioned in each county to oversee the work. Similar exhortations occurred in every Northern state. A Lincoln triumph in and of itself was not sufficient; the victory margin had to be of such magnitude that it would crush the hopes of those traitors looking to foment revolution in case of a Republican victory. "They have threatened it and they mean it," warned Porter. In Pennsylvania, John Pilsifer advised the chairman of the Union League of Philadelphia's Committee of Publication that because of League posters and pamphlets, numerous men in Schuylkill County who had voted for "the so-called democratic ticket" in the prior election were now switching to Lincoln and Johnson. Michigan's Grand Council continued to urge the "vast importance and immediate necessity" of furnishing Michigan residents with "proper" political reading material. Not merely partisan matter, but those papers and pamphlets that bore upon the nation's unconditional preservation along with the rebellion's wickedness and unconstitutionality. Such printed matter was to be immediately "sown broadcast over the length and breadth of the state."[14]

As it had in the war's early months, much of the Protestant church continued to be a prominent spokesperson for the administration. Furthermore, it had the money, manpower, and buildings to host political meetings. Its centrality to community life made Sunday services the perfect distribution outlet for publication society or Union League campaign literature, which included reprints of recent speeches promoting a religious necessity for the ongoing war. In the torrid 1864 presidential campaign, there often appeared to be little separation between church and state as preachers increasingly blurred the biblical line between Caesar and Christ. Republicans and Union League members throughout the North certainly would have concurred with the pastor, who stated that any man casting a vote for the Democrats would do "the rebel cause more service, if possible, than he would by joining the rebel army."[15]

Perhaps inevitably, some Union League men were too zealous in their hunt for disloyalty, often using their new membership to mete out personal malice against a particular neighbor who they believed may have wronged them in the past. This revenge was inevitably disguised by the perpetrator's claim that he was only rooting out treason. Lynchings were not unheard of, such as the League men in Kansas who hung two Rebel sympathizers. In Greene County, Missouri, some fanatical League members announced that any man who planned to vote for McClellan was a traitor to his country and that it would be an act of mercy for Union League men to shoot such creatures. It was instances such as these that compelled Democrats to organize and to harbor disdain and fear toward the Leagues. Cooler heads generally prevailed with such threats, however. More likely, violence usually took the form of Union League ruffians destroying Democratic newspaper offices and printing presses. From Des Moines, Iowa, eastward, League men scoured their respective towns looking for any disloyal enemies.[16]

As the Union Leagues continued their home front war, the Union Army continued to suppress any peace Democrat newspaper or literature found within the camps. From his Atlanta headquarters, Gen. William Sherman advised Gen. George Thomas in Union-held Nashville to "give a good horse-whipping to any editor who would dare advise our soldiers to avoid their honorable contracts of enlistment, confiscate his press, and use his types for printing quartermasters' blanks." After Ohio Democrats sent McClellan ballots to their men in the field, they were stunned to see the boxes later returned to them, unopened.[17]

Loyal and influential Lincoln men did all they could to tilt the election. The War Department sought and granted furloughs to reliably Republican soldiers in camps and hospitals so they could go home to vote in those states where the election was considered too close to call. As Indiana had not approved soldiers voting outside the state, Lincoln even wrote to William Sherman in Atlanta, inquiring if the general might be able to release some Republican-leaning Indiana men so they could go home to vote. Furloughs for Democratic-leaning soldiers were never forthcoming, however. Meanwhile, Democrats at home learned to watch their tongues. "Treason cannot be uttered here, as in days gone by, for they know they will be punished," remarked an Ohio man prior to the election. Those whose comments were too controversial often found themselves jailed by Union provost marshals for the flimsiest of reasons, though only until the election was over.[18]

With only a few weeks to go till the election, the Union Leagues' publication arms were working hand in glove with the Union Congressional Committee to win the message war. On June 29, that committee announced a list of nineteen recent speeches, ready for "judicious distribution" throughout the country. The pamphlets were all eight or sixteen pages long and priced at either $1 or $2 per hundred copies. The price included envelopes and franking privilege. If specific names were included, the pamphlets would be sent directly to the recipient at the committee's expense. As for other methods of circulation, the Congressional Committee left the decision to the Union Leagues' discretion. By September 7, another fifteen pamphlets were prepared, all available in English or German, and sent postage-paid to the recipient. "The plans and purposes of the Copperheads having been disclosed by the action of [their] Chicago Convention," warned the committee's secretary, "should at once be laid bare before the loyal people of the country."[19]

Meanwhile, with the campaign in its home stretch, every state Union Committee and Union League was being urged by the Republican and League leadership in Washington to "perfect their organizations." Local councils were urged to inject new vigor and purpose into their cause. League men stood on street corners and handed out scores of pro-Union newspapers and pamphlets in order to "combat the deceptive and perilous sophistries" of the treasonous enemy. "We are now sending out from fifty to a hundred thousand documents a day," exclaimed Congressional Committee member Elihu Washburne in mid-September. "Every man who has a tongue and a hand, must go to work and work constantly," Washburne further urged. "Not a man whom it is possible to convert should be left unconverted." In New York City, the Loyal Leagues worked side by side with the Union Congressional Committee and the Union National Committee to send 200,000 copies of "loyal" pro-war newspapers to Union troops in Virginia during October, while Francis Lieber was overseeing the distribution of thousands of the Loyal Publication Society's German-language pamphlets to the city's German workingmen. He was gratified to learn that when the German version of *Lincoln or McClellan?* was reprinted in full in the *New York Tribune,* German men crowded around the *Tribune* bulletin board all day long to read it. Not to be outdone, the Union League of Philadelphia sent out a thirty-page pamphlet solely to Pennsylvanians explaining in great detail why they should vote for Lincoln. For a year and a half, Union League men had labored on behalf of Republican candidates in state elections. With the all-important presidential election winding down, James Edmunds exhorted his "brothers" on October 18 to "Once more rally around the *Flag,* and your work will be complete." Over 140 years before the advent of the Internet and social media, the distribution of political messaging on such a widespread scale constituted the era's version of today's viral messaging.[20]

At the same time, the Democrats' propaganda campaign was also changing. The pamphlets produced by the Society for the Diffusion of Political Knowledge had initially set forth their positions in a calm, rationed discourse, such as Robert C. Winthrop's eloquent speech defending George McClellan. That work had purportedly appeared in multiple printings approaching 200,000 copies. By the fall of 1864, however, the Democrats at large had thrown such caution to the wind. The gloves were off and they were now reprinting speeches and editorials as scathing as anything published by their opponents. Yet all argued to save the Union via Democratic positions and values; none promoted Southern secession and independence.[21]

Partisan Democratic newspapers were another matter, however. While visiting Chicago in the days before the election, a Frenchman fluent in English concluded that reading the *Chicago Times* was no different than reading Rebel propaganda. "You would think you were reading the Richmond papers," he wrote.[22]

Yet in spite of the myriad constitutional, financial, or military issues that Democrats might have been harping upon, it seemed as if their primary rallying point was stoking fear of blacks among white voters. "The people are again to be surfeited with this nausea of the nigger," complained the *Detroit Free Press*, arguing that Yankee abolitionist desires trumped all other concerns that the Lincoln administration should have been focusing on. Chief among Democratic efforts was the publication of a widely distributed pamphlet titled *The Lincoln Catechism*. With its subtitle of *Herein the Eccentricities & Beauties of Despotism are Fully Set Forth*, the forty-eight-page pamphlet featured sarcastic questions and answers targeting Lincolnian policy and "Loyal Leaguers" that were certain to generate laughs among its antiblack audience. Even though administration officials branded *The Lincoln Catechism* pamphlet as treasonable, it was nonetheless issued by a New York publisher who even took out a copyright. Apparently looking to double down on their efforts, Democrats concocted another propaganda piece titled *Miscegenation: The Theory of the Blending of the Races, Applied to the American White Man and the Negro*, which was anonymously penned by the *New York World*'s managing editor. The pamphlet was an entire fabrication, having been designed to appear both "scientific" and congratulatory toward Lincoln and the Emancipation Proclamation. Its overall theme offered an explanation on how the inevitable mixing of the black and white races would create a new, superior brown race. Included in its racist stew was an analysis of why blond women were invariably attracted to black male slaves. The author's hope was that any public statements of approval by abolitionists or Republicans could be parlayed back against them by pointing out to much of the racist North just what a Republican victory would bring. In any case, the SDPK soon released a follow-up pamphlet alleging Republican endorsement of miscegenation. For Democrats, the need for such dire warnings was both genuine and obvious, given what they considered was at stake in the upcoming election.[23]

From the Republican and Union League position, however, such Democratic antiblack rants were not only predictable but hypocritical as well. For all of their public hand-wringing over miscegenation, Democrats, North or South, never mentioned the unspoken truth of white slave owners routinely exploiting their patriarchal authority by forcing themselves upon black female slaves and the "amalgamated" children who followed. An Indiana colonel was amazed to learn that Warrenton, Virginia, was noted for the great number of "white" slaves who were born there. "When we see the children together, it is in many instances impossible to distinguish the owner from the slave," he reported. A former Texas slave later echoed that reality, recalling how his white masters had all the black "girls" they wanted, including one black woman, who had four children, one right after the other, from her white master. "Their children was brown," the slave recounted to his white interviewer, "but one of them was white as you is." At the other end of the social spectrum stood women like Mary Chesnut, the famed South Carolina diarist who mingled at the pinnacle of Confederate high society, but would have nonetheless agreed with the old Texas slave. She declared to her diary that slavery was monstrous, and disparaged those genteel Southern lords who lived with their wives and concubines all under one roof. Chesnut reserved special scorn for the South's first ladies who could readily identify the father of all the mulatto children in any fine household, many of whom looked exactly like the white children, "but those in her own she seems to think drop from the clouds, or pretends so to think." More important to the Republicans was their conviction that such racial escapades illustrated how the Democratic Party had refused to accept how slavery had torn the country apart and that its end was necessary for reunification. Such overt anti-Lincoln, antiblack propaganda reminded the more Radical Republican and Union League men of the ample work still remaining once the shooting war ended.[24]

The Union Leagues' tactic of aggressively promoting their cause by distributing pro-Union pamphlets and arranging for Republican speakers while attempting to downplay, if not outright suppress, Democratic propaganda was having an effect as the campaign ground on. The Democratic *Detroit Free Press* warned its readers that the country was about to be "flooded with abolition documents" and how it was imperative that every Democratic voter do his duty to rescue the country from its impending peril. Adding insult to injury was the contention that much of the Republican propaganda was being sent out at taxpayers' expense. Over one hundred government clerks were alleged to have taken over all of the vacant committee rooms in the capital and were spending $18,000 per day to send pro-Lincoln literature across the country. "There is no lack of greenbacks here among the Lincolnites," the *Indianapolis Daily State Sentinel* reported. "The printing presses on the other side of the avenue being constantly kept busy to keep up the supply." In fact, eighty bags per day of propaganda was earmarked just for Sherman's army. The apparent lack of a similar party machine worried Democratic National Central Committee Chairman Charles Mason, who expressed deep concerns for his party's success in the crucial Pennsylvania vote after learning from one of the state's interior counties that Republicans were blanketing the state with their propaganda while no Democratic equivalents were seen anywhere. When he asked his committee why this was so, the mealy response was only that none could be sent. Furthermore, those few that were sent were allegedly not properly adapted to the voters. This concern over a lack of organization for distributing literature, expressed as early as mid-July by the *Bedford Gazette*, stood in stark contrast to the well-oiled machines of the Union Leagues and their fellow publication societies. The last thing either party wanted was a potential voter showing up at the polls on election day in a confused state.[25]

The act of voting in the mid-nineteenth century was completely unlike the orderly and personal ritual enjoyed by the well-behaved, twenty-first-century citizenry who assemble at modern polling precincts. Casting one's vote then was a public, not private, process witnessed by any who desired to watch. A citizen cast his vote by obtaining a ballot directly from his chosen party—known as a "party ticket"—that featured all of the candidates' names printed on it. It was the political party's responsibility to supply voters with their tickets either in advance of the election at preannounced locations, or party operatives would hand them out at the polling station on the day of the election. A political party's ticket was often printed on different color paper than the opposition tickets for ease of identification.[26]

The polling station was usually some prominent building, often the courthouse in a county's largest town, or perhaps even a saloon or other popular meeting place in smaller villages. In order to cast his vote, a voter typically had to step up onto a small outdoor platform and hand his party ticket through the chosen building's outdoor window to the waiting election officials in the corresponding and locked room inside the building. The entire area around the outdoors platform and building was deemed a public space that was often contested ground between the various political parties. Given this arrangement, a voter's choice was often easily visible to all. Jeers or even threats against the voter by opposition loyalists sometimes followed. The building served as the formal separation between the voting

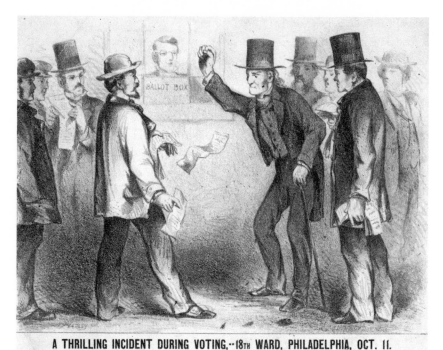

A THRILLING INCIDENT DURING VOTING,--18ᴛʜ WARD, PHILADELPHIA, OCT. II.

An old man over seventy years of age advanced to the window, leaning tremblingly on his staff, when an officious copperhead vote distributor approached him and thrusting a ticket in his face said, "Here is an old Jackson Democrat who always votes a straight ticket."

The old man opened the ballot and held it with trembling fingers until he had read one or two of the names, when he flung it from him with loathing, and in a voice husky with emotion, exclaimed: "I despise you more than I hate the rebel who sent his bullet through my dead son's heart! You miserable creature! Do you expect me to dishonor my poor boy's memory, and vote for men who charges American soldiers, fighting for their country, with being hirelings and murderers?"

"A thrilling incident during voting": An elderly man (with raised hand) is approached by a Copperhead vote distributor, who thrusts a ticket at him, saying, "Here is an old Jackson Democrat who always votes a straight ticket." The elderly man replies, "I despise you more than I hate the rebel who sent his bullet through my dead son's heart! You miserable creature! Do you expect me to dishonor my poor boy's memory, and vote for men who charges American soldiers, fighting for their country, with being hirelings and murderers?" (Library of Congress Prints and Photographs Division)

public outside and election officials inside with the latter giving little concern to what transpired beyond their room. In some geographic areas where one party dominated, burly men literally blocked the voter's access to the platform if they felt he was casting a vote for the opposition.[27]

George Boker was certainly aware of this process. In the days leading up to the election, he urged his League brothers to ensure that all Union League men spent the entire week before the election confirming all loyal men in their precinct, ward, or township were able and prepared to vote the Union ticket. The *Agitator* in Wellsboro, Pennsylvania, counseled all Union League men and any others in charge of Union Party ballots to keep one-half in safe reserve on election day, just in case there were any "accidents." The League men were warned to be especially vigilant against desperate Democrats who might try to circulate fraudulent tickets among the gullible. These Union League men, as well as Republican "party agents" had to be aware just how many voters were uneducated, maybe even illiterate, and had no understanding of how party politics and the grand issues of the day intersected to affect their daily lives. Party policies were watered down into simple slogans calculated to resonate with such voters. That they showed up to vote at all was often a victory and as long as they voted the Republican ticket, Republican and Union League operatives were indifferent as to which message brought about that vote. Alcohol was often offered to prospective voters, either as a courtesy to known loyalists or as a bribe to others. Such stratagems were in place throughout the country. One worker later recollected how "Night and day, without cessation, young men like myself, in halls, upon street corners, and from cart-tails, were haranguing, pleading, sermonizing, orating, arguing, extolling our cause and our candidate, and denouncing our opponents." All of these men were to devote the entire election day, as well as the day prior, to making sure every loyal man in their vicinity was coming out to vote for the Republican, aka Union, Party.[28]

Democrats were hardly conceding, of course. George Harlow, cofounder of the original Tazewell, Illinois, Union League, warned Illinois's Gov. Richard Yates that "The Union men of this county (Tazewell) are doing all in their power to carry it for the Union this fall; but I must confess if we do not have help the results are very doubtful. . . . The Copperheads have plenty of money and are using it lavishly. . . . If we can get the Soldiers home we send you will be safe result from the apparent apathy that seems to exist in this matter."[29]

Republicans and the Union Leagues sensed the election would be too close to call with only civilians voting. They identified an important ally in their citizen soldiers in uniform and accordingly, were fighting mightily within legislatures to make sure the boys in blue had a say in the election. Before the war, most soldiers had simply not been allowed to vote in the field. Moreover, the concept of absentee ballots had yet to be created. In the current conflict, this reality suited Democrats, who feared a mob-like "bayonet vote" would inevitably favor the commander-in-chief. Republicans obviously felt otherwise and bombarded the soldiers with campaign material, including a Republican-prepared pamphlet titled *A Few Plain Words with the Rank and File of the Union Armies,* which lauded the citizen soldier's historical integrity while playing up the soldiers' current antagonism toward Copperheads. Lincoln certainly agreed, reminding a crowd that "no classes of people seem so nearly unanimous as the soldiers in the field and the seamen afloat." His leading general, Ulysses S. Grant, also felt his men should have the same voting privilege as any man at home. "Nay, more," explained Grant, "for they have sacrificed more for their country."[30]

Given the growing groundswell on the matter, nineteen Northern states had enacted legislation permitting soldiers to vote away from their homes. Yet the sense of intimidation felt by home front Democrats certainly extended to those of similar political sympathies in the field. There was immense pressure to vote for the Union ticket. Since voting was a public act, few Democratic-leaning privates cherished garnering their comrades' enmity or the wrath of their Republican officers. An additional conundrum was that while some soldiers considered themselves firm, dyed-in-the-wool Democrats, they could not bring themselves to vote for a party that seemed so inimical to them and that had condemned their battlefield efforts as a failure.[31]

Not knowing whether they would be able to go home and vote, some regiments held mock votes in the field to see where their sentiments lay. A private in the 129th Illinois Infantry reported days before the election that in his regiment, Lincoln received 286 votes while McClellan garnered only thirty. He learned only days earlier how another regiment in his brigade, the 79th Ohio Infantry, offered only five votes to McClellan, the rest to Lincoln. Like scores of his comrades, one young Union private in the 1st New York Light Artillery wondered why the Copperheads were so against soldiers voting since they appeared so confident of a McClellan victory. Angered that such people viewed Union soldiers as merely "Lincoln hirelings," he advised his parents that "before they talk Copperheadism to a man in blue, they must first find out if he is a soldier or a slink."[32]

With less than three weeks until the election, the Union League of Philadelphia sent another circular to ULA councils throughout the North instructing them on how they could ensure each soldier from their town exercised his right to vote, which was clearly equated to a Republican/Union Party vote. Initially, the local League was asked to ensure that each soldier's name from their district was duly recorded on the assessment lists and that his property taxes were properly paid. If all was in order, the receipt was to be immediately sent to the soldier along with proxies for those who could vote by sealed ballot. League members were to visit every local house with a soldier in the field and compare all those names with the assessors list.

The League's circular stressed the soldier could vote only if he was duly assessed within ten days of the election and if his taxes were paid with receipt in hand as proof of the transaction.[33]

As election day neared, Grand National Council President James Edmunds exuded confidence as he considered the extensive networks of men and material his ULA had so diligently created on behalf of the administration. Their field reports were positive. He assured Connecticut's Mark Howard that with a fair vote, Lincoln would carry every state. On the other hand, he admitted how voter fraud might give McClellan three, maybe four states at most. As for the Philadelphia circular, Edmunds responded to the outside instructions by calmly reassuring Lincoln that his organization knew what they were doing in light of growing concern over how Pennsylvania might vote. He reminded Lincoln, "Ours, the 'Union League of America' is an organization of all work & no public demonstration," whereas "The Philadelphia Union League is one of great demonstration & considerable local work." Edmunds praised the Philadelphia men and reiterated his complete confidence in them, but also stressed to his president and friend that he should have no worries over the election's result. ULA men were at that moment securing votes in every part of the state and throughout Philadelphia. "You can have no doubt that I rely confidently upon the vote of Pa. & if we are not cheated Little Mac shall not have one vote," Edmunds reassured his friend, the president.[34]

Despite such assurances, the administration was concerned that Copperhead violence might break out in attempts to disrupt the election. Such fears were not unfounded. There were, of course, the deadly July 1863 New York draft riots to serve as a reminder. Antiwar riots had also taken place in 1863 in both Detroit and Boston. Since then, other violent acts perpetrated by disgruntled Copperheads and pro-Rebel saboteurs had occurred, including a bloody antidraft riot in Charleston, Illinois, on March 28, 1864, that left six Union soldiers dead and twenty more wounded after they were ambushed by armed Copperheads.[35]

Confederate agents had hijacked a Detroit passenger ship in September 1864 with the ultimate plan of seizing the USS *Michigan* on Lake Erie and then using the warship to free Rebel prisoners being held on Johnson's Island. More Rebel sympathizers hiding in Canada had attacked the tiny Vermont town of St. Albans, stealing over $200,000 from its banks and then trying to burn the village before fleeing. Union counterintelligence agents reported additional Confederate-sponsored attacks were in the works that sought to burn Northern towns. Throughout all of this, draft enforcement

officials had been shot and killed while attempting to carry out their enrollment tasks in rural areas.[36]

To counter the threat, Northern provost marshals planned to have troops
stationed anywhere violence was feared, which generally happened to be anywhere a Democratic victory was possible. Michigan's provost marshal, Lt.
Col. Bennett Hill, reported how he had organized each Union League council
into a home-guard company with the chapter leaders reporting directly to
him. "In [Detroit] alone, four thousand loyal men could have been called together in half an hour," Hill asserted. To outfit those men, Hill revealed his
state had a thousand stand of arms with ten rounds in every cartridge box,
under constant guard and ready for use. Detroit's *Free Press* reported that the
Union League of America's New York state council had urged its subordinate
chapters to organize military companies and then "arm and drill with the
utmost diligence." To Detroit's leading Democratic journal, these civilian–
military joint ventures were nothing more than "an armed conspiracy."[37]

In most cases, the soldiers' stated goal was to maintain an orderly election; however, they also sensed that those men most likely to try and disrupt
the voting were the same men most suspected of disloyalty. Not allowing
those men to vote for whatever reason could be concocted was viewed as the
easiest path to a well-ordered and calm process. James Edmunds implored
Lincoln on this need: "Some vigorous & prompt action may be required of
the Military Authorities in particular localities, especially in New York and
Maryland. Should this be the case I trust there will be no hesitation. There
is power in a bold hand at this time."[38]

Edmunds's concern for New York was well heeded. Fearing riots simi-
lar to those that tore the city apart in July 1863, Edwin Stanton ordered the
Union Army to occupy New York City with close to six thousand troops in
the days leading up to the election, all of whom were led by appropriately
loyal officers. This "special duty" force included units sent directly from the
Army of the Potomac. In command was Gen. Benjamin Butler, a reliably
Radical New York politician who had previous experience in such matters.
As military governor of New Orleans in 1862, Butler had enforced a harsh
occupation, which earned him the sobriquet "Beast Butler" from the Cres-
cent City's Confederate residents. The Union League Club of New York approved Butler's new duty, though Democrats were well aware of the general's reputed disregard for legal process and protested accordingly. All of this
prompted George Strong to humorously note in his diary, "It is quite natural

that rats should hold terriers unconstitutional and scandalous." As November 8 dawned, Lincoln was cautiously optimistic, though not overconfident. It was time to tally the votes.[39]

The popular vote conveyed a convincing though not overwhelming reelection victory for Abraham Lincoln with the president winning 55 percent of the ballots cast, tallying 2,213,665 votes to McClellan's 1,802,237. Lincoln's electoral vote win was far more decisive—221 to 21—winning in twenty-two of the twenty-five loyal and neutral border states. Only Delaware, Kentucky, and McClellan's home state of New Jersey went for the general. "There is no patriotic citizen who is not impressed and invigorated by this evident truth; no traitor who is not stricken and humiliated by the overwhelming rebuke which a sagacious people have administered to him," pronounced an ecstatic George Boker in his year-end report for the Philadelphia Union League. It was apparent that the fall military successes from Atlanta to the Shenandoah had bolstered spirits, giving the North new resolve to see the war through to the end. Republicans everywhere simultaneously proclaimed their jubilance while breathing a sigh of relief.[40]

Even more gratifying to Lincoln was the soldier vote, which showed a much wider margin of victory for Lincoln than had the civilian count. Those men in blue who cast ballots voted for the president by over a three-to-one margin (about 78 percent to 22 percent). In a few states this "bayonet vote" provided the margin of victory. After hearing from Lincoln how Maryland soldiers in the Army of Potomac had overwhelmingly voted for the administration, a War Department official in Baltimore thanked the president for the good news, and then succinctly summed up why the soldier vote was so crucial in the first place: "The soldiers are quite as dangerous to Rebels in the rear as in front." Lincoln had sensed this sentiment all along, confident his Union soldiers would vote in the same direction that they fired their muskets—against the butternut enemy and his alleged home front sympathizers.[41]

To Democrats, however, the military voting process had been rife with fraud, which is what they feared from the start. They suspected, and with good reason, that only Union League and Republican propaganda was distributed to the troops at the front while the Democratic equivalents that even reached the camps were simply tossed out or burned. Republican officers were alleged to have given not-so-subtle hints that soldiers who voted with Democratic ballots might soon find themselves on the front lines. Secretary of War Stanton all but admitted to this by telling the tale of one colonel who had landed a cushy quartermaster's position in Illinois, but when Stanton learned he was canvassing for McClellan, the man was demoted to captain and sent into the South. With an eye toward self-preservation, many Democratic soldiers opted to simply not vote. Assistant Secretary of War Charles Dana later admitted that his department's direct involvement in the contest was "almost painful" to watch and how "all the power and influence" of Edwin Stanton's office was brought to bear on Lincoln's re-election. Such proactive "on the ground" work by the Union Leagues, the publication societies, the Republican/Union Party, coupled with probable sabotage against Democratic soldiers being freely allowed to vote their conscience, led to the huge Lincoln win.[42]

Congressional Democrats were generally diplomatic in defeat. Sen. John Sherman informed his famous brother, Gen. William T. Sherman, that those he had spoken with were "willing to acquiesce cheerfully" to any new measures deemed necessary. Others privately admitted they would have lost even if every vote cast had been counted fair and square. Lincoln responded in kind, stressing that he held no ill will toward his opponents, but only the belief that they had acted according to their conscience. McClellan likewise appeared gracious, noting "the public had voted with their eyes wide open."[43]

The same magnanimous feelings were exhibited by a few of the Radical Republicans who had vehemently opposed Lincoln only several months prior. Salmon Chase offered his sincere congratulations to Lincoln. So did New York Union Leaguer Theodore Tilton, who reminded the president's secretary how he had nearly killed himself laboring on Lincoln's behalf in the campaign's final week. It was time to begin the diligent work of forgetting or, at least, covering up their one-time opposition.[44]

Democratic newspapers, conversely, were stunned and bitter at the magnitude of Lincoln's electoral win. Sour grapes regarding the results and the Union Leagues' involvement were everywhere. Indiana's *Fort Wayne Sentinel* considered the election "ruinous" to the nation and how the sun was now setting on the American experiment. Fearing what would now transpire over the next few years, the *Illinois State Register* declared the results as "the heaviest calamity that ever befell this nation" and then proclaimed "no living creature can hold the democratic party responsible." In its election postmortem, Ohio's *Ashland Union* referred to the Union Leagues as "that offspring of the Spanish Inquisition" and then alleged that the Leagues' "terrible and damnable oaths" were the reason so many men failed to vote their honest sentiments. At Columbus, the *Daily Ohio Statesman* warned its readers only days before the election that the "Loyal Leaguers" were scheming to vote in citizens attire in the morning and then again in soldiers' uniforms during the afternoon. After Lincoln's win, the paper complained how Loyal League "sycophants" had been operating their "political guillotines" without letup by warning Democratic office holders that a McClellan vote would cost them their positions. In Bloomsburg, Pennsylvania, the *Star of the North* angrily reported how the local Union League council "was never in more perfect working order" as its members had swarmed over polling sites purportedly warning workingmen that if McClellan won, they would all lose their jobs since local factories would be forced to close. The *Columbian Register* in New Haven, Connecticut, alleged that the Leagues had existed solely "to carry the Presidential election *by force,* if they found that bribery, and wholesale fraud, and the direct power of an army of office holders and government contractors was likely to fail them." In New York, the *World* railed against the Union Leagues' tactics. Though admitting the people had spoken and that it would put forth an "honorable submission to the will of the majority," the paper was especially bitter toward the League's "bigoted agency," "organized social exclusion," and how its "poisoned shafts of calumny" were used indiscriminately to demonize opponents' public reputations. Well aware of the old maxim that all is fair in love and politics, the most vicious and hyperpartisan mouthpiece of the Democratic Party was now accusing the Union Leagues of dirty pool. "We are compelled to enter our deliberate protest against a kind of warfare so alien to the spirit of the age and the genius of our institutions," it wrote.[45]

While Democrats had stood by their principles centering on constitutional conservatism—and firmly believing those principles held broad appeal—the message was lost in what historian Joel Silbey called "the welter of Republican [i.e., Union League] propaganda." Historically, and even today, once a party's candidate has been determined, the party attempts to move toward the political center in order to attract the largest number of wavering or undecided voters. With a party platform written almost entirely by its peace-at-any-price faction, it made little effort to move toward a less controversial position, and what effort was made was successfully blocked by the Republican–Union League counterattacks. When Republicans and their Union League allies alleged at the time that Democrats "had the smell of treason on their garments," it was a sincere belief and not a calculated falsehood spoken solely to win votes. The Union Leagues and their publishing society colleagues convinced the voting public that Democratic loyalty was indeed conditional. As a prominent Democrat later recalled of 1864, "It was not fashionable to be a Democrat. The glory of Lincoln and the Republican Party was shining like a midday sun. A Democrat was nothing but a Copperhead. He was considered little less than a traitor." Thus, the 1863–64 political campaigns were the circumstances that brought about Union League charges of disloyalty against Democrats, not the cause. Though many Republican and Democratic voters may have been dissatisfied with Lincolnian policies, this election was a case of "the devil I know is better than the one I do not know."[46]

As he had done the previous year, Lincoln had proclaimed a national "Day of Thanksgiving" in October, which was to be observed on the last Thursday in November 1864. It was an especially apropos moment, for the nation had just successfully concluded a democratic election in the midst of a civil war, an accomplishment that the world had never experienced before. In addition, with the Confederacy's armies on the ropes everywhere and its people lacking in virtually every necessity, the bloody war's end seemed close at hand.

Seeking to build on Lincoln's proclamation, the Union League Club of New York quickly turned its eyes back to the war and the Union soldiers and sailors. On November 3, the club began plans to send a Thanksgiving dinner to every possible Union man in uniform in the Armies of the Potomac, James, and Shenandoah. Those sailors on Atlantic coast blockade duty were also included; however, Western army men were not included solely because of logistics. The effort garnered the support of each commanding general and admiral and when the effort was completed, the Union League pointed with pride toward its logistical success. Over $56,000 was raised for the effort with scores of Northern citizens contributing anywhere from $1 or several jars of food to $100 or more. The effort resulted in approximately 225,000 pounds of poultry and all the trimmings being sent to the grateful men at the front.[47]

By attempting to provide a traditional Thanksgiving meal to Northern soldiers and sailors, the Union League Club of New York in particular and the Union League movement in general illustrated one of their strengths and better qualities: the ability to gather large resources in a short time outside of government bureaucracy for the benefit of a chosen cause. Of course, in any undertaking of such scale, there were misfires. Some soldiers and units received minimal supplies, if any, which the League readily acknowledged. An

Iowa officer called the whole affair "a damned humbug" and was aghast that he received only "two old Ganders" to feed twenty-eight hungry men. For the most part, however, the Union League delivered on its goal with scores of letters and notes of thanks being sent from the field. Starving Confederates, often within shouting distance of their Union enemy, enjoyed no such meal. In its eighty-five-page published report of the undertaking, the Union League Club of New York considered its effort a grand success. They even managed to take a friendly jab at their Philadelphia rivals, noting how the latter had been invited to cooperate. Much back-and-forth correspondence between the two Leagues followed, but in the end "no tangible result" was obtained.[48]

To use a popular modern phrase, the value of the immense number of civilian "boots on the ground" and campaign functions furnished to the Lincoln campaign by the Union Leagues and the Loyal Leagues cannot be overstated. Gustave Koerner, Lincoln's good friend and U.S. ambassador to Spain, described the Union Leagues as "perfectly organized" and a "powerful influence" after seeing their operations for the first time when he returned home from Europe in time for the 1864 election. William Stoddard aptly described the Union Leagues as "the most perfect party skeleton put together for utter efficiency of political machine work." The size of the Union Leagues in sheer manpower was enormous, yet unlike the blue-uniformed Union Army, League men (and women) were always somewhat hidden within Northern society. Many of the Loyal Leagues or Union Leagues considered themselves secret in nature, others perhaps less so. In any event, to their partisan Democratic enemies, League members were always cloaked as the friendly neighbor, or influential townsfolk such as the local judge, newspaper editor, or clergyman. All of these citizens seemed to be on guard against what they defined as treason and were successful in impressing their definition onto the public at large. Democrats, of course, had their own printing presses and political benefactors, but they lacked one crucial element that benefited the Union Leagues for two years going: the complete support and blessing of the president and party in power.[49]

Though he intentionally wrote his 1890 memoir of his time spent as Lincoln's secretary in the present tense, Stoddard was correct when he described in retrospect how "The Union League [was] to be the rearguard of the Boys in Blue, and its numberless 'councils' [were] to be as camp-fires. All that the loyal voting elements required was to be mustered in and drilled and disciplined, and the coming political battle-fields [were] now to be securely won beforehand." After the votes were tallied, ULA President James

Edmunds remarked how the Leagues had served as "a very powerful engine in the canvass, and, in the opinion of members, was the organization of all others that brought about this glorious result." The Union Leagues were, as Stoddard later wrote, "The most complete political machine ever known."[50]

Their colleagues at the three publication societies were likewise critical in making the case *for* Lincoln and perhaps more decisively, *against* the Democrat–Copperhead factions in a manner similar to the negative political commercials that dominate television, radio, and the Internet during today's political campaigns. It is worth reminding the reader that as mentioned in the "Introduction," modern public opinion analysis has illustrated that it is more effective to stir the people *against* a particular issue rather than *for* a specific cause. The Union Leagues and their allied publication societies successfully worked this principle in the minds of many voters by utterly blanketing the North with pro-Lincoln, anti-Democrat editorials and propaganda.

The Union League of Philadelphia's Board of Publications led the way. Though it published only seven pamphlets between April and August 1864, the Board made up for it by releasing twenty in the campaign's homestretch months of September and October. Between December 1, 1863, and November 8, 1864, the Board issued 1,044,904 copies of its various propaganda pamphlets, both in English and German. In addition, it distributed 560,000 copies of its *Union League Gazette* newspaper to civilians and soldiers throughout the land.[51]

New York's smaller Loyal Publication Society also scored successes. A Herkimer, New York, correspondent thanked the Society for sending him its publications. "They have exerted a very powerful influence in our rural lodges," he acknowledged. From Evansville, Indiana, another missive proclaimed how the country owed a debt of gratitude to the Society. Its work had a "very decided" influence, "tending powerfully to reduce the copperhead majority, which had always reigned supreme." In all, the Loyal Publication Society issued 470,000 copies of its thirty-three new works in 1864. Francis Lieber was a tireless workhorse, overseeing the translation of three key pamphlets into his native German language and one into Dutch as well. He also saw to it that most of the others conformed to his Radical Republican ideology. When the Society closed its doors for good in 1866, Henry Bellows noted that almost every Loyal Publication Society member was also a member of the Union League Club of New York.[52]

The New England Loyal Publication Society (NELPS) sent out two to three broadsides a week in 1864 until the presidential election was over, in addition to other pro-Lincoln propaganda sent to them for distribution. In its May 1865 report, the NELPS noted that broadsides were being regularly sent to the editors of 874 loyal newspapers in thirty-three states, three territories, and the District of Columbia. Another 556 were distributed to other recipients such as foreign newspapers, American consuls, various associations, and prominent individuals. In an attempt to gauge the effectiveness of its mailings, the Society sent out a questionnaire with return postage in January 1865 to the editors on its mailing list. It asked if, and generally how often, had the broadsides been utilized by the newspapers, if the overall political opinion in the newspaper's region was comparable to the Society's, and what was the opinion of the paper's readership with regard to freed blacks obtaining citizenship rights. The Society reported it had received 356 replies with just under 50 percent affirming they used the broadsides frequently. The *Indianapolis Gazette*'s response was typical in this regard, its editor replying, "I have made frequent use of them, generally publishing them as editorial—and often very glad to get them—both because their sentiment suited, and because they helped me to fill up my paper with good material." Twenty-seven percent reported using the broadsides occasionally with the remaining 23 percent stating seldom or never. From that last grouping, the *Palladium* in Richmond, Indiana, mockingly noted that since the broadsides were printed on only one side of first-rate quality paper, the blank side served wonderfully for the newspaper's own notices or editorials, and even as excellent wrapping paper. By publishing such a letter, we see that Norton was not without a sense of humor. Norton estimated at war's end that the bottom-line cost of printing and distributing the broadsides stood at just under three cents each.[53]

The New England Loyal Publication Society, New York's Loyal Publication Society, and the Union League of Philadelphia's Board of Publications had in the aggregate prepared, published, and distributed some two million pieces of pro-Union, anti-Democrat literature during 1864. Though the Union League of America's publishing efforts were minimal compared to the publication societies, their Washington, D.C., National Council headquarters distributed another 214,900 campaign pamphlets while acting as a clearinghouse for their brother societies. Other pro-Union organizations added to the flood. *New York Times* editor Henry J. Raymond was also the chairman of the Republican Party's national committee, known as the National Union Executive Committee. Raymond set up headquarters at the Astor House, home of his newspaper, and distributed scores of campaign documents from there while working hand in glove with the Union Party

Congressional Committee. The chair of that latter committee, Iowa's Sen. James Harlan, claimed his committee sent out over six million pieces of campaign literature as well.[54]

The aggregate total of literature sent by these allied groups is truly amazing when compared to the overall voting bloc: All of these sources, taken as a whole, distributed over three pieces of pro-Republican or anti-Democrat propaganda for every single individual who voted for Lincoln in the 1864 presidential election. When one considers that newspapers and pamphlets were routinely shared and read by many individuals beyond the initial recipient, it becomes apparent that the Union League and Publication Society viewpoint was read by millions of Americans, well over the four million total who voted in the election. In fact, Lincoln scholar William F. Zornow estimated that in the years 1863–64, in excess of ten million pieces of pro-Union literature were distributed to the masses. "No one can overestimate the magnitude of the silent work which was performed by this deluge of loyal literature," wrote George Boker in the Union League of Philadelphia's 1864 year-end report. "There is scarcely a homestead so retired into which one or more of our documents have not found a way of entrance, to the enlightenment of its secluded inmates."[55]

The Grand Secretary for the Washington-based Union League of America, W. R. Irwin, knew he was on to something when he had written prior to the 1864 Baltimore convention that "The League is the best means for the distribution of documents that has ever been devised. It saves much time and expense in the way of putting up and mailing." For Irwin, the key was in the numbers. "I can have fifty [pamphlets] put up in one package, send it to a Council; at their weekly meetings they are distributed among the members and by them placed in the hands of the proper parties."[56]

Whether these political opinion pieces were in a newspaper editorial, pamphlet, or broadside format, the sheer quantity of pro-Union, pro-Lincoln, and anti-Democrat printed material overwhelmed the thirty-nine pamphlets distributed by the Society for the Diffusion of Political Knowledge, the Democrats' lone national publication group. In any event, much of that Democratic literature had been banned from army camps or occasionally "lost" somewhere within the postal system. In what could be compared to the modern era's media battles between political action committees and their affiliated parties, the Union Party (Republicans) vastly outspent and outworked their Democratic opponents, significantly contributing to their electoral landslide victory.[57]

Chapter 12

"It Is a Fatal Mistake to Hold That This War Is Over Because the Fighting Has Ceased"

The Union League in Reconstruction

Lincoln's reelection was momentous for the Republican Party and its various allies. It signaled the Peace Democrats' end as a viable political opponent. The people had spoken; the nation's course was set for the next four years, with no knowledge of the presidential disaster only five months away. The bloody war continued on, however.

While many sensed the Confederacy was fading and Northern victory inevitable, when that glorious day would arrive was still anybody's guess. "For the time being we have silenced that opposition, *but not annihilated it,*" cautioned the ULA as a reminder that there was still ample work to do. If the North was secure, it was now the Union League's primary mission to follow the armies as they advanced deeper into Rebel-held areas. Much loyal work had already been accomplished in the Union-held areas of Arkansas and Tennessee; its work was indispensable in Missouri and Kansas for as the Union armies moved southward and secured geography, Unionist men came out of hiding to form loyal Union clubs who assisted the military in any way feasible. For instance, the Union Association of New Orleans was organized following the city's capture in 1862. Their efforts culminated in a rally on November 15, 1862, at the St. Charles Theater with Gen. Benjamin Butler, Governor Shepley, and Adm. David Farragut as honored guests. After Vicksburg, Mississippi, fell to Union forces in July 1863, that city's first Union League was formed in February 1864. In February 1865, Gen. Godfrey Weitzel reported that the Union League president for the Wilmington, North Carolina, council had surreptitiously provided him with excellent intelligence regarding the enemy's defensive works. Near the war's end, a secret Richmond Loyal League delegation met with Union troops as they prepared to enter the city. These Southern-born Unionist men became a cornerstone for the Union League of America's activities in the South. Now, its 1864 year-end report proclaimed, was the time to start focusing in on other loyalist regions. "As our military conquests increase, we shall have more difficult ground to cultivate—more ignorance to combat—more disloyalty to encounter," the League's leadership asserted.[1]

Part of that necessary work was aiding the Union loyalists in the South or border states who had found themselves under Southern boot heels for much of the war. Those who escaped murder or being tossed into jails often fled into the mountains, where they eked out a hardscrabble existence. Now it was the Union League who was looking to work with the Union military to offer assistance, often conferring with each other to determine where help was needed most. Other assistance included using League machinery to help recruit new soldiers where needed.[2]

An immediate focus on the political front was the debate over a constitutional amendment to abolish slavery. The Union League was unwavering in its commitment to this end, as well as a belief that there could be no armistice with the Rebels, no assumption of their debts when the war ended, and no measure of foreign aid to negotiate peace.[3]

Another important event was the creation of the Bureau of Refugees, Freedmen, and Abandoned Lands on March 3, 1865. Better known as simply the Freedmen's Bureau, this agency was intended to last only one year with the mission of assisting newly freed slaves make the transition from bondage to citizenship. Establishing schools for freedmen and offering help in finding work, food, clothing, medicine, and lost relatives were the Bureau's essential duties, along with acting as an arbiter in disputes between freedmen or between freedmen and whites. Most Southern Freedmen's Bureau representatives were active Union soldiers, some of whom found their way into the Union Leagues.[4]

Robert E. Lee's surrender at Appomattox on April 9 signaled the beginning of the end of military hostilities, though not necessarily the end of the rebellion, as the North would soon discover. Celebrations and resolutions echoed through every Northern city and hamlet. The Union Leagues and all loyal men felt vindicated because the perseverance they preached had brought about this glorious result. Those antiwar Democrats who had carped inces-

THE FREEDMEN'S BUREAU.—Drawn by A. R. Waud.—[See Page 167.]

The Freedmen's Bureau (Library of Congress Prints and Photographs Division from *Harper's Weekly*)

santly that Lincoln's war policies would never bear fruit now faced some private reassessment, for the war's convincing end had a way of changing one's perspective.[5]

As a member of the Union League Club of New York's Applications Committee, George Strong relished how men who were unabashed Copperheads two years earlier and ardent McClellan supporters from just the previous fall were now eagerly applying for admission to the Club. It appeared to Strong that every candidate presented himself as a zealous Union man right from the rebellion's start. "What a pity we had not known this a year ago," Strong confessed to his diary, no doubt with tongue firmly planted in cheek. "We should have been saved much uneasiness." These attempts to jump on the bandwagon and recast one's public and self-image were common. Regardless of the era, many men in influential positions often mistake a weather vane for the national flag. In the years to come, many Northerners would "recall" that they had always been committed abolitionists from before the war, with some proclaiming their home had served as an Underground Railroad safe haven. Everyone always loves a winner.[6]

. . .

Lincoln's November 1864 reelection coupled with the Civil War's conclusion in May 1865 marked the end of an era for the Union Leagues and all of the other pro-loyalty organizations the Leagues had influenced. With those two landmark events, the need for the Leagues as a "boots-on-the-ground," partisan political force in the North began to fade away. When George Boker wrote that "The rebellion is no more. It died hard, it died justly, it died, as all good men desired that it should, by the edge of the sword," he spoke directly to the Union Leagues' self-proclaimed, essential reason for existence, which was suppressing a treasonous rebellion while promoting a new idea of nationalistic loyalty. That new vision had been fulfilled, if only temporarily.[7]

As summer 1865 gave way to fall, the Midwestern small-town Union Leagues became the first to dissolve, their reasons for existence now ended. Even with the war over, Democratic papers remembered the enmity they felt toward the Leagues and noted their passing with glee. "May thy soul march where John Brown's soul is marching, and may no singing, however sweet, ever awaken thee to curse thy country again!" wrote the *Dayton Daily Empire* as its bitter farewell to the Leagues.[8]

For the elite clubs in Philadelphia, New York, and Boston, their existence continued unabated. The Union League Club of New York chose to battle municipal corruption at the state and local level while promoting freedmen suffrage in the South. Though the Club continued to be staunchly pro-Republican and nationalistic in its outlook, the emotional war-footing that the members had thrived on likewise began a slow but steady weakening. By September 1866, George Strong felt the Club he cofounded was ever more radical and degenerating. He lamented that the "first-rate men" who had battled home front treason in 1863 were mostly gone. Though the Club's membership and gatherings seemed as large as ever, Strong felt they were now "made up mostly of people who look and talk like low politicians and wire-pullers." In Philadelphia, George Boker also sensed an emotional letdown, cautioning one and all that the Union League must not become "a congregation of insipid idlers and nerveless pleasure-seekers."[9]

Meanwhile, Lincoln's plan for the South's reconstruction was magnanimous and forgiving, far more so than the Radicals wanted to see. The president, however, was felled by the assassin's bullet on April 16, triggering Vice-President Andrew Johnson's ascension into the White House. The fifty-six-year-old Johnson was an ardent War Democrat from Tennessee and was the only senator from a seceded state who had not resigned his seat in 1861. Lincoln repaid that loyalty by making Johnson Tennessee's mili-

tary governor in 1862 after his Senate term ended and then again by select-
ing him as Lincoln's 1864 running mate. Politics was also a consideration,
prompting Lincoln to select Johnson due to the belief that he could siphon
off an ample number of Democratic votes away from the peace faction in
the 1864 election. Though a committed, antislavery Unionist, Johnson subscribed to the era's commonly held racist convictions and was therefore opposed to the idea of racial equality. Now that he held the executive branch's
reins of power, Johnson's reconstruction intent was to continue Lincoln's
olive branch offerings, not to elevate the black man, however, but purely
as a means of reestablishing economic stability and white dominance in
the defeated South. In spite of Congress's recent passage of the Thirteenth
Amendment to the Constitution abolishing slavery, Johnson saw no role for
blacks in the forthcoming Reconstruction.[10]

Johnson wasted no time putting his plan in place. On May 29, he announced two proclamations that bypassed Congress since that body was in
recess. Much of his edicts were similar to what Lincoln had put forth almost a
year and a half earlier. Provisional governors were installed who would oversee the reorganization. This "Presidential Reconstruction" offered amnesty to
all white Southerners who took a loyalty oath. High-ranking ex-Confederate
officers and governmental officials were excluded from that offer, along with
those who owned $20,000 or more in property. Those men could, however,
appeal directly to the president for a pardon. The Union League of America's
new official newspaper, the *Great Republic*, reported that by January 1867,
Johnson had granted roughly eighteen thousand such pardons. Southerners
were also free to form their own new state governments and elect federal legislators as long as secession and slavery were formally repudiated in the new
state constitutions. Former slaves, however, were given few rights.[11]

Though the small-town, Midwestern Union League councils were slowly
closing up shop, the Union League of America's Washington-based Grand
National Council had every intention of maintaining its existence, overall radical ideology, and influence. With the Civil War's great questions
now answered, however, the ULA realized that a major sea change in its
focus was required for it to remain a viable political force. The League's
gaze shifted from promoting loyalty and combating treason in the Northern states toward organizing freedmen under the Republican banner in the
states of the defeated Confederacy.

For the revamped, southward-looking Union League, Johnson's executive orders were troubling. Republicans considered it imperative that the

reconstructed South not produce legislators or policies inimical to "Northern interests," i.e., Republicans, or to the former slaves. Northern businessmen now dominated Washington so they also had no desire to see an agrarian and rejuvenated South upset their lucrative apple cart. All could see that the South's legislators, once reseated in Congress, would hold the nation's balance of power in their hands. To some of Congress's Radical Republicans and their business allies, the humbled South presented a golden economic opportunity to secure business interests in a Republican-dominated region that would last for generations via millions of newly registered black voters. Others with more abolitionist leanings saw the opportunity to fulfill their dreams of racial equality. Whether capitalistic or moralistic, the issues over which North and South fought the Civil War and initiated Reconstruction were, to a large degree, a revolution of, by, and for white men generated by black exploitation. Radicalism became the sole similarity between the Northern Union Leagues of the Civil War years and the Southern Union Leagues in the postwar, Reconstruction era.[12]

The Radicals were shrewd enough to realize that the latter goal depended on the former for without black votes, the Republicans were destined to remain a minority party throughout the Democratic-dominated white South. The Union League of America and its organizational machinery became the primary grassroots tool in this new political war. Funding could not be forgotten, however. The ULA knew that without congressional aid, they would not be able to long compete against the South's aristocracy, who controlled most of the region's purse strings, political experience, and social influence.[13]

The League's centralized Grand National Council became the guiding force for the new movement. Existing Union League organizers traveled south along with new members comprised of Freedmen's Bureau representatives, schoolteachers, and preachers. Union military officers still stationed in the South signed on, as well as ex-Union soldiers who had decided to remain in Dixie and were committed to the Union League's progressive ideals. Yet the League's new effort started off with a more moderate tone than its Radical goals may have suggested. The Union League certainly wanted blacks to gravitate toward Republican Party objectives, but there was concern that any festering black aggressiveness could prove troublesome, both to white planters as well as the white yeoman farmers whom the League was trying to recruit. After all, the Civil War's crushing military defeat along with black emancipation in only four years represented a complete upheaval in Southern culture and way of life that had developed over countless generations. In order to downplay this dangerous mix, the Union League leadership instructed its field activists and organizers to present the League as a benevolent society along the lines of the Freedmen's Bureau and Aid Societies. This inoffensive face hid their Radical mission and avoided confrontation with disgruntled Southerners whose ultimate support would be critical to League success.[14]

While many of the League's field organizers and activists were individuals truly dedicated to the betterment of freed bondsmen, there was a shadier element who slipped through the cracks and joined solely to enrich themselves by taking advantage of the social chaos that still reined. These Northern white individuals were disdained in the South and given the epithet of "carpetbagger," a sordid Yankee who had seemingly packed everything he owned into a carpet salesman's oversized sample bag and headed south to exploit the region for personal gain in any way possible as it strove to rebuild. A carpetbagger and a white Union League man, regardless of the latter's intent, soon became synonymous to Southerners.

The Union League's Washington leadership and its field agents were still an entirely white order and as it spread southward after the war, much of its local membership was initially comprised of the white middle-class and working poor who lived in the uphill and mountain counties. Most of these men were the hardscrabble farmers whose families had never owned slaves and became the most disillusioned with the Confederacy's "rich man's war, poor man's fight" conscription policies. Desertion and draft evasion became rampant in those regions as the war progressed. They loathed the wealthy planter and judged him as the guilty party who had brought about Southern devastation, solely to keep slavery intact so that "King Cotton" exports could keep flowing. These disaffected white, working-class yeomen were those that President Johnson, most of Congress, and the Union League of America hoped would become the new dominant force in reconstructed white Southern politics.[15]

Not surprisingly, those Southerners who had supported the Confederacy viewed the region's Unionists in a different light. To ex-Confederate Chief of Ordnance Josiah Gorgas, the new Union Leagues were mainly comprised of those ex-soldiers who "always skulked during the war" and were now turning their backs on their own people. This homegrown version of the carpetbagger became known to Southerners as "scalawags": men who were born and raised in the South but then allied themselves to the black Republican Yankees after the war ended as a means of securing wealth or position. As

League councils began to take hold in the South in 1866 and 1867, Southern white Unionists rose in local League hierarchy "like scum upon the pot," recalled a Georgia physician. The scalawag was scorned by Southerners as a traitor to his land, his people, and perhaps most importantly, his race. Other men proposed joining the League under false pretenses, solely as a means of plotting subterfuge against it. However, most Southerners were deterred against this tact believing they would most likely be considered scalawags. Both found their way into early Union League leadership positions in the South. By 1866, roughly 80 percent of the mountain population in the Southern states had become League members.[16]

Unfortunately for Democrat Andrew Johnson and the Republican Party, the results he expected in his May 1865 presidential edicts failed to materialize. Congressional Radicals became incensed and Johnson himself dismayed when it became clear that white Southern voters were placing local affairs back into the hands of prominent planters and ex-Confederates rather than the Unionists Johnson had counted on, which was no surprise considering that the government had failed to enfranchise blacks, which would have given Republicans the ballot margins they needed. Both Johnson and Congress had, in fact, overestimated the depth of Southern Unionist sentiment. Concurrently, the white aristocracy who led the South into a bloody four-year war to maintain a way of life predicated on slavery was simply not going to roll over and relinquish every vestige of its culture, even though its military rebellion had failed. The conservative white South would continue that struggle by other methods, as historian George Rable noted by altering Clausewitz's well-known maxim, "for the South, peace became war carried on by other means."[17]

As part of an early, postwar Southern tour that included a stop in northeast Florida, recently seated Supreme Court Chief Justice Salmon Chase wrote to President Johnson in mid-May 1865 warning of that specific Southern mindset. Chase met with David Yulee, a wealthy, "fire-eating" Floridian who had served as a U.S. senator prior to the war. Yulee admitted that while national reunion and slavery's death were final, some manner of "coercing labor" had to be initiated to replace slavery. Moreover, it was imperative that Southern white men remain in power because if not, according to Yulee, "the Southern states will be Africanized and ruined." On a more positive note, Chase wrote that he saw "colored citizens" forming Union Leagues everywhere. Recalling how the Union Leagues had influenced Northern affairs during the war, Chase advised Johnson that the new Southern Leagues could "form a power which no wise statesman will disregard."[18]

Even more troubling than the ex-Rebels coming back into power were new "Black Codes" that the revised state legislatures were passing. Based on the conviction that free blacks were idlers wholly unprepared for citizenship, the codes sought to maintain white dominance over black movement. The old slavery system may have been abolished, but this new structure was much the same, just under a new facade. Under the codes, blacks were denied the right to vote, forbidden to serve on juries, or testify against whites in a court of law. Planters demanded that freed blacks sign annual labor contracts, thus returning many former slaves back to the plantation. Those unemployed blacks who refused to sign contracts were routinely arrested for vagrancy and sentenced to chain gangs. "It is a fatal mistake to hold that this war is over because the fighting has ceased," declared Boston Union Club member and noted attorney Richard Dana in 1865 after learning of what was transpiring. This growing realization among blacks and white Radicals that the gains won from war could now be lost gave new energy to the Union League movement.[19]

As Reconstruction turned more state and local governments back into the hands of former Rebels, Union League members feared for their safety for it was believed that the former would look to settle old scores with the latter. At its annual Washington meeting in December 1865, the ULA's Executive Committee admitted that its minimal success to date in recruiting white councils was due to the society's generally chaotic state. This included white workingmen's inability to fully grasp the League's mission, which was due in large measure to Dixie's planter class maintaining control over the masses, whom the latter was not yet willing to disobey. This was all the more frustrating since the Freedmen's Bureau head, Gen. Oliver O. Howard, was willing to have Bureau agents distribute Union League literature.[20]

In discussing its results, the ULA reported that only ten councils were formed in South Carolina, composed almost entirely of freed slaves. Yet the League's early efforts in the Palmetto State did offer a ray of hope to both the League and the freedmen, proclaiming how "It provides them with the best of political schools . . . and the moral power of the social system." Just as important, the council noted that efforts to date had shown the freedmen the importance of the Union League. "It will give them the power of self-protection and mutual assistance, which they cannot get in any other way." A black sailor in Wilmington, North Carolina, privately confirmed the council's concerns in his diary, recording that though there were two Union League councils in that woebegone town, all recent meetings were cancelled due to the lack of a quorum.[21]

The Radical legislators could only stand by and watch throughout the summer and fall of 1865, but when Congress reconvened in December, they refused to seat the recently elected Southern congressmen. Furthermore, they demanded that Johnson's program be scrapped. They wanted a more forceful Reconstruction plan that granted black suffrage and barred former Confederates from holding elected office. A compromise between the more moderate and Radical elements in Congress resulted in the 1866 Civil Rights bill, which essentially voided the hated Black Codes by granting blacks every right accorded white men, including birthright citizenship. The right to vote, however, was again the one notable exclusion. The existing Southern state legislatures could remain in power as long as they granted these essential civil rights to blacks.

To everyone's shock, Johnson vetoed the bill and then stubbornly refused any type of compromise. Johnson's racism rose to the surface, claiming blacks were unworthy of citizenship rights and, furthermore, the questions on the table were a states' rights matter that was inappropriate for federal government consideration. The congressional Radicals were in no mood to listen to such an argument, coming as it was on the heels of a bloody civil war that settled much of that very topic. Yet moderate Republicans and Democrats saw the Union League's agitations as directly contributing to the growing legislative tension. Democratic-leaning Secretary of the Navy Gideon Welles was no admirer of the Union League during the war and was especially dismayed now, complaining to his diary how "The Union League has contributed largely to present difficulties," for, as Welles believed, they were "an irresponsible faction, organized for mischief."[22]

Nonetheless, Congress obtained the two-thirds majority vote necessary to override Johnson's veto that April, a first in the history of American law. Congress moved forward without Johnson, passing the Fourteenth Amendment in June 1866, which guaranteed equal protection to all men in the eyes of the law, though it still denied blacks the right to vote. If Southern states refused to pass the amendment, their congressional representation would suffer. Again, Southern white intransigence against racial equality rose to the fore. Andrew Johnson likewise deplored Congress's actions and urged Southern states to defy Congress. The ULA's New York state council

The Union League procession passing Independence Hall, Philadelphia, and cheering the flag raised by Abraham Lincoln in 1861. (*Harper's Weekly*, September 22, 1866)

responded by denouncing Johnson, accusing the president of having "prostituted his high office to the purpose of faction and disloyalty."

The Union League of Philadelphia also reentered the fray by publishing a widely disseminated pamphlet whose title asked the rhetorical question, *Is the South Ready for Restoration?* The answer was not yet. The pamphlet's anonymous author spoke for the Radicals and the Union League movement by declaring, "the South has learned nothing and forgotten nothing. Unabashed, unhumiliated, unrepentant, it comes up to us with its old swagger, yielding nothing and demanding everything, listening to no reason and threatening revolution and confusion. It acknowledges only the empire of force." Nine of the ten Southern states required to ratify the amendment refused to do so. Only Tennessee ended up ratifying the amendment. Andrew Johnson and Congress were headed to an inevitable showdown. Meanwhile, freed slaves in the South were compelled to place their interests first.[23]

Regardless of the Washington wrangling or the objectives that Northern white politicians may have set for themselves, freed blacks quickly established their own set of priorities, which became the driving force for Southern League expansion. In the agrarian South, true black freedom meant access to

land. The right to till their own farms meant independence from the plantation bondage system and the white overlords who went with it. White planters, meanwhile, did all they could to keep the new realities as much like the
old system as possible by often refusing to sell or rent land to blacks. White
merchants who did business with blacks felt their neighbors' disapproval
or were ostracized. This growing black unrest toward social conditions that
were all too familiar with bondage spawned a black political movement that
the Leagues were able to tap into rather than create. White Union League
leaders, often with the help of ex-Union black soldiers, began to create black-
only Union Leagues. Blacks knew that until they achieved voting rights and
obtained their own land, they remained in a quasi-slavery state. Their growing confidence in knowing what their local communities needed and wanted
led to a more assertive black role within the Leagues. Much of that community discussion occurred in the church, another social institution that freed
people were increasingly setting up under their own control. Though slaves
and their white masters had sometimes attended the same church, the pews
themselves were highly segregated with blacks being pushed to the back and
upper balcony. With their new freedom in hand, blacks soon left those con-
gregations that they saw as tainted with racism. The mere act of leaving demonstrated their freedom to both themselves and their former white masters.
Where they were to go next was a secondary matter for the time being.[24]

As blacks became more knowledgeable of local and state politics, white
leadership within the black-only Union Leagues began to dissipate. Their
growing political awareness translated into blacks seeking a greater role
within the council. Since officers were generally elected by member vote,
black men seeking a leadership role had little difficulty in obtaining support from their brother members. It was an educational process, for ac-
quiring knowledge of any sort was paramount to freed blacks, especially
learning how to read. If a man knew how to read, then he could engage in
business or contracts without being cheated, all of which was another element of true independence. As word of new councils spread, freed blacks
would often travel twenty miles or more to hear Union League speakers
or other educated men read newspapers and announcements to them. All
of this "gone to meeting" travel proved vexing to local white farmers, who
remained in their fields and sometimes proved problematic to Freedmen's
Bureau agents, who were more concerned with the former slaves' physical welfare than their political indoctrination. One agent complained that
since his district's primary mission was to prevent famine, the several days

that freedmen spent traveling to and from Union League gatherings would have been better spent at home working their plots and keeping the weeds from overtaking their corn. His advice to those who traveled great distances was to begin "Loyal Leagues" in their own neighborhood.[25]

In spite of time and distance, those former slaves who journeyed the miles considered their political education worth the trip. Often the orators were educated black men with church-affiliated credentials. In many instances, freedmen reported it was the first time anyone, white or black, had ever explained their new civil and political rights to them. Union League officials acknowledged these educational goals, therefore they strove to align their political objectives with the black community's current needs by setting up schoolhouses and supplying teachers. Those councils who were most successful did so by tapping into the culture and customs within the black community. The true carpetbagger soon found himself exposed and shown the door.[26]

The second key issue to the newly freed black community was self-defense against a white population that in many instances refused to accept former slaves acting upon their new role of free citizens. Informal militias and martial drilling soon took hold as a constant reminder to blacks of the risks they faced. League meetings were generally held at night and at places that would attract minimal attention. Armed sentinels ringed the meetinghouse, which was often a black church or schoolhouse. In South Carolina, for example, the Union League—now nicknamed the Loyal League and of no relation to the 1863 New York organization of the same name—was also the Negro militia.[27]

Given the relentless intransigence on the part of Johnson and the South, the congressional Radicals passed their own Reconstruction bill over the president's veto in March 1867. Known formally as the Military Reconstruction Act of 1867, or colloquially as congressional Reconstruction, it was far more punishing toward the South than anything Lincoln or Johnson had imagined, and represented precisely what each president had strove to avoid. The act divided the South into five military-run districts, each headed by a renowned Union general. Only those Southerners approved by Congress could vote, which were primarily white Unionists and, for the first time, freed black men. Any elected official had to pledge loyalty to the Union. New state constitutions were mandated that were to serve as precursors to each state ratifying the Thirteenth and Fourteenth constitutional amendments.

Another key tenet of the 1867 Act was to deny the president the right to discharge officials who were placed into office with congressional consent, unless that body agreed to the dismissal. Johnson immediately ignored what was known as the Tenure of Office Act by firing Secretary of War Edwin Stanton, who had long been a Radical favorite. It was the final straw in the simmering battle between the congressional Radicals and the president. Congress charged Johnson with a list of "high crimes and misdemeanors" and initiated impeachment proceedings in the spring of 1868. The movement failed by a single vote, but Johnson and the Democrats were damaged in the process, which resulted in the election of Republican Ulysses S. Grant to the presidency in November 1868.

The 1867 congressional Reconstruction Act provided the impetus and a major turning point for the postwar Union League. James Edmunds argued that since the League had always put forth a secretive and mysterious facade, it provided the perfect cover to instill Republican loyalty among the new freedmen. The *Great Republic* argued that very point prior to the Act's passage, pointing out that there were six million loyal black and white men in the South. It was imperative they become properly organized in order that their voting power could be brought to bear for the loyal states. "This is the work for the Union League of America, which must be promptly performed," the paper asserted. When the congressional Reconstruction Act was passed in March, the ULA counted 300,000 members in the South ready to work.[28]

Thomas W. Conway, a staunch Radical and former Freedmen's Bureau commissioner in Louisiana, was named as the League's new special organizer for the South. His mission was to ensure that the Union League gospel was being preached throughout the region. Edmunds had also secured the Republican Congressional Committee's full cooperation, but the Committee and the ULA soon learned an important lesson: Bombarding the region with political pamphlets would not work as it had in the North during the Civil War. Since the new black voters were politically inexperienced and largely illiterate, it became obvious that the Union League would have to change its message delivery method. Its target audience would hear speakers instead of being expected to read pamphlets. This resulted in numerous Radical congressmen joining Conway to explain both the rights and responsibilities of citizenship. Furthermore, when Conway arrived in the South, he carried with him a personal letter of introduction from Oliver O. Howard asking that his Freedmen's Bureau agents assist Conway in any possible manner.[29]

The League had also made a major decision to desegregate its Southern councils. Whereas the early chapters were white-only, which had then been followed by black-only councils, new and existing councils were now avail-

Thomas W. Conway (Author's collection)

able to both whites and blacks. This new directive prompted an immediate backlash from Southern white members. Many chose to abandon the Union League or if they stayed, did so only in fully segregated chapters. Those who operated on a biracial basis, such as the council in Hamburg, North Carolina, still kept a close tally of its white and "colored" members. Most of those who left had joined the Union League in 1865–66 as a means of furthering their own political welfare, with the hoped-for additional bonus of seeing the ex-Confederate gentry knocked down a peg or two on the political ladder. They cared little, if at all, for black rights. In fact, most League organizers also cared little for black equality. Their primary concern was directed toward ensuring blacks embraced the national radical Republican agenda.[30]

Nevertheless, freed blacks flocked toward the Union Leagues as a means of political organization once they learned of the Military Reconstruction Act due to its promise of voting rights. Its secretive nature also provided a form of cover. This reassurance, coupled with growing dissatisfaction over conservative white unwillingness to grant them a seat at the civic table, provided the required incentive for the Union League to become a mass

movement in the South. Union League recruitment activity, which had occurred primarily near larger cities, now fanned out across the plantation
belt, where most former slaves still lived. League-sponsored voter registra-
tion drives were commonplace. "You never saw a people more excited on
the subject of politics than are the Negroes of the South. They are perfectly
wild," wrote one plantation overseer.[31]

The ULA had not forgotten how the mysticism of its initiation rite had
attracted Northern white men during the Civil War. It now took every solemn observance in its ritual manual to entice black freedmen seeking membership. Tales abounded as to how League organizers went from one black
village to the next, warning naive residents that their old masters had plans
afoot to enslave them yet again and that only Union League membership
would save them. Candles and incense provided the sight and smell to a
secret induction ceremony that revolved around an American flag draped
over an altar. An open Bible and a copy of the Declaration of Independence
were placed on the flag. Like the earlier wartime initiation rituals, an anvil,
sickle, or any other "emblems of industry" available were to accompany
the scene. The council's marshal and applicants read prayers and recited
pledges to the country and the Union League. After the ceremony, "Grips,
signs and passwords were given to the freedmen" and they were then told
that they had "received something beyond the reach and conception of
their former masters," recalled a past witness. Meetings often occurred in
black churches or schools, but if no similar building was available, the initiation occurred in the woods, with the new initiates solemnly pledging
their fealty to the United States Government.[32]

Congress's actions were cheered by the Southern Union Leagues. Alabama's Grand Council passed resolutions praising Congress for its "patriotic action" that would allow "true Union men" to reorganize the state government on fair terms. It decried the rebellion as the highest crime known
to law and that its leaders still lived only by "the clemency of an outraged
but merciful government." Still, the council was willing to welcome any to
the Republican Party who were willing to disown all of the principles upon
which the rebellion began.[33]

The Augusta, Georgia, council reported "a very large and harmonious"
meeting that cheered the new Act. The council passed resolutions urging
that blacks be allowed to register to vote as soon as possible and that a copy
of the resolutions should be sent to Augusta's mayor for prompt action.[34]

Tennessee posed a typical race relations scenario within the Southern states. Its legislature was filled by Radicals after the war, yet as the late 1867 elections approached, new battles emerged. Fall 1867 marked the first time that freedmen had the right to vote. The Union Leagues reminded black voters just who their true friends were and that a bright future lay in store for freedmen if they were true to the Republican Party. White conservatives retorted that League promises were bald lies, that the Republicans had no intention of helping blacks and were simply bamboozling them for their own gains. It was a conundrum for blacks, most of whom were illiterate. The majority ended up siding with Republicans because they were willing to take the chance that there was some truth to Republican promises. With Democrats, however, black men and women remembered all too well what was in store for them in that direction.

In North Carolina, the Republican Party was established in 1867 at approximately the same time as the Union League. Gov. William Woods Holden endorsed Union League activity while agitating for black equality. Like elsewhere, the pushback from white conservatives became intense. The Radical rhetoric and political education of their former slaves enraged Southerners. Few whites would conduct business with blacks and those who did demanded immediate cash payment. An elderly black man in Orange County, North Carolina, for example, sought to borrow funds from fellow freedmen against his fall crop since no white conservative would grant anyone who voted Republican, especially blacks, a loan. Since few blacks were receiving cash for their labors, the old man reported, many were in a desperate financial condition.[35]

Even Florida with its small population experienced significant Union League activity. There was even some competition in the form of a more conservative loyalty group formed by Thomas Osborn—the head of Florida's Freedmen's Bureau—that was known as the Lincoln Brotherhood. First formed in Tallahassee, the secret organization utilized every secretive Union League ritual, including armed sentinels at meetinghouses along with signs and countersigns for entry. The Brotherhood spread throughout north Florida in 1866 before merging with Florida's Loyal League the following year.[36]

Daniel Richards, a white Radical from Illinois, first came to Florida in 1866 as a tax commissioner and immediately saw the Leagues' influence in existence. Union League organizing activity prompted white violence against blacks of such hatred that Richards feared a race war more likely than any other eventuality. In fact, Richards had complained to friend and Illinois Rep. Elihu Washburne that his most pressing challenge was preventing well-armed freedmen from seeking vengeance against whites. "The Blacks know their strength and power that anytime they can drive every rebel into the sea, or kill him," wrote Richards. Florida conservatives' fury toward racial equality was so intense that they would gladly give up their congressional representation if it meant gaining control over Florida's state government. Anything to them, reported Richards, was preferable to giving blacks equal voice, for whites realized that meant the end of their power and dominance.[37]

Returning to Florida in 1867 as one of Florida's primary Union League organizers, Richards tore into white conservatives in his speeches. He accused them of plotting to return blacks to slavery if only given the chance. For freedmen, the only way they could protect their families and newfound rights was to vote for the Republican Party. In order to do that, they were told they first had to join the Union League, a falsehood considered necessary to keep freedmen aware and motivated. White Southerners alleged that the League's black-oriented initiation ceremony played against the ignorant blacks' darkest superstitions. Some conservative Floridians reacted by threatening emigration to the British Honduras rather than live with freedman as social equals. Others advised white planters not to hire black Union League members.[38]

This growing Union League–led mass movement on behalf of organizing blacks and educating them on their newfound civil rights sent shockwaves through the Southern white community. South Carolina's provisional governor, Benjamin F. Perry, considered the Leagues "diabolical," as they strove to separate the freedman from "the influence of his true friends and neighbors."[39]

That freedmen had and still were creating militias to defend themselves was intolerable, for nothing generated more white fear than tales of black men under arms. For generations, the white South's greatest fear was an armed insurrection initiated by any of the region's four million slaves. As an effect of that ingrained dread, Southerners were willing to believe the worst regarding black motives and intentions. Now, right in their midst, white Southerners heard repeated rumors of how blacks were preparing to pillage white communities. This fear only added to the anger created by the sight of lowly scalawags openly hobnobbing with hated carpetbaggers. If suffering a humiliating defeat in the Civil War was not bad enough, the old Confederacy's slaveocracy now witnessed one of their worst nightmares coming to pass: The vile Yankee government's guns and bayonets protecting a coalition comprised of the planters' former chattel—now armed and drilling—and the region's "low white trash."

James Edmunds and Southern Republican newspapers stressed to nervous Southerners that the Union League only represented temperance, education, and an adherence to the rule of law and to lawful authority. "The League by its teachings stimulates loyalty to Republican progress and principles; it produces organized and concerted action . . . and asserts the duty and dignity of labor," Edmunds wrote. As far as he was concerned, the ULA's goals and methods were fully transparent and open to public inspection. The Leagues' "only secret consists in the fact that its opponents are excluded from the deliberation of its councils." Simply, the League was not seeking anything but to help cultivate Southern resources. Thomas Conway brought this message with him in his 1867 organizing mission. In North Carolina at least, the ULA's assertions rang true. No conviction or even an indictment was ever brought against the League or a member for any of the depredations alleged against it by conservative whites. This is even more remarkable considering that functioning civil courts and grand juries existed at the time that were comprised almost entirely of white men.[40]

Nevertheless, these promises carried little sway with conservative white Southerners. They were unable to see black freedmen as anything other than shiftless and morally depraved creatures impinging upon whites' divine rights. Moreover, conservative whites felt that the few dollars blacks did legitimately earn usually ended up in the pockets of fraudulent land surveyors or Freedmen's Bureau agents, whom a *New York Herald* correspondent described as "a useless, expensive, and cumbersome humbug." This pitched battle in Congress, state capitals, newspapers, and small-town meeting halls over the proper place of former slaves was the lone hindrance to peaceful reunification. "The Union Leagues throughout the South and their incendiary radical orators who go about like so many roaring lions, seeking out the negroes to harangue them," wrote the *Herald*, "are chiefly to blame for this state of things."[41]

Southern fear that black freedmen would seek armed revenge against their past overlords was transformed into rage by the sight of blacks gathering at the polls to vote as equals. The mathematics were irrefutable. If the Republican-oriented Union Leagues were allowed to have their way, white Southern Democrats felt they would find themselves in a politically subservient position similar to what their slaves had endured for generations. Robert

Fitzgerald, a free Northern black man and schoolteacher, saw this trepidation at his North Carolina polling station in April 1868. He counted five black Republican voters present for every one white conservative. Fitzgerald soon overheard a bitter conservative remark that today may be the black man's day, but tomorrow will be the white man's. Fitzgerald almost pitied the man, recording in his diary that "those days of distinction between colors is about over in this now free country." For the time being, Fitzgerald had no idea just how wrong he was.[42]

In order to strike back, white Southerners ostracized any employer, neighbor, retailer, or newspaper that sympathized with Republican views, a tactic that was utilized so effectively by the wartime Union Leagues against their Northern enemies. This method was part of the larger battle against black suffrage, which was being waged for two reasons. The more practical reason was that white Southerners realized that if freedmen gained voting equality within the Republican Party, white Democratic political power would be marginalized. On a more base emotional level, conservative white Southerners, who for two centuries or more were raised to believe in white dominance over blacks, could not accept the new racial paradigm that was thrust into their culture almost overnight. When allegations started to spread that Union League men and freed blacks were committing depredations against white citizens, Southern men convinced themselves that retaliation was vital. Their response was to create their own "secret society," soon to be known nationwide as the Ku Klux Klan.

The infamous Klan was first formed as a social club in Pulaski, Tennessee, in 1866, but soon became a paramilitary force who sought to maintain white dominance against any black advancement. Clad in masks and robes of various designs, the night-riding Klan sought to instill terror in its enemies through intimidation, threats, assault, as well as murder, rape, and arson. Its targets included free blacks loyal to the Republican Party, Union League council leaders, Republican-leaning newspapermen, and practically any public official or private civilian who was committed to black advancement or preached racial equality. That many of the Klan's victims were active in politics was coincidental to the fact that those targets were promoting a new social order that was anathema to conservative white Southern culture. All of these individuals were deemed a threat to the regional racial order that existed for generations.[43]

Klan threats and violence took a slow but steady toll on local Union League councils from 1867 to 1869. Council leaders were considered prime targets. Many were killed, which precipitated a downward decline in membership. Alabama state senator and alleged scalawag Charles Hays wrote after learning of two such murders, "I do not know how long it will be before you will hear of my assassination but one thing you may count on with certainty and that is that I shall die *game.*" Exhausted by his six years at the ULA's helm, James Edmunds saw the writing on the wall and retired as Grand National Council president in early 1869. He accepted the position of Washington, D.C., postmaster and served in that role until his death in 1879. Edmunds was replaced as ULA president by fifty-year-old John W. Geary, the current Republican governor of Pennsylvania and an ex-Union general. At its March 1869 annual conference in Washington, the ULA's Committee of the Condition of the League at the South admitted that Klan violence and intimidation against its members had seriously hampered operations. In most Southern states, no meetings had occurred for months.[44]

Louisiana and Mississippi were in the worst condition. Intimidation and violence had eliminated all vestiges of the ULA's organization. Georgia's state council was still functioning, but no subordinate council had submitted an activity report for quite some time. The Committee reported that, according to Georgia's leading Republicans, the ULA was dissolved in order to pacify the Rebels. In the upper South, the Committee reported no knowledge of any activity in Virginia, Maryland, or Delaware.[45]

Councils within the other Southern states were still functioning, some better than others. The Union League in Florida was considered "very active and efficient." The same good news was reported for Alabama and Tennessee, though in all three states, the Committee was unaware of the precise number of active councils. Texas reported the most detailed information with sixty-four active councils, though most of those were in the state's western portion. Missouri counted 350 councils, though how many of those were actually performing work was unknown. The Committee did note that Missouri's state council had failed to meet in almost a year.[46]

North and South Carolina's results were a mixed bag. The success of League activity and its impact on electing Republicans in both states in the 1868 elections were positive, though no meetings had taken place since due to the Klan's ongoing activity. The violence only worsened in the Tarheel State. South Carolina's situation was comparable with the state's western half shut down due to ongoing violence. Though the Union League of America continued to exist into the early 1870s, serving more as a means of securing patronage, it never again reached its 1867–68 postwar zenith.[47]

By 1870, the Reconstruction-era Ku Klux Klan was broken up by the U.S. military. Yet in the Klan's case, it expired knowing it had succeeded in eliminating Union League influence, which resulted in the return of white rule. In later congressional testimony, ex-Confederate generals and one-time Klan members, Nathan Bedford Forrest and John Gordon, both asserted that the Klan had held no political agenda. Rather, it had formed simply as a defensive measure against repeated Republican and Union League depredations against white Southerners.[48]

By the time of the 1872 presidential campaign, the Union League movement was all but dead in the North and South. The lone exceptions were in the North's large cities such as New York and Philadelphia, which had slowly transformed themselves into social clubs. In the South, Klan violence had practically pummeled the Union Leagues out of existence.

As discussed earlier in this chapter, yeoman whites abandoned the Union League in droves once chapter leaders desegregated their local councils, an act that was as much about racial equality as political expedience. Yet in the overall political picture, the Union League's Republican white leadership realized that the Southern black vote was more important in the long run than the white in order to gain the political dominance they sought. They succeeded in this early initiative, forming viable League chapters all across Dixie during their halcyon days of 1865–67.

Thus, from the disaffected perspective of the Old South, "The carpetbagger found that he could control the Negro without the help of the scalawag," wrote historian Walter L. Fleming in 1919. Fleming's analysis embodied the early twentieth-century view of the Reconstruction-era Union League's efforts as put forth by the "Dunning School" of thought. Named after Columbia University's William A. Dunning, the "school" referred to Dunning's graduate students, who represented the first generation of university-trained historians to study Reconstruction using primary sources and accepted historical methodology. Though now discredited in the twenty-first century by a far more progressive academy, their many dissertations and published writings dominated the public's perception of Reconstruction for much of the twentieth century.[49]

The Dunning School viewpoint held that the postwar Union Leagues were the malign machination of Radicals and carpetbaggers who pursued political benefit by duping ignorant blacks into voting for the Republican Party; that some Union League men who organized blacks in the South held a sincere belief in racial equality was never acknowledged by these scholars. Forcing political rights upon African Americans through congressional Reconstruction was deemed a disaster because the illiterate former slave was unprepared for the civic responsibilities that accompanied citizenship rights. If only the "unscrupulous whites" who led the Union League, the Freedmen's Bureau, and any other Yankee busybody group had just kept their hands off the South, white Southerners and freed blacks would have created a peaceable region together, or so their belief went. The unspoken malice lurking within all of this early scholarship was that black racial inferiority was considered a given by both author and reader.[50]

To carry out their diabolical ends, white League leaders played off of black superstitions by attracting freedmen to the League's mystical and secret initiation rites. Their one chance to escape bondage was to join the Union League, whose secretive initiation rites would cast a spell around the black man that would prevent any further enslavement. Countering those evil designs after 1867 was the Ku Klux Klan, who, to generations of white Southerners, was often portrayed as the "white knight" riding to the rescue of the beleaguered South.[51]

Post-Reconstruction history clearly shows the fallacy of that Dunning image. When an emotionally exhausted North withdrew the last Union soldiers from Southern states in 1877, black legal and civil rights began a precipitous decline. Every Republican-elected state government was ultimately swept out of office, to be replaced by Democrats hostile to racial equality precepts. White Southerners smugly referred to this new era as "Redemption." Democrats enacted new voting requirements such as literacy laws and poll taxes that effectively took away African American voting rights. All manner of services, including restaurants, hotels, and public transportation, became segregated and in many instances "white only" under new "separate but equal" laws. The Ku Klux Klan saw a resurgence in the early twentieth century that sought to continue white dominance in the South not only against blacks, but now Jews and immigrants as well.

If it had not been for the bold initiatives adopted by congressional Radicals following the end of the war—of which the Union League of America was a key part—blacks would have suffered continuously. The civic equality that former slaves briefly tasted from 1867 through the mid-1870s would never have occurred. And while many Republicans were focused primarily on political victory in the South, the Union League's twin goals of racial equality and Republican political superiority were not mutually exclusive. Congress's

Southern Reconstruction bid did not fail so much as it was overthrown by the conservative white South. Led by Ku Klux Klan violence, the takeover was an actual coup d'état. In the process, the Union League and its newly freed African American beneficiaries both became martyred brothers to the cause of racial equality. While the 1862–65 Northern-based Union Leagues could claim unqualified home front victory against their Civil War enemies, the postwar Reconstruction battle in the South represented the death knell for the Union League of America. African Americans were forced to wait almost a full century until they regained the civil and social rights that were purchased, if only briefly, at such high cost during the tumultuous 1860s.

Conclusion

***

This work has attempted to show that from the summer of 1862 through Lincoln's November 1864 reelection, the Union Leagues and like-minded Northern patriotic groups were created, organized, and took action as *a response to* what they considered the treasonous speech and violent actions of antiwar, antiblack, and antidraft Northern dissidents. Much of that violence was directed against pro-Union, loyal men. As a consequence, pro-Union Northern citizens became convinced that home front treason was on the march. Those convictions were punctuated by the summer 1862 antidraft violence in the lower Midwest; the 1863 antidraft and antiblack rioting in Detroit, New York, and elsewhere; and then the Peace Democrats' control of the 1864 Democratic convention and the concurrent Sons of Liberty conspiracy. The nefarious Knights of the Golden Circle and its ideological descendants put forth a "fire in the rear" threat, which the average civilian men who joined their local Union League councils knew to be real and widespread. The Civil War's Union League movement became the zeitgeist in the Northern home-front battle against seditious dissent and insurrection.

As a result, the Union Leagues and their various "brother" organizations declared war against the Copperhead–Peace Democrat faction that meant to destroy their beloved Union. The battle was for the hearts and minds of the Northern public. While it may not have been open warfare with marching armies like the ones Billy Yank and Johnny Reb were engaged in down South, it was nonetheless a war within *the* war where political and religious pamphlets, newspaper editorials, and public speeches substituted for weapons. In the Midwestern states of Indiana, Illinois, and Ohio, however, Union League men were often compelled to pick up the musket and form their own home-guard units in order to, as they had phrased it, "put down treason."

The home front, public opinion victory that the Union Leagues helped to obtain made it possible, in part, for Northern armies to have the time necessary to achieve victory on Southern battlefields. This paradigm was understood by a Union League of Philadelphia historian who later wrote, "The sword of Government was rivaled in potency by the pen of the Union League."[1]

The hyperpartisan Union Leagues that began 1864, fully girded for Lincoln's reelection, abandoned their previous nonpartisan statements as well as the "no party now" ideals of 1861 and spring 1863. Just as the Union armies eventually crushed their Confederate opponents into oblivion, the Union Leagues figuratively did likewise to their enemies in the North's home front war. When Secretary of State William Seward said in a speech the day before the 1864 presidential election that "Faction in civil war is unmitigated treason," he gave voice to a core Union League belief that they successfully conveyed to a majority of the North's voting public. The Democratic Party would spend a generation trying to scrub away the traitor label painted on them by Republicans and the Union Leagues.[2]

Many men who sat in the halls of Congress, served in state legislatures or the military, edited influential newspapers, or were part of Lincoln's inner circle all became Union League members after they realized its grassroots formation was genuine and lasting. This synergetic relationship allowed the Union Leagues to become far more successful in delivering their version of the truth to the Northern people than the Democrats were. In our modern era, this accomplishment is referred to as "controlling the spin." The Union Leagues' ability to influence the bulk of the Northern media, and "spin" the loyalty versus treason message to their liking helps us understand the psychological power of messaging in the twenty-first century.

The Union League movement's core mission was to promote unconditional loyalty to the Union and the Lincoln administration. In the small-town councils formed throughout the Midwest and far West, a second though no less important objective was to create a means for loyal, pro-Union men to band together for their physical safety and that of their families against anti-Lincoln, Copperhead–KGC violence. This need was fundamental to the secretive nature of these councils. The Union Leagues worked diligently to stifle dissent and label any antiwar or anti-Lincoln Democrat as treasonous. Their demand that the public support the administration and its armies in *all* of their efforts offers a case study that asks the modern reader if the political ends justify the political means during an internal civil war in which the nation's very existence may be at stake.

The Union League of Philadelphia freely answered this philosophical question in the affirmative by explaining how the war taught valuable lessons in constitutional law that lay people could easily understand. They were shown that "the government must have power to save the nation; that whatever is necessary to that end is constitutional; that the people are the nation; and that the constitution exists for the people." Given the struggle's desperate nature, many Northerners came to view slavery's destruction as essential to winning the war, even if that meant a few theoretical constitutional infractions. "The life is more than meat, the body is more than raiment, and the Country is more than the Constitution," wrote historian and attorney John C. Ropes in early 1863 while debating the Emancipation Proclamation's legality. The good people who felt that way may be wrong, Ropes admitted, "but they may also be patriotic; and they may be right."[3]

By the beginning of 1864, Francis Lieber believed the nature of the rebellion and the mortal threat it posed to the republic had surpassed the framers' visions when they created the Constitution. As beloved as that document was, it was insufficient in dealing with the current crisis. Saving the Union was paramount, which meant utilizing extralegal measures if necessary. "We must cut and hew through the thicket as best we can," observed Lieber. He reasoned that when the war was over, the Constitution could be properly amended to deal with such future crises—which Lieber considered an imperative—or the nation could silently adopt what had transpired when, not Lincoln, but rather "the people had assumed dictatorial power."[4]

If the Lincoln administration—on behalf of the people Lieber spoke of—bent the constitutional letter of the law or if some truly innocent man languished briefly in jail without charge as a warning to others, then that was the price to be paid if the end result was the preservation of the United States and its restoration to a new singular whole. Any manner of *conditional* support was likened to treason. Democratic insistence for unadulterated devotion to narrow, traditional interpretations of constitutional principles—and the consequences be damned—was like Nero fiddling as Rome burned. While home front Democrats carped and complained, the Union Leagues did whatever was necessary to put out the inferno. The Union League movement took to heart Ralph Waldo Emerson's remark that "Good men must not obey the laws too well."[5]

So, then, were the Union Leagues' actions righteous and noble? Did they offer a means of proudly preserving the nation? Or were their threats, ostracism, suppression, and press destruction little more than political thuggery that sought to destroy their opponent by any means necessary? Secretary of State William Seward offered his insight to these questions when he wrote to Charles Francis Adams in February 1865: "The agitators for war in time of peace, and for peace in time of war, are not necessarily, or perhaps ordinarily, unpatriotic in their purposes or motives. Results alone determine whether they are wise or unwise."[6]

Modern readers may answer those questions for themselves; however, I would suggest that their answer may be determined in part by how they view the philosophical question, "Do the ends justify the means?"—especially during a war when a nation's survival is at stake. Seward was there and experienced the upheavals firsthand. He left no doubt as to how he felt, as did the civilian Union Leagues. They managed the North's "free speech" issue in a way the Lincoln administration could never overtly do.

The nation's hope for lasting peace in April 1865 was ultimately dashed by another decade of conservative white resistance throughout Dixie. Still, one of the most important long-term consequences of the American Civil War was the nation's transformation from an antebellum collection of autonomous states into a republic with power resting primarily with the federal government. Much of the old "states' rights" debates were settled by the Civil War, obviously including the right to own human chattel and a state's purported right to secede. The two words "United States" transitioned from a plural noun into a singular one.[7]

This emerging nationalism, a "new birth of freedom" with the federal government leading the way, is what Frederick Olmsted and his Union League Club of New York cofounders envisioned in late 1862. Four years of bloody strife brought an end to human bondage and a renewed sense that Americans were again living in one country, all under one glorious flag, a cornerstone moment in our nation's history, in which the North's Union League movement played a significant and consequential part.

Notes

Foreword

1. Lincoln, "Address Before the Young Men's Lyceum of Springfield, Illinois," Jan. 27, 1838, in Basler, *Collected Works*, 1:108–15.

2. Lincoln, "Eulogy on Henry Clay," July 6, 1852, in ibid., 2:126; Lincoln, "Annual Message to Congress," Dec. 1, 1862, in ibid., 5:537.

3. Sullivan Ballou to Sarah, July 14, 1861, in Kass, Kass, and Diana Schaub, *What So Proudly We Hail*, 304–6; McPherson, *For Cause and Comrades*, 19, 110.

4. Some of the best recent work on these questions is Lawson, *Patriot Fires;* Smith, *No Party Now;* Neely, *The Union Divided;* Neely, *Lincoln and the Triumph of the Nation;* Gallman, *Defining Duty in the Civil War;* and Sandow, *Contested Loyalty.*

5. Gallagher, *The Union War*, 2, 6, 53.

6. For an assessment of this scholarship, see White, "Copperheads."

Introduction

1. Wilson, *My Six Convicts: A Psychologist's Three Years in Fort Leavenworth*, 216–23.

2. Ibid.; Grodzins, *The Loyal and the Disloyal*, 3.

3. For example, see Sprague, *What Is Treason?;* Cooper, *The Loyalty Demanded by the Present Crisis;* Anonymous, *Loyalty: What Is It?;* Nagler, "Loyalty and Dissent," 331.

4. Basler, ed., *The Collected Works of Abraham Lincoln*, 4:331–32.

5. Dell, *Lincoln and the War Democrats*, 9–16; Rawley, *The Politics of Union*, 90; Weber, *Copperheads*, 3–4; Lathrop, *The Life and Times of Samuel J. Kirkwood*, 240.

6. Weyl, *Treason*, 284–85; Baker, *Affairs of Party*, 338–39; Klement, "Copperheads in the Upper Midwest during the Civil War," 6–7.

7. Sprague, *What Is Treason?*, 2.

8. Weyl, *Treason*, 264.

9. *U.S. Constitution*, Art. 3, Sec., 3; White, *Abraham Lincoln and Treason*, 53.

10. See Nelson, *The Old Man*, 150; McGlone, *John Brown's War Against Slavery.*

11. Fletcher, *Our Secret Constitution*, 76–79; Also see Blair, "Friend or Foe," 27–51, and White, "'To Aid Their Rebel Friends,'" PhD diss., Univ. of Maryland, 2008.

12. *Cleveland Morning Leader*, Oct. 31, 1862; Summers, *A Dangerous Stir*, 29; *Doylestown Democrat*, June 30, 1863, as quoted in White, "To Aid Their Rebel Friends," 314–15.

13. Halliday, *Habeas Corpus*, 1–2; White, *Abraham Lincoln and Treason in the Civil War*, 52–57; Randall, *Constitutional Problems under Lincoln*, 74–95; Rawley, *The Politics of Union*, 60; Neely Jr., *The Fate of Liberty*, vii–xvii.

14. Blake, "Ten Firkins of Butter and Other 'Traitorous' Aid," 289–90.

15. Weyl, *Treason*, 2; Abraham Lincoln to Erastus Corning and Others, [June] 1863, Abraham Lincoln Papers, Manuscripts Division, Library of Congress, Washington, D.C., online at LOC American Memory, hereafter referred to as Lincoln Papers; Ayer, *The Great Northwestern Conspiracy*, 98; Blondheim, "'Public Sentiment Is Everything,'" 870.

16. Thompson, *Revolution Against Free Government*, 16–18.

17. Stoddard, *Inside the White House in War Times*, 133; Grant, *North Over South*, 153; Lawson, "'A Profound National Devotion,'" 340; Duquette, *Loyal Subjects*, 22–23.

18. Though the word *propaganda* carries significant negative connotation in our modern era, I use it in the more classical sense to simply mean "the shaping of public opinion." See Paludan, *"The Better Angels of Our Nature,"* 1–2.

19. Union League of Philadelphia, *Articles of Association and By-Laws of the Union League of Philadelphia*, 3; Irion, *Public Opinion and Propaganda*, 455; Key Jr., *Politics, Parties, & Pressure Groups*, 154–61; Bellows, *Historical Sketch of the Union League Club of New York*, 15.

20. Basler, *The Collected Works of Abraham Lincoln*, 3:27.

21. For instance, see White, *Abraham Lincoln and Treason in the Civil War*; Blair, *With Malice toward Some* and Gallman, *Defining Duty in the Civil War*.

22. For example, see Stampp, *The Era of Reconstruction 1865–1877*, 156–66.

1. *"Quiet Men Are Dangerous"*

1. Kendall, *Members Only*, 2–3; Clawson, *Constructing Brotherhood*, 4; Reidenbach, "A Critical Analysis of Patriotism as an Ethical Concept," 11–12.

2. Beckert, *The Monied Metropolis*, 58; Milne-Smith, *London Clubland*, 9; also see Townsend, *Mother of Clubs*.

3. Union League, *Address of the National Executive Committee*.

4. See Keehn, *Knights of the Golden Circle*, 1–15, 77. This is the most contemporary, scholarly analysis of the KGC; *K.G.C.: An Authentic Exposition of the Origin, Objects, and Secret Work of the Organization Known as the Knights of the Golden Circle*.

5. Franklin, *The Autobiography of Benjamin Franklin*, 80; see Anbinder, *Nativism and Slavery*.

6. Arthur Newell to George Newell, Oct. 6, 1864, Newell Family Papers, William L. Clements Library, Univ. of Michigan, Ann Arbor; Ridley, *The Freemasons*, 188–89. Also see Jeffers, *Freemasons*, and Halleran, *The Better Angels of Our Nature*.

7. Carnes, *Secret Ritual and Manhood in Victorian America*, 3–14; Kendall, *Members Only*, 34; McConnell, *Glorious Contentment*, 31, 87; Harwood, "Secret Societies in America," 623.

8. Carnes, *Secret Ritual*, 3–14.

9. Lause, *A Secret Society History of the Civil War*, 130.

10. Speed, *The Union Cause in Kentucky 1860–1865*, 17–18; *Covington Journal*, "Union Club," July 7, 1860; *Louisville Daily Journal*, July 19 and 26, 1860.

11. Kelly, "The Secret Union Organization in Kentucky in 1861," 3:282–85; Matthews, *Nine Months in the Infantry Service*, 8; Speed, *The Union Cause in Kentucky*, 164–65.

12. *Holmes County Farmer*, Aug. 30, 1860; *Dayton (Ohio) Daily Empire*, Sept. 6, 1860; see *Proceedings of the State U.C. of Ohio,*

13. See Forbes, *The Missouri Compromise and Its Aftermath;* Wunder and Ross, *The Nebraska-Kansas Act of 1854.*

14. Christensen, Foley, Kremer, and Winn, "Claiborne Jackson," in *Dictionary of Missouri Biography*, 423–25; *Glasgow (Missouri) Weekly Times*, Nov. 22, 1860.

15. Blair, "Missouri's Unionists at War," 5:6971; Sherman, *Memoirs of General William T. Sherman*, 1:169.

16. Broadhead, "St. Louis during the Civil War," 13; Blair, "Missouri's Unionists at War," 69–71; Boërnstein, *Memoirs of a Nobody*, 267–68, 275–76.

17. Rathbun, "'The Wide Awakes,'" 327–35. Rathbun was a founding member of the original Hartford Wide Awakes. Anbinder, *Nativism and Slavery*, 269.

18. Trexler, "Slavery in Missouri 1804–1865," 165–67; Boërnstein, *Memoirs of a Nobody*, 262–63; Rowan, *Germans for a Free Missouri*, 147; Snead, *The Fight for Missouri*, 65; Smith, *The Francis Preston Blair Family in Politics*, 2:23–24, 31–32.

19. Grinspan, "Young Men for War," 357–78.

20. *Cleveland Morning Leader*, Sept. 6, 1860; *New York Herald*, Sept. 16 and 26, 1860.

21. Quoted in Keehn, *Knights of the Golden Circle*, 71, 87; David Hunter to Abraham Lincoln, Dec. 18, 1860, Lincoln Papers; George P. Bissell to Abraham Lincoln, Dec. 30, 1860, Lincoln Papers.

22. Rathbun, "The Wide Awakes," 327–35; Grinspan, "Young Men for War," 357–78; Klement, *Dark Lanterns*, 35.

23. Union League of America, *Proceedings of the National Convention, Union League of America, Held at Cleveland, May 20 and 21, 1863*, 11–12, 22; Gibson, "Lincoln's League," 10–11.

24. Chandler, "Vigilante Rebirth," 10; various correspondents to Simon Cameron, Aug. 28, 1861, U.S. War Department, *The War of the Rebellion*, ser. 1, vol. 50, pt. 1, 589–90 (hereafter cited as *O.R.*); R. B. Hall to Simon Cameron, June 7, 1861, *O.R.*, ser. 2, vol. 2, 9.

2. *"There Can Be No Neutrals in This War; Only Patriots or Traitors"*

1. Henry Clay (1777–1852) served as a U.S. senator and congressman from Kentucky, including three terms as Speaker of the House. He was considered one of the great orators of his age and an ardent champion of Kentucky's interests.

2. Garrett Davis to George McClellan, June[?] 8, 1861, *O.R.*, ser. 1, vol. 2, 678; Townsend, *Lincoln and the Bluegrass*, 282; Lewis, *For Slavery and Union*, 2–3.

3. Bahde, "Our Cause Is a Common One," 66–98.

4. Astor, *Rebels on the Border*, 87–88.

5. Leech, *Reveille in Washington 1861–1865*, 56–57.

6. McPherson, *Ordeal by Fire*, 163; General Orders no. 4, *O.R.*, ser. 1, vol. 2, 602.

7. Crawford diary, Mar. 6, 1861, Samuel Wylie Crawford Papers; John Sherman to William T. Sherman, May 30, 1861, William T. Sherman Papers; Howard, *Autobiography of Oliver Otis Howard*, 1:104.

8. Quigley Jr., *Pure Heart*, xxii; Dunham, *The Attitude of the Northern Clergy toward the South 1860–1865*, 110–15, 134; Moore, *The Rebellion Record*, 1:75.

9. Griffin, *Their Brothers' Keepers*, 242–44; Hall, *The Organization of American Culture, 170 –1900*, 221; Howard, *Religion and the Radical Republican Movement 1860–1870*, 1, 4; Fredrickson, *The Inner Civil War*, 141; Reidenbach, "A Critical Analysis of Patriotism," 14; Smith, "Beyond Politics," 146, 152; Moorhead, *American Apocalypse*, 39, 151–52.

10. Hyman, *Union and Confidence*, 81–82. Also see Neely, *The Fate of Liberty*.

11. Rawley, *The Politics of Union*, 17; Julian, *Political Recollections*, 195–96; Brinton, *Personal Memoirs of John H. Brinton*, 19; *Washington Evening Star*, Dec. 13, 1860; *Washington National Republican*, Dec. 24, 1860; Crawford, "Politicians in Crisis," 238.

12. Tripler, *Eunice Tripler*, 143; Abraham Lincoln executive orders, Feb. 14, 1862, in Lubin, *The Words of Abraham Lincoln*, 320–22.

13. *Letters of the Hon. Joseph Holt, the Hon. Edward Everett, and Commodore Charles Stewart, on the Present Crisis*, 14; Taft diary, Apr. 12, 1861, Manuscripts Division, Library of Congress; Gurowski, *Diary*, 24; Beale, *Diary of Gideon Welles*, 1:10. This is the restored version of Welles's diary, which was originally published in 1911, but was later shown to have had scores of additions and deletions by Welles in the post–Civil War years.

14. Jones, *A Rebel War Clerk's Diary*, 1:13, 14–15; Gibboney, *Littleton Washington's Journal*, 185; Neely, *The Fate of Liberty*, 26.

15. Coopersmith, "For God and Liberty," 51; Gallman, *Defining Duty in the Civil War*, 3.

16. Banasik, *Missouri in 1861*, 10; (Douglas quote) Moore, *The Rebellion Record*, 1:298–99; Neely Jr., *The Union Divided*, 7–20.

17. *Daily Green Mountain Freeman*, Apr. 19, 1861, reprinted from *Boston Post;* Barnes, *The Love of Country*, 43; *Indianapolis Daily Journal*, Apr. 16, 1861, quoted in Stampp, *Indiana Politics during the Civil War*, 73; Robert McClelland to "Dear Augusta," Apr. 19, 1861, Robert McClelland Papers.

18. Quoted in Stampp, *Indiana Politics*, 92; (Wood quote) Moore, *Rebellion Record*, 1:89–90.

19. Oakes, *Freedom National*, 33; see Sen. James Lane's description of a Radical, U.S. *Congressional Globe*, 1862, 37th Cong., 2nd sess., July 7, 3151; Long, *The Jewel of Liberty*, 21–22. "Fire-eater" was a term used to describe Southerners who were strong secession advocates prior to the Civil War.

20. Oakes, *Freedom National*, 79–80, 110; Waugh, *Reelecting Lincoln*, 54; Williams, *Lincoln and the Radicals*, 5–6.

21. Williams, *Lincoln and the Radicals*, 5–6; Thomas J. Goss, *The War within the Union High Command*, 146–47; Benjamin Wade to his wife, Dec. 29, 1851, Benjamin Wade Papers; Howard, *Religion and the Radical Republican Movement*, 3–4; Moorhead, *American Apocalypse*, 147; Hyman, *To Try Men's Souls*, 156.

22. Rawley, *The Politics of Union*, 34, 41.

23. Beale, *The Diary of Edward Bates*, 4:185–87; Hyman, *To Try Men's Souls*, 140.

24. General Orders no. 13, *O.R.*, ser. 3, vol. 1, 133–34; Chittenden, *Invisible Siege*, 18.

25. Julian, *Political Recollections*, 244; quoted in Hyman, *To Try Men's Souls*, 140; Wesley, *The Politics of Faith during the Civil War*, 51–53; Charles O'Connor to James A. Bayard, July 2, 1861, Thomas F. Bayard Papers.

26. Brooks, *Washington in Lincoln's Time*, 11; William B. Hesseltine, "The Pryor–Potter Duel," 400–409.

27. U.S. Congress, House, *Loyalty of Clerks and Other Persons Employed by the Government*, 37th Cong., 2nd sess., House Report no. 16, 1–4; Benjamin French to Abraham Lincoln, Oct. 15, 1861, Lincoln Papers.

28. U.S. Congress, *Loyalty of Clerks*, 1–4; U.S. *House Journal*, 1861, 37th Cong., 1st sess., July 30; quoted in Leech, *Reveille in Washington*, 160–61; *Washington Evening Star*, July 31, 1861.

29. U.S. *Congressional Globe*, 1861, 37th Cong., 2nd sess., Dec. 30, 178–80; U.S. Congress, *Loyalty of Clerks*, 1–4; Leech, *Reveille in Washington*, 161.

30. Maynadier, *Reply of Lt. Col. Maynadier to the Charges in the Report of the Potter Committee; New York Times*, Sept. 16, 1861.

31. Chipman, *State of the Union Delivered Before the Detroit Democratic Association*, 5.

3. *"A Fire of Liberty Burning Upon the Altar"*

1. Studies of the 1862 Western theater campaigns and battles are extensive. See Hafendorfer, *Mill Springs;* Cooling, *Forts Henry and Donelson.*

2. Shea and Hess, *Pea Ridge;* Hall, *Sibley's New Mexico Campaign;* Cunningham, *Shiloh and the Western Campaign of 1862;* Schiller, *Sumter Is Avenged! The Siege and Reduction of Fort Pulaski;* Hearn, *The Capture of New Orleans, 1862.*

3. Gen. Thomas W. Sherman letter dated Mar. 25, 1862, *O.R.*, ser. 1, vol. 6, 250; Gen. John A. McClernand to the Illinois Cong. Delegation, July 9, 1862, Elihu B. Washburne Papers (hereafter referred to as Washburne Papers); Marvel, *Lincoln's Autocrat*, 178–80.

4. See Hennessy, *First Battle of Manassas;* "Bull Run to Washington: The Great Skedaddle by a Survivor," *National Tribune*, Aug. 20, 1881.

5. For George McClellan biographies, see Rafuse, *McClellan's War*, and Sears, *George B. McClellan.*

6. Burlingame and Ettlinger, *Inside Lincoln's White House*, 28–29; Detroit Post and Tribune, *Zachariah Chandler*, 224–25.

7. Irvin McDowell memorandum in Raymond, *The Life and Public Services of Abraham Lincoln*, 773.

8. See Beatie, *Army of the Potomac*, vol. III.

9. Sears, *To the Gates of Richmond*, 355.

10. See Hennessy, *Return to Bull Run;* Taylor, *He Hath Loosed the Fateful Lightning;* Warner, *Generals in Blue*, 258–59, 376–77, 475–76.

11. Bowery Jr., *The Civil War in the Western Theater 1862*, 40–43.

12. Marvel, *Lincoln's Darkest Year*, 299–302; Greene, *Letters from a Sharpshooter*, 146.

13. John Pope to Henry Halleck, Sept. 2, 1862, *O.R.*, ser. 1, vol. 12, ser. 3, 796–97.

14. Phillips, *The Rivers Ran Backward*, 5–10; Hubbart, *The Older Middle West, 1840–1880*, 9–11; Waugh, *Reelecting Lincoln*, 210; Klement, "Midwestern Opposition to Lincoln's Emancipation Policy," 111; Tredway, *Democratic Opposition to the Lincoln Administration in Indiana*, 1–4.

15. Phillips, *The Rivers Ran Backward*, 199; Stampp, *Indiana Politics during the Civil War*, 78–80; Hubbart, *The Older Middle West*, 180.

16. Towne, *Surveillance and Spies in the Civil War*, 12; also see Silbey, *A Respectable Minority*, 99–114.

17. Dickerson, "The Illinois Constitutional Convention of 1862," 385–442.

18. E. Stover to Elihu B. Washburne, June 28, 1862, Washburne Papers; Weber, *Copperheads*, 49.

19. Lawson, "A Profound National Devotion," 340; Marvel, *Lincoln's Autocrat*, 221.

20. Sandow, "Damnable Treason or Party Organs," 56; Edward Salomon to Abraham Lincoln, Dec. 1, 1862, Lincoln Papers.

21. Oliver Morton to Thomas Scott, Aug. 31, 1861, *O.R.*, ser. 3, vol. 1, 473–74; Oliver Morton to Edwin Stanton, June 25, 1862, *O.R.*, ser. 3, vol. 2, 109–10, 176–77; James F. Wilson to Edwin Stanton, July 28, 1862, *O.R.*, ser. 3, vol. 2, 265–66; D. L. Phillips to J. K. DuBois, June 28, 1862, Richard Yates Wabash College Papers (hereafter referred to as Yates Wabash Papers). Gen. William Kerley Strong was in command of the Union Army's District of Cairo; Warner, *Generals in Blue*, 484.

22. McPherson, *Battle Cry of Freedom*, 493–94.

23. *Detroit Free Press*, Jan. 26, 1861.

24. Richard Yates to Edwin Stanton, Aug. 11, 1862, *O.R.*, ser. 3, vol. 2, 351.

25. *New York Commercial Advertiser*, Aug. 19, 1862, quoted in Smith, "Generative Forces of Union Propaganda," 258; Scott, *Forgotten Valor*, 346–47; Dickerson, "The Illinois Constitutional Convention of 1862," 50–51; Hamilton, "The Union League," 111; *Harper's Weekly*, Apr. 12, 1862.

26. Keehn, *Knights of the Golden Circle*, 167–68; Towne, *Surveillance and Spies in the Civil War*, 14–16.

27. Quoted in Towne, *Surveillance and Spies in the Civil War*, 17; various handbills and broadsides of the Indiana North Union Club, Henry K. English Collection; Subordinate U.C. No. 6 charter, Civil War Union Club of Indiana Collection.

28. *Proceedings of the State Grand Council of the U.L.A. of Illinois at its Second Annual Session*, 9–10; *Raftsman's Journal*, Oct. 23, 1861; Union League of America, *Proceedings of the National Convention, Union League of America, Held at Cleveland, May 20 and 21, 1863*, 22; *New York Times*, Oct. 26, 1861; *Chicago Tribune*, Apr. 11, 1862; Humes, *The Loyal Mountaineers of Tennessee*, 146–60.

29. *Proceedings of the State Grand Council of the U.L.A. of Illinois*, 9–10.

30. Ibid., 10.

31. Freeman cited in Clawson, *Constructing Brotherhood*, 7–8.

32. Printed list of rejected candidates, Union League of America Collection, Kansas Historical Society, Topeka; for examples of minutes and membership lists, see Salem Union League Records, Phillips Library; Record Book, Loyal Union League, Henry County, Iowa, 1863–4, Special Collections & University Archives.

33. Union League of America, *Form of a Council*.

34. *Indiana State Sentinel*, July 28, 1862.

35. *Illinois State Journal*, Oct. 20, 1862.

36. Horace Beach to Rueben Gold Thwaites, July 9, 1896, Civil War Loyalty Flag Collection 1951.213, Wisconsin Historical Society, Madison; *Proceedings of the State Grand Council of the U.L.A. of Illinois*, 9–11.

37. *Proceedings of the State Grand Council of the U.L.A. of Illinois*, 9–11.

38. *Proceedings of the State Grand Council of the U.L.A. of Illinois*, 12–13; Lanman and Morrison, *Biographical Annals of the Civil Government of the United States*, 552.

39. These historians include Frank Klement, who made a career of downplaying

the Copperhead threat while portraying the Union Leagues as cynical Republican inventions. Also see Marvel, *The Great Task Remaining*, 114, and Silvestro, "None but Patriots: The Union Leagues in Civil War and Reconstruction."

40. Gray, *The Hidden Civil War*, 143–44.

41. Ben Price to George Julian, Mar. 29, 1863, Correspondence of Joshua R. Giddings and George Washington Julian, Manuscripts Division; Rawley, *The Politics of Union*, 93; *New York World*, Sept. 6, 1862.

42. R. E. Lee routinely referred to his Northern adversaries as "those people."

43. *Civilian and Telegraph*, Sept. 4, 1862; *New York Daily Tribune*, Sept. 13, 1862.

44. There are numerous accounts of the Antietam Campaign. See Carman, *The Maryland Campaign of September 1862*, and Sears, *Landscape Turned Red*.

45. Raymond, *The Life and Public Services of Abraham Lincoln*, 761.

46. Sebrell II, *Persuading John Bull*, 167–68.

47. Pease, *The Diary of Orville Hickman Browning*, 1:578, 592.

48. *Indiana State Sentinel*, Sept. 29, 1862; *Stark County Democrat*, Sept. 24, 1862.

49. Laas, *Wartime Washington*, 223.

50. Engs and Brooks, *Their Patriotic Duty*, 143; Lemcke, *Reminiscences of an Indianian*, 196; Blanchard, *Counties of Morgan, Monroe, and Brown, Indiana*, 72; Klement, *The Limits of Dissent*, 106; Howard, *Religion and the Radical Republican Movement*, 41–42.

51. Moran, *Interracial Intimacy*, 25–26; Wood, *Black Scare*, 60–65; Lemire, *"Miscegenation,"* 139–40.

52. Indiana North Union Club to Joseph K. English, Sept. 26, 1862, Henry K. English Collection. Joseph K. English (1824–1903) served as Indianapolis city treasurer during the Civil War years.

53. Blondheim, "Public Sentiment Is Everything," 877; Williams, *Lincoln and the Radicals*, 230; Long, *The Civil War Day by Day*, 175.

54. Williams, *Lincoln and the Radicals*, 232; Andrews, *The North Reports the Civil War*, 31.

55. Williams, "Benjamin F. Wade and the Atrocity Propaganda of the Civil War," 33–43; Smith, "Generative Forces of Union Propaganda," 103–5; Doster, *Lincoln and Episodes of the Civil War*, 243.

56. Burton, *The City of Detroit, Michigan, 1701–1922*, 2:1083; quoted in Stampp, *Indiana Politics during the Civil War*, 148–49; quoted in Howard, *Religion and the Radical Republican Movement*, 42–43.

57. Basler, *The Collected Works of Abraham Lincoln*, 5:442.

58. Katz, *August Belmont*, 116–18; Mitchell, *Horatio Seymour of New York*, 244; Silbey, *A Respectable Minority*, 65.

59. John Sherman to William T. Sherman, Nov. 16, 1862, William T. Sherman Papers.

60. Weber, *Copperheads*, 68–69; Stampp, *Indiana Politics during the Civil War*, 156–57.

61. Neely Jr., *The Boundaries of American Political Culture in the Civil War Era*, 82; Paludan, *"A People's Contest,"* 231–35.

62. Belmont, *Letters, Speeches and Addresses of August Belmont*, 85; Katz, *August Belmont*, 112.

63. Cutler, *Life and Times of Ephraim Cutler*, 296–97; John Goram to Elihu Washburne, Dec. 24, 1862, Washburne Papers; Silber and Sievens, *Yankee Correspondence*, 115–16.

64. Quoted in Burlingame, *Abraham Lincoln: A Life*, 2:446.

4. *"A Refuge Rather Than a Resort for Loyalty"*

1. Union League of Philadelphia, *First Annual Report of the Board of Directors of the Union League of Philadelphia*, 3; Montgomery Meigs to Ambrose Burnside, Dec. 30, 1862, *O.R.*, ser. 1, vol. 21, 917.

2. Pierce, *Memoir and Letters of Charles Sumner*, 4:114.

3. Lawson, "A Profound National Devotion," 338–62; *Harpers Weekly*, Apr. 20, 1861; Griffin, *Their Brothers' Keepers*, xii–xiii; Hall, *Organization of American Culture*, 225–28.

4. Trollope, *North America*, 1:451; Whiteman, *Gentlemen in Crisis*, 5–6.

5. Philadelphia Club, *The Philadelphia Club 1834–1934*, 41; Norton, *War Elections 1862–1864*, 42.

6. White, *A Philadelphia Perspective: The Civil War Diary of Sidney George Fisher*, 177; Boker, *Proceedings of a Meeting of the Union Club of Philadelphia*, 12; Lathrop, *History of the Union League of Philadelphia*, 20; Wecter, *The Saga of American Society: A Record of Social Aspiration 1607–1937*, 258.

7. Lewis, "John Innes Clark Hare," 712; Union League of Philadelphia, *Chronicle of the Union League of Philadelphia 1862–1902*, 40, 42; *Reception Tendered by the Members of the Union League of Philadelphia to George H. Boker*, 38; Whiteman, *Gentlemen in Crisis*, 18.

8. Minutes of meeting, Dec. 27, 1862, Union League Archives, The Heritage Center of the Union League of Philadelphia, Pa.; Union League of Philadelphia, *Chronicle of the Union League of Philadelphia*, 46; Whiteman, *Gentlemen in Crisis*, 26; Benson, *The Union League during the War*, 10.

9. Union League of Philadelphia, *Chronicle of the Union League of Philadelphia*, 62.

10. Krutch, "George Henry Boker," 458, 466; Burt, *The Perennial Philadelphians*, 372–73; Union League of Philadelphia, *Chronicle of the Union League of Philadelphia*, 22; Union League of Philadelphia, *First Annual Report*, 4.

11. John Russell Young to John Forney, undated (though late 1862), John Russell Young Papers, Manuscripts Division, Library of Congress, Washington, D.C.

12. George Boker to John Russell Young, Feb. 20 and 28, 1863, John Russell Young Papers.

13. Union League of Philadelphia, *Chronicle of the Union League of Philadelphia*, 303; the *Press*, Feb. 24, 1863; copy of typeset letter from George Boker to William Meredith dated Mar. 5, 1863, Meredith Family Papers, Historical Society of Pennsylvania, Philadelphia.

14. *"Our Federal Union, It Must be Preserved": Speech of Thomas Swann Delivered before the Union League of Philadelphia, March 2, 1863*; Ferdinand J. Dreer, "Extracts from His Journal," Union League Archives, The Heritage Center of the Union League of Philadelphia, Pa., 1; White, *Diary of Sidney George Fisher*, 185.

15. Strausbaugh, *City of Sedition*, 10–22; Migliore, "The Business of Union," 15–18; Dittenhoefer, *How We Elected Lincoln*, 1–2.

16. Beckert, *The Monied Metropolis*, 87–88; Irwin, May, and Hotchkiss, *A History of the Union League Club of New York City*, 10–11.

17. Beckert, "The Making of New York City's Bourgeoisie, 1850–1866," 163–70.

18. Cannon, *Personal Reminiscences of the Rebellion, 1861–1866*, 191–94.; Union Club, *Union Club of the City of New York 1836 to 1986*, 1, 66–67.

19. Stillé, *History of the United States Sanitary Commission*, 532–33. Also see Maxwell, *Lincoln's Fifth Wheel*.

20. Stillé, *History of the United States Sanitary Commission*, 63–64; Attie, *Patriotic Toil*, 57–65; Bellows, *Historical Sketch of the Union League Club of New York*, 8.

21. Bellows, *Historical Sketch of the Union League Club*, 6–7; Nevins, *Diary of the Civil War 1860–1865*, 276 (hereafter referred to as Strong Diary); Hall, *The Organization of American Culture*, 226–27; McCrary, "The Party of Revolution," 333; Attie, *Patriotic Toil*, 56–57.

22. Migliore, "The Business of Union," 49–50; U.S. Census Dept., *Population of the United States in 1860*, xxxii; Gordon, *The Orange Riot*, 13–14.

23. Crawford, *William Howard Russell's Civil War*, 24; Sheppard, *The Partisan Press*, 152; quoted in Thomas, *Delmonico's*, 89; Hayes, *Samuel Francis Du Pont*, 2:449; Irwin et al., *A History of the Union League Club of New York City*, 9.

24. Bellows, *Historical Sketch of the Union League Club*, 5, 8–11; Nevins, Strong Diary, 276; Censer, *The Papers of Frederick Law Olmsted*, IV, 466–71; Bernstein, *The New York City Draft Riots*, 155, 261; Griffin, *Their Brothers' Keepers*, xii–xiii.

25. Union League of Philadelphia, *Chronicle of the Union League of Philadelphia*, 47–50; Censer, *The Papers of Frederick Law Olmsted*, IV:505–6; Frederick Olmsted to Samuel Howe, Jan. 3, 1863, letterbook, Frederick Law Olmsted Papers, Manuscripts Division, Library of Congress, Washington, D.C. Fort Lafayette was situated in New York harbor and served as a Civil War prison for the North's political prisoners.

26. Circular quoted in Howard Jr., *The Union League Club*, 3–4; Union League Club of New York, *Report of the Executive Committee, Constitution, By-Laws and Roll of Members, July 1864*, 5–6; Bellows, *Historical Sketch of the Union League Club*, 52–53.

27. Nevins, Strong Diary, 292–93, 302; Censer, *The Papers of Frederick Law Olmsted*, IV:507. Attie, *Patriotic Toil*, 176–77.

28. Isa., 9:6.

29. *New York Times*, Feb. 6, 1863; Bellows, *Unconditional Loyalty*, 4–6, 12; Maxwell, *Lincoln's Fifth Wheel*, 197–99; Gallman, *Defining Duty in the Civil War*, 257; Moorhead, *American Apocalypse*, 11.

30. "Union Leagues," *New York Times*, Feb. 26, 1863.

31. Seward, *Seward at Washington as Senator and Secretary of State*, 159; Union League Club of New York, *Report of the Executive Committee*, 6; Nevins and Thomas, Strong Diary, 321.

32. Hughes, *Letters of John Murray Forbes*, 2:70; Pearson, *An American Railroad Builder*, 112–13.

33. Somerset Club, *A Brief History of the Somerset Club of Boston*, 3–4; Union Club of Boston, *A Report of the Celebration of the Fiftieth Anniversary of the Founding of the Union Club of Boston 1863–1913*, 12–13; Thorndike, *The Past Members of the Union Club of Boston*, 6. Brimmer served as the secretary of Boston's Union Club.

34. Norton, *Letters of Charles Eliot Norton*, 1:259; Grace Heath to Francis Lee, Mar. 15, 1863, Francis L. Lee Papers, Massachusetts Historical Society, Boston; Ware, *Political Opinion in Massachusetts during Civil War and Reconstruction*, 120–21; John Sherman to William T. Sherman, July 18, 1863, William T. Sherman Papers.

35. Circular quoted in Heslin, "The New England Loyal Publication Society," 90;

Thorndike, *Past Members of the Union Club of Boston*, 7; Norton, *Letters of Charles Eliot Norton*, 1:260–61.

36. Norton, *Letters of Charles Eliot Norton*, 1:260–61; Silvestro, "None but Patriots," 55. Silvestro cites the Union Club's original Articles of Association, then in the private possession of Robert Montgomery, club president; Edward Everett journal, Feb. 17, 1863, Massachusetts Historical Society, Boston. The Jacobins were a progressive, revolutionary faction that developed out of the French Revolution.

37. Everett, *An Address Delivered at the Inauguration of the Union Club, 9 April, 1863*, 3; *Barnstable (Mass.) Patriot*, Apr. 21, 1863; Hughes, *Letters of John Murray Forbes*, 2:93; Edward Everett journal, Feb. 17, 1863.

5. *"We Are Learning to Draw the Line Between Treason and Loyalty"*

1. *Raftsman's Journal*, Mar. 25, 1863; *Western Reserve Chronicle*, Mar. 25, 1863; Lathrop, *History of the Union League of Philadelphia*, 31, 46; Anonymous, "Philadelphia: The Republican Party Has a Homecoming," 64.

2. *New York World*, Feb. 9, 1863, and Apr. 24, 1863.

3. Phelan, "Manton Marble of the New York *World*," 1–2, 24–27; Heaton, *The Story of a Page*, 2.

4. James A. Dix to Manton Marble, Mar. 6, 1863, Manton Marble Papers, Manuscripts Division, Library of Congress, Washington, D.C.; McJimsey, *Genteel Partisan*, 9–10; Nevins, *Strong Diary*, 309–10; quoted in Phillips, *The Rivers Ran Backward*, 227.

5. *New York World*, Feb. 9, 1863; *Portsmouth Times*, Apr. 18, 1863; *Daily Ohio Statesman*, Mar. 4, 1863; *Bedford Gazette*, Mar. 6 and Apr. 17, 1863; Spann, *Gotham at War*, 166; Bundy, *The Nature of Sacrifice*, 260–61; *The Pilot* quoted in Samito, *Commanding Boston's Irish Ninth*, 226n.

6. Orville H. Browning to Edgar Cowan, Mar. 19, 1863, Lincoln Collection—Lincoln Miscellaneous Manuscripts, Special Collections, Univ. of Chicago Library, Illinois.

7. Lathers quoted in Bernstein, *The New York City Draft Riots*, 134; Hughes, *Letters of John Murray Forbes*, 2:80; *New York Daily Tribune*, July 15, 1861.

8. Boker, *Proceedings of a Meeting of the Union Club of Philadelphia*, 22; Nevins, *Strong Diary*, 319.

9. Porzelt, *The Metropolitan Club of New York*, 6; Nevins, *Strong Diary*, 319.

10. Union League of Philadelphia, *Chronicle of the Union League of Philadelphia*, 35.

11. Union League of Philadelphia, *First Annual Report*, 4; White, *A Philadelphia Perspective*, 109.

12. Mark DeWolfe Howe to George Boker, Feb. 17, 1863, Union League Archives, The Heritage Center of the Union League of Philadelphia, Pa.; Boker, *Proceedings of a Meeting*, 22, 38; Benson, *The Union League during the War*, 8; Tousey, *Indices of Public Opinion 1860–1870*, 56–58.

13. Hyman, *Era of the Oath*, xiii. For a prime example regarding educators, see Becker, "'Disloyalty' and the Dayton Public Schools," 58–68; Hamilton, "The Union League," 113.

14. Shankman, *The Pennsylvania Anti-War Movement 1861–1865*, 104; Scott, *A Visitation of God*, 130, 268–69; Scott, "'His Loyalty Was But Lip Service,'" 300; Dunham, *The*

Attitude of the Northern Clergy toward the South, 143–50; also see Andreasen, "Civil War Church Trials," 214–42; quoted in Wesley, *The Politics of Faith during the Civil War*, 72–73.

15. Quoted in Hyman, *Era of the Oath*, xiii.

16. Ibid.; original copy of Union League of Philadelphia Articles of Association dated Dec. 27, 1862, Union League folder, box 7-A, Society Miscellaneous Collection, Historical Society of Pennsylvania, Philadelphia; meeting minutes, Oct. 3, 1863, Union League of America—Council no. 13 records 1863–65, Massachusetts Historical Society, Boston; *Evening Union*, Aug. 20 and Sept. 15, 1863.

17. *Cass County Republican*, Mar. 26, 1863; *Daily Evansville Journal*, Apri.7, 1863; quoted in Smith, *No Party Now*, 80–81.

18. *Elyria Independent Democrat*, Mar. 4, 1863; Wallis, *Writings of Severn Teackle Wallis*, 2:267.

19. *Detroit Free Press*, Mar. 31, 1863; Joseph Wise to "Cousin Tillie," June 14, 1863, Wise-Clark Family Papers, Special Collections & University Archives, Univ. of Iowa Library, Iowa City.

20. Boker and Whipple quoted in Union League of Philadelphia, *Chronicle of the Union League of Philadelphia*, 58–59, 71; Weber, *Copperheads*, 26; Bryant II and Voss, *The Letters of William Cullen Bryant*, IV:304; Hammond, *Diary of a Union Lady 1861–1865*, 241.

21. Palmer, *The Selected Letters of Charles Sumner*, 2:150–51; John Sherman to William T. Sherman, May 7, 1863, William T. Sherman Papers. Sherman refers to Confederate sympathizers as Butternuts. The term also applied to those Southern soldiers who wore homespun uniforms of a butternut color. The phrase "dissent is the highest form of patriotism" has often been attributed to Thomas Jefferson, but scholars at the Thomas Jefferson Foundation have refuted this. Their research points to 1961 as the earliest use of the phrase. See http://www.monticello.org/site/jefferson/dissent-highest-form-patriotism-quotation.

22. James, *The Principles of Psychology*, 1:292–93; Williams, *Ostracism*, 3–4, 175; quoted in Milne-Smith, *London Clubland*, 6. Social ostracism was hardly a tactic against dissent used only in the North. With its "Old South" codes of honor and conduct, Southern elites' rampant use of ostracism against pro-Unionists or those opposed to secession was every bit the equal of the Union Leagues, if not more so. See Sheehan-Dean, *Why Confederates Fought* and Wyatt-Brown, *Southern Honor*.

23. Nevins, *Strong Diary*, 295–96; Armstrong, "Report of the Guest Committee," 78.

24. Quoted in Altschuler and Blumin, *Rude Republic*, 152.

25. Frank, *With Ballot and Bayonet*, 165; Costa and Kahn, "Shame and Ostracism," 1–4, http://www.nber.org/papers/w10425.

6. *"This Is the Time for Pamphleteers and Essayists"*

1. Beckert, "Making of New York City's Bourgeoisie," 171–72; Bigelow, *Letters and Literary Memorials of Samuel J. Tilden*, 1:169; Thomas, *Delmonico's*, 91–92; Society for the Diffusion of Political Knowledge, *Handbook of the Democracy for 1863 & '64*, 2; quoted in Baker, *Affairs of Party*, 170; Flick, *Samuel Jones Tilden*, 140–41. Tilden became the twenty-fifth governor of New York, serving from 1875 to 1876.

2. Silverman, *Lightning Man*, 391–403; Samuel F. B. Morse to "My Dear Cousin," Feb. 7, 1863, and to Amos Kendall, Feb. 14, 1863, Letterbooks, Samuel F. B. Morse

Papers, Manuscripts Division, Library of Congress, Washington, D.C. Kendall was a lawyer, onetime Morse business manager, and prominent Democrat.

3. *New York Evening Post,* Feb. 7, 1863; Hughes, *Letters and Recollections of John Murray Forbes,* 2:79.

4. *New York World,* Feb. 10 and 11, 1863; Turnure, "Untitled Examination of the Society for the Diffusion of Political Knowledge and the Union Leagues," David Mitchell Turnure Papers, New York Historical Society, New York.

5. McJimsey, *Genteel Partisan,* 46–47; Bigelow, *Letters and Literary Memorials of Samuel J. Tilden,* 1:172.

6. Society for the Diffusion of Political Knowledge, *Handbook of the Democracy,* 2; Samuel F. B. Morse to "Dear Sir," June 1, 1863, Letterbooks, Morse Papers.

7. Loyal Publication Society, *Proceedings at the First Anniversary Meeting of the Loyal Publication Society, February 13, 1864,* 8–9; Stoddard, *The Life and Letters of Charles Butler,* 318–19; Freidel, *Francis Lieber,* 347–48.

8. Loyal Publication Society, *Proceedings at the First Anniversary Meeting,* 8; John Austin Stevens obituary, *New York Times,* June 17, 1910.

9. Nevins, *Strong Diary,* 297–98, 386; Migliore, "The Business of Union," 198.

10. Loyal Publication Society, *Proceedings at the First Anniversary Meeting,* 8, 10, 16–17; Freidel, "The Loyal Publication Society," 10; Ware, "Committees of Public Information," 65–67; Owen, *The Future of the Northwest in Connection with the Scheme of Reconstruction without New England: An Address to the People of Indiana.*

11. Hughes, *Letters of John Murray Forbes,* 1:217; Hughes, *Letters and Recollections of John Murray Forbes,* 1:324–28; Smith, "Broadsides for Freedom," 294.

12. John Forbes to various, Mar. 9, 1863, New England Loyal Publication Society Manuscript Letters Collection, Boston Public Library, Mass.; Hughes, *Letters of John Murray Forbes,* 2:55; Hughes, *Letters and Recollections of John Murray Forbes,* 2:3–5; Norton, *Letters of Charles Eliot Norton,* 1:222–23, 259; Smith, "Broadsides for Freedom," 294, 297.

13. Ware, "Committees of Public Information," 65–67; Nagler, "Loyalty and Dissent," 336; Frederick L. Olmsted to John Forbes, Mar. 11, 1863, New England Loyal Publication Society Manuscript Letters Collection, Boston Public Library, Mass.

14. Smith, "Broadsides for Freedom," 298; John Forbes to Charles Norton, Mar. 22, 1863, New England Loyal Publication Society Manuscript Letters Collection.

15. Subscription Request, 1863, Publication Committee folder, Union League Archives, The Heritage Center of the Union League of Philadelphia, Pa.; Union League of Philadelphia, *First Annual Report,* 6–7; Lathrop, *History of the Union League of Philadelphia,* 64.

16. Union League of Philadelphia Publication Committee Meeting Minutes, Mar. 2 and 12, 1863, Union League Archives, The Heritage Center of the Union League of Philadelphia, Pa.; Lathrop, *History of the Union League of Philadelphia,* 64–66; Hardie, "The Influence of the Union League of America on the Second Election of Lincoln," 32; White, *A Philadelphia Perspective,* 183.

17. Whiteman, *Gentlemen in Crisis,* 36; Lathrop, *History of the Union League of Philadelphia,* 67; Freidel, *Union Pamphlets of the Civil War 1861–1865,* 1:16–17.

18. Whiteman, *Gentlemen in Crisis,* 29–30; Gallman, *Defining Duty in the Civil War,* 9–10.

19. For examples of early pamphlets, see Bailyn, *Pamphlets of the American Revolution, 1750–1776;* Freidel, *Union Pamphlets of the Civil War,* 1:1; Silbey, *The American Party Battle,* 2:xii–xiii; Neely Jr., *Lincoln and the Triumph of the Nation,* 20–23; Shaw, *Our Beloved Country,* xxiii–xxxiv.

20. Silbey, *The American Party Battle,* 2:xv–xvi; McPherson, *For Cause and Comrades,* 11; Gallman, *Defining Duty in the Civil War,* 6.

21. Morton to W. Wallace, May 2, 1863, Henry K. English Collection.

22. Stampp, *Indiana Politics,* 82, 86–87.

23. Christensen, Foley, Kremer, and Winn, "Montgomery Blair (1813–1883)," 83–84.

24. Blake, "Ten Firkins of Butter," 290; Roberts, *"This Infernal War,"* 73–74 Newton Fox to Perrin Fox, Mar. 5, 1863, Fox Family Correspondence, Bentley Historical Library, Univ. of Michigan, Ann Arbor; Calvin Cowgill report, "Historical Reports of the State Acting Assistant Provost Marshal General and District Provost Marshals, 1865," Records of the Provost Marshal General's Bureau (RG 110), (M1163—Indiana), National Archives, Chicago, 18–19; *Plymouth Weekly Democrat,* July 2, 1863; Bulla and Borchard, *Journalism in the Civil War Era,* 168.

25. Cutler, *Life and Times of Ephraim Cutler,* 298; Joseph Medill to Elihu Washburne, Feb. 19, 1863, Washburne Papers; Bulla and Borchard, *Journalism in the Civil War Era,* 168; *O.R.,* ser. 2, vol. 1, 563; *O.R.,* ser. 2, vol. 2, 500–501; *O.R.,* ser. 2, vol. 2, 82; Whiteman, *Gentlemen in Crisis,* 36.

26. John Boynton to C. K. Judson, July 7, 1862, Washburne Papers.

27. Quoted in Sandow, *Deserter Country,* 80.

28. Roberts, *"This Infernal War,"* 72.

29. Loving, *Civil War Letters of George Washington Whitman,* 104; quoted in Wiley, *The Life of Billy Yank,* 286; Kallgren and Crouthamel, *"Dear Friend Anna,"* 56–57.

30. Anson Shuey letter to wife, Mar. 8, 1864, box 105, folder 10, Civil War Document Collection, United States Army Military History Institute, Carlisle, Pa.; Temple, *The Civil War Letters of Henry C. Bear,* 9; Greene, *Letters from a Sharpshooter,* 249.

31. Fisk, *Anti-Rebel,* 149–50; Engs and Brooks, *Their Patriotic Duty,* 189; Capron, "War Diary of Thaddeus H. Capron, 1861–1865," 365.

32. Andrew Davis to Sarah Davis, Mar. 6, 1863, Andrew F. Davis Papers, Special Collections & University Archives, Univ. of Iowa Library, Iowa City.

33. Samuel Tilden to Martin Kalbfleisch, June 11, 1863, Samuel J. Tilden Papers, Manuscripts and Archives Division, New York Public Library; McJimsey, *Genteel Partisan,* 48.

34. Athearn, *Soldier in the West,* 96–97; *Dayton Daily Empire,* Mar. 14, 1863.

35. Beasecker, *"I Hope to Do My Country Service,"* 184; Weber, *Copperheads,* 101–2, 131.

7. "The 'Loyal Leagues' Are Really Effecting Public Opinion"

1. Nagler, "Loyalty and Dissent," 329; Frank, *With Ballot and Bayonet,* 165, 169; Ramold, *Across the Divide,* 115; Union League of America, New York State Council, *Proceedings of the State Council of the Union League of America for the State of New York at Its First Annual Session,* 14.

2. Engs and Brooks, *Their Patriotic Duty*, 213; *Indiana State Sentinel*, May 13, 1863; George Collins to "My Dear Mother," Feb. 1, 1863, Collins Family Papers, Carl A. Kroch Library, Cornell Univ., Ithaca, New York; Quint, *The Potomac and the Rapidan*, 24–25.

3. Charles Mason diary, May 13, 1863, Charles Mason Remey Family Papers, Manuscripts Division, Library of Congress, Washington, D.C; Belmont, *A Few Letters and Speeches of the Late Civil War*, 84–85.

4. Freidel, *Francis Lieber*, 344–45; Freidel, *Union Pamphlets of the Civil War*, 1:11.

5. See Lieber, *No Party Now; But All for Our Country;* Nevins, *The War for the Union*, III:167; Paludan, *"A People's Contest,"* 237; Smith, *No Party Now*, 78.

6. Everett, *An Address Delivered at the Inauguration of the Union Club*, 3; Binney, *Letter from Horace Binney to the General Committee of Invitation and Correspondence*, 90, 137; *Plymouth Weekly Democrat*, July 2, 1863; Mitchell, *Horatio Seymour*, 298; *Herkimer Democrat*, July 22, 1863.

7. Summers, *A Dangerous Stir*, 28; Beale, *The Diary of Edward Bates*, 321–22; Burlingame and Ettlinger, *Inside Lincoln's White House*, 235.

8. Quoted in Migliore, "The Business of Union," 201.

9. Beckert, *The Monied Metropolis*, 51, 126; Nevins, Strong Diary, 297, 298n, 319.

10. "Draft proposal for forming the Loyal League of Union Citizens, dated New York, Feb. 28, 1863," Loyal League of Union Citizens Collection, New-York Historical Society, New York; Prosper Wetmore to George Boker, Mar. 27, 1863, Union League Archives, The Heritage Center of the Union League of Philadelphia, Pa.

11. See Loyal League of Union Citizens, *Loyal Meeting of the People of New York*.

12. *New York Times*, Mar. 7 and 10, 1863; Brummer, "Political History of New York State during the Period of the Civil War," 296–97.

13. Nevins, Strong Diary, 303; Loyal National League, *By-Laws of the Loyal National League*, 1; Stevens (uncredited), Review of *Proceedings at the Dinner of the Early Members of the Union League Club of the City of New York*, 395–96.

14. See Loyal National League, *Proceedings at the Organization of the Loyal National League at the Cooper Institute;* Warner, *Generals in Blue*, 86–87, 198.

15. Orville H. Browning to Edgar Cowan, Mar. 19, 1863, Lincoln Collection—Lincoln Miscellaneous Manuscripts.

16. Loyal National League, *Proceedings at the Organization of the Loyal National League*, 16, 42; *New York Times*, Mar. 21, 1863.

17. *Brooklyn Daily Eagle*, Apr. 4, 1863; *Detroit Free Press*, Apr. 23, 1863; Curtis, "The True Conditions of American Loyalty," 10.

18. Nevins, Strong Diary, 312; Smith, "Generative Forces of Union Propaganda," 271; Chase, *Letter from Hon. S. P. Chase, Secretary of the Treasury, to the Loyal National League*.

19. Bellows, *Historical Sketch of the Union League Club*, 32; "Great Union Rally at Toledo," *Illinois State Journal*, Mar. 23, 1863; *New York World*, July 25, 1863; O. W. Smith to Samuel F. B. Morse, May 28, 1863, Morse Papers.

20. *New York Daily Tribune*, Mar. 24, 1863; The *Independent*, Apr. 23, 1863. For a list of officers for each Loyal League, see Loyal National League, *Proceedings at the Organization of the Loyal National League at the Cooper Institute*, 48; and Loyal League of Union Citizens, *Loyal Meeting of the People of New York*, 62.

21. Union League of Philadelphia, *Immense Meeting in Favor of the Union; Inaugu-ration of the National Union Club;* Amasa McCoy to John Sherman, Mar. 3, 1863, John Sherman Papers, Manuscripts Division, Library of Congress, Washington, D.C.; Union League of Philadelphia, *First Annual Report,* 10.

22. Union League of Philadelphia, *Immense Meeting in Favor of the Union; Inaugura-tion of the National Union Club, Speech of Benjamin H. Brewster, Delivered at the Musical Fund Hall, Philadelphia, Wednesday Evening, March 11, 1863,* 3; the *Press,* Mar. 12, 1863.

23. Altschuler and Blumin, *Rude Republic,* 8.

24. *New York Daily Tribune,* July 10, 1863.

25. Gov. Andrew Curtin to Edwin Stanton, Oct. 25, 1862, "Pennsylvania Volunteers of the Civil War," www.pacivilwar.com/draftletter.html; For a full account of the Detroit riot, see Taylor, *"Old Slow Town,"* 94–103.

26. Capt. Lucius S. Goodrich report, "Historical Reports of the State Acting As-sistant Provost Marshal General and District Provost Marshals, 1865," Records of the Provost Marshal General's Bureau (RG 110), (M1163—Connecticut), National Archives, Chicago, 10–11; C. Tower to Col. James B. Fry, June 10, 1863, "Pennsylvania Volunteers of the Civil War," www.pacivilwar.com/draftletter2.html; Churchill, "Liberty, Conscription, and a Party Divided," 297; Towne, *Surveillance and Spies,* 94; *Raftsman's Journal,* June 17, 1863.

27. Stoddard (though published anonymously as by "A Volunteer Special"), *The Volcano under the City,* 19–20.

28. Rosenwaike, *Population History of New York City,* 42; Spann, *The New Metropolis,* 24; Duvergier de Hauranne, *A Frenchman in Lincoln's America,* 1:32; Seymour quoted in Cook, *The Armies of the Streets,* 53. Also see pp. 3–17 for an analysis of Irish living conditions prior to the riot.

29. Stoddard, *The Volcano under the City,* 8; "Memories of the *New York Times,*" *New York Times,* Mar. 27, 1898; *New York Times,* July 14, 1863.

30. Hennesey, *American Catholics,* 148; Massie, *America,* 66; White, *A Philadelphia Perspective,* 169.

31. *New York Times,* July 14, 1863; Nevins, Strong Diary, 335–36; Stoddard, *The Volcano under the City,* 81, 83–86.

32. Josyph, *The Wounded River,* 159–63.

33. Cook, *The Armies of the Streets,* 176, 193–98; Bernstein, *The New York City Draft Riots,* 24; see *O.R.,* ser. 1, vol. 27, pt. 2, 875–912 for Union military correspondence pertaining to the New York riots.

34. Committee of Merchants for the Relief of Colored People, *Report of the Com-mittee of Merchants for the Relief of Colored People,* 3, 31.

35. Costello, *Our Police Protectors,* 204; Nevins, Strong Diary, 343; Bernstein, *New York City Draft Riots,* 44, 157; Stoddard, *The Volcano under the City,* 36–37.

36. F. L. Olmsted to Edwin L. Godkin, July 15, 1863, Edwin Lawrence Godkin Pa-pers, Houghton Library, Harvard Univ., Cambridge, Mass. Olmsted refers to leading Democrats who, in his opinion, had abetted the recent New York riots through their criticism of the draft and the Lincoln administration; *New York Times,* July 16, 1863.

37. Irwin et al., *A History of the Union League Club of New York City,* 30; "The Union League Club," *New York Times,* Aug. 30, 1863.

38. Smith, *Civil War Letters of Col. Elijah H. C. Cavins,* 175; "grape," aka grapeshot, and "cannister" were types of artillery ammunition, usually small steel balls packed together that turned the cannon into a giant shotgun; Sears, *Mr. Dunn Browne's Experiences in the Army,* 125.

8. *"Neutrality Is Allied to Treason; Indifference Becomes a Crime; and Whoever Is Not with Us Is Against Us"*

1. *Proceedings of the State Grand Council of the U. L. A. of Illinois,* 12; Orville H. Browning to Edgar Cowan, Mar. 19, 1863, Lincoln Collection—Lincoln Miscellaneous Manuscripts.

2. Various to Richard Yates, Jan. 6, 1863, Yates Wabash Papers; A. Babcock to Jacob Ammen, Apr. 23, 1863, Jacob Ammen Papers, Abraham Lincoln Presidential Library, Springfield, Ill; Phillips, *The Rivers Ran Backward,* 272–74; Mrs. Rankin M. McPheeters to husband, Feb. 1, 1863, McPheeters Family Papers, United States Army Military History Institute, Carlisle, Pa.

3. Gilje, *Rioting in America,* 86.

4. *Proceedings of the State Grand Council of the U.L.A. of Illinois,* 12; P. P. Enos to Lyman Trumbull, Feb. 6, 1863, Lyman Trumbull Papers, Manuscripts Division, Library of Congress, Washington, D.C.; *Chicago Tribune,* Feb. 3, 1863; B. H. Mills to Richard Yates, Jan. 30, 1863, Yates Wabash Papers; quoted in Gray, *Hidden Civil War,* 144.

5. *Proceedings of the State Grand Council of the U.L.A. of Illinois,* 13–14.

6. Ibid., 13–16; Nevins, *The War for the Union,* III:163.

7. Union League of America, *Proceedings of the National Convention, Union League of America, Held at Cleveland, May 20 and 21, 1863,* 4–7; *Cleveland Morning Leader,* May 21, 1863.

8. *Proceedings of the State Grand Council of the U.L.A. of Illinois,* 14–15; Union League of America, *Proceedings of the National Convention, Union League of America, Held at Cleveland, May 20 and 21, 1863,* 17–18.

9. Smith, "A Strong Band Circular," 557–64; *Ottawa (Illinois) Free Trader,* Feb. 21, 1863; John D. Bartlett Jr., W. P. Bailey, and L. M. Bartlett to Richard Yates, Feb. 17, 1863, Yates Family Papers, Abraham Lincoln Presidential Library, Springfield, Ill.

10. Union League of America, *Proceedings of the National Convention, Union League of America, Held at Cleveland, May 20 and 21, 1863,* 9; Gibson, "Lincoln's League," 113.

11. *Detroit Free Press,* Mar. 31, 1863; *Daily Ohio Statesman,* Apr. 24, 1864.

12. *Cincinnati Gazette* quoted in *Cleveland Morning Leader,* May 22, 1863; *Portage County Democrat,* May 27, 1863; *Cleveland Morning Leader,* June 3, 1863, discussing *Daily Cleveland Herald* comments.

13. *Centralia Sentinel,* Aug. 6, 1863.

14. Stoddard, *Inside the White House in War Times,* 129; Donald, *Inside Lincoln's Cabinet,* 192.

15. Drehle, *Rise to Greatness,* 238.

16. Detroit Post and Tribune, *Zachariah Chandler,* 312–18; Lanman, *The Red Book of Michigan,* 437; Harris, *Public Life of Zachariah Chandler, 1851–1875,* 112; Edmunds obituary, *New York Times,* Dec. 15, 1879.

17. U.S. Census Dept., *Population of the United States in 1860*, xxxi–xxxii; Villard, *Memoirs of Henry Villard*, 1:154; Sherman, *Recollections of Forty Years in the House, Senate and Cabinet*, 1:318; Riddle, *Recollections of War Times: Reminiscences of Men and Events in Washington, 1860–1865*, 8; Oliphant, *Episodes in a Life of Adventure*, 51.

18. Trefousse, *The Radical Republicans*, 60–62.

19. See Shelden, *Washington Brotherhood*, for a full analysis of antebellum Washington comradery; Laas, *Wartime Washington*, 14.

20. Horatio Taft diary, Feb. 11, 1863; Dustin Cheever diary, Apr. 4, 1863, Dustin Grow Cheever Papers, Andersen Library, Univ. of Wisconsin, Whitewater; Keehn, *Knights of the Golden Circle*, 47; Neely's Pulitzer Prize–winning work was *The Fate of Liberty: Abraham Lincoln and Civil Liberties*. Neely conclusion taken from Neely, *The Union Divided*, 60–61.

21. Copy of typeset letter from George Boker to William Meredith, dated Mar. 5, 1863, Meredith Family Papers, Historical Society of Pennsylvania, Philadelphia; Union League of Philadelphia, *Chronicle of the Union League of Philadelphia*, 71–72.

22. *Proceedings of the State Grand Council of the U.L.A. of Illinois*, 11–12; Bohrnstedt, *Soldiering with Sherman*, 45; *Washington Chronicle* quoted in *Cass County Republican*, Apr. 16, 1863.

23. *Minutes of the Proceedings of the State Council of the Union League of America for the State of New Hampshire, Since its Organization January 2, 1863*, 1–4; Smith, "Generative Forces of Union Propaganda," 275; Loyal Publication Society, *The Venom and the Antidote*. For well over a generation, Frank Klement (1908–94) was considered a leading scholar on Copperhead–KGC activity in the North during the Civil War. Throughout his entire oeuvre, Klement's overarching argument was that the anti-Lincoln Copperhead threat was overblown. Moreover, Klement claimed that the various Democratic "dark lantern" societies, such as the KGC, were little more than paper-based organizations with no real substance and that Republicans knew it. He asserted that much of the evidence was scanty and even fabricated by Republican partisans as a cynical means of whipping up anti-Democrat hysteria. This book challenges Klement's thesis by showing that the average loyal Northern citizen, i.e., a Union League man, had ample reason at the time to believe in and react accordingly to the Copperhead–KGC allegations. Many loyal men witnessed or read about the Copperheads' violent antidraft rioting. Some of these men were physically attacked and saw their homes and barns burned to the ground. They knew the subversion and insurrection was real. This fear regarding physical safety was a key reason for the Midwestern Union Leagues' formation in the first place. As scholar Stephen Towne put forth in his recent *Surveillance and Spies in the Civil War*, there is no documentary proof that shows Republican civil or military leaders ever conspired to concoct or magnify evidence against their Democratic rivals (307–8); also see Summers, *A Dangerous Stir*, 25–30, on why partisans subscribed the worst possible motives to their political opponents.

24. James Edmunds to Mark Howard, Feb. 10, 1863, James M. Edmunds Collection, Archives of Michigan, Lansing.

25. D. W. Houston, "The Union League of America in Kansas," Union League of America Collection, Kansas Historical Society, Topeka, 2–4; Union Club (Brownville, Neb.), 1863 Minutes, Nebraska State Historical Society, Lincoln.

26. 1863–70 Minutes Volume, Union League Records, Rhode Island Historical Society Library, Providence; Report of the committee and letter of support from John A. Andrew, dated June 4, 1863, Waltham Union League records, 1862–63, Massachusetts Historical Society, Boston.

27. Delaware County Historical Society, *Proceedings of the Delaware County Historical Society 1895–1901*, 1:161; Union League of America, Pennsylvania Council No. 1 (York, Pa.), Records, 1863–65, York County Historical Society, Pa.; *Pittston Gazette*, July 16, 1863; *Proceedings of the State Grand Council U.L.A. of the State of Pennsylvania*, 12; Scharf, *History of Delaware: 1609–1888*, 1:373; *Smoky Hill and Republican Union*, May 23, 1863; *Nebraska Advertiser*, May 7, 1863; *Der Demokrat*, Mar. 19, 1863; George W. O'Brien to Samuel Kirkwood, Apr. 7, 1863, Samuel J. Kirkwood Papers, State Historical Society of Iowa, Des Moines; meeting minutes, July 30, 1863, Loyal Union League, Henry County, Iowa, 1863–64, Special Collections & University Archives, Univ. of Iowa Library, Iowa City; Records, 1863, Union League of the Town of Burnett (Dodge County, Wis.), Wisconsin Historical Society, Madison; Wisconsin ULA Grand Secretary to Clinton, Wi. Council Secretary, printed circular dated June 23, 1863, Dustin Grow Cheever Papers.

28. Brown, *Reminiscences of Senator William N. Stewart of Nevada*, 165–66; *Virginia Evening Bulletin*, July 27, 1863; S. H. Parker to Addison Gibbs, Dec. 9, 1863, and Hiram Smith to Gibbs, Jan. 27, 1864, Addison Crandall Gibbs Papers, Oregon Historical Society, Portland; John M. Allen to Lincoln, Oct. 14, 1863, Lincoln Papers.

29. George Wright to Lorenzo Thomas, Apr. 20, 1863, *O.R.*, ser. 1, vol. 50, pt. 1, 407. Wright commanded the Union Army's Department of the Pacific during the Civil War; Gen. L. H. Allen to Henry Halleck, June 8, 1863, *O.R.*, ser. 1, vol. 50, pt. 2, 475–76; Chandler, "Vigilante Rebirth," 11; William C. Kibbe to Henry Halleck, *O.R.*, ser. 1, vol. 50, 107–8; Robert Robinson to John Mason, *O.R.*, ser. 1, vol. 50, 938; *Proceedings of the Grand Council of the Union League of America for the State of California at Its Annual Session, Held in San Francisco, August 4th and 5th, 1863*, 7, 9; Prosch, *Reminiscences of Washington Territory*, 51–52.

30. Keehn, *Knights of the Golden Circle*, 10, 142–44; the *Daily Exchange*, July 16, 1859; Crawford, *William Howard Russell's Civil War*, 35; Dix, *Memoirs of John Adams Dix*, 2:36.

31. Marks and Schatz, *Between North and South*, 80–81.

32. Ibid.

33. Ibid., 85; Jérôme Bonaparte to "My Dear Son," Jan. 31, 1863, box 9, Jerome Napoleon Bonaparte Papers, Maryland Historical Society, Baltimore; de Hauranne, *A Frenchman in Lincoln's America*, 2:482–83.

34. Jérôme Bonaparte to "My Dear Son," Mar. 14, Apr. 19, and May 19, 1863, box 9, Jerome Napoleon Bonaparte Papers; Union Club of Baltimore, *Constitution and By-Laws*.

35. Copy of Gen Robert C. Schenck orders dated Mar. 11, 1863, to John I. C. Hare, Hare-Willing Family Papers, American Philosophical Society Library, Philadelphia, Pa; Frank Vandiver, *The First Public War, 1861–1865*, 10; Warner, *Generals in Blue*, 422–23.

36. Agnew, *Our National Constitution*, 21; Nevins, Strong Diary, 300.

37. Maj. Gen. Robert Schenck orders, *O.R.*, ser. 1, vol. 27, pt. 3, 361–62; Union Club of Baltimore, Handwritten transcript of letter dated July 27, 1863, from Maj. Gen. R. Schenck, Record Books 1863–72, vol. II, Maryland Historical Society, Baltimore.

38. (Willcox order) Moore, *Rebellion Record*, vol. 7, Documents: 336; Scott, *Forgotten Valor*, 453–54; Warner, *Generals in Blue*, 558–59.

39. Fuller, "Historical News, Notes, and Comment," 18–20; *Monroe Monitor,* Aug. 19, 1863, quoted in *Detroit Free Press,* Aug. 23, 1863; *Abstract of the Proceedings of the Grand Council of the U.L.A. for the State of Michigan,* 1, 5.

40. Bennett Hill to James Fry, Nov. 9, 1863, *O.R.,* ser. 3, vol. 3, 1008; Also see Taylor, *"Old Slow Town,"* 156–61.

41. *Detroit Advertiser and Tribune,* Dec. 17, 1863; Lexington, Michigan Union League Council Charter, John C. Waterbury Papers, Bentley Historical Library, Univ. of Michigan, Ann Arbor.

42. *Detroit Free Press,* June 30, 1863; "1864 speech of John M. Potter to the Union League of Romeo, Michigan," Briggs Family Papers, Bentley Historical Library, Univ. of Michigan, Ann Arbor; Michigan Pioneer and Historical Society, *Michigan Historical Collections,* 26:415; quoted in Klement, *Dark Lanterns,* 54.

43. James A. Thomas to parents, Sept. 3 and 8, 1863, James A. Thomas Letters, Filson Historical Society, Louisville, Ky.

44. Hayes, "Incidents of the Battle of Cedar Creek," 4:237; *Proceedings of the State Grand Council of the U.L.A. of Michigan . . . 1864,* 13; *National Tribune,* June 5, 1902; Warner, *Generals in Blue,* 390–91.

45. Rhodes, *All for the Union,* 221; Peck Jr., "A Recruit Before Petersburg," 289; Furry, *The Preacher's Tale,* 97–98; Andersen, *The Civil War Diary of Allen Morgan Geer,* 116.

9. "We Are Not a Partisan, Yet We Are a Political Organization"

1. Union League of Philadelphia, *Chronicle of the Union League of Philadelphia,* 75–76; Union League to Abraham Lincoln, May 5, 1863, *O.R.,* ser. 3, vol. 3, 193–94.

2. Ent, *The Pennsylvania Reserves in the Civil War,* 70; Union League circular dated July 6, 1863, Union League Archives, The Heritage Center of the Union League of Philadelphia, Pa.

3. See Spurgeon, *Soldiers in the Army of Freedom;* Lathrop, *History of the Union League of Philadelphia,* 76–79.

4. Gallman, *Mastering Wartime,* 47, 49; Lathrop, *History of the Union League of Philadelphia,* 78–79.

5. Lathrop, *History of the Union League of Philadelphia,* 79–80.

6. Giesberg, *Army at Home,* 9–10; Massey, *Bonnet Brigades,* 5–12.

7. E. Clyde to J. C. Redfield et al., Sept. 7, 1863, Union League of America Collection, Kansas Historical Society, Topeka.

8. Ladies' Union League (Madison, Wis.), Papers, 1862–64, Wisconsin Historical Society Archives, Madison; Hurn, *Wisconsin Women in the War Between the States,* 68; Kiper, *Dear Catharine, Dear Taylor,* 165; Ladies' Union League minutes for 1863–64, First Congregational Church (Marine Mills, Minn.) Records, Minnesota Historical Society, St. Paul.

9. Scott, Diary, May [n.d.], 1863, 193–95; *Indiana State Sentinel,* May 6, 1863.

10. *Mount Vernon Republican,* June 25, 1863; *Illinois State Journal,* May 12 and 29, 1863; *Civilian & Telegraph,* Apr. 23, 1863.

11. Phillips, *The Rivers Ran Backward,* 279; *Addresses at the Inauguration of the Women's Loyal League of Bridgeport, April 17th, 1863,* 2, 7.

12. Gordon, *The Selected Papers of Elizabeth Cady Stanton and Susan B. Anthony*, 1:483.

13. Quoted in Hamand, "The Woman's National Loyal League," 39–41.

14. Women's National Loyal League, *Proceedings of the Meeting of the Loyal Women of the Republic*, 10, 15, 18.

15. Ibid., 19–21, 23.

16. David McKinney to Jeanette McKinney, Aug. 9, 1863, David McKinney Papers, William L. Clements Library, Univ. of Michigan, Ann Arbor; David Grier to Anna McKinney, June 30, 1863, Grier Family Papers, Missouri History Museum, St. Louis; Stanton, Anthony et al., *History of Woman Suffrage: 1861–1876*, 3; Hamand, "The Woman's National Loyal League," 48.

17. Women's National Loyal League, *Proceedings of the Meeting of the Loyal Women of the Republic*, 15.

18. Quoted in Lyftogt, *From Blue Mills to Columbia*, 104–5. Silber, *Daughters of the Union*, 153–54.

19. Kirkland, *A Few Words in Behalf of the Loyal Women of the United States by One of Their Own*, 5; Giesberg, *Army at Home*, 124–26.

20. Women's Loyal National League circular, 1863, Miscellaneous Manuscripts Collection, Manuscripts Division, Library of Congress, Washington, D.C.

21. *Proceedings of the State Grand Council of the U. L. A. of Illinois at its Second Annual Session*, 16.

22. Robert H. Milroy to Union League, Oct. 25, 1863, General Robert H. Milroy Collection, Jasper County Public Library, Rensselaer, Indiana; Warner, *Generals in Blue*, 326.

23. Mahoney, *From Hometown to Battlefield in the Civil War Era*, 353; Oldt and Quigley, *History of Dubuque County, Iowa*, 299–300; *Patriot & Union*, June 15, 1863.

24. Thornbrough and Corpuz, *Diary of Calvin Fletcher*, VIII:5–6.

25. J. B. Grinnell to Samuel Kirkwood, Aug. 18, 1862, *O.R.*, ser. 3, vol. 2, 403–4; Samuel Kirkwood to Edwin Stanton, Mar. 10, 1863, *O.R.*, ser. 3, vol. 3, 62.

26. Oliver P. Morton to Edwin Stanton, Mar. 10, 1863, *O.R.*, ser. 3, vol. 3, 423; Towne, *Surveillance and Spies*, 87.

27. Witness report of Nancy Quick, Mar. 21, 1863, Jacob Ammen Papers, Abraham Lincoln Presidential Library, Springfield, Ill.; Roberts, *"This Infernal War,"* 75; J. C. Scott, William H. Mason, and others to Ambrose Burnside, Apr. 23, 1863, Ammen Papers; R. U. Mallory and S. G. Nesbitt to Jacob Ammen, May 19, 1863, Ammen Papers; J. M. Kelly to Col. J. K. Dubois, May 22, 1863, Ammen Papers; J. G. McCoy to Richard Yates, June 26, 1863, Yates Family Papers; Phillips, *The Rivers Ran Backward*, 170.

28. James Oakes to James B. Fry, July 16, 1863, *O.R.*, ser. 3, vol. 3, 500–501; Richard Yates to Edwin Stanton, Aug. 5 and 17, 1863, *O.R.*, ser. 3, vol. 3, 626–27, 685.

29. Richard Yates to Edwin Stanton, Oct. 10 and 14, 1863, Yates Wabash Papers.

30. For discussions on fear of conspiracy within the American experiment, see Bailyn, *The Ideological Origins of the American Revolution;* and Davis, *The Fear of Conspiracy*.

31. Lathrop, *History of the Union League of Philadelphia*, 57–58.

32. James Edmunds to Mark Howard, July 20, 1863, Dudley S. Ingraham Papers, Thomas J. Dodd Research Center, Univ. of Connecticut, Storrs; Wisconsin ULA Grand Council to subordinate council, printed circular dated Milwaukee 1863, Dustin Grow Cheever Papers.

33. General Orders No. 38, *O.R.*, ser. 1, vol. 23, pt. 2, 237; General Orders No. 9, *O.R.*, ser. 2, vol. 5, 485. Also see Bulla, *Lincoln's Censor*.

34. *Indiana State Sentinel*, June 22, 1863; Mason, Diary, Oct. 22, 1863; Weber, *Copperheads*, 121.

35. Burlingame, *At Lincoln's Side*, 66.

36. Howard, *Religion and the Radical Republican Movement*, 57–58; Croffut and Morris, *The Military and Civil History of Connecticut during the War of 1861–65*, 457–59; Marvel, *The Great Task Remaining*, 20–21; also see Warshauer, "Copperheads in Connecticut," 60–80.

37. Weber, Copperheads, 121–22; Klement, *Limits of Dissent*, 235, 250–52; Leavitt, *Decision of Judge Leavitt, of Ohio*.

38. Nevins, Strong Diary, 368–69; *Proceedings . . . State Council of the Union League of America for the State of New York*, 10–11.

39. Niven et al., *The Salmon P. Chase Papers*, 4:153; Mason, Diary, Nov. 5, 1863.

40. Union League of America, *Proceedings of the Annual Meeting of the Grand National Council, Union League of America, Held at Washington, December 9–11, 1863;* Mason, Diary, Nov. 15, 1863.

41. Henry C. Bowen to Salmon Chase, Nov. 16, 1863, Lincoln Collection—Lincoln Miscellaneous Manuscripts, Special Collections, Univ. of Chicago Library, Illinois.

42. The Odd Fellows were a secret fraternal society formed in England in the eighteenth century. Its first American chapters were created in the early nineteenth century.

43. Nicolay and Hay, *Abraham Lincoln*, 8:315–16.

44. Burlingame and Ettlinger, *Inside Lincoln's White House*, 119.

45. Loyal National League, *The Sumter Anniversary, 1863*, 128–29; Smith, "Generative Forces of Union Propaganda," 369–70; Zornow, *Lincoln and the Party Divided*, 32; Smith, *Chase and Civil War Politics*, 2:17.

46. Union League of America, *Proceedings of the Annual Meeting . . . December 9–11, 1863*, 10–11; Union League of Philadelphia, *First Annual Report*, 5.

47. Union League of America, *Proceedings of the Annual Meeting . . . December 9–11, 1863*, 10; Union League of America, *Proclamation: U.L.A. Grand National Council Chamber to "Brothers," January 1, 1864;* U.S. Census Dept., *Population of the United States in 1860*, iv.

48. Union League of America, *Proceedings . . . State Council of the Union League of America for the State of New York*, 36; Smith, "Generative Forces of Union Propaganda," 366–67.

49. Union League of America, *Proclamation: U.L.A. Grand National Council Chamber to "Brothers," January 1, 1864.*

50. Ibid.

51. Meeting minutes, Dec. 4 and 19, 1863, Union League of America, Pennsylvania Council No. 1 (York, Pa.), Records, 1863–65, York County Historical Society, Pa.; Thomas M. Vincent memorandum, Mar. 11, 1864, Lincoln Papers; Basler, *Collected Works of Abraham Lincoln*, 7:216–17.

52. Union League of America, *Proclamation: U.L.A. Grand National Council Chamber to "Brothers," January 1, 1864.*

53. Ibid.

54. Union League of Philadelphia, *Chronicle of the Union League of Philadelphia*, 154–56; Union League of Philadelphia, *First Annual Report*, 7.

55. Loyal Publication Society, *Proceedings at the First Anniversary Meeting of the Loyal Publication Society*, 4, 19–20.

56. New England Loyal Publication Society, *Pamphlet Addressed to William Endicott, Jr.* This two-page printed pamphlet pertains to NELPS circulation and expenses for the preceding fiscal year.

57. Ibid.

58. Society for the Diffusion of Political Knowledge, *Handbook of the Democracy for 1863 & '64*.

10. *"We Are Organizing Our Leagues and Getting Ready for the Great Fight of 1864"*

1. *Cleveland Plain Dealer*, Sept. 6, 1864.

2. Oakes, *Forever National*, xvi–xx, 53; Burlingame, *Lincoln Observed*, 22.

3. Charles Beasley to Lincoln, Jan. 8, 1864, Lincoln Papers; Blaine, *Twenty Years of Congress*, 1:514.

4. Oakes, *Forever National*, xviii; *Cleveland Morning Leader*, Feb. 1, 1864; Nicolay and Hay, *Abraham Lincoln*, 8:312.

5. Smith, *Chase and Civil War Politics*, 2:106.

6. Burlingame and Ettlinger, *Inside Lincoln's White House*, 141; Union League of Philadelphia, *Second Annual Report of the Board of Directors of the Union League of Philadelphia*, 4.

7. James M. Edmunds to Zachariah Chandler, Mar. 5, 1959, Zachariah Chandler Papers, Manuscripts Division, Library of Congress, Washington, D.C.; James M. Edmunds to "Friend Howard," Jan. 24, 1864, James M. Edmunds Collection, Archives of Michigan, Lansing. "Shadow of turning" is a biblical phrase to describe variance or deviation; James M. Edmunds to "Friend Howard," Feb. 10, 1864, Dudley S. Ingraham Papers; Smith, *Chase and Civil War Politics*, 2:109.

8. Niven, *The Salmon P. Chase Papers*, 4:303–5; Basler, *Collected Works of Abraham Lincoln*, 7:212–13; Smith, *Chase and Civil War Politics*, 2:116.

9. Niven, *The Salmon P. Chase Papers*, 4:315, 329; Julian, *Political Recollections*, 237–38.

10. Beale, *The Diary of Edward Bates*, 347; H. G. McPike to Lyman Trumbull, Feb. 1, 1864, Lyman Trumbull Papers, Manuscripts Division, Library of Congress, Washington, D.C.; James H. Lane to James Edmunds, Jan. 20, 1864, James M. Edmunds Correspondence, Bentley Historical Library, Univ. of Michigan, Ann Arbor.

11. Lowell, *The President's Policy*; Basler, *Collected Works of Abraham Lincoln*, 7:132; Henry C. Lea to Abraham Lincoln, Apr. 18, 1864, Lincoln Papers.

12. Union League of Philadelphia, *Chronicle of the Union League of Philadelphia*, 63–65; Bellows, *Historical Sketch of the Union League Club*, 18.

13. Union League Club of New York, *Report of the Committee on Volunteering*, 3–7; Union League Club of New York, *Banquet Given by Members of the Union League Club of 1863 and 1864*, 12; Cannon, *Personal Reminiscences of the Rebellion*, 186–87.

14. Union League Club of New York, *Report of the Committee on Volunteering*, 3–7.

15. Union League to Edwin Stanton, *O.R.*, ser. 3, vol. 3, 1106–7; Union League Club of New York, *Report of the Committee on Volunteering*, 6–7; Cannon, *Personal*

Reminiscences of the Rebellion, 187; Union League Club of New York, *Banquet Given by Members of the Union League Club*, 15.

16. C. W. Foster to Union League, *O.R.*, ser. 3, vol. 3, 1117–18; Union League Club of New York, *Report of the Committee on Volunteering*, 9.

17. Cannon, *Personal Reminiscences of the Rebellion*, 188; Union League Club of New York, *Banquet Given by Members of the Union League Club*, 18–19; C. W. Foster to Union League, *O.R.*, ser. 3, vol. 4, 4.

18. Habberton, Diary, Mar. 5, 1864, John Habberton Papers, United States Army Military History Institute, Carlisle, Pa.; Union League Club of New York, *Report of the Committee on Volunteering*, 13.

19. Habberton, Diary, Feb. 26, 1864.

20. Cannon, *Personal Reminiscences of the Rebellion*, 188–89; Habberton, Diary, Mar. 5, 1864.

21. Union League Club of New York, *Report of the Committee on Volunteering*, 24; Cannon, *Personal Reminiscences of the Rebellion*, 190; *The Liberator*, Mar. 18, 1864.

22. Union League Club of New York, *Banquet Given by Members of the Union League Club*, 7; Bernstein, *New York City Draft Riots*, 71.

23. Quoted in Union League Club of New York, *Banquet Given by Members of the Union League Club*, 20. Of the thirty-seven examples discovered during 1863–64 in the *New York Herald*, see Mar. 27, July 10, July 11, and Aug. 1, 1863; *New York Tribune*, Mar. 5, 1864; Smith, *The Civil War Letters of Col. Elijah H. C. Cavins*, 113.

24. Nevins, Strong Diary, 313; Chase, *Letter from Hon. S. P. Chase*.

25. Roberts, *"This Infernal War,"* 189; Beale, *The Diary of Gideon Welles*, 2:41, 43; Brooks, *Lincoln Observed*, 109; Nicolay and Hay, *Abraham Lincoln*, 4:416–20; *New York Times*, June 1, 1864.

26. Union League of America, *Meeting of the Grand National Council, Baltimore, June 6, 1864*, 1, 5–6.

27. Stoddard, "The Story of a Nomination," 138:270–71; Holzer, *Lincoln's White House Secretary*, 335–38.

28. Stoddard, "The Story of a Nomination," 270–71; Stoddard, *Inside the White House in War Times*, 238–39; Hardie, "The Influence of the Union League of America on the Second Election of Lincoln," 44. In Stoddard's full autobiography, *Lincoln's White House Secretary: The Adventurous Life of William O. Stoddard*, much of which was previously unpublished, editor Harold Holzer suggests historians should take some of Stoddard's more startling pronouncements with a grain of salt (7–8). I assert that Stoddard's declaration portraying the Baltimore ULA convention as the *real* opening to the National Union Convention is a case in point.

29. W. R. Irwin to John Bagby, Apr. 28, 1864, John C. Bagby Correspondence 1849–1866, Abraham Lincoln Presidential Library, Springfield, Ill.; Stoddard, *Inside the White House in War Times*, 238–41.

30. See *Proceedings at the Annual Meeting of the Grand Council of the Union League of the State of Connecticut Held at New Haven, May 18, 1864*, 9–10; quoted in Long, *The Jewel of Liberty*, 23; Trefousse, *The Radical Republicans*, 234.

31. Oakleaf, *National Union Convention of 1864 and Why Lincoln Was Not Nominated by Acclamation*, 3–10; Beale, *Diary of Gideon Welles*, 2:47; Laas, *Wartime Washington*, 389.

For a complete transcript of the proceedings, see Murphy, *Presidential Election, 1864, Proceedings of the National Union Convention Held in Baltimore, Md., June 7th and 8th, 1864.*

32. Beale, *The Diary of Edward Bates,* 374–75; Beale, *Diary of Gideon Welles,* 2:47.

33. W. R. Irwin to Abraham Lincoln, June 8, 1864, Lincoln Papers; Basler, *Collected Works of Abraham Lincoln,* 7:383–84.

34. Union League of America, *Grand Lincoln and Johnson Ratification Meeting at Washington City, D.C., June 15, 1864.*

35. Neely Jr., *The Boundaries of American Political Culture in the Civil War Era,* 90.

36. Adams, *Letter from Washington 1863–1865,* 142.

37. Union League of America, *Speaker Colfax and the Union League Committee;* United States Congress, *Journal of the House of Representatives,* 38th Cong., 1st sess., 505–10.

38. Waugh, *Reelecting Lincoln,* 207–8.

39. *Secret Circular, Executive Committee of the Union League of America, New York, July 8, 1864,* James Henry Harris Papers, State Archives of North Carolina, Raleigh.

40. John W. Reid file, letter dated Apr. 13, 1864, Union Provost Marshal Citizens File, Microfilm #M345, National Archives, Washington, D.C.; Maj. Frank Bond to Gen. C. Fisk, Apr. 29, 1864, *O.R.,* ser. 1, vol. 24, pt. 3, 352; John Pendleton file, letter dated Apr. 16, 1864, Union Provost Marshal Citizens File, Microfilm #M345, National Archives, Washington, D.C.; Warner, *Generals in Blue,* 154–55.

41. Cooper, *The Loyalty Demanded by the Present Crisis;* Wakelyn, *Southern Unionist Pamphlets and the Civil War,* 380.

42. Foulke, *Life of Oliver P. Morton,* 1:361; Churchill, "Liberty, Conscription, and a Party Divided," 296–97.

43. *Grand Haven News,* Mar. 16, 1864.

44. Society for the Diffusion of Political Knowledge, *Handbook of the Democracy for 1863 & '64,* 2, 17, 29; *Bedford Gazette,* July 15, 1864; Wilmer Atkinson and Howard Jenkins to Jay Cooke, June 2, 1864, Jay Cooke Papers, Historical Society of Pennsylvania, Philadelphia; Smith, "Generative Forces of Union Propaganda," 410.

45. *Daily Ohio Statesman,* July 11, 1864; *Der Lacha Caunty Patriot,* July 19, 1864.

46. Samuel B. Lawrence to Gen. Lew Wallace, July 6, 1864, *O.R.,* ser. 1, vol. 37, pt. 2, 73, 92; Union Club of Baltimore Collection, Minutes and Company Roll, July 10–15, 1864, Maryland Historical Society, Baltimore.

47. H. W. Halleck to Gen. Christopher Augur, July 12, 1864, *O.R.,* ser. 1, vol. 37, pt. 2, 228; Furguson, *Freedom Rising,* 312.

48. Union Club of Baltimore Collection, Minutes and Company Roll, July 10–15, 1864.

49. Henry Halleck to Ulysses Grant, Aug. 11, 1864, *O.R.,* ser. 1, vol. 42, pt. 2, 111–12.

50. Joseph Medill to Elihu Washburne, Apr. 26, 1864, Washburne Papers; Butler, *Private and Official Correspondence of Gen. Benjamin F. Butler,* 5:35.

11. "Once More Rally Around the Flag, *and Your Work Will Be Complete"*

1. Basler, *Collected Works of Abraham Lincoln,* 7:514.

2. Butler, *Private and Official Correspondence of Gen. Benjamin F. Butler,* 5:67–69; Niven, *Salmon P. Chase Papers,* 1:491, 4:423; "Secret Movement to Supersede Abra-

ham Lincoln in '64," *New York Sun,* June 30, 1889; Pearson, *The Life of John A. Andrew,* 2:159–60; Perry, *The Life and Letters of Francis Lieber,* 350.

3. Loyal Publication Society, *Proceedings at the Second Anniversary Meeting of the Loyal Publication Society, February 11, 1865,* 9, 13–14; Lieber, *Lincoln or McClellan?*

4. Burlingame, *At Lincoln's Side,* 92.

5. Union League of Philadelphia, *Chronicle of the Union League of Philadelphia,* 156–57.

6. Lathrop, *History of the Union League of Philadelphia,* 81; Union League of Philadelphia, *Second Annual Report,* 6–7; Union League of Philadelphia, *Third Annual Report,* 9–10.

7. Zornow, "Treason as a Campaign Issue in the Re-election of Lincoln," 350–51; *Official Proceedings of the Democratic National Convention, Held in 1864 at Chicago;* Union League of Philadelphia, *Congressional Record of George H. Pendleton; New York Semi-Weekly Tribune,* Sept. 6, 1864.

8. Waugh, *Reelecting Lincoln,* 298–301; also see *Official Proceedings of the Democratic National Convention* for McClellan's full statement; Sears, *The Civil War Papers of George B. McClellan,* 614–15.

9. *Union League Gazette* 1, no. 7 (Oct. 1864): 1.

10. Burlingame and Ettlinger, *Inside Lincoln's White House,* 234; *New York Times,* Sept. 8, 1864; *New York Semi-Weekly Tribune,* Sept. 6, 1864; Lincoln memorandum, Aug. 23, 1864, Lincoln Papers.

11. William T. Sherman to Henry Halleck, Sept. 3, 1864, *O.R.* ser. 1, vol. 38, pt. 5, 777; Donald, *Inside Lincoln's Cabinet,* 253.

12. Halbert Paine to Capt. C. H. Potter, Aug. 21, 1864, in "Manuscripta Minora," vol. 2, Halbert E. Paine Papers, 1861–15, LSU Libraries, Baton Rouge, La.; Oscar Dinwiddie, "Reminiscences," Union League Club of Chicago Archives, Ill. See Towne, *Surveillance and Spies in the Civil War,* 263–75, for the most recent scholarly analysis of the Chicago plot and related arms seizure.

13. Union League of Philadelphia, *The Great Northern Conspiracy of the "O.S.L.";* also see Churchill, "Liberty, Conscription, and a Party Divided," 295–303; Towne, *Surveillance and Spies in the Civil War,* 308.

14. Union League of America, Connecticut State Council, *Letter from a Union League Activist Advocating the Re-election of President Abraham Lincoln,* 15; John Pilsifer to Lindley Smyth, Oct. 27, 1864, Documents and Papers Relating to the Union League of America; *Proceedings of the State Grand Council of the U.L.A. of Michigan U.L.A. at its Special Meeting, March 2, 1864.*

15. Rable, *God's Almost Chosen Peoples,* 353–55; quoted in Moorhead, *American Apocalypse,* 156.

16. Ewing Jr. to Maj. Gen. Schofield, Oct. 1, 1863, *O.R.,* ser. 1, vol. 22, pt. 2, 587; Holcombe, *History of Greene County Missouri,* 474–75; *Ashland Union,* May 4, 1864; Kiper, *Dear Catharine, Dear Taylor,* 283.

17. William Sherman to George Thomas, Aug. 5, 1864, *O.R.,* ser. 1, vol. 38, pt. 5, 376–77; Summers, *A Dangerous Stir,* 30.

18. Dana, *Recollections of the Civil War,* 261; Abraham Lincoln to William Sherman, Sept. 19, 1864, Lincoln Papers; Marvel, *Lincoln's Autocrat,* 326–27; Engs and Brooks, *Their Patriotic Duty,* 303.

19. Union Congressional Committee publicity letter for 1864 campaign, Lincoln Financial Foundation Collection, Allen County Public Library, Fort Wayne, Ind.; *Indianapolis Daily Journal*, Sept. 7, 1864.

20. The *Alleghanian*, Oct. 6, 1864; Elihu Washburne to Edward Warner, Sept. 15, 1864, Edward B. Warner Papers, Illinois History and Lincoln Collections, Univ. of Illinois, Urbana; Loyal League printed circular on supplying loyal newspapers to the Army of the Potomac, Oct. 1864, and Albert G. Richardson to Lincoln, Oct. 24, 1864, Lincoln Papers; Freidel, *Francis Lieber*, 351–53; Union League of Philadelphia, *Address by the Union League of Philadelphia, to the Citizens of Pennsylvania, in Favor of the Re-election of Abraham Lincoln;* James Edmunds to "Brothers," printed circular dated Oct. 18, 1864, Lincoln Papers.

21. Freidel, *Union Pamphlets of the Civil War*, 1:15; "Great Speech of Hon. Robert C. Winthrop," Campaign Doc. No. 23, in Society for the Diffusion of Political Knowledge, *Handbook of the Democracy*, n.p.; Weber, *Copperheads*, 83.

22. De Hauranne, *A Frenchman in Lincoln's America*, 1:495.

23. *Detroit Free Press*, Aug. 16, 1864; Anonymous, *The Lincoln Catechism;* Freidel, *Union Pamphlets*, 1:16; Anonymous, *Miscegenation;* Society for the Diffusion of Political Knowledge, *Miscegenation Indorsed by the Republican Party.*

24. Smith, *Civil War Letters of Col. Elijah H. C. Cavins*, 177; quoted in Boswell, "Black Women during Slavery to 1865," 19; Woodward, *Mary Chesnut's Civil War*, 29.

25. *Detroit Free Press*, Aug. 16, 1864; *Indianapolis Daily State Sentinel*, Oct. 12, 1864; Mason, Diary, Oct. 9, 1864; *Bedford Gazette*, July 15, 1864.

26. Bensel, *The American Ballot Box in the Mid-Nineteenth Century*, 14–20.

27. Ibid.; Altschuler and Blumin, *Rude Republic*, 174–76.

28. George Boker to unknown, Oct. 26, 1864, Union League folder, box 7-A, Society Miscellaneous Collection, Historical Society of Pennsylvania, Philadelphia; the *Agitator*, Nov. 2, 1864; Dittenhoefer, *How We Elected Lincoln*, 87–88; Bensel, *The American Ballot Box in the Mid-Nineteenth Century*, 2–3, 17, 20.

29. George H. Harlow to Richard Yates, Oct. 23, 1864, Yates Papers (Wabash).

30. DeRosa, "A Million Thinking Bayonets," 26–27; Union Congressional Committee, *A Few Plain Words with the Rank and File of the Union Armies;* Basler, *Collected Works of Abraham Lincoln*, 8:53; Ulysses Grant to Edwin Stanton, Sept. 27, 1864, *O.R.*, ser. 1, vol. 42, pt. 2, 1045–46.

31. White, *Emancipation, the Union Army, and the Reelection of Abraham Lincoln*, 103–11.

32. DeRosier Jr., *Through the South with a Union Soldier*, 156, 159; Clarence Johnson to parents, Nov. 1, 1864, Clarence H. Johnson Letters, The Library of Virginia, Richmond.

33. Union League of Philadelphia, Soldiers vote circular dated Oct. 20, 1864, Union League Archives, The Heritage Center of the Union League of Philadelphia, Pa.

34. James Edmunds to "Friend Howard," Oct. 31, 1864, James M. Edmunds Collection, Archives of Michigan, Lansing; James Edmunds to Lincoln, Nov. 1, 1864, Lincoln Papers.

35. See Charleston, Ill., Riot Records, James S. Schoff Civil War Collection, William L. Clements Library, Univ. of Michigan, Ann Arbor, for soldier and civilian depositions.

36. Taylor, *"Old Slow Town,"* 156–80; Churchill, "Liberty, Conscription, and a Party Divided," 297.

37. Bennett Hill report, "Historical Reports of the State Acting Assistant Provost Marshal General and District Provost Marshals, 1865," Records of the Provost Marshal General's Bureau (RG 110), (M1163—Michigan), National Archives, Chicago, 3; *Detroit Free Press*, Nov. 4, 1864.

38. James Edmunds to Lincoln, Nov. 2, 1864, Lincoln Papers; Bensel, *The American Ballot Box in the Mid-Nineteenth Century*, 219–20.

39. Longacre, "The Union Army Occupation of New York City, November 1864," 133–58; Marvel, *Lincoln's Autocrat*, 353–54; Nevins, Strong Diary, 509.

40. McPherson, *Battle Cry of Freedom*, 803–6; Union League of Philadelphia, *Second Annual Report*, 3.

41. Basler, *Collected Works of Abraham Lincoln*, 8:100.

42. Silbey, *A Respectable Minority*, 160–61; Dana, *Recollections of the Civil War*, 261; White, *Emancipation, the Union Army, and the Reelection of Abraham Lincoln*, 103–11.

43. De Hauranne, *A Frenchman in Lincoln's America*, 1:170–71; John Sherman to William T. Sherman, Dec. 18, 1864, William T. Sherman Papers; Sears, *Civil War Papers of George B. McClellan*, 618; Summers, *A Dangerous Stir*, 39.

44. Salmon P. Chase to Lincoln, Nov. 14, 1864, Lincoln Papers; Theodore Tilton to John Nicolay, Nov. 12, 1864, Lincoln Papers.

45. *Fort Wayne Sentinel*, quoted in *Indianapolis Daily Journal*, Nov. 14, 1864; *Illinois State Register*, Nov. 10, 1864; *Ashland Union*, Nov. 16, 1864; *Daily Ohio Statesmen*, Nov. 3 and 10, 1864; *Bloomsburg Star of the North*, Nov. 16, 1864; *Columbian Register*, Nov. 19, 1864; *New York World*, Nov. 21, 1864.

46. Quoted in Watterson, *History of the Manhattan Club*, xxiii–xxiv; Silbey, *A Respectable Minority*, 164–67. Also see Summers, *A Dangerous Stir*, 3, 26, for commentary on the paranoid thread in American politics.

47. See Union League Club of New York, *Report of the Committee on Providing a Thanksgiving Dinner for the Soldiers and Sailors*; Smith, *Starving the South*, 145–62.

48. Union League Club of New York, *Report of the Committee on Providing a Thanksgiving Dinner for the Soldiers and Sailors*, 15, 25; Kiper, *Dear Catharine, Dear Taylor*, 317.

49. McCormack, *Memoirs of Gustave Koerner*, 2:433; Stoddard, *Inside the White House in War Times*, 131–32; Blair, *With Malice toward Some*, 202–3.

50. Stoddard, *Inside the White House in War Times*, 133; quoted in Klement, "Copperheads in the Upper Midwest during the Civil War," 15; Stoddard, *Abraham Lincoln*, 363.

51. Union League of Philadelphia, *Chronicle of the Union League of Philadelphia*, 156–57; Union League of Philadelphia, *Second Annual Report*, 5–6.

52. Loyal Publication Society, *Proceedings at the Second Anniversary Meeting*, 11, 13–14, 21; Freidel, *Francis Lieber*, 346; Bellows, *Historical Sketch of the Union League Club*, 90.

53. New England Loyal Publication Society, *Report of the Executive Committee of the New England Loyal Publication Society, May 1, 1865*, 1–27.

54. Union League of America, *Resolutions Adopted by the National Union League of America, at Its Annual Session, Held in Washington City, D.C., Dec. 14 and 15, 1864*, 9–10; Henry Raymond to Elihu Washburne, June 20, 1864, Washburne Papers; James Harlan to Elihu Washburne, Nov. 19, 1864, Washburne Papers; Silvestro, "None but Patriots," 132.

55. Zornow, *Lincoln and the Party Divided*, 182; Union League of Philadelphia, *Second Annual Report*, 6.

56. W. R. Irwin to John Bagby, Apr. 28, 1864, Bagby Collection.

57. Society for the Diffusion of Political Knowledge, *Handbook of the Democracy*, contents; Neely, *Lincoln and the Triumph of the Nation*, 20; Zornow, *Lincoln and the Party Divided*, 181.

12. *"It Is a Fatal Mistake to Hold That This War Is Over Because the Fighting Has Ceased"*

1. Union League of America, *Resolutions Adopted by the National Union League of America, at Its Annual Session, Held in Washington City, D.C., Dec. 14 and 15, 1864*, 13–14; Baggett, *The Scalawags*, 113; Vicksburg, Miss. Union League no. 1 to Lincoln, Feb. 15 and 24, 1864, Lincoln Papers; United States Congress, *Report of the Joint Committee on the Conduct of the War*, 5:68; Bruce, "The Capture and Occupation of Richmond," 14:134.

2. *O.R.*, ser. 1, vol. 49, pt. 1, 733–34; W. Hancock to L. Thomas, *O.R.*, ser. 3, vol. 4, 1088–89.

3. Lieber, *A Letter to Hon. E. D. Morgan*.

4. Howard, *Autobiography of Oliver Otis Howard*, 2:194–308. Maj. Gen. O. O. Howard headed the Freedmen's Bureau from May 1865 to July 1874; also see Cimbala and Miller, *The Freedmen's Bureau and Reconstruction*, and Cimbala, *The Freedmen's Bureau*.

5. See Downs, *After Appomattox*.

6. Nevins, Strong Diary, 581.

7. Union League of Philadelphia, *Third Annual Report of the Board of Directors of the Union League of Philadelphia*, 3.

8. *Dayton Daily Empire*, Aug. 21, 1865.

9. Bellows, *Historical Sketch of the Union League Club of New York*, 85–86; Nevins and Thomas, *The Diary of George Templeton Strong*, 99–100; Union League of Philadelphia, *Third Annual Report*, 18.

10. Bergeron, *Andrew Johnson's Civil War and Reconstruction*, 7.

11. Abbott, *The Republican Party and the South*, 47; *Great Republic*, Jan. 17, 1867.

12. McKitrick, *Andrew Johnson and Reconstruction*, 55–56; Drumm, "The Union League in the Carolinas," 10–11; Fleming, "The Union League of America," 3–4.

13. Abbott, *The Republican Party and the South*, 42–43; Fleming, "The Union League of America," 3–4.

14. Fitzgerald, *The Union League Movement in the Deep South*, 14–15, 32.

15. Warren, *Reminiscences of a Mississippi Carpet-Bagger*, 41; Fitzgerald, "'He Was Always Preaching the Union,'" 230.

16. Wiggins, *The Journals of Josiah Gorgas*, 211; Hull, *Annals of Athens, Georgia*, 320.

17. Rable, *But There Was No Peace*, 15. Carl von Clausewitz (1780–1831), was a Prussian general and military theorist well known to the general public for his quote, "War is the continuation of politics by other means."

18. Simpson, Graf, and Muldowny, *Advice after Appomattox*, 34–35.

19. Fleming, "The Black Codes of 1865–66," 3; Dana Jr., *Speeches in Stirring Times and Letters to a Son*, 246.

20. Union League of America, *Proceedings of the Annual Meeting of the Grand National Council, Union League of America, Held at Washington, December 13, 1865*, 9–10; George

Sterns to Oliver O. Howard, Oct. 4, 1865, Oliver Otis Howard Papers, George J. Mitchell Department of Special Collections & Archives, Bowdoin College Library, Brunswick, Maine. Hereafter referred to as O. O. Howard Papers; O. O. Howard to George Sterns, Oct. 9, 1865, O. O. Howard Papers; also see Oliver O. Howard to Freedmen's Bureau Officers & Agents, Apr. 12, 1867, O. O. Howard Papers.

21. Union League of America, *Proceedings of the Annual Meeting of the Grand National Council . . . December 13, 1865,* 9–10; Gould IV, *Diary of a Contraband,* 82.

22. Beale, *Diary of Gideon Welles,* 2:444.

23. Union League of America, New York State Council, *Proceedings of the State Council of the Union League of America for the State of New York: at the Special Session, held at Syracuse, on Tuesday, September 4, 1866,* 6; Anonymous, *Is the South Ready for Restoration?,* 20.

24. Fitzgerald, *The Union League Movement in the Deep South,* 26–27, 31.

25. Hahn, *A Nation under Our Feet,* 184–86; McWhiney, Moore, and Pace, *"Fear God and Walk Humbly,"* 375; De Forest, *A Union Officer in the Reconstruction,* 99–100.

26. John Costin to Thomas Tullock, May 25, 1867, "Black Ministers and the Organization of the Republican Party in the South in 1867."

27. Fitzgerald, *The Union League Movement in the Deep South,* 37–38, 66–67.

28. Union League of America, *Proceedings of the National Council of the Union League of America at its Sixth Annual Session, Held in the City of Washington D.C., March 2nd and 3rd, 1869,* 9; *Great Republic,* Jan. 31, 1867; Fitzgerald, *The Union League Movement in the Deep South,* 12, 47, 153.

29. Oliver O. Howard to Freedmen's Bureau Officers & Agents, Apr. 12, 1867, O. O. Howard Papers; Owens, "The Union League of America: Political Activities in Tennessee, the Carolinas, and Virginia," 32–33, 480. Owens cites the Union League of America's *Fifth Annual Report* from December 1867. In his 1989 book, *The Union League Movement in the Deep South,* author Michael Fitzgerald noted that the *Fifth Annual Report* had vanished from the Library of Congress's collections, though Owens, fortunately, reprinted portions of it as an appendix in her 1943 dissertation. As of 2016, I was likewise unable to locate a copy of the ULA's 1867 report.

30. Hamburg, N.C., Council of the ULA, Record Book 1867, Brower Family Papers; Hahn, *A Nation under Our Feet,* 187.

31. Quoted in Foner, *Reconstruction,* 283–84.

32. Fleming, "The Ritual of the Union League," 17–27; Wallace, *Carpet Bag Rule in Florida,* 45; Cason, "The Loyal League in Georgia," 132; Warren, *Reminiscences of a Mississippi Carpet-Bagger,* 44.

33. Fleming, "Resolutions of the Alabama Grand Council of the Union League, April, 1867," 34–35.

34. *Great Republic,* Apr. 4, 1867.

35. Fitzgerald, Diary, May 19, 1868, Fitzgerald Family Papers, Southern Historical Collection, Univ. of North Carolina, Chapel Hill.

36. Wallace, *Carpet Bag Rule in Florida,* 42–44. As discussed in Chapter 6, the Northern Union Leagues and Loyal Leagues that rose to prominence in 1863 were two distinct organizations. In the postwar South, however, the terms were used interchangeably to refer to the Union League of America.

37. Osborn, "Letters of a Carpetbagger in Florida, 1866–1869," 240, 248.

38. Shofner, *Nor Is It Over Yet*, 169–70, 172.

39. The *Southern Enterprise*, May 23, 1867.

40. *Great Republic*, Apr. 18, 1867; Elliott and Smith, *Undaunted Radical*, 361–63.

41. Wood, *Reminiscences of Reconstruction in Texas*, 14; the *Opelousas Courier*, Nov. 23, 1867.

42. Fitzgerald, Diary, Apr. 22, 1868.

43. Parsons, *Ku Klux*, 7, 115. The popular image of a Klan uniform as a flowing white robe with a matching pointed mask was created by the Klan in the twentieth century.

44. United States Congress, *Ku Klux Klan Conspiracy Report*, 1:20; Rogers Jr., *Black Belt Scalawag*, 70; Union League of America, *Proceedings of the National Council . . . Sixth Annual Session . . . 1869*, 11; James Edmunds obituary, *New York Times*, Dec. 15, 1879.

45. Union League of America, *Proceedings of the National Council . . . Sixth Annual Session . . . 1869*, 12–13.

46. Ibid.

47. Ibid.; Fitzgerald, Diary, Sept. 1, 1869.

48. Wish, *Reconstruction in the South*, 156, 158.

49. Quoted in Fleming, *The Sequel of Appomattox*, 181; Foner, "Foreword," ix–xii.

50. Foner, "Foreword," ix–xii; Wish, *Reconstruction in the South*, xxxviii; Fleming, *Civil War and Reconstruction in Alabama*, 553.

51. Fitzgerald, *The Union League Movement in the Deep South*, 3; Fleming, "The Ritual of the Union League," 17–27; Cason, "The Loyal League in Georgia," 132.

Conclusion

1. Union League of Philadelphia, *Chronicle of the Union League*, 73.

2. Baker, *The Works of William Seward*, 5:507; Silbey, *A Respectable Minority*, 227, 243; Rawley, *The Politics of Union*, 90.

3. Union League of Philadelphia, *Address by the Union League of Philadelphia, to the Citizens of Pennsylvania*, 25; Gray and Ropes, *War Letters, 1862–1865*, 73.

4. Perry, *Life and Letters of Francis Lieber*, 340.

5. Emerson, *The Prose Works of Ralph Waldo Emerson*, 1:525.

6. Seward to Charles Francis Adams, Feb. 7, 1865, *O.R.*, ser. 1, vol. 46, pt. 2, 471.

7. McPherson, *Battle Cry of Freedom*, 859.

Bibliography

Unpublished Manuscript and Archival Sources

Ammen, Jacob. Papers. Abraham Lincoln Presidential Library, Springfield, Ill.

Bagby, John C. Correspondence 1849—66. Abraham Lincoln Presidential Library, Springfield, Ill.

Bayard, Thomas F. Papers. Manuscripts Division, Library of Congress, Washington, D.C.

Bonaparte, Jerome Napoleon. Papers. Maryland Historical Society, Baltimore.

Briggs Family. Papers. Bentley Historical Library, University of Michigan, Ann Arbor.

Broadhead, James O. "St. Louis during the Civil War." Missouri History Museum, St. Louis.

Brower Family. Papers. Southern Historical Collection, University of North Carolina, Chapel Hill.

Chandler, Zachariah. Papers. Manuscripts Division, Library of Congress, Washington, D.C.

Charleston, Illinois, Riot Records. James S. Schoff Civil War Collection, William L. Clements Library, University of Michigan, Ann Arbor.

Cheever, Dustin Grow. Papers. Andersen Library, University of Wisconsin, Whitewater.

Civil War Loyalty Flag. Collection 1951.213. Wisconsin Historical Society, Madison.

Civil War Union Club of Indiana. Collection. Manuscript Section, Indiana Division, Indiana State Library, Indianapolis.

Collins Family. Papers. Carl A. Kroch Library, Cornell University, Ithaca, N.Y.

Cooke, Jay. Papers. Historical Society of Pennsylvania, Philadelphia.

Crawford, Samuel Wylie. Papers. Manuscripts Division, Library of Congress, Washington, D.C.

Davis, Andrew F. Papers. Special Collections & University Archives, University of Iowa Library, Iowa City.

Dinwiddie, Oscar. "Reminiscences." Union League Club of Chicago Archives, Illinois.

Documents and Papers Relating to the Union League of America, and to the Orwigsburg, Schuylkill County, Pa., Branch, 1863–1866. Eberly Family Special Collections Library, Pennsylvania State University, University Park.

Edmunds, James M. Collection. Archives of Michigan, Lansing.

———. Correspondence. Bentley Historical Library, University of Michigan, Ann Arbor.

English, Henry K. Collection. Manuscript Section, Indiana Division, Indiana State Library, Indianapolis.

Everett, Edward. Journals. Massachusetts Historical Society, Boston.

First Congregational Church (Marine Mills, Minn.). Records. Minnesota Historical Society, St. Paul.

Fitzgerald Family. Papers. Southern Historical Collection, University of North Carolina, Chapel Hill.

Fox Family. Correspondence. Bentley Historical Library, University of Michigan, Ann Arbor.

Gibbs, Addison Crandall. Papers. Oregon Historical Society, Portland.

Giddings, Joshua R., and George Washington Julian. Manuscripts Division, Library of Congress, Washington, D.C.

Godkin, Edwin L. Papers. Houghton Library, Harvard University, Cambridge, Massachusetts.

Grier Family. Papers. Missouri History Museum, St. Louis.

Habberton, John. Papers. United States Army Military History Institute, Carlisle, Pennsylvania.

Hare-Willing Family. Papers. American Philosophical Society Library, Philadelphia, Pennsylvania.

Harris, James Henry. Papers. State Archives of North Carolina, Raleigh.

Howard, Mark. Papers. Connecticut Historical Society, Hartford.

Howard, Oliver Otis. Papers. George J. Mitchell Department of Special Collections & Archives, Bowdoin College Library, Brunswick, Maine.

Ingraham, Dudley S. Papers. Thomas J. Dodd Research Center, University of Connecticut, Storrs.

Johnson, Clarence H. Letters. The Library of Virginia, Richmond.

Kirkwood, Samuel J. Papers. State Historical Society of Iowa, Des Moines.

Ladies' Union League. Papers, 1862–64. Wisconsin Historical Society Archives, Madison.

Lee, Francis L. Papers. Massachusetts Historical Society, Boston.

Lincoln, Abraham. Papers. Manuscripts Division, Library of Congress, Washington, D.C. (American Memory)

Lincoln Collection—Lincoln Miscellaneous Manuscripts. Special Collections, University of Chicago Library, Illinois.

Loyal League of Union Citizens. Records, 1863. New York Historical Society, New York.

Loyal Union League, Henry County, Iowa. Minute Book, 1863–64. Special Collections & University Archives, University of Iowa Library, Iowa City.

Marble, Manton. Papers. Manuscripts Division, Library of Congress, Washington, D.C.

McClelland, Robert. Papers. Bentley Historical Library, University of Michigan, Ann Arbor.

McKinney, David. Papers. William L. Clements Library, University of Michigan, Ann Arbor.

McPheeters Family. Papers. United States Army Military History Institute, Carlisle, Pa.

Meredith Family. Papers. Historical Society of Pennsylvania, Philadelphia.

Milroy, Gen. Robert H. Collection. Jasper County Public Library, Rensselaer, Indiana.

Miscellaneous Manuscripts Collection. Manuscripts Division, Library of Congress, Washington, D.C.

Morse, Samuel F. B. Papers. Manuscripts Division, Library of Congress, Washington, D.C.

New England Loyal Publication Society. Manuscript Letters Collection. Boston Public Library, Massachusetts.

Newell Family. Papers. William L. Clements Library, University of Michigan, Ann Arbor.

Paine, Halbert E. Papers, 1861–1915. LSU Libraries, Baton Rouge, Louisiana.

Records of the Provost Marshal General's Bureau. Record Group 110 (M1163). National Archives, Chicago, Illinois.

Remey, Charles Mason. Family Papers. Manuscripts Division, Library of Congress, Washington, D.C.

Salem Union League. Records, MM 16, Phillips Library, Peabody Essex Museum, Salem, Massachusetts.

Scott, Elvira Ascenith Weir. Diary. State Historical Society of Missouri, Columbia.

Sherman, John. Papers. Manuscripts Division, Library of Congress, Washington, D.C.

Sherman, William T. Papers. Manuscripts Division, Library of Congress, Washington, D.C.

Shuey, Anson B. "War Letters." Civil War Document Collection, United States Army Military History Institute, Carlisle, Pennsylvania.

Society Miscellaneous Collection. Historical Society of Pennsylvania, Philadelphia.

Taft, Horatio Nelson. Diary. Manuscripts Division, Library of Congress, Washington, D.C.

Thomas, James A. Letters. Filson Historical Society, Louisville, Kentucky.

Tilden, Samuel J. Papers. Manuscripts and Archives Division, New York Public Library, New York.

Trumbull, Lyman. Papers. Manuscripts Division, Library of Congress, Washington, D.C.

Turnure, David Mitchell. Papers. New York Historical Society, New York.

Union Club (Brownville, Nebraska). 1863 Minutes. Nebraska State Historical Society, Lincoln.

Union Club of Baltimore. Minutes and Company Roll, 1864 July 10–15.

———. Record Books, 1863–72. Maryland Historical Society, Baltimore.

Union Congressional Committee. 1864 Campaign Letter. Lincoln Financial Foundation Collection, Allen County Public Library, Fort Wayne, Indiana.

Union League of America. Collection. Kansas Historical Society, Topeka.

Union League of America—Council #13. Records, 1863–65. Massachusetts Historical Society, Boston.

Union League of America, Pennsylvania Council No. 1 (York, Pa.). Records, 1863–65. York County Historical Society, Pennsylvania.

Union League Archives. Correspondence. The Heritage Center of the Union League of Philadelphia, Pennsylvania.

———. Meeting Minutes. The Heritage Center of the Union League of Philadelphia, Pennsylvania.

Union League of the Town of Burnett (Dodge County, Wisconsin). Records, 1863. Wisconsin Historical Society, Madison.

Union League Records. Rhode Island Historical Society Library, Providence.

Union Provost Marshal Citizens File. Microfilm M345. National Archives, Washington, D.C.

Wade, Benjamin. Papers. Manuscripts Division, Library of Congress, Washington, D.C.

Waltham Union League. Records, 1862–63. Massachusetts Historical Society, Boston.

Warner, Edward B. Papers. Illinois History and Lincoln Collections, University of Illinois, Urbana.

Washburne, Elihu B. Papers. Manuscripts Division, Library of Congress, Washington, D.C.

Waterbury, John C. Papers. Bentley Historical Library, University of Michigan, Ann Arbor.

Wise-Clark Family. Papers. Special Collections & University Archives, University of Iowa Library, Iowa City.

Yates, Richard. Wabash College Papers. Abraham Lincoln Presidential Library, Springfield, Illinois.

———. Yates Family Papers. Abraham Lincoln Presidential Library, Springfield, Illinois.
Young, John Russell. Papers. Manuscripts Division, Library of Congress, Washington, D.C.

Published Federal Government Documents

United States Congress. *Congressional Globe.* 37th Congress.
———. House Reports. 37th Congress.
———. *Journal of the House of Representatives.* 37th and 38th Congress.
———. *Ku Klux Klan Conspiracy Report of the Joint Select Committee to Inquire into the Condition of Affairs in the Late Insurrectionary States.* 13 vols. Washington, D.C.: Government Printing Office, 1872.
———. *Report of the Joint Committee on the Conduct of the War.* 8 vols. 1863–66. Reprint, Wilmington, N.C.: Broadfoot Publishing, 1998–2000.
United States War Department. *The War of the Rebellion: A Compilation of the Official Records of the Union and Confederate Armies.* 128 vols. Washington, D.C.: Government Printing Office, 1881–1902.
U.S. Census Dept., *Population of the United States in 1860; Compiled from the Original Returns of the Eighth Census.* Washington, D.C.: Government Printing Office, 1864.
U.S. Constitution.

Newspapers

The Agitator (Pennsylvania)
The Alleghanian (Pennsylvania)
Ashland Union (Ohio)
Barnstable Patriot (Massachusetts)
Bedford Gazette (Pennsylvania)
Bloomsburg Star of the North (Pennsylvania)
Brooklyn Daily Eagle (New York)
Cass County Republican (Michigan)
Centralia Sentinel (Illinois)
Chicago Tribune (Illinois)
Civilian & Telegraph (Maryland)
Cleveland Morning Leader (Ohio)
Cleveland Plain Dealer (Ohio)
Columbian Register (Connecticut)
Covington Journal (Kentucky)
Daily Evansville Journal (Indiana)
Daily Exchange (Maryland)
Daily Green Mountain Freeman (Vermont)
Daily Ohio Statesman
Dayton Daily Empire (Ohio)
Der Demokrat (Iowa)
Der Lacha Caunty Patriot (Pennsylvania)
Detroit Advertiser and Tribune (Michigan)
Detroit Free Press (Michigan)

Doylestown Democrat (Pennsylvania)
Elyria Independent Democrat (Ohio)
Evansville Daily Journal (Indiana)
Evening Union (D.C.)
Fort Wayne Sentinel (Indiana)
Glasgow Weekly Times (Missouri)
Grand Haven News (Michigan)
Great Republic (D.C.)
Harper's Weekly (New York)
Herkimer Democrat (New York)
Holmes County Farmer (Ohio)
Illinois State Journal
Illinois State Register
The Independent (New York)
Indiana State Sentinel
Indianapolis Daily Journal (Indiana)
Indianapolis Daily State Sentinel (Indiana)
Indianapolis Gazette (Indiana)
The Liberator (Massachusetts)
Louisville Daily Journal (Kentucky)
Monroe Monitor (Michigan)
Mount Vernon Republican (Ohio)
National Tribune (D.C.)
Nebraska Advertiser
New York Commercial Advertiser
New York Daily Tribune
New York Evening Post
New York Herald
New York Semi-Weekly Tribune
New York Sun
New York Times
New York World
Opelousas Courier (Louisiana)
Ottawa Free Trader (Illinois)
Patriot & Union (Pennsylvania)
Pittston Gazette (Pennsylvania)
Plymouth Weekly Democrat (Indiana)
Portage County Democrat (Ohio)
Portsmouth Times (Ohio)
The Press (Pennsylvania)
Raftsman's Journal (Pennsylvania)
Smoky Hill and Republican Union (Kansas)
Southern Enterprise (South Carolina)
Stark County Democrat (Ohio)
Union League Gazette (Pennsylvania)
Virginia Evening Bulletin (Nevada)
Washington Evening Star (D.C.)
Washington National Republican (D.C.)
Western Reserve Chronicle (Ohio)

Dissertations and Theses

Beckert, Sven. "The Making of New York City's Bourgeoisie, 1850—1866." PhD diss., Columbia University, 1995.

Brummer, Sidney D. "Political History of New York State during the Period of the Civil War." PhD diss., Columbia University, 1911.

Coopersmith, Andrew S. "For God and Liberty: Propaganda and Ideology in Civil War America." PhD diss., Harvard University, 1999.

DeRosa, Christopher S. "A Million Thinking Bayonets: Political Indoctrination in the United States Army." PhD diss., Temple University, 2000.

Drumm, Austin Marcus. "The Union League in the Carolinas." PhD diss., University of North Carolina, 1955.

Gibson, Guy James. "Lincoln's League: The Union League Movement during the Civil War." PhD diss., University of Illinois, 1957.

Hardie, Ann Smith. "The Influence of the Union League of America on the Second Election of Lincoln." MA thesis, Louisiana State University, 1937.

Heslin, James J. "The New England Loyal Publication Society: An Aspect in the Molding of Public Opinion during the Civil War." PhD diss., Boston University, 1952.

Migliore, Paul. "The Business of Union: The New York Business Community and the Civil War." PhD diss., Columbia University, 1975.

Owens, Susie Lee. "The Union League of America: Political Activities in Tennessee, the Carolinas, and Virginia, 1865–1870." PhD diss., New York University, 1943.

Phelan, Sister Mary C. "Manton Marble of the New York *World*." PhD diss., Catholic University, 1957.

Reidenbach, Clarence. "A Critical Analysis of Patriotism as an Ethical Concept." PhD diss., Yale University, 1918.

Silvestro, Clement M. "None but Patriots: The Union Leagues in Civil War and Reconstruction." PhD diss., University of Wisconsin, 1959.

Smith, George Winston. "Generative Forces of Union Propaganda: A Study in Civil War Pressure Groups." PhD diss., University of Wisconsin, 1939.

Trexler, Harrison A. "Slavery in Missouri 1804–1865." PhD diss., Johns Hopkins University, 1914.

White, Jonathan W. "'To Aid Their Rebel Friends': Politics and Treason in the Civil War North." PhD diss., University of Maryland, 2008.

Union League, Publication Society, and Related Pamphlets

Abstract of the Proceedings of the Grand Council of the U.L.A. for the State of Michigan. Detroit: Grand Council of the ULA, 1863.

Addresses at the Inauguration of the Women's Loyal League of Bridgeport, April 17th, 1863. Bridgeport, Conn.: Samuel B. Hall, 1863.

Agnew, Daniel. *Our National Constitution: Its Adaptation to a State of War or Insurrection.* Philadelphia: C. Sherman, Son & Co., 1863.

Anonymous. *Is the South Ready for Restoration?* Philadelphia: Union League of Philadelphia, 1866.

———. *The Lincoln Catechism, Wherein the Eccentricities & Beauties of Despotism are Fully Set Forth: A Guide to the Presidential Election of 1864.* New York: J. F. Feeks, 1864.

————. *Loyalty: What Is It? To Whom or What Due?* N.p.: N.p., 1863.

————. *Miscegenation: The Theory of the Blending of the Races, Applied to the American White Man and Negro.* New York: H. Dexter, Hamilton & Co., 1864.

Armstrong, William H. "Report of the Guest Committee." *Annual Report of the Union League of Philadelphia, 1905.* Philadelphia: Union League of Philadelphia, 1905.

Bellows, Henry W. *Unconditional Loyalty.* New York: Anson D. F. Randolph, 1863.

Binney, Horace. *Letter from Horace Binney to the General Committee of Invitation and Correspondence of the Union League of Philadelphia.* Philadelphia: N.p., 1863.

Boker, George H. *Proceedings of a Meeting of the Union Club of Philadelphia.* Philadelphia: J. B. Lippincott & Co., 1871.

Chase, Salmon P. *Letter from Hon. S. P. Chase, Secretary of the Treasury, to the Loyal National League.* New York: N.p., 1863.

Committee of Merchants for the Relief of Colored People, *Report of the Committee of Merchants for the Relief of Colored People, Suffering from the Late Riots in the City of New York.* New York: George A. Whitehorne, 1863.

Cooper, Rev. Jacob. *The Loyalty Demanded by the Present Crisis.* Philadelphia: Henry B. Ashmead Printers, 1864.

Curtis, George T. "The True Conditions of American Loyalty." *Papers from the Society for the Diffusion of Political Knowledge,* no. 5. New York: SDPK, 1863.

Inauguration of the National Union Club, Speech of Benjamin H. Brewster, Delivered at the Musical Fund Hall, Philadelphia, Wednesday Evening, March 11, 1863. Philadelphia: King & Baird, 1863.

Kirkland, Caroline M. *A Few Words in Behalf of the Loyal Women of the United States by One of Their Own.* New York: Loyal Publication Society, 1863.

Leavitt, Humphrey. *Decision of Judge Leavitt, of Ohio, in the Vallandigham Habeas Corpus Case.* Philadelphia: Union League of Philadelphia, 1863.

Lieber, Francis. *A Letter to Hon. E. D. Morgan: On the Amendment of the Constitution Abolishing Slavery. Resolutions, Passed by the New York Union League Club, Concerning Conditions of Peace with the Insurgents.* New York: Loyal Publication Society, 1865.

————. *Lincoln or McClellan?: Appeal to the Germans in America.* New York: Loyal Publication Society, 1864.

————. *No Party Now; But All for Our Country.* New York: C. S. Westcott & Co., 1863.

Lowell, James R. *The President's Policy.* Union League of Philadelphia, no. 71. Philadelphia: N.p., 1864.

Loyal League of Union Citizens. *Loyal Meeting of the People of New York: To Support the Government, Prosecute the War, and Maintain the Union, Held at the Cooper Institute, Friday Evening, March 6, 1863.* New York: George F. Nesbitt & Co., 1863.

Loyal National League. *By-Laws of the Loyal National League.* New York: Loyal National League, 1863.

————. *Proceedings at the Organization of the Loyal National League at the Cooper Institute, Friday Evening, March 20, 1863.* New York: C. S. Westcott & Co., 1863.

————. *The Sumter Anniversary, 1863: Opinions of Loyalists Concerning the Great Question of the Times.* New York: C. S. Westcott & Co., 1863.

Loyal Publication Society. *Proceedings at the First Anniversary Meeting of the Loyal Publication Society, February 13, 1864.* New York: Loyal Publication Society, 1864.

————. *Proceedings at the Second Anniversary Meeting of the Loyal Publication Society, February 11, 1865.* New York: Loyal Publication Society, 1865.

————. *The Venom and the Antidote,* No. 9. New York: Loyal Publication Society, 1863.

Minutes of the Proceedings of the State Council of the Union League of America for the State of New Hampshire, Since its Organization January 2, 1863. Concord, N.H.: State Council of the Union League of America for the State of New Hampshire, 1864.

New England Loyal Publication Society. *Pamphlet Addressed to William Endicott, Jr., Treasurer of the New England Loyal Publication Society, from J. B. Thayer, Secretary dated February 1, 1864.* Boston: New England Loyal Publication Society, 1864.

———. *Report of the Executive Committee of the New England Loyal Publication Society, May 1, 1865.* Boston, Mass.: New England Loyal Publication Society, 1865.

Official Proceedings of the Democratic National Convention, Held in 1864 at Chicago. Chicago: Times Steam Pub. House, 1864.

"Our Federal Union, It Must be Preserved": Speech of Thomas Swann Delivered before the Union League of Philadelphia, March 2, 1863. Baltimore: Bull & Tuttle, 1863.

Owen, Robert Dale. *The Future of the Northwest in Connection with the Scheme of Reconstruction without New England: An Address to the People of Indiana.* New York: E. O. Jenkins, 1863.

Proceedings at the Annual Meeting of the Grand Council of the Union League of the State of Connecticut Held at New Haven, May 18, 1864. New Haven, Conn.: Thomas J. Stafford, 1864.

Proceedings of the Grand Council of the Union League of America for the State of California at Its Annual Session, Held in San Francisco, August 4th and 5th, 1863. San Francisco: Grand Council of the Union League of America for the State of California, 1863.

Proceedings of the State Grand Council of the U.L.A. of Illinois at its Second Annual Session. Springfield, Ill.: Grand Council of the ULA of Illinois, 1863.

Proceedings of the State Grand Council of the ULA of Michigan ULA at its Special Meeting, March 2, 1864. Detroit: Grand Council of the ULA of Michigan, 1864.

Proceedings of the State Grand Council U.L.A. of the State of Pennsylvania at its Annual Session Held in Pittsburg June 29, 1864. Philadelphia: Pennsylvania State Grand Council, 1864.

Proceedings of the State UC of Ohio. Cincinnati: N.p., 1862.

Society for the Diffusion of Political Knowledge. *Handbook of the Democracy for 1863 & '64.* New York: SDPK, 1864.

———. *Miscegenation Indorsed by the Republican Party, Campaign Document no. 11.* N.p.: SDPK, 1864.

Sprague, Peleg. *What Is Treason?: A Charge to the Grand Jury.* Salem, Mass.: Charles W. Swasey, 1863.

Thompson, Joseph P. *Revolution Against Free Government Not a Right But a Crime.* New York: Union League, 1864.

Union Congressional Committee. *A Few Plain Words with the Rank and File of the Union Armies.* Washington, D.C.: Union Congressional Committee, 1864.

Union League. *Address of the National Executive Committee of the Union League to the Citizens of the United States.* New York: Benjamin Urner, 1860.

Union League of America. *Form of a Council.* Washington, D.C.: Union League of America, 1863.

———. *Grand Lincoln and Johnson Ratification Meeting at Washington City, D.C., June 15, 1864.* Washington, D.C.: Union League of America, 1864.

———. *Meeting of the Grand National Council, Baltimore, June 6, 1864.* Washington, D.C.: N.p., 1864.

———. *Proceedings of the Annual Meeting of the Grand National Council, Union League of America, Held at Washington, December 9–11, 1863.* Washington, D.C.: Union League of America, 1863.

———. *Proceedings of the Annual Meeting of the Grand National Council, Union League of*

America, Held at Washington, December 13, 1865. Washington, D.C.: Union League of America, 1865.

———. *Proceedings of the National Council of the Union League of America at its Sixth Annual Session, Held in the City of Washington D.C., March 2nd and 3rd, 1869.* Washington, D.C.: Union League of America, 1869.

———. *Proceedings of the National Convention, Union League of America, Held at Cleveland, May 20 and 21, 1863.* Washington, D.C.: Union League of America, 1863.

———. *Proclamation: ULA Grand National Council Chamber to "Brothers," January 1, 1864.* Washington, D.C.: Union League of America, 1864.

———. *Resolutions Adopted by the National Union League of America, at Its Annual Session, Held in Washington City, D.C., Dec. 14 and 15, 1864.* Washington, D.C.: Union League of America, 1864.

———. *Speaker Colfax and the Union League Committee: With the Letter of President Lincoln, to A.G. Hodges, of Kentucky.* Washington, D.C.: Union League of America, 1864.

Union League of America, Connecticut State Council. *Letter from a Union League Activist Advocating the Re-election of President Abraham Lincoln.* New Haven, Conn.: Union League of America, 1864.

Union League of America, New York State Council. *Proceedings of the State Council of the Union League of America for the State of New York at Its First Annual Session, Held in the City of New York on the 25th day of November, 1863.* New York: Davies and Kent, 1864.

———. *Proceedings of the State Council of the Union League of America for the State of New York: at the Special Session, held at Syracuse, on Tuesday, September 4, 1866.* New York: Union League of America, New York State Council, 1866.

Union League Club of New York. *Banquet Given by Members of the Union League Club of 1863 and 1864, to Commemorate the Departure for the Seat of War of the Twentieth Regiment of United States Colored Troops Raised by the Club.* New York: George F. Nesbitt & Co., 1886.

———. *Report of the Committee on Volunteering.* New York: Union League Club of New York, 1864.

———. *Report of the Executive Committee, Constitution, By-Laws and Roll of Members, July 1864.* New York: Union League Club of New York, 1864.

Union League of Philadelphia. *Address by the Union League of Philadelphia, to the Citizens of Pennsylvania, in Favor of the Re-election of Abraham Lincoln.* Philadelphia: King & Baird, 1864.

———. *Articles of Association and By-Laws of the Union League of Philadelphia.* Philadelphia: King & Baird, 1863.

———. *Congressional Record of George H. Pendleton.* Philadelphia: Union League of Philadelphia, 1864.

———. *First Annual Report of the Board of Directors of the Union League of Philadelphia.* Philadelphia: King & Baird, 1863.

———. *The Great Northern Conspiracy of the "O.S.L.".* Philadelphia: Union League of Philadelphia, 1864.

———. *Immense Meeting in Favor of the Union; Inauguration of the National Union Club.* Philadelphia: Leader & Creamer, 1863.

———. *Immense Meeting in Favor of the Union; Inauguration of the National Union Club, Speech of Benjamin H. Brewster, Delivered at the Musical Fund Hall, Philadelphia, Wednesday Evening, March 11, 1863.* Philadelphia: King & Baird, 1863.

———. *Second Annual Report of the Board of Directors of the Union League of Philadelphia.* Philadelphia: Henry B. Ashmead, 1864.

———. *Third Annual Report of the Board of Directors of the Union League of Philadelphia.* Philadelphia: Henry B. Ashmead, 1865.

Women's National Loyal League. *Proceedings of the Meeting of the Loyal Women of the Republic, Held in New York, May 14, 1863.* New York: Phair & Co., 1863.

Published Primary Sources

Adams, Lois Bryan. *Letter from Washington 1863–1865.* Edited by Evelyn Leasher. Detroit: Wayne State University Press, 1999.

Andersen, Mary Ann. *The Civil War Diary of Allen Morgan Geer, Twentieth Regiment, Illinois Volunteers.* Bloomington, Ill.: McClean County Historical Society, 1977.

Bailyn, Bernard, ed. *Pamphlets of the American Revolution, 1750–1776.* 2 vols. Cambridge, Mass.: Harvard University Press, 1965.

Baker, George E., ed. *The Works of William Seward.* 5 vols. Boston: Houghton, Mifflin and Co., 1890.

Banasik, Michael E., ed. *Missouri in 1861: The Civil War Letters of Franc B. Wilkie, Newspaper Correspondent.* Iowa City: Camp Press Bookshop, 2001.

Barnes, Rev. Albert. *The Love of Country: A Sermon Delivered in the First Presbyterian Church, Philadelphia, April 28, 1861.* Philadelphia: C. Sherman & Son, 1861.

Basler, Roy, ed. *The Collected Works of Abraham Lincoln.* 9 vols. New Brunswick, N.J.: Rutgers University Press, 1953.

Beale, Howard K., ed. *The Diary of Edward Bates 1859–1866.* Vol. 4, *Annual Report of the American Historical Association for the Year 1930.* Washington, D.C.: Government Printing Office, 1933.

———. *Diary of Gideon Welles.* 3 vols. New York: W. W. Norton & Co., 1960.

Beasecker, Robert, ed. *"I Hope to Do My Country Service": The Civil War Letters of John Bennitt, M.D., Surgeon, 19th Michigan Infantry.* Detroit: Wayne State University Press, 2005.

Bellows, Henry W. *Historical Sketch of the Union League Club of New York.* New York: G. P. Putnam's Sons, 1879.

Belmont, August. *A Few Letters and Speeches of the Late Civil War.* New York: Privately printed, 1870.

———. *Letters, Speeches and Addresses of August Belmont.* New York: Privately printed, 1890.

Benson, Edwin N. *The Union League during the War.* Philadelphia: W. P. Koebel, 1888.

Bigelow, John, ed. *Letters and Literary Memorials of Samuel J. Tilden.* 2 vols. New York: Harper & Brothers, 1908.

Blaine, James G. *Twenty Years of Congress: From Lincoln to Garfield.* 2 vols. Norwich, Conn.: Henry Bill Publishing, 1884.

Blair, Montgomery. "Missouri's Unionists at War." In *Battles and Leaders of the Civil War,* vol. 5, edited by Peter Cozzens, 67–90. Urbana: University of Illinois Press, 2002.

Boërnstein, Heinrich, *Memoirs of a Nobody: The Missouri Years of a Austrian Radical, 1849–1866.* Translated and edited by Steven Rowan. St. Louis: Missouri Historical Society Press, 1997.

Bohrnstedt, Jennifer C., ed. *Soldiering with Sherman: The Civil War Letters of George C. Cram.* DeKalb: Northern Illinois University Press, 2000.

Brinton, John H. *Personal Memoirs of John H. Brinton, Major and Surgeon U.S.V., 1861–1865.* New York: Neale Publishing Co., 1914.

Brooks, Noah. *Washington in Lincoln's Time.* New York: The Century Co., 1895.

Brown, George R., ed. *Reminiscences of Senator William N. Stewart of Nevada.* New York: Neale Publishing Co., 1908.

Bruce, George A. "The Capture and Occupation of Richmond." In *Papers of the Military Historical Society of Massachusetts,* vol. 14. 1918. Reprint, Wilmington, N.C.: Broadfoot Publishing Co., 1990.

Bryant, William Cullen, II, and Thomas G. Voss, eds. *The Letters of William Cullen Bryant.* 6 vols. New York: Fordham University Press, 1975–92.

Burlingame, Michael, ed. *At Lincoln's Side: John Hay's Civil War Correspondence and Selected Writings.* Carbondale: Southern Illinois University Press, 2000.

———, ed. *Lincoln Observed: Civil War Dispatches of Noah Brooks.* Baltimore: Johns Hopkins University Press, 1998.

Burlingame, Michael, and John R. Turner Ettlinger, eds. *Inside Lincoln's White House: The Complete Civil War Diary of John Hay.* Carbondale: Southern Illinois University Press, 1997.

Butler, Benjamin F. *Private and Official Correspondence of Gen. Benjamin F. Butler during the Period of the Civil War.* 5 vols. Norwood, Mass.: Plimpton Press, 1917.

Cannon, Le Grand B. *Personal Reminiscences of the Rebellion, 1861–1866.* New York: Burr Printing House, 1895.

Capron, Thaddeus H. "War Diary of Thaddeus H. Capron, 1861–1865." *Journal of the Illinois State Historical Society* 12, no. 3 (October 1919): 330–406.

Censer, Jane Turner, ed. *Defending the Union 1861–1863.* Vol. IV of *The Papers of Frederick Law Olmsted,* edited by Charles Eliot Beveridge. Baltimore: Johns Hopkins University Press, 1986.

Chipman, J. Logan. *State of the Union Delivered Before the Detroit Democratic Association, Feb. 18, 1863.* Detroit: Free Press Steam Printing House, 1863.

Chittenden, Lucius E. *Invisible Siege: The Journal of Lucius E. Chittenden April 15, 1861—July 14, 1861.* San Diego: Americana Exchange Press, 1969.

Crawford, Martin, ed. "Politicians in Crisis: The Washington Letters of William S. Thayer, December 1860—March 1861." *Civil War History* 27, no. 3 (September 1981): 231–47.

———. *William Howard Russell's Civil War: Private Diary and Letters, 1861–1862.* Athens: University of Georgia Press, 1992.

Cutler, Julie Perkins. *Life and Times of Ephraim Cutler.* Cincinnati: Robert Clarke & Co., 1890.

Dana, Charles. *Recollections of the Civil War.* 1898. Reprint, New York: D. Appleton & Co., 1913.

Dana Jr., Richard Henry. *Speeches in Stirring Times and Letters to a Son.* Boston: Houghton Mifflin Co., 1910.

De Forest, John William. *A Union Officer in the Reconstruction.* New Haven, Conn.: Yale University Press, 1948.

DeRosier, Arthur H., Jr., ed. *Through the South with a Union Soldier.* Johnson City: East Tennessee State University Research Advisory Council, 1969.

Dittenhoefer, Abram J. *How We Elected Lincoln: Personal Recollections of Lincoln and Men of His Time.* New York: Harper & Brothers, 1916.

Dix, Morgan, ed. *Memoirs of John Adams Dix.* 2 vols. New York: Harper & Brothers, 1883.

Donald, David, ed. *Inside Lincoln's Cabinet: The Civil War Diaries of Salmon P. Chase.* New York: Longmans, Green and Co., 1954.

Doster, William. *Lincoln and Episodes of the Civil War.* New York: G. P. Putnam's Sons, 1915.

Duvergier de Hauranne, Ernest. *A Frenchman in Lincoln's America.* 2 vols. Chicago: Lakeside Press, 1974–75.

Elliott, Mark, and John David Smith, eds. *Undaunted Radical: The Selected Writings and Speeches of Albion W. Tourgée.* Baton Rouge: Louisiana State University Press, 2010.

Emerson, Ralph Waldo. *The Prose Works of Ralph Waldo Emerson.* 2 vols. Boston: Fields, Osgood and Co., 1870.

Engs, Robert F., and Corey M. Brooks, eds. *Their Patriotic Duty: The Civil War Letters of the Evans Family of Brown County, Ohio.* New York: Fordham University Press, 2007.

Everett, Edward. *An Address Delivered at the Inauguration of the Union Club, 9 April, 1863.* Boston: Little, Brown, and Co., 1863.

Fisk, Wilbur. *Anti-Rebel: The Civil War Letters of Wilbur Fisk.* New York: Emil Rosenblatt, 1983.

Fleming, Walter L., ed. "The Black Codes of 1865–66." In Fleming, *Documents Relating to Reconstruction,* No. 8, 3.

———. *Documents Relating to Reconstruction.* Morgantown: West Virginia University Press, 1904.

———. "Resolutions of the Alabama Grand Council of the Union League, April, 1867." In Fleming, *Documents Relating to Reconstruction,* No. 3, 34–35.

———. "The Ritual of the Union League." In Fleming, *Documents Relating to Reconstruction,* No. 3, 17–27.

———. "The Union League of America." In Fleming, *Documents Relating to Reconstruction,* No. 3, 3–5.

Franklin, Benjamin. *The Autobiography of Benjamin Franklin.* Cambridge, Mass.: Riverside Press, 1886.

Furry, William, ed. *The Preacher's Tale: The Civil War Journal of Rev. Francis Springs, Chaplain, U.S. Army of the Frontier.* Fayetteville: University of Arkansas Press, 2001.

Gibboney, Douglas Lee, ed. *Littleton Washington's Journal: Life in Antebellum Washington, Vigilante San Francisco and Confederate Richmond.* Bloomington, Ind.: Xlibris, 2001.

Gordon, Ann D., ed. *The Selected Papers of Elizabeth Cady Stanton and Susan B. Anthony.* 6 vols. New Brunswick, N.J.: Rutgers University Press, 1997.

Gould, William Benjamin, IV, ed. *Diary of a Contraband: The Civil War Passage of a Black Sailor.* Stanford, Calif.: Stanford University Press, 2002.

Gray, John Chipman, and John Codman Ropes. *War Letters, 1862–1865.* Boston: Houghton Mifflin Co., 1927.

Greene, William B. *Letters from a Sharpshooter.* Belleville, Wis.: Historic Publications, 1993.

Gurowski, Adam. *Diary, from March 4, 1861 to November 12, 1862.* Boston: Lee and Shepard, 1862.

Hammond, Harold E., ed. *Diary of a Union Lady 1861–1865.* New York: Funk & Wagnalls Co., 1962.

Hayes, John D., ed. *Samuel Francis Du Pont: A Selection from His Civil War Letters.* 3 vols. Ithaca, N.Y.: Cornell University Press, 1969.

Hayes, Rutherford B. "Incidents of the Battle of Cedar Creek." In S*ketches of War History, 1861–1865: Papers Read before the Commandery of the State of Ohio, Military Order of the Loyal Legion of the United States.* 9 vols. Cincinnati: Robert Clarke and Company, 1888–1916.

Holzer, Harold, ed. *Lincoln's White House Secretary: The Adventurous Life of William O. Stoddard.* Carbondale: Southern Illinois University Press, 2007.

Howard, Joseph, Jr., ed. *The Union League Club: Historical and Biographical 1863–1900.* New York: Union Historical Assoc., 1900.

Howard, Oliver Otis. *Autobiography of Oliver Otis Howard.* 2 vols. New York: Baker & Taylor, 1907.

Hughes, Sarah Forbes, ed. *Letters and Recollections of John Murray Forbes.* 2 vols. Boston: Houghton Mifflin, 1899.

———, ed. *Letters of John Murray Forbes.* 3 vols. Boston: George H. Ellis, 1905.

Jones, John B. *A Rebel War Clerk's Diary at the Confederate States Capital.* 2 vols. Philadelphia: J. B. Lippincott, 1866.

Josyph, Peter, ed. *The Wounded River: The Civil War Letters of John Vance Lauderdale, M.D.* East Lansing: Michigan State University Press, 1993.

Julian, George W. *Political Recollections.* Chicago: Jansen, McClurg & Co., 1884.

Kallgren, Beverly H., and James L. Crouthamel, eds. *"Dear Friend Anna": The Civil War Letters of a Common Soldier from Maine.* Orono: University of Maine Press, 1992.

Kelly, R. M. "The Secret Union Organization in Kentucky in 1861." In *Sketches of War History, 1861–1865: Papers Read before the Commandery of the State of Ohio, Military Order of the Loyal Legion of the United States.* 9 vols. Cincinnati: Robert Clarke and Company, 1888–1916.

Kiper, Richard L., ed. *Dear Catharine, Dear Taylor: The Civil War Letters of a Union Soldier and His Wife.* Lawrence: University Press of Kansas, 2002.

Laas, Virginia Jean, ed. *Wartime Washington: The Civil War Letters of Elizabeth Blair Lee.* Urbana: University of Illinois Press, 1991.

Lemcke, Julius A. *Reminiscences of an Indianian.* Indianapolis: The Hollenbeck Press, 1905.

Letters of the Hon. Joseph Holt, the Hon. Edward Everett, and Commodore Charles Stewart, on the Present Crisis. Philadelphia: W. S. & A. Martien, 1861.

Loving, Jerome M., ed. *Civil War Letters of George Washington Whitman.* Durham, N.C.: Duke University Press, 1975.

Lubin, Martin, ed. *The Words of Abraham Lincoln: Speeches Letters, Proclamations, and Papers of Our Most Eloquent President.* New York: Tess Press, 2005.

Marks, Bayly Ellen, and Mark Norton Schatz, eds. *Between North and South: A Maryland Journalist Views the Civil War: The Narrative of William Wilkins Glenn, 1861–1869.* Rutherford, N.J.: Fairleigh Dickinson University Press, 1976.

Matthews, Robert P. *Nine Months in the Infantry Service: The Civil War Journal of R. P. Matthews.* Springfield, Mo.: Greene County Historical Society, 1999.

Maynadier, Lieut. Col. William. *Reply of Lt. Col. Maynadier to the Charges in the Report of the Potter Committee.* Washington, D.C.: H. S. Bowen, 1862.

McCormack, Thomas J., ed. *Memoirs of Gustave Koerner 1809–1896.* 2 vols. Cedar Rapids, Iowa: Torch Press, 1909.

McWhiney, Grady, Warner O. Moore, and Robert F. Pace, eds. *"Fear God and Walk Humbly": The Agricultural Journal of James Mallory, 1843–1877.* Tuscaloosa: University of Alabama Press, 1997.

Moore, Frank, ed. *The Rebellion Record: A Diary of American Events.* 12 vols. 1861–68. Reprint, New York: Arno Press, 1977.

Murphy, D. F., reporter. *Presidential Election, 1864, Proceedings of the National Union Convention Held in Baltimore, Md., June 7th and 8th, 1864.* New York: Baker & Godwin, 1864.

Nevins, Allen, ed. *Diary of the Civil War 1860–1865: George Templeton Strong.* New York: Macmillan Co., 1962.

Nevins, Allen, and Milton H. Thomas, eds. *The Diary of George Templeton Strong: The Post War Years 1865–1875.* New York: Macmillan Co., 1952.

Nicolay, John G., and John Hay. *Abraham Lincoln: A History.* 10 vols. New York: The Century Co., 1890.

Niven, John, et al., eds. *The Salmon P. Chase Papers.* 5 vols. Kent, Ohio: Kent State University Press, 1997.

Norton, Charles E. *Letters of Charles Eliot Norton.* 2 vols. Boston: Houghton Mifflin Company, 1913.

Oliphant, Laurence. *Episodes in a Life of Adventure: Or, Moss from a Rolling Stone.* London: William Blackwood & Sons, 1887.

Osborn, George C., ed. "Letters of a Carpetbagger in Florida, 1866–1869." *The Florida Historical Quarterly* 36, no. 3 (January 1958): 239–85.

Palmer, Beverly W., ed. *The Selected Letters of Charles Sumner.* 2 vols. Boston: Northeastern University Press, 1990.

Pease, Theodore C., ed. *The Diary of Orville Hickman Browning.* 2 vols. Springfield: Illinois State Historical Library, 1927.

Peck, George B., Jr. "A Recruit Before Petersburg." In *Personal Narratives of Events in the War of the Rebellion, Being Papers Read Before the Rhode Island Soldiers and Sailors Historical Society,* 2:3–78. 10 vols. 1878–1915. Reprint, Wilmington, N.C.: Broadfoot Publishing, 1993.

Perry, Thomas S., ed. *The Life and Letters of Francis Lieber.* Boston: James R. Osgood & Co., 1882.

Pierce, Edward L. *Memoir and Letters of Charles Sumner.* 4 vols. Boston: Roberts Brothers, 1893.

Prosch, Charles. *Reminiscences of Washington Territory.* Seattle: N.p., 1904.

Quint, Alonzo H. *The Potomac and the Rapidan.* Boston: Crosby and Nichols, 1864.

Rathbun, Julius G. "'The Wide Awakes': The Great Political Organization of 1860." *Connecticut Quarterly* 1 (October 1895): 327–35.

Reception Tendered by the Members of the Union League of Philadelphia to George H. Boker, Minister of the United States to Turkey. Friday Evening, December 22, 1871. Philadelphia: Collins Printer, 1872.

Rhodes, Elisha Hunt. *All for the Union: A History of the 2nd Rhode Island Volunteer Infantry.* Edited by Robert H. Rhodes. Lincoln, R.I.: Andrew Mowbray Inc., 1985.

Riddle, Albert G. *Recollections of War Times: Reminiscences of Men and Events in Washington, 1860–1865.* New York: G. P. Putnam's Sons, 1895.

Roberts, Timothy Mason, ed. *"This Infernal War": The Civil War Letters of William and Jane Standard.* Kent, Ohio: Kent State University Press, 2018.

Rowan, Steven, ed. and trans. *Germans for a Free Missouri: Translations from the St. Louis Radical Press, 1857–1862.* Columbia: University of Missouri Press, 1983.

Samito, Christian G., ed. *Commanding Boston's Irish Ninth: The Civil War Letters of Colonel Patrick R. Guiney, Ninth Massachusetts Volunteer Infantry.* New York: Fordham University Press, 1998.

Scott, Robert Garth, ed. *Forgotten Valor: The Memoirs, Journals and Civil War Letters of Orlando B. Willcox.* Kent, Ohio: Kent State University Press, 1999.

Sears, Stephen W., ed. *The Civil War Papers of George B. McClellan.* New York: Ticknor & Fields, 1989.

———. *Mr. Dunn Browne's Experiences in the Army: The Civil War Letters of Samuel W. Fiske.* New York: Fordham University Press, 1998.

Seward, Frederick W. *Seward at Washington as Senator and Secretary of State: A Memoir of His Life with Selections from His Letters 1861–1872.* New York: Derby & Miller, 1891.

Shaw, Jon, ed. *Our Beloved Country: Civil War Pamphlets Published in Philadelphia.* Philadelphia: University of Pennsylvania Press, 2010.

Sherman, John. *Recollections of Forty Years in the House, Senate and Cabinet.* 2 vols. Chicago: Werner Co., 1895.

Sherman, William T. *Memoirs of General William T. Sherman.* 2 vols. New York: D. Appleton & Co., 1875.

Silber, Nina, and Mary Beth Sievens, eds. *Yankee Correspondence: Civil War Letters between New England Soldiers and the Home Front.* Charlottesville: University Press of Virginia, 1996.

Simpson, Brooks D., Leroy P. Graf, and John Muldowny, eds. *Advice after Appomattox: Letters to Andrew Johnson 1865–66.* Knoxville: University of Tennessee Press, 1987.

Smith, Barbara A., comp. *The Civil War Letters of Col. Elijah H. C. Cavins, 14th Indiana.* Owensboro, Ky.: Cook-McDowell Publications, 1981.

Snead, Thomas L. *The Fight for Missouri: From the Election of Lincoln to the Death of Lyon.* New York: Charles Scribner's Sons, 1886.

Stanton, Elizabeth Cady, Susan Brownell Anthony et al., eds. *History of Woman Suffrage.* 3 vols. Rochester, N.Y.: Self-published, 1881.

Stevens, John Austin, Jr. [Uncredited]. "Review of *Proceedings at the Dinner of the Early Members of the Union League Club of the City of New York: Thursday, May 20th, 1880.*" *The Magazine of American History* 6 (1881): 395–96.

Stillé, Charles J. *History of the United States Sanitary Commission.* Philadelphia: J. B. Lippincott & Co., 1866.

Stoddard, William O. *Inside the White House in War Times.* New York: Charles L. Webster & Co., 1890.

———. "The Story of a Nomination." *The North American Review* 138, (1884): 263–73.

———. ("A Volunteer Special"), *The Volcano under the City.* New York: Fords, Howard, & Hulbert, 1886.

Temple, Wayne C., ed. *The Civil War Letters of Henry C. Bear, a Soldier in the 116th Illinois Volunteer Infantry.* Harrogate, Tenn.: Lincoln Memorial University Press, 1961.

Thornbrough, Gayle, and Paula Corpuz, eds. *The Diary of Calvin Fletcher.* Vol. VIII, *1863–1864.* Indianapolis: Indiana Historical Society, 1981.

Thorndike, S. Lothrop. *The Past Members of the Union Club of Boston, and a Brief Sketch of the History of the Club,* July, 1893. Boston: Union Club of Boston, 1893.

Tousey, Sinclair. *Indices of Public Opinion 1860–1870.* New York: Privately printed, 1871.

Tripler, Eunice. *Eunice Tripler: Some Notes of Her Personal Recollections.* New York: Grafton Press, 1910.

Trollope, Anthony. *North America.* 2 vols. London: Chapman & Hall, 1862.

Union Club of Baltimore. *Constitution and By-Laws.* Baltimore: John D. Toy, 1863.

Union Club of Boston. *A Report of the Celebration of the Fiftieth Anniversary of the Founding of the Union Club of Boston 1863–1913.* Cambridge, Mass.: Riverside Press, 19—.

Villard, Henry. *Memoirs of Henry Villard.* 2 vols. Boston: Houghton, Mifflin, and Co., 1904.

Wallace, John. *Carpet Bag Rule in Florida: The Inside Workings of the Reconstruction of Civil Government in Florida after the Close of the Civil War.* Jacksonville, Fl.: Da Costa Publishing, 1888.

Wallis, Severn Teackle. *Writings of Severn Teackle Wallis.* 4 vols. Baltimore: John Murphy & Co., 1896.

Warren, Henry W. *Reminiscences of a Mississippi Carpet-Bagger.* Holden, Mass.: Davis Press, 1914.

White, Jonathan W., ed. *A Philadelphia Perspective: The Civil War Diary of Sidney George Fisher.* New York: Fordham University Press, 2007.

Wiggins, Sarah W. *The Journals of Josiah Gorgas, 1857–1878.* Tuscaloosa: University of Alabama Press, 1995.

Wilson, Donald Powell. *My Six Convicts: A Psychologist's Three Years in Fort Leavenworth.* New York: Rinehart & Co., 1948.

Wish, Harvey, ed., *Reconstruction in the South, 1865–1877: First-Hand Accounts of the American Southland after the Civil War.* New York: Farrar, Straus & Giroux, 1965.

Wood, William D. *Reminiscences of Reconstruction in Texas; and, Reminiscences of Texas and Texans Fifty Years Ago.* N.p.: N.p., 1902.

Woodward, C. Vann, ed. *Mary Chesnut's Civil War.* New Haven, Conn.: Yale University Press, 1981.

Published Secondary Sources

Abbott, Richard H. *The Republican Party and the South, 1855–1877.* Chapel Hill: University of North Carolina Press, 1986.

Altschuler, Glenn C., and Stuart M. Blumin. *Rude Republic: Americans and Their Politics in the Nineteenth Century.* Princeton, N.J.: Princeton University Press, 2000.

Anbinder, Tyler. *Nativism and Slavery: The Northern Know Nothings and the Politics of the 1850s.* New York: Oxford University Press, 1992.

Andreasen, Bryon C. "Civil War Church Trials: Repressing Dissent on the Northern Home Front." In *An Uncommon Time: The Civil War and the Northern Home Front,* edited by Paul A. Cimbala and Randall M. Miller, 214–42. New York: Fordham University Press, 2002.

Andrews, J. Cutler. *The North Reports the Civil War.* Pittsburgh: University of Pittsburgh Press, 1955.

Anonymous. "Philadelphia: The Republican Party Has a Homecoming." *Life Magazine,* June 24, 1940.

Astor, Aaron. *Rebels on the Border: Civil War, Emancipation, and the Reconstruction of Kentucky and Missouri.* Baton Rouge: Louisiana State University Press, 2012.

Athearn, Robert G., ed. *Soldier in the West: The Civil War Letters of Alfred Lacey Hough.* Philadelphia: University of Pennsylvania Press, 1957.

Attie, Jeanie *Patriotic Toil: Northern Women and the American Civil War.* Ithaca, N.Y.: Cornell University Press, 1998.

Ayer, I. Winslow. *The Great Northwestern Conspiracy in All Its Startling Details.* Chicago: Rounds and James Printers, 1865.

Baggett, James A. *The Scalawags: Southern Dissenters in the Civil War and Reconstruction.* Baton Rouge: Louisiana State University Press, 2003.

Bahde, Thomas. "'Our Cause Is a Common One': Home Guards, Union Leagues, and Republican Citizenship in Illinois, 1861–1873." *Civil War History* 56 (March 2010): 66–98.

Bailyn, Bernard. *The Ideological Origins of the American Revolution.* Cambridge, Mass.: Harvard University Press, 1967.

Baker, Jean. *Affairs of Party: The Political Culture of Northern Democrats in the Mid-Nineteenth Century.* Ithaca, N.Y.: Cornell University Press, 1983.

Beatie, Russel H. *Army of the Potomac.* Vol. III, *McClellan's First Campaign March—May 1862.* New York: Savas Beatie, 2007.

Becker, Carl M. "'Disloyalty' and the Dayton Public Schools." *Civil War History* 11, no. 1 (March 1965): 58–68.

Beckert, Sven. *The Monied Metropolis: New York City and the Consolidation of the American Bourgeoisie, 1850–1896.* New York: Cambridge University Press, 2003.

Bensel, Richard F. *The American Ballot Box in the Mid-Nineteenth Century.* New York: Cambridge University Press, 2004.

Bergeron, Paul H. *Andrew Johnson's Civil War and Reconstruction.* Knoxville: University of Tennessee Press, 2011.

Bernstein, Iver. *The New York City Draft Riots: Their Significance for American Society and Politics in the Age of the Civil War.* New York: Oxford University Press, 1990.

Blair, William. "Friend or Foe: Treason and the Second Confiscation Act." In *Wars within a War: Controversy and Conflict over the American Civil War,* edited by Joan Waugh and Gary Gallagher, 27–51. Chapel Hill: University of North Carolina Press, 2009.

————. *With Malice toward Some: Treason and Loyalty in the Civil War Era.* Chapel Hill: University of North Carolina Press, 2014.

Blake, Kellee L. "Ten Firkins of Butter and Other 'Traitorous' Aid." *Prologue: The Journal of the National Archives* 30, no. 4 (Winter 1998): 289–93.

Blanchard, Charles, ed. *Counties of Morgan, Monroe, and Brown, Indiana: Historical and Biographical.* Chicago: F. A. Battey & Co., 1884.

Blondheim, Menahem. "'Public Sentiment Is Everything': The Union's Public Communications Strategy and the Bogus Proclamation of 1864." *The Journal of American History* 89, no. 3 (December 2002): 869–99.

Boswell, Angela. "Black Women during Slavery to 1865." In *Black Women in Texas History,* edited by Bruce A. Glasrud and Merline Pitre, 13–37. College Station, Texas: A&M University Press, 2008.

Bowery, Charles R., Jr. *The Civil War in the Western Theater 1862.* Washington, D.C.: Center of Military History—U.S. Army, 2014.

Bulla, David W. *Lincoln's Censor: Milo Hascall and Freedom of the Press in Civil War Indiana.* West Lafayette, Ind.: Purdue University Press, 2008.

Bulla, David W., and Gregory A. Borchard. *Journalism in the Civil War Era.* New York: Peter Lang, 2010.

Bundy, Carol. *The Nature of Sacrifice: A Biography of Charles Russell Lowell, Jr., 1835–1864.* New York: Farrar, Straus and Giroux, 2005.

Burlingame, Michael. *Abraham Lincoln: A Life.* 2 vols. Baltimore: Johns Hopkins University Press, 2008.

Burt, Nathaniel. *The Perennial Philadelphians: An Anatomy of an American Aristocracy.* Boston: Little, Brown & Co., 1963.

Burton, Clarence, ed. *The City of Detroit, Michigan, 1701–1922.* 5 vols. Detroit: S. J. Clarke Publishing Co., 1922.

Carman, Ezra A. *The Maryland Campaign of September 1862.* 3 vols. Edited by Thomas G. Clemens. El Dorado, Calif.: Savas Beatie, 2010–17.

Carnes, Mark C. *Secret Ritual and Manhood in Victorian America.* New Haven, Conn.: Yale University Press, 1989.

Cason, Roberta F. "The Loyal League in Georgia." *The Georgia Historical Quarterly* 20, no. 2 (June 1936): 125–53.

Chandler, Robert J. "Vigilante Rebirth: The Civil War Union League." *The Argonaut* 3, no. 1 (Winter 1992): 10–18.

Christensen, Lawrence O., William E. Foley, Gary Kremer, and Kenneth H. Winn, eds. "Montgomery Blair (1813–1883)." In *Dictionary of Missouri Biography.* Columbia: University of Missouri Press, 1999.

Churchill, Robert. "Liberty, Conscription, and a Party Divided: The Sons of Liberty Conspiracy 1863–1864." *Prologue: The Journal of the National Archives* 30, no. 4 (Winter 1998): 295–303.

Cimbala, Paul A. *The Freedmen's Bureau: Reconstructing the American South after the Civil War.* Huntington, N.Y.: Krieger Pubs., 2005.

Cimbala, Paul A., and Randall M. Miller, eds. *The Freedmen's Bureau and Reconstruction: Reconsiderations.* New York: Fordham University Press, 1999.

Clawson, Mary Ann. *Constructing Brotherhood: Class, Gender, and Fraternalism.* Princeton, N.J.: Princeton University Press, 1989.

Cook, Adrian. *The Armies of the Streets: The New York City Draft Riots of 1863.* Lexington: University Press of Kentucky, 1974.

Cooling, Benjamin Franklin. *Forts Henry and Donelson: The Key to the Confederate Heartland.* Knoxville: University of Tennessee Press, 1987.

Costello, Augustine E. *Our Police Protectors: History of the New York Police from the Earliest Period to the Present Time.* New York: Chas. F. Roper and Co., 1884.

Croffut, William A., and John M. Morris. *The Military and Civil History of Connecticut during the War of 1861–65.* New York: Ledyard Bill, 1868.

Cunningham, O. Edward. *Shiloh and the Western Campaign of 1862.* Edited by Gary D. Joiner and Timothy B. Smith. New York: Savas Beatie, 2007.

Davis, David Brion, ed. *The Fear of Conspiracy: Images of Un-American Subversion from the Revolution to the Present.* Ithaca, N.Y.: Cornell University Press, 1971.

Delaware County Historical Society. *Proceedings of the Delaware County Historical Society 1895–1901.* Vol. 1. Chester, Pa.: Delaware County Historical Society, 1902.

Dell, Christopher. *Lincoln and the War Democrats: The Grand Erosion of Conservative Tradition.* Rutherford, N.J.: Fairleigh Dickinson University Press, 1975.

Detroit Post and Tribune. *Zachariah Chandler: An Outline Sketch of His Life and Public Services.* Detroit: Post and Tribune Co., 1880.

Dickerson, O. M. "The Illinois Constitutional Convention of 1862." *University Studies* 1, no. 9 (March 1905): 385–442.

Downs, Gregory. *After Appomattox: Military Occupation and the Ends of War.* Cambridge, Mass.: Harvard University Press, 2015.

Drehle, David Von. *Rise to Greatness: Abraham Lincoln and America's Most Perilous Year.* New York: Henry Holt and Co., 2012.

Dunham, Chester F. *The Attitude of the Northern Clergy toward the South 1860–1865.* 1942. Reprint, Philadelphia: Porcupine Press, 1974.

Duquette, Elizabeth. *Loyal Subjects: Bonds of Nation, Race, and Allegiance in Nineteenth-Century America.* New Brunswick, N.J.: Rutgers University Press, 2010.

Ent, Uzal W. *The Pennsylvania Reserves in the Civil War: A Comprehensive History.* Jefferson, N.C.: McFarland, 2014.

Fitzgerald, Michael W. "'He Was Always Preaching the Union': The Wartime Origins of White Republicanism during Reconstruction." In *The Yellowhammer War: The Civil War and Reconstruction in Alabama,* edited by Kenneth Noe, 220–39. Tuscaloosa: University of Alabama Press, 2013.

———. *The Union League Movement in the Deep South: Politics and Agricultural Change during Reconstruction.* Baton Rouge: Louisiana State University Press, 1989.

Fleming, Walter L. *Civil War and Reconstruction in Alabama.* New York: Columbia University Press, 1905.

———. *The Sequel of Appomattox: A Chronicle of the Reunion of the States.* New York: United States Publishers, 1919.

Fletcher, George P. *Our Secret Constitution: How Lincoln Redefined American Democracy.* New York: Oxford University Press, 2001.

Flick, Alexander C. *Samuel Jones Tilden: A Study in Political Sagacity.* Port Washington, N.Y.: Kennikat Press, 1939.

Foner, Eric. "Foreword." In *The Dunning School: Historians, Race, and the Meaning of Reconstruction*, edited by John David Smith and J. Vincent Lowery, ix–xii. Lexington: University Press of Kentucky, 2013.

———. *Reconstruction: America's Unfinished Revolution 1863–1877*. New York: Harper & Row, 1988.

Forbes, Robert Pierce. *The Missouri Compromise and Its Aftermath: Slavery and the Meaning of America*. Chapel Hill: University of North Carolina Press, 2007.

Foulke, William D. *Life of Oliver P. Morton: Including His Important Speeches*. 2 vols. Indianapolis: Bowen-Merrill, 1899.

Frank, Joseph A. *With Ballot and Bayonet: The Political Socialization of American Civil War Soldiers*. Athens: University of Georgia Press, 1998.

Fredrickson, George M. *The Inner Civil War: Northern Intellectuals and the Crisis of the Union*. New York: Harper & Row, 1965.

Freidel, Frank. *Francis Lieber: Nineteenth Century Liberal*. Baton Rouge: Louisiana State University Press, 1947.

———. "The Loyal Publication Society: A Pro-Union Propaganda Agency." *The Mississippi Valley Historical Review* 26, no. 3 (December 1939): 359–76.

———. *Union Pamphlets of the Civil War 1861–1865*. 2 vols. Cambridge, Mass.: Harvard University Press, 1967.

Fuller, George N., ed. "Historical News, Notes, and Comment." *Michigan History Magazine* 6, no. 1 (1922): 3–57.

Furguson, Ernest B. *Freedom Rising: Washington in the Civil War*. New York: Alfred A. Knopf, 2004.

Gallagher, Gary W. *The Union War*. Cambridge, Mass.: Harvard University Press, 2011.

Gallman, J. Matthew. *Defining Duty in the Civil War: Personal Choice, Popular Culture, and the Union Home Front*. Chapel Hill: University of North Carolina Press, 2015.

———. *Mastering Wartime: A Social History of Philadelphia during the Civil War*. 1990. Reprint, Philadelphia: University of Pennsylvania Press, 2000.

Giesberg, Judith. *Army at Home: Women and the Civil War on the Northern Home Front*. Chapel Hill: University of North Carolina Press, 2009.

Gilje, Paul. *Rioting in America*. Bloomington: Indiana University Press, 1996.

Gordon, Michael A. *The Orange Riots: Irish Political Violence in New York City, 1870 and 1871*. Ithaca, N.Y.: Cornell University Press, 1993.

Goss, Thomas J. *The War within the Union High Command: Politics and Generalship during the Civil War*. Lawrence: University Press of Kansas, 2003.

Grant, Susan-Mary. *North over South: Northern Nationalism and American Identity in the Antebellum Era*. Lawrence: University Press of Kansas, 2000.

Gray, Wood. *The Hidden Civil War: The Story of the Copperheads*. New York: Viking Press, 1942.

Griffin, Clifford S. *Their Brothers' Keepers: Moral Stewardship in the United States, 1800–1865*. New Brunswick, N.J.: Rutgers University Press, 1960.

Grinspan, Jon. "Young Men for War: The Wide Awakes and Lincoln's 1860 Presidential Campaign." *Journal of American History* 96 (September 2009): 357–78.

Grodzins, Morton. *The Loyal and the Disloyal: Social Boundaries of Patriotism and Treason*. Chicago: University of Chicago Press, 1956.

Hafendorfer, Kenneth A. *Mill Springs: Campaign and Battle of Mill Springs, Kentucky*. Louisville, Ky.: KH Press, 2001.

Hahn, Steven. *A Nation under Our Feet: Black Political Struggles in the Rural South from Slavery to the Great Migration*. Cambridge, Mass.: Harvard University Press, 2003.

Bibliography

Hall, Martin Hardwick. *Sibley's New Mexico Campaign.* Austin: University of Texas Press, 1960.

Hall, Peter D. *The Organization of American Culture, 1700—1900: Private Institutions, Elites, and the Origins of American Nationality.* New York: New York University Press, 1982.

Halleran, Michael A. *The Better Angels of Our Nature: Freemasonry in the American Civil War.* Tuscaloosa: University of Alabama Press, 2010.

Halliday, Paul D. *Habeas Corpus: From England to Empire.* Cambridge, Mass.: Harvard University Press, 2010.

Hamand, Wendy F. "The Woman's National Loyal League: Feminist Abolitionists and the Civil War." *Civil War History* 35, no. 1 (1989): 39–58.

Hamilton, E. Bentley. "The Union League: Its Origin and Achievements in the Civil War." In *Transactions of the Illinois State Historical Society for the Year 1921,* 110–15. Springfield, Ill.: Phillips Bros., 1922.

Harris, Wilmer C. *Public Life of Zachariah Chandler, 1851–1875.* Lansing: Michigan Historical Commission, 1917.

Harwood, W. S. "Secret Societies in America." *The North American Review* 164, (April 1997): 617–25.

Hearn, Chester G. *The Capture of New Orleans, 1862.* Baton Rouge: Louisiana State University Press, 1995.

Heaton, John L. *The Story of a Page: Thirty Years of Public Service and Public Discussion in the Editorial Columns of the New York World.* New York: Harper & Brothers, 1913.

Hennesey, James. *American Catholics: A History of the Roman Catholic Community in the United States.* New York: Oxford University Press, 1983.

Hennessy, John J. *First Battle of Manassas: An End to Innocence July 18–21, 1861.* Mechanicsburg, Pa.: Stackpole Books, 2015.

———. *Return to Bull Run: The Campaign and Battle of Second Manassas.* New York: Simon & Schuster, 1993.

Hesseltine, William B. "The Pryor—Potter Duel." *The Wisconsin Magazine of History* 27, no. 4 (June 1944): 400–409.

Holcombe, R. I., ed. *History of Greene County Missouri, Written and Compiled from the Most Authentic Official and Private Sources.* St. Louis, Mo.: Western Historical Co., 1883.

Howard, Joseph, Jr., ed. *The Union League Club: Historical and Biographical 1863–1900.* New York: J. J. Wohltman, 1900.

Howard, Victor B. *Religion and the Radical Republican Movement 1860–1870.* Lexington: University Press of Kentucky, 1990.

Hubbart, Henry B. *The Older Middle West, 1840–1880.* New York: D. Appleton & Co., 1936.

Hull, Augustus Longstreet. *Annals of Athens, Georgia, 1801–1901.* Athens: Banner Job Office, 1906.

Humes, Thomas W. *The Loyal Mountaineers of Tennessee.* Knoxville, Tenn.: Ogden Bros. & Co., 1888.

Hurn, Ethel A. *Wisconsin Women in the War Between the States.* Madison: Wisconsin Historical Commission, 1911.

Hyman, Harold M. *Era of the Oath: Northern Loyalty Tests during the Civil War and Reconstruction.* Philadelphia: University of Pennsylvania Press, 1954.

———. *To Try Men's Souls: Loyalty Tests in American History.* Berkeley: University of California Press, 1959.

———. *Union and Confidence: The 1860s.* New York: Thomas Y. Crowell Co., 1976.

Irion, Frederick C. *Public Opinion and Propaganda.* New York: Thomas Y. Crowell Co., 1950.

Irwin, Will, Earl May, and Joseph Hotchkiss. *A History of the Union League Club of New York City.* New York: Dodd, Mead & Co., 1952.

James, William. *The Principles of Psychology.* 2 vols. London: Macmillan & Co., 1890.

Jeffers, H. Paul. *Freemasons: A History and Exploration of the World's Oldest Secret Society.* New York: Citadel Press, 2005.

Kass, Amy A., Leon R. Kass, and Diana Schaub, eds. *What So Proudly We Hail: The American Soul in Story, Speech, and Song.* Newark, Del.: ISI Books, 2011.

Katz, Irving. *August Belmont: A Political Biography.* New York: Columbia University Press, 1968.

Keehn, David C. *Knights of the Golden Circle: Secret Empire, Southern Secession, Civil War.* Baton Rouge: Louisiana State University Press, 2013.

Kendall, Diana Elizabeth. *Members Only: Elite Clubs and the Process of Exclusion.* Lanham, Md.: Rowman & Littlefield, 2008.

Key, V. O., Jr. *Politics, Parties, & Pressure Groups.* 5th ed. New York: Thomas Y. Crowell Co., 1964.

K.G.C.: An Authentic Exposition of the Origin, Objects, and Secret Work of the Organization Known as the Knights of the Golden Circle. Kentucky: U.S. National U.C., 1862.

Klement, Frank L. *Dark Lanterns: Secret Political Societies, Conspiracies, and Treason Trials in the Civil War.* Baton Rouge: Louisiana State University Press, 1984.

———. *The Limits of Dissent: Clement L. Vallandigham and the Civil War.* Lexington: University Press of Kentucky, 1970.

———. *Lincoln's Critics: The Copperheads of the North.* Edited by Steven K. Rogstad.Shippensburg, Pa.: White Mane, 1999.

Krutch, Joseph W. "George Henry Boker." *The Sewanee Review* 25, no. 4 (October 1917): 457–68.

Lanman, Charles. *The Red Book of Michigan: A Civil, Military and Biographical History.* Detroit: E. B. Smith & Co., 1871.

Lanman, Charles, and Joseph M. Morrison. *Biographical Annals of the Civil Government of the United States.* New York: J. M. Morrison, 1887.

Lathrop, George P. *History of the Union League of Philadelphia, from Its Origin and Foundation to the Year 1882.* Philadelphia: J. B. Lippincott & Co., 1884.

Lathrop, Henry W. *The Life and Times of Samuel J. Kirkwood, Iowa's War Governor.* Iowa City, Iowa: Henry W. Lathrop, 1893.

Lause, Mark A. *A Secret Society History of the Civil War.* Urbana: University of Illinois Press, 2011.

Lawson, Melinda. *Patriot Fires: Forging a New American Nationalism in the Civil War North.* Lawrence: University Press of Kansas, 2002.

———. "'A Profound National Devotion': The Civil War Union Leagues and the Construction of a New National Patriotism." *Civil War History* 48, no. 4 (December 2002): 338–62.

Leech, Margaret. *Reveille in Washington 1861–1865.* 1941. Reprint, New York: Book-of-the-Month Club, 1989.

Lemire, Elise. *"Miscegenation": Making Race in America.* Philadelphia: University of Pennsylvania Press, 2002.

Lewis, Patrick A. *For Slavery and Union: Benjamin Buckner and Kentucky Loyalties in the Civil War.* Lexington: University Press of Kentucky, 2015.

Lewis, William D. "John Innes Clark Hare." *The American Law Register* 54, no. 12 (December 1906): 711–17.

Long, David E. *The Jewel of Liberty: Abraham Lincoln's Re-election and the End of Slavery.* Mechanicsburg, Pa.: Stackpole Books, 1994.

Long, E. B. *The Civil War Day by Day: An Almanac, 1861–1865.* New York: Doubleday, 1971.

Longacre, Edward G. "The Union Army Occupation of New York City, November 1864." *New York History* 65, no. 2 (April 1984): 133–58.

Lyftogt, Kenneth L. *From Blue Mills to Columbia: Cedar Falls and the Civil War.* Ames: Iowa State University Press, 1993.

Mahoney, Timothy R. *From Hometown to Battlefield in the Civil War Era: Middle Class Life in Midwest America.* New York: Cambridge University Press, 2016.

Marvel, William. *The Great Task Remaining: The Third Year of Lincoln's War.* Boston: Houghton Mifflin, 2010.

———. *Lincoln's Autocrat: The Life of Edwin Stanton.* Chapel Hill: University of North Carolina Press, 2015.

———. *Lincoln's Darkest Year: The War in 1862.* Boston: Houghton Mifflin, 2008.

Massey, Mary E. *Bonnet Brigades.* New York: Alfred A. Knopf, 1966.

Massie, James William. *America: The Origin of Her Present Conflict; Her Prospect for the Slave and Her Claim for Anti-Slavery Sympathy.* London: John Snow, 1864.

Maxwell, William Quentin. *Lincoln's Fifth Wheel: The Political History of the U.S. Sanitary Commission.* New York: Longmans, Green & Co., 1956.

McConnell, Stuart. *Glorious Contentment: The Grand Army of the Republic, 1865–1900.* Chapel Hill: University of North Carolina Press, 1992.

McCrary, Peyton. "The Party of Revolution: Republican Ideas about Politics and Social Change, 1862–1867." *Civil War History* 30, no. 4 (December 1984): 330–50.

McGlone, Robert E. *John Brown's War Against Slavery.* New York: Cambridge University Press, 2009.

McJimsey, George T. *Genteel Partisan: Manton Marble, 1834–1917.* Ames: Iowa State University Press, 1971.

McKitrick, Eric L. *Andrew Johnson and Reconstruction.* 1960. Reprint, New York: Oxford University Press, 1988.

McPherson, James M. *Battle Cry of Freedom.* New York, Oxford University Press, 1988.

———. *For Cause and Comrades: Why Men Fought in the Civil War.* New York: Oxford University Press, 1997.

———. *Ordeal by Fire: The Civil War and Reconstruction.* New York: Alfred Knopf, 1982.

Michigan Pioneer and Historical Society. *Michigan Historical Collections,* vol. 26. Lansing, Mich.: Robert Smith & Co, 1896.

Milne-Smith, Amy. *London Clubland: A Cultural History of Gender and Class in Late-Victorian Britain.* London: Palgrave Macmillan, 2011.

Mitchell, Stewart. *Horatio Seymour of New York.* Cambridge, Mass.: Harvard University Press, 1938.

Moorhead, James H. *American Apocalypse: Yankee Protestants and the Civil War 1860–1869.* New Haven, Conn.: Yale University Press, 1978.

Moran, Rachel F. *Interracial Intimacy: The Regulation of Race and Romance.* Chicago: University of Chicago Press, 2001.

Moses, Zebina. *The Sons of Michigan and the Michigan State Association of Washington D.C.* Washington, D.C.: Michigan State Association, 1912.

Nagler, Jörg. "Loyalty and Dissent: The Home Front in the American Civil War." In *On the Road to Total War: The American Civil War and the German Wars of Unification,* edited by Stig Förster and Jörg Nagler, 329–56. Cambridge: Cambridge University Press, 1997.

Neely, Mark E., Jr. *The Boundaries of American Political Culture in the Civil War Era.* Chapel Hill: University of North Carolina Press, 2005.

————. *The Fate of Liberty: Abraham Lincoln and Civil Liberties.* New York: Oxford University Press, 1991.

————. *Lincoln and the Triumph of the Nation: Constitutional Conflict in the American Civil War.* Chapel Hill: University of North Carolina Press, 2011.

————. *The Union Divided: Party Conflict in the Civil War North.* Cambridge, Mass.: Harvard University Press, 2002.

Nelson, Truman. *The Old Man: John Brown at Harper's Ferry.* New York: Holt, Rinehart and Winston, 1973.

Nevins, Allen. *The War for the Union.* Vol. III, *The Organized War 1863–1864.* New York: Charles Scribner's Sons, 1971.

Norton, Lee. *War Elections 1862–1864.* New York: International Publishers, 1944.

Oakes, James. *Freedom National: The Destruction of Slavery in the United States, 1861–1865.* New York: W. W. Norton & Co., 2013.

Oakleaf, Joseph B. *National Union Convention of 1864 and Why Lincoln Was Not Nominated by Acclamation.* Moline, Ill.: Carlson Printing, 1924.

Oldt, Franklin, and P. J. Quigley, eds. *History of Dubuque County, Iowa.* Chicago: Goodspeed Historical Assoc., n.d.

Paludan, Phillip Shaw. *"A People's Contest": The Union and Civil War 1861–1865.* New York: Harper & Row, 1988.

————. *"The Better Angels of Our Nature": Lincoln, Propaganda and Public Opinion in the North during the American Civil War.* Fort Wayne, Ind.: The Lincoln Museum, 1992.

Parsons, Elaine Frantz. *Ku Klux: The Birth of the Klan during Reconstruction.* Chapel Hill: University of North Carolina Press, 2015.

Pearson, Henry G. *An American Railroad Builder: John Murray Forbes.* Boston: Houghton Mifflin, 1911.

————. *The Life of John A. Andrew, Governor of Massachusetts 1861–1865.* 2 vols. Boston: Houghton Mifflin, 1904.

Philadelphia Club. *The Philadelphia Club 1834–1934.* Philadelphia: Privately printed, 1934.

Phillips, Christopher. *The Rivers Ran Backward: The Civil War on the Middle Border and the Making of American Regionalism.* New York: Oxford University Press, 2016.

Porzelt, Paul. *The Metropolitan Club of New York.* New York: Rizzoli Publications, 1982.

Quigley, William F., Jr., *Pure Heart: The Faith of a Father and Son in the War for a More Perfect Union.* Kent, Ohio: Kent State University Press, 2016.

Rable, George C. *But There Was No Peace: The Role of Violence in the Politics of Reconstruction.* 1984. Reprint, Athens: University of Georgia Press, 2007.

————. *God's Almost Chosen Peoples: A Religious History of the American Civil War.* Chapel Hill: University of North Carolina Press, 2010.

Rafuse, Ethan S. *McClellan's War: The Failure of Moderation in the Struggle for the Union.* Bloomington: Indiana University Press, 2005.

Ramold, Steven J. *Across the Divide: Union Soldiers View the Northern Home Front.* New York: New York University Press, 2013.

Randall, James G. *Constitutional Problems under Lincoln.* New York: D. Appleton and Co., 1926.

Rawley, James A. *The Politics of Union: Northern Politics during the Civil War.* Hinsdale, Ill.: Dryden Press, 1974.

Raymond, Henry J. *The Life and Public Services of Abraham Lincoln.* New York: Derby and Miller Publishers, 1865.

Ridley, Jasper. *The Freemasons.* London: Constable and Robinson, 2005.

Rodgers, William Warren, Jr. *Black Belt Scalawag: Charles Hays and the Southern Republicans in the Era of Reconstruction.* Athens: University of Georgia Press, 1993.

Rosenwaike, Ira. *Population History of New York City.* Syracuse, N.Y.: Syracuse University Press, 1972.

Sandow, Robert M., ed. *Contested Loyalty: Debates over Patriotism in the Civil War North.* New York: Fordham University Press, 2018.

Sandow, Robert M. "Damnable Treason or Party Organs: Democratic Secret Societies in Pennsylvania." In *This Distracted and Anarchical People: New Answers for Old Questions about the Civil War-Era North,* edited by Andrew L. Slap and Michael T. Smith, 42–59. New York: Fordham University Press, 2013.

———. *Deserter Country: Civil War Opposition in the Pennsylvania Appalachians.* New York: Fordham University Press, 2009.

Scharf, John Thomas. *History of Delaware: 1609–1888.* 2 vols. Philadelphia: L. J. Richards and Co., 1888.

Schiller, Herbert M. *Sumter Is Avenged! The Siege and Reduction of Fort Pulaski.* Shippensburg, Pa.: White Mane Publishing, 1995.

Scott, Sean A. *A Visitation of God: Northern Civilians Interpret the Civil War.* New York: Oxford University Press, 2011.

———. "'His Loyalty Was But Lip Service': Loyalty Oaths and the Military Arrests of Two Ministers in Occupied Virginia during the Civil War." *Virginia Magazine of History and Biography* 122, no. 4 (2014): 298–335.

Sears, Stephen W. *George B. McClellan: The Young Napoleon.* New York: Ticknor & Fields, 1988.

———. *Landscape Turned Red.* New York: Ticknor & Fields, 1983.

———. *To the Gates of Richmond: The Peninsula Campaign.* New York: Ticknor & Fields, 1992.

Sebrell, Thomas E., II. *Persuading John Bull: Union and Confederate Propaganda in Britain, 1860–1865.* New York: Lexington Books, 2014.

Shankman, Arnold M. *The Pennsylvania Anti-War Movement 1861–1865.* Rutherford, N.J.: Fairleigh Dickinson University Press, 1980.

Shea, William L., and Earl J. Hess. *Pea Ridge: Civil War Campaign in the West.* Chapel Hill: University of North Carolina Press, 1992.

Sheehan-Dean, Aaron. *Why Confederates Fought: Family and Nation in Civil War Virginia.* Chapel Hill: University of North Carolina Press, 2007.

Shelden, Rachel A. *Washington Brotherhood: Politics, Social Life, and the Coming of the Civil War.* Chapel Hill: University of North Carolina Press, 2013.

Sheppard, Si. *The Partisan Press: A History of Media Bias in the United States.* Jefferson, N.C.: McFarland & Co., 2008.

Shofner, Jerrell H. *Nor Is It Over Yet: Florida in the Era of Reconstruction 1863–1877.* Gainesville: University Press of Florida, 1974.

Silber, Nina. *Daughters of the Union: Northern Women Fight the Civil War.* Cambridge, Mass.: Harvard University Press, 2005.

Silbey, Joel H. *A Respectable Minority: The Democratic Party in the Civil War Era, 1860–1868.* New York: W. W. Norton & Co., 1977.

———. *The American Party Battle: Election Campaign Pamphlets 1828–1876.* 2 vols. Cambridge, Mass.: Harvard University Press, 1999.

Silverman, Kenneth. *Lightning Man: The Accursed Life of Samuel F. B. Morse.* New York: Alfred A. Knopf, 2003.

Smith, Adam I. P. "Beyond Politics: Patriotism and Partisanship on the Northern Home Front." In *An Uncommon Time: The Civil War and the Northern Home Front,* edited by Paul A. Cimbala and Randall M. Miller, 145–69. New York: Fordham University Press, 2002.

———. *No Party Now: Politics in the Civil War North.* New York: Oxford University Press, 2006.

Smith, Andrew F. *Starving the South: How the North Won the Civil War.* New York: St. Martin's Press, 2011.

Smith, Donna V. *Chase and Civil War Politics.* 2 vols. Columbus, Ohio: F.J. Heer Printing Co., 1931.

Smith, George Winston. "A Strong Band Circular." *The Mississippi Valley Historical Review* 29, no. 4 (March 1943): 557–64.

———. "Broadsides for Freedom: Civil War Propaganda in New England." *The New England Quarterly* 21, no. 3 (September 1948): 291–312.

Smith, John David, and J. Vincent Lowery, eds. *The Dunning School: Historians, Race, and the Meaning of Reconstruction.* Lexington: University Press of Kentucky, 2013.

Smith, William E. *The Francis Preston Blair Family in Politics.* 2 vols. New York: Macmillan Co., 1933.

Somerset Club. *A Brief History of the Somerset Club of Boston, with a List of Past and Present Members, 1852–1913.* Cambridge, Mass.: Riverside Press, 1914.

Spann, Edward K. *Gotham at War: New York City, 1860–1865.* Wilmington, Del.: Scholarly Resources, 2002.

———. *The New Metropolis: New York City, 1840–1857.* New York: Columbia University Press, 1981.

Speed, Thomas. *The Union Cause in Kentucky 1860–1865.* New York: G. P. Putnam's Sons, 1907.

Spurgeon, Ian M. *Soldiers in the Army of Freedom: The 1st Kansas Colored, The Civil War's First African American Combat Unit.* Norman: University of Oklahoma Press, 2014.

Stampp, Kenneth M. *The Era of Reconstruction 1865–1877.* New York: Alfred Knopf, 1965.

———. *Indiana Politics during the Civil War.* Indianapolis: Indiana Historical Bureau, 1949.

Stoddard, Francis Hovey *The Life and Letters of Charles Butler.* New York: Charles Scribner's Sons, 1903.

Stoddard, William O. *Abraham Lincoln: The True Story of a Great Life.* New York: Fords, Howard & Hulbert, 1884.

Strausbaugh, John. *City of Sedition: The History of New York City during the Civil War.* New York: Twelve Books, 2016.

Summers, Mark W. *A Dangerous Stir: Fear, Paranoia, and the Making of Reconstruction.* Chapel Hill: University of North Carolina Press, 2009.

Taylor, Paul. *He Hath Loosed the Fateful Lightning: The Battle of Ox Hill (Chantilly), September 1, 1862.* Shippensburg, Pa.: White Mane Publishers, 2003.

———. *"Old Slow Town": Detroit during the Civil War.* Detroit: Wayne State University Press, 2013.

Thomas, Lately. *Delmonico's: A Century of Splendor.* Boston: Houghton Mifflin Co., 1967.

Towne, Stephen. *Surveillance and Spies in the Civil War: Exposing Confederate Conspiracies in America's Heartland.* Athens: Ohio University Press, 2015.

Townsend, Reginald. *Mother of Clubs: Being the History of the First Hundred Years of the Union Club of the City of New York 1836–1936.* New York: William Rudge, 1936.

Townsend, William H. *Lincoln and the Bluegrass: Slavery and Civil War in Kentucky.* Lexington: University of Kentucky Press, 1955.

Tredway, G. R. *Democratic Opposition to the Lincoln Administration in Indiana.* Indianapolis: Indiana Historical Bureau, 1973.

Trefousse, Hans L. *The Radical Republicans: Lincoln's Vanguard for Racial Justice.* New York: Alfred A. Knopf, 1969.

Union Club. *Union Club of the City of New York 1836 to 1986.* New York: Privately printed, 1986.

Union League Club of New York. *Report of the Committee on Providing a Thanksgiving Dinner for the Soldiers and Sailors.* New York: Union League Club of New York, 1865.

Union League of Philadelphia. *Chronicle of the Union League of Philadelphia 1862–1902.* Philadelphia: Union League of Philadelphia, 1902.

Vandiver, Frank. *The First Public War, 1861–1865: An Address before the Conference of the Public Relations Society of America.* New York: Foundation for Public Relations Research and Education, 1962.

Wakelyn, Jon L. *Southern Unionist Pamphlets and the Civil War.* Columbia: University of Missouri Press, 1999.

Ware, Edith Ellen. "Committees of Public Information." *Historical Outlook* 10 (1919): 65–67.

———. *Political Opinion in Massachusetts during Civil War and Reconstruction.* New York: Columbia University Press, 1916.

Warner, Ezra J. *Generals in Blue.* 1964. Reprint, Baton Rouge: Louisiana State University Press, 1989.

Warshauer, Matthew. "Copperheads in Connecticut: A Peace Movement That Imperiled the Union." In *This Distracted and Anarchical People: New Answers for Old Questions about the Civil War-Era North,* edited by Andrew L. Slap and Michael T. Smith, 60–80. New York: Fordham University Press, 2013.

Watterson, Henry. *History of the Manhattan Club: A Narrative of the Activities of Half a Century.* New York: Henry Watterson, 1916.

Waugh, John C. *Reelecting Lincoln: The Battle for the 1864 Presidency.* New York: Crown Publishers, 1997.

Weber, Jennifer L. *Copperheads: The Rise and Fall of Lincoln's Opponents in the North.* New York: Oxford University Press, 2006.

Wecter, Dixon. *The Saga of American Society: A Record of Social Aspiration 1607–1937.* New York: Charles Scribner's Sons, 1937.

Wesley, Timothy L. *The Politics of Faith during the Civil War.* Baton Rouge: Louisiana State University Press, 2013.

Weyl, Nathaniel. *Treason: The Story of Disloyalty and Betrayal in American History.* Washington, D.C.: Public Affairs Press, 1950.

White, Jonathan W. *Abraham Lincoln and Treason in the Civil War: The Trials of John Merryman.* Baton Rouge: Louisiana State University Press, 2011.

———. "Copperheads." *Essential Civil War Curriculum.* Virginia Tech, 2015.

———. *Emancipation, the Union Army, and the Reelection of Abraham Lincoln.* Baton Rouge: Louisiana State University Press, 2014.

Whiteman, Maxwell. *Gentlemen in Crisis: The First Century of the Union League of Philadelphia 1862–1962.* Philadelphia: Union League of Philadelphia, 1975.

Wiley, Bell Irvin. *The Life of Billy Yank: The Common Soldier of the Union.* 1952. Reprint, Baton Rouge: Louisiana State University Press, 1971.

Williams, Harry. "Benjamin F. Wade and the Atrocity Propaganda of the Civil War." *Ohio History Journal* 48, no. 1 (January 1939): 33–43.

Williams, Kipling D. *Ostracism: The Power of Silence.* New York: The Guilford Press, 2001.

Williams, T. Harry. *Lincoln and the Radicals.* Madison: University of Wisconsin Press, 1941.

Wood, Forrest G. *Black Scare: The Racist Response to Emancipation and Reconstruction.* Berkeley: University of California Press, 1968.

Wunder, John R., and Joann M. Ross, eds. *The Nebraska–Kansas Act of 1854.* Lincoln: University of Nebraska Press, 2008.

Wyatt-Brown, Bertram. *Southern Honor: Ethics and Behavior in the Old South.* New York: Oxford University Press, 1982.

Zornow, William F. *Lincoln and the Party Divided.* Norman: University of Oklahoma Press, 1954.

———. "Treason as a Campaign Issue in the Re-election of Lincoln." *The Abraham Lincoln Quarterly* 5, no. 6 (June 1949): 348–63.

Internet Sources

"Black Ministers and the Organization of the Republican Party in the South in 1867: Letters from the Field." Rutherford B. Hayes Presidential Center. http://www.rbhayes .org/hayes/content/files/Hayes_Historical_Journal/blackministersrepublican_party .html#go back 11.

Costa, Dora L., and Matthew E. Kahn. "Shame and Ostracism: Union Army Deserters Leave Home." Working Paper 10425, National Bureau of Economic Research, April 2004. http://www.nber.org/papers/w10425.

"Dissent is the Highest Form of Patriotism," The Jefferson Monticello. http://www .monticello.org/site/jefferson/dissent-highest-form-patriotism-quotation.

"Pennsylvania Volunteers of the Civil War." www.pacivilwar.com.

Index